The President's Wife
MARY   TODD   LINCOLN

Photograph by Mathew B. Brady.
National Life Foundation, Fort Wayne, Indiana

Mrs. Mary Todd Lincoln early in 1862, just before the death of her son Willie in the White House. It illustrates her well-known love of low décolletage and her use of flowers, so fashionable at the time.

The
President's Wife

MARY TODD LINCOLN

A Biography

Ishbel Ross

G. P. PUTNAM'S SONS
New York

SBN: 399-11132-8

LIBRARY OF CONGRESS CATALOG
CARD NUMBER: 72-97309

Contents

Illustrations will be found following page 222

Acknowledgments

IN ASSEMBLING MATERIAL on Mary Todd Lincoln, the research trail leads from Lexington, Kentucky, where she was born in 1818, to Frankfort, Louisville, Fort Wayne, Springfield, Chicago, Batavia, Boston, Providence, New York, Philadelphia, Washington and Los Angeles. The Lincoln documentation is overwhelming, and wherever it exists, echoes of Mrs. Lincoln come through, some faint, some strong.

She was so newsworthy in her own right that newspaper and magazine articles about her abound in both the scholarly and popular press. Although few books have been written about her, she was the most publicized of Presidents' wives up to the time of Mrs. John F. Kennedy. She was commented on, often unjustly but sometimes with high praise, in many political books and social records of the day, since the Civil War brought correspondents to Washington from various parts of the world and the White House was a showcase where Mrs. Lincoln and her family life were closely observed.

The official Lincoln papers in the Library of Congress and the National Archives include a number of her letters and bills, and there are also many references to her in other Civil War collections. I am most grateful to Dr. Roy P. Basler, chief of the Manuscript Division of the Library of Congress and a noted expert on Lincoln-iana, for his help and guidance in my quest for Mary Lincoln material. The staff of this division gave its usual courteous and painstaking assistance. Among the manuscript collections consulted in the national library for this biography were the following:

Hamilton Fish	Robert T. Lincoln
John G. Nicolay	Gideon Welles
Vinnie Ream Hoxie	Benjamin B. French
J. P. Usher	Mrs. Lucretia Garfield
Jacob W. Shuckers	Simon Cameron
John Hill Wheeler	Salmon Portland Chase
Fields and Garrison	Herndon-Weik
John Davis Batchelder	Zachariah Chandler
Breckinridge family	Benjamin F. Butler

In this connection I am particularly indebted to H. B. Fant, archivist, National Historical Publications Commission, and to Miss Kate M. Stewart, of the Manuscript Division of the Library of Congress, for their help and interest.

Nowhere in the country perhaps is one more conscious of Mary Todd Lincoln than in Springfield, where she is richly and variously documented in the Illinois State Historical Library. More than a hundred of her letters and several by her sons may be found in this library, which has 7,500 Lincoln books and pamphlets and memorabilia of Mrs. Lincoln, including one of her handsomest dresses. Her social and political links with Illinois may be traced through regional manuscript collections, and the encompassing files of the *Journal of the Illinois State Historical Society*, the *Abraham Lincoln Quarterly* and kindred publications.

I am particularly indebted to William K. Alderfer, State Historian of Illinois, and to James T. Hickey, curator of the Lincoln Collection at the Illinois State Historical Library, for assistance given me on my visit to Springfield. I should also like to thank Mrs. Mildred V. Schulz, head librarian, and Paul Spence, manuscript curator.

Mrs. Lincoln's early history is strongly felt in the house where she lived from 1844 to 1861 before going to Washington to preside at the White House. With its furnishings faithfully reproduced, it looks much as it did in the time of Abraham Lincoln, and in 1972 it was dedicated as a historical landmark. Miss Virginia Stuart Brown, custodian of the house for many years, was still its gracious hostess. George W. Doyle and Mrs. Doyle, whose tours of the Lincoln shrines have brought firsthand knowledge of Mrs. Lincoln to thousands of visitors from all parts of the world, were enlightening on my visits to the Lincoln house, to the Lincoln Tomb in Oak Ridge Cemetery, to New Salem, and to other landmarks closely identified with Mrs. Lincoln's history.

Chicago, like Springfield, has many Mary Lincoln associations, and the unique and beautiful Newberry Library is of prime interest to all students of Lincolniana. I am deeply grateful to Dr. Ralph G. Newman for his help and advice in this field in which he is so well informed and active as a collector, dealer and authority on the Lincolns. This library has been a meeting ground for Lincoln scholars and collectors, and countless valuable documents have passed through his hands. Nothing bearing on the Lincoln family escapes his attention, and he acts in an advisory capacity on Lincolniana.

Chicago also has the dean of Lincoln scholars in Paul M. Angle, and the Chicago Historical Society, with which he has long been associated, is rich in its Civil War records. His collaboration with Carl Sandburg, his intimate knowledge of Springfield, and his study of Mary Lincoln make his writings essential groundwork for any study in this field. I am most appreciative of help received from the Chicago Historical Society and also from the University of Chicago Library.

The Lincoln Life Foundation in Fort Wayne, Indiana, with its vast collection of pictures, documents and memorabilia, draws many strings together for the researcher, and Dr. Gerald McMurtry, its director and a noted Lincoln authority, gave me generous assistance and access to a variety of documents, pictures and scrapbooks bearing on Mrs. Lincoln's history.

Lexington, Kentucky, where she passed her early years, still has many echoes of Mary Todd, and the house where she lived stands in lonely disrepair, awaiting restoration. Mrs. William H. Townsend, whose husband wrote the illuminating *Lincoln and His Wife's Home Town*, received me most hospitably in the house that for years was a repository of Todd and Helm material, and her daughter Mary Genevieve, who is Mrs. J. H. Murphy, Jr., and lives in the old Helm house outside Lexington surrounded by family relics, was also most responsive to my inquiries.

J. Winston Coleman, Jr., noted chronicler of Kentucky life, was generous in his advice and assistance. Few understand as he does the atmosphere in which Mary Todd grew up. Charles W. Hackensmith, author, professor and an authority on the history of the Todd and Helm families, was enlightening and helpful when I called on him. Art Lawson guided me to old records in the Lexington Public Library.

I am indebted to Dr. Jacqueline Bull, in charge of Special Collections in the Margaret King Library, University of Kentucky, and to Miss Roemel Henry, librarian of the Frances Carrick Thomas Library at Transylvania College, for their interest and help in my quest for material. Through Miss Henry I had access to a brilliant thesis on Mary Todd Lincoln done by Miss Teresa L. Reed in her senior year at Transylvania College. A Lincoln enthusiast who continues to work in this field, Miss Reed, who lives in Lexington, was generous in letting me read her thesis. I am also indebted to Miss Katherine Lambert, formerly with the Kentucky Parks Department in Frankfort, for keeping me informed of plans for the restoration of the Todd house in Lexington.

The Filson Club in Louisville has a wealth of manuscript material on the Todd family, and I am grateful to Miss Evelyn R. Dale, the club's curator, and to James R. Bentley, curator of manuscripts, for their help and advice. Mary Todd Lincoln material was also forthcoming at the Kentucky Historical Society in Frankfort.

A number of historical societies and libraries across the country were generous in their aid, and I should like to acknowledge in particular the material given me by Stuart C. Sherman, John Hay Librarian, and Mrs. Virginia M. Trescott, Special Collections, Brown University; by Rodney G. Dennis, Curator of Manuscripts, The Houghton Library, Harvard University; by Miss Winifred Collins, Massachusetts Historical Society; by Archie Motley, director of Manuscript Department, Chicago Historical Society; by Margaret McFadden, Special Collections, University of Chicago Library; and by Harriet McLoone, Huntington Library, San Marino, California.

The New York Public Library, with its fine collection of Civil War books, historical journals and Lincolniana of all kinds, yielded a rich harvest of material. I should also like to thank Miss Sylvia Hilton, Miss Helen Ruskell and the staff of the New York Society Library for their never-failing help and understanding of a writer's needs. Robert P. Borges, of the Mercantile Library, and his staff were at all times most resourceful and kind in their response to my requests.

Mrs. Lincoln's letters have changed hands so often through

collectors and dealers that few are now in private hands. Among the most noted collectors of Lincolniana have been Oliver Barrett, Foreman M. Lebold, Justin G. Turner and Ralph G. Newman. I owe special thanks to Mrs. Katrina van Asmus Kindel, of Grand Rapids, Michigan, who was kind enough to give me permission to use her Mary Todd Lincoln letters. She has been collecting Lincolniana for years and is one of Mrs. Lincoln's warmest advocates, believing her to have been greatly misunderstood.

David Kirschenbaum, of the Carnegie Book Shop, New York, kindly gave me permission to use Mrs. Lincoln's letter to Mrs. Sally Orne, March 15, 1866, regarding President Johnson and the assassination plot against her husband.

I should also like to thank Philip D. Sang of River Forest, Illinois, for permission to use his Simon Cameron and Mrs. Lincoln letters in "Mary Todd Lincoln, a Tragic Portrait," published in *The Journal of Rutgers University Library*, April, 1961. Donald Sinclair, of Special Collections at Rutgers, was also most cooperative.

Many of Mary's letters have disappeared or have been crumpled beyond legibility, but she was such a persistent letter writer that it is safe to assume there may be more in existence than the 609 so effectively presented in *Mary Todd Lincoln: Her Life and Letters* by Justin G. Turner and Linda Levitt Turner. Fully aware of her own indiscretion when she dashed off hasty notes of recrimination, Mrs. Lincoln sometimes added: "Burn this." Yet a number of those she condemned have survived. They are not her angriest letters; they simply reflect a growing sense of caution as she was buffeted about. No other President's wife has left such revealing correspondence, with the exception of Abigail Adams. Because she was Mrs. Abraham Lincoln her letters, trivial or tragic, lighthearted or angry, have historical interest, beyond being the revelation of a complex and tortured nature.

Anyone writing a biography of Mary Todd Lincoln owes a deep debt of gratitude to the late Ruth Painter Randall, who profoundly and sympathetically researched Mrs. Lincoln's life history and in *Mary Lincoln: Biography of a Marriage* did much to clear up the myths and canards surrounding the personal life of the Lincolns. I found Mrs. Randall's books on the Lincoln family invaluable guides in the preparation of this biography.

I. R.

I

A Bluegrass Girl

MARY TODD, DESTINED to be the most misunderstood and slandered of Presidents' wives, was born to wealth in the world of Southern planters and politicians. In marrying Abraham Lincoln she was swept from a luxurious girlhood in Kentucky, where she had been trained in all the social graces, to a hardy life in the Middle West, and eventually into the sadness and fury of the Civil War. Through it all she was a keen participant in the swift development of America in the mid-nineteenth century.

Her faith and belief in the man she always called "Mr. Lincoln" were obsessive. Never for a moment did she doubt the road that he would travel; the heights he might attain; the promise inherent in his unfathomable nature. So strong was her drive, so constant her influence and ambition that many of her contemporaries believed she helped shape the national image of Abraham Lincoln. Their history shows how often she swayed his judgment in their early years together as she backed him determinedly in the significant decisions that led him finally to the Presidency. Once there, the picture changed dramatically, her power waned, and Mary lost ground as adviser and political helpmate.

In the White House she became an easy target for her husband's enemies, since her fluent tongue and unstable nature made her vulnerable in periods of stress. His friends, conceding her gift for prodding him into action, deplored the embarrassment she caused him with her moods and tempers, her jealousy and fabled ex-

13

travagance. The true Mary Lincoln, as pathetic as she was brilliant at times, has been lost to view in the blurred image of her paradoxical nature, and the historical record has been heavily weighted against her.

Pride and ambition were her dominant qualities. At her best no one questioned her warmth and charm, her scholarship, sparkling conversation and subtle understanding. Conversely, few who knew her well from girlhood to old age failed to comment on her demonic temper, her sarcastic wit and instinct for show and entertainment. From her earliest years Mary Todd loved fun, excitement and parties. She was an exhibitionist in an atmosphere of Victorian decorum; a perfectionist who had to excel.

Her father, Robert Smith Todd, was her first object of adoration; Henry Clay her second; and Abraham Lincoln her third. To all three she was fiercely loyal, one of the few consistencies in her divided nature. Her family ties linked her to prominent families in Kentucky, Illinois and Pennsylvania, and she grew up with a well-defined sense of social status. But at the age of seven she came to grips with sorrow and wrote in later years of a "desolate" childhood. This may have been due to the loss of her mother at that time and to the fact that she soon had a stepmother who treated her well but whom she disliked.

Actually there was never a time in Mary's life until her last years when she was not surrounded by kinfolk, friends or guardians who saw to it that she was neither neglected nor forgotten. To think of her girlhood as being "desolate"—her own characteristically extravagant term—was to be blind to the social customs of the world in which she lived. She met more interesting and notable people than most girls of her age, and she was fully exposed to the political giants of the day in the Whig stronghold of Kentucky. It was an atmosphere infused with a strong drive for the White House, with her father and his associates working ceaselessly for Henry Clay. Mary was well aware of the political activity around her as she listened to the talk at her father's dinner table, and if she was quoted on a number of occasions—sometimes in earnest, often in jest—as saying that one day she would be the wife of a President, there was more than the usual excuse for this vain boast.

As things turned out, she became a *mater dolorosa*, the first President's wife to lose a husband by assassination, almost a century before the same fate overtook Jacqueline Kennedy. Her days in the White House were brief and cataclysmic as she became the most discussed and abused of Presidents' wives. Brainy and ambitious though she was for her generation, the chances are that she would have been one of the countless mothers who lived, loved, sorrowed, brought up their children, and died in the Middle West without notice, had she not met and married Lincoln in the prairie town of Springfield.

The destruction of Mary Lincoln was a gradual and dramatic process, closely observed by the public because of her husband's stature and her own affinity for disaster. The loss of her mother was only a prelude to her sorrows. Death was close to her all through the Civil War as friends and relatives fell in battle, fighting at cross-purposes for the North and the South. Three of her four sons died during her lifetime, one of them in the White House. From the night President Lincoln was shot by her side in a theater box in 1865 she became the very symbol of sorrow to the nation at large. Her ceaseless mourning and emotionalism broke down her last defenses, and Mary Lincoln, who had made sensational use of her powers as a White House hostess, died in misery and lost in the veil of madness, at the Edwards' house in Springfield, a few feet from the spot where she and Abraham Lincoln had been married in 1842.

In the intervening years she had traveled a long way from her sunny days in the Todd home on West Short Street in Lexington, where she was born on December 13, 1818. Only two months earlier Nancy Hanks Lincoln had died and left a nine-year-old boy named Abraham to work his way into the history of the country, with Mary Todd as his mate. She was the third daughter and fourth of seven children born to Robert Todd and his gentle wife, Eliza Ann Parker Todd. The last child died in infancy, leaving two boys, Levi and George, and four girls—Elizabeth, Mary, Frances and Ann. They all came close together, but there were plenty of servants to care for everyone, so Mary never had to iron her ruffles, bake bread, or polish silver. She had blooded horses to ride and a carriage to take her wherever she wanted to go.

The blood of rebels coursed through Mary's veins, for she was descended on both sides of her family from related Todds who had fled at different times from religious persecution in Scotland. By chance her father and mother had the same great-grandfather, John Todd, so the strain of rebellion was strong in Mary, and she never forgot it. This was part of her inheritance and was ingrained in her nature. All the Todds were hotheaded and outspoken.

Their ancestors were Covenanters who had fought the Duke of

Monmouth at Bothwell Bridge, fled to the north of Ireland, established families there, and eventually transferred the family strain to America when John Todd's grandsons, Andrew and Robert, settled in 1737 in Montgomery County, Pennsylvania. Robert's three sons, John, Robert and Levi, were sent south to Virginia to be educated by John Todd, a famous Presbyterian minister of the colonies who helped establish Transylvania Seminary, later Transylvania University. This noted divine was Mary Lincoln's great-uncle.

He used his influence with Patrick Henry, governor of Virginia, to get army posts for the three young Todds, and they were soon engaged in combat with the Indians and the British. John was killed in the Battle of Blue Licks. Young Robert Smith Todd, serving with the Fifth Regiment, Kentucky Volunteers, was home on sick leave during the War of 1812 when he fell in love with seventeen-year-old Eliza Ann Parker, of the same family strain. No sooner were they married than he headed off to do battle with the Indians. On his return he built a home for his bride adjoining the imposing brick house of his mother-in-law on West Short Street in Lexington, and there Mary Lincoln was born.

Mrs. Elizabeth Porter Parker was to loom large in her life and to influence her future. She was descended from the Robert Todd who had fled from Scotland in 1679. His second wife was Isabelle Bodley, and his second daughter, Elizabeth Todd, married William Parker. These were Mary's ancestors on her mother's side, and Mrs. Parker, who outlived her husband by many years, was a determined woman and a figure of consequence in Lexington. She was generally known as the Widow Parker.

On the paternal side Mary's most noted ancestor was her grandfather, General Levi Todd, who had been active in the military operations of the pioneers and had succeeded Daniel Boone in command of the Kentucky militia. He had built a fine house on the Richmond Pike that he named Ellerslie after a Scottish village identified with his family. Originally their name had been spelled Tod, meaning Fox, but this was changed to Todd after they settled in the new land. Lincoln in time would jest that one *d* was good enough for God, but not for the Todds.

They soon intermarried with established Kentucky families and became dominant in the state through land ownership and political and social activities. It had been much the same with the Todds in Pennsylvania. Mary's great-grandfather, General Andrew Porter, was a friend of George Washington's, and the Porters gave Pennsylvania a governor and two Cabinet officers.

It was part of the family history that they reaped honors along the way. There were judges, legislators, doctors, lawyers and preachers in Mary's ancestry—and a few rogues, too. Her father was not a man of outstanding talents, but he was so involved in local affairs that he sustained the family tradition. Although he studied law after the War of 1812, he never practiced it, but he served as State Senator and clerk of the House of Representatives. He was a banker, a farmer, a manufacturer, but above all, he was an active politician in the group around Clay. Courtly in manner, he was a quiet man, tall but stooping, with a high complexion and thick neck. His daughters all adored him, and they fashioned dolls' clothes with the bright silks and muslins he brought to them from New Orleans. Mary collected dolls and avidly sought possessions, even in her earliest years. She was also something of a tomboy, climbing trees, chasing birds and butterflies.

This carefree existence came to an end suddenly when she was whisked away to Mrs. Parker's one night, only to learn the next day that her mother had died, giving birth to a son who would survive her by fourteen months. Mary was stunned. After seeing her mother's still face, she was never again able to face death without showing convulsive grief. She became difficult to handle, although she was still part of a well-ordered household. Mammy Sally had charge of the children, assisted by small Judy. Chaney, cranky but an inspired cook, presided in the kitchen. Nelson, who served as butler and coachman, did the marketing and drove the children around. Jane Sanders, their black housekeeper, preserved harmony on all fronts.

Todd's sister, Mrs. Charles M. Carr, kept an eye on the children, and an unmarried sister-in-law, Ann Maria Parker, moved into the Todd house to uphold the Parker interests. All too soon it became apparent that Mary's father was intent on finding a new mother for his children—a common situation in an era when so many young wives died in childbirth. Gossip soon focused on Elizabeth Humphreys, the highly cultivated and good-looking daughter of Dr. Alexander Humphreys, a Virginian who settled in Frankfort. Todd had met her there while he was working for the legislature. One of her uncles, James Brown, who represented Louisiana in the Senate and later was Minister to France, was Mrs. Henry Clay's brother-in-law.

Mrs. Parker watched with anger and outrage this quick renewal of love so soon after her daughter's death. Every move made by Todd was watched, and he urged Betsy Humphreys to forestall trouble by marrying him at once. In spite of the formidable Mrs. Parker the marriage came off at the Humphreys' house in Frankfort on November 1, 1826, with John Jordan Crittenden, soon to be known as one of Kentucky's leading statesmen, acting as best man. He would figure sadly in Mary's life during her White House days, since he allied himself with Stephen A. Douglas and veered away from her husband.

Todd and his bride returned to find Eliza's four daughters studying them with considerable hostility, but the new Mrs. Todd took hold serenely. She was a sophisticated woman, and in their later years she and Mary would find common interests in their love of books and learning, of flowers and fine household possessions. But when Mary was eight, sparks flew, and the widow Parker helped feed the flame. Whether she was torn with jealousy over her father's new love or still mourned her lost mother, Mary ran wild and defied her stepmother, who had a strong sense of convention and decorum. She did not cherish pets or approve of hoydenish ways in little girls, and she was baffled by her stepdaughter's tantrums and self-assertion. Mary was a fury when crossed but an angel if handled with loving care, something that Abraham Lincoln seemed to understand better than anyone else.

Things went more smoothly when her father decided to move some distance from the watchful Mrs. Parker. He took a larger house on Main Street for his growing family. Babies were born with the frequency characteristic of the times, until Mary had three half brothers and five half sisters. The total number was nine, but one died in infancy. These were the relatives who brought her endless woe during the Civil War, tying her to the South in spite of all her protestations of complete devotion to the Union. In these early days, with slaves around them and black children sharing in their games, Mary played with Samuel, who would die at Shiloh; with David, who would be fatally wounded at Vicksburg; with Alexander, who would lose his life at Baton Rouge; as well as with her own brother, mischievous Levi, who would give Lincoln a great deal of trouble in the future.

The Todd children of both wives had all the advantages known to the more affluent residents of Kentucky. They had the best of town and country life, with long days of play on the grounds of their

L-shaped mansion, with its large double parlors and graceful décor. A white gravel walk ran from the library to the conservatory, and the children's special delight was a little stream that ran through the grounds, making a wading pool, where they chased minnows and splashed about in the sunshine. Honeysuckle vines clung to the arbor, and at long intervals Mary and her sisters were allowed to stay up for the magic of the night-blooming cereus unfolding. Lilacs, roses, verbena, and heliotrope scented the air in season as Mary sat by her bedroom window reading poetry with all the intensity of her ardent nature. She was the liveliest and most active of the children, and there was no repose in her except for the hours she passed with books.

Most exciting of all were their trips to the country home of the Reverend Robert Stuart, minister of the Presbyterian Church at Walnut Hills, a few miles from Lexington. He taught languages at Transylvania, and his boys and girls were always exchanging visits with the Todds. They rode horses in shady lanes, had boisterous picnics and nutting expeditions in the woods, picked grapes in season, went sleigh riding in winter, and in the evenings they gathered around an enormous hearth to roast corn or apples, to play games, and to do conundrums. Mary was always the focal figure when someone was called on to perform, for she was adept at mimicry and imaginative about costumes. Before she was seven, she had learned how best to tuck a flower in her hair and whisk a tiny fan.

She and her sister Elizabeth threw themselves heart and soul into the excitement of occasional trips to Crab Orchard Springs in Kentucky. Spas were in high fashion at the time, and Mrs. Todd, who was fragile from constant childbearing, sought the benefit of the mineral waters whenever she could. Her brother, Dr. Alexander Humphreys, Jr., usually met them there with his family from New Orleans. Spa life, which she would come to know intimately in her later years, began early for Mary as she and Elizabeth promenaded in dainty organdy frocks with blue satin sashes. Wide-brimmed leghorn hats with dangling ribbons shaded their softly rounded faces.

In later years, when her name had become identified with elaborate attire, Mary's passion for clothes as a child was recalled. She could not wait to grow up, and one day she and Elizabeth stuffed their Sunday dresses with willow reeds to create the effect of hoops. Their stepmother caught them setting off for church in this grotesque attire, and when they were told to change at once, Mary wept and raged. All fashionable women wore hoops at this time, and as one of Mary's friends said, "She wanted what she wanted when she wanted it and no substitute."

Katherine Helm, whose mother, Emilie Todd Helm, was Mary's half sister, gives a romantic picture of her dressing up in a rose silk frock, with a Byronic collar and puff sleeves, to attend the races, a forbidden jaunt. A huge hat with a rose plume rested precariously on her dark hair as she started to climb down the vine from her window. But her stepmother caught her, and again there was a wild scene. Her stormy nature was better understood by her stepgrandmother, Mrs. Alexander Humphreys, who lived in Frankfort and at the age of seventy-three was akin in spirit to the French *grandes dames* of the eighteenth century. Mary was impressed with the perfection of her diction and manners and with the fact that she studied Voltaire in the original French. When Mary was eighteen, this dowager took her and her cousin, Elizabeth Humphreys, to a ball in Frankfort. Fashionably dressed in satin, with a lace cap resting lightly on her snowy hair, she dazzled them by leading the grand march with style and vigor. She made an unforgettable impression on Mary, who said that if only she could be like Grandmother Humphreys, she would be perfectly satisfied with herself.

From the time they first met, ambition stirred in Mary as she listened to this witty woman, who spoke the language of George Sand and whose associations were not too distant from the days of the American Revolution. Mary was already a scholar at heart, but as her education progressed from one phase to another, she gave thoughtful attention to the issues of the day. However rebellious she had been after her father's remarriage, things changed for the better when her formal schooling began. She was a clever girl, eager for knowledge and quick to absorb it, so that she settled into the role of student with ease and success. Throughout her life she seemed to find a sustaining sense of accomplishment in scholarship, and she was uncommonly well educated for her day.

She was eight when she first attended the academy of Dr. John Ward, an Episcopal clergyman, who had in his care more than a hundred boys and girls from Lexington's leading families. Although a strict disciplinarian, he was ahead of his time in his methods. His classes assembled at five in the morning, and in winter Mary and her cousin, Elizabeth Humphreys, who had come to Lexington to stay with the Todds and take classes at Dr. Ward's, trudged through snow to the two-story building where the spartan round of recitation went on. Years later, when she was Mrs. Elizabeth Humphreys Norris, wife of a judge, the visiting cousin would write a memoir of these days. In her aging years she grieved over the public image of Mrs. Lincoln, for she knew it to be false.

The girls studied together by candlelight, and Elizabeth could never forget the speed with which Mary memorized, or the delight she took in reciting poetry. Mary was analytical in her reading but quickly succumbed to the British poets and romantic legends. Elizabeth would be only halfway through her studies when Mary, her homework finished, would also have completed the ten rounds of a cotton sock required of the girls each evening.

In later years Elizabeth insisted that, although Mary's impulses were lightning fast and she made no attempt to conceal her feelings, she had never seen her in one of her fabled rages. "Without designing to wound she now and then indulged in sarcastic, witty remarks that cut but there was no malice in it," said Elizabeth. She recalled her engaging looks at that time—clear blue eyes, creamy skin with the soft flush of health, brown hair, and a face so intelligent that one did not easily forget it. "Her form was fine," Elizabeth added, "and no old master ever modeled a more perfect arm and hand."

Mary's zeal for learning never interfered with the feminine arts that were hers by instinct and inheritance. Although she called herself a "regular blue," she was apologetic for her intellectual drive in a world so dedicated to the whims of men and the home. She learned more of the graces after registering at Madame Mentelle's boarding school in 1832, the year in which the first break occurred in the family pattern and the door was opened for her eventual meeting with Abraham Lincoln.

Her sister Elizabeth, aged sixteen, had fallen in love with Ninian Wirt Edwards, son of the governor of Illinois and a student at Transylvania College. They were married just as Mary entered Madame Mentelle's, and they moved to Springfield, a significant event in the Todd history. The legend grew that Elizabeth was anxious to get away from her stepmother. Lincoln at this time was living in New Salem and was boarding at the Rutledge Tavern.

Mary developed fast at Madame Mentelle's, becoming the assured, sophisticated and well-read girl she was when she met Lincoln. The finishing process had been carefully worked out for Kentucky's most cherished daughters. Although lacking little on the social side, Mary was also a model student, getting top marks with ease in all her subjects. Her academic instruction was thorough. Augustus Waldemare Mentelle, son of a professor at the National and Royal Academy and historiographer to the king, had fled from France with his wife, Madame Victorie Charlotte LeClerc Mentelle, after the Revolution. They reached Lexington with their family in 1798 and never ceased to mourn the guillotining of their rulers.

Their school was modestly advertised in the beginning, promising a "truly useful and solid English education in all its branches" as well as instruction in French. The fee for boarding, washing and tuition was $120 a year. Conversation for the most part was in French, and Mary acquired a fluency in this language that served her well during her years in the White House. She gravitated naturally to leading roles in the French plays staged at the school and was an instinctive show-off at a time when conversation was a studied art. The Mentelles gave courses in conversation and letter writing, and Mary Lincoln's versatility in both fields became proverbial through the years. Her penmanship was graceful, clear as copperplate. She crisscrossed her lines with the exactitude of needlepoint, but her syntax and punctuation did little credit to her French instructors. Mary's erratic use of ellipses and capital letters was as dismaying as her excessive use of commas, exclamation points and hyphens. But aside from these eccentricities she became a tireless correspondent, and every phase of her troubled life is reflected in the hundreds of letters she penned. "Pass my imperfections lightly by," she wrote with lighthearted grace to a friend in 1840, but the war years taught her to ask that many of her·letters be "consigned to the flames."

Her most enjoyable hours at Madame Mentelle's were spent on the dance floor as the pupils were led through the mazes of the quadrille, Circassian circle, the round and top waltzes, the schottische, and various regional dances. Mary was featherlight on her feet, an inspired dancer, one of the accomplishments that caught Abraham Lincoln's attention when he first met her at a ball.

She went home regularly on weekends. Nelson, in his blue swallowtail coat with brass buttons, drove her a mile and a half along the Richmond Pike to the Todd house on Friday afternoons, then took her back on Sunday mornings. When her sister Frances followed Elizabeth to Springfield and there married Dr. William S. Wallace, Ann alone remained with Mary. Ann was still too young to be allowed to share in the endless political discussions which her sister heard at their father's dinner table. But by 1849 Ann, too, had left home and had become the wife of Clark Moulton Smith, a prosperous Springfield merchant.

Mary was no stranger to Henry Clay. He had been in and out of her life from her earliest years, and one of the pleasures of being at Madame Mentelle's was the knowledge that she could see him starting out from Ashland for his daily drive into town. She was familiar with the treasures that he had brought back to Lexington after signing the Treaty of Ghent in 1814. The gold-brocaded satin draperies from Lyons were recalled by Mary when she refurbished the White House. The gold-bronze candlesticks, the French sofa, and the American Empire tables that were fitted together for large dinners were identified in her mind with Clay's stately home. His paneled library was a delight to this book-minded girl, but above all his personality had her bewitched. "Mr. Henry Clay," said Mary, "is the handsomest man in town and has the best manners of anybody—except my father."

She seemed to have political prescience from the start as she listened to governors, jurists, Congressmen, diplomats, scholars and soldiers discussing the issues of the day in her father's house, but Clay was the one who made the most lasting impression. As leader of the Whig Party he drew in celebrities, and one political event followed another in Lexington. Her father almost invariably was involved. In 1828, when she was ten, he and some friends were raising money for Clay's defense on a charge of having consorted with Aaron Burr. On July 4 of the following year the citizens of Lexington gave him a dinner. And in September, 1832, just after Mary became one of Madame Mentelle's students, there was wild excitement locally over a campaign visit by Andrew Jackson. She would never forget Old Hickory's chiseled face as he rode in an open carriage while women waved hickory sticks and handkerchiefs, and horsemen, military companies, clubs and orders marched to blaring bands. The big rally and barbecue were free-style campaigning, in the fashion of the 1830's, with a feast of roast pig, baskets of fried chicken, pickles, cakes and pie. Kegs of whiskey and buckets of beer sparked up the celebration.

Mary, unable to conceal her Whig sympathies, was wildly excited when she predicted that Jackson would be snowed under and that they would freeze his long face so that he would never smile again. It amused her father's friends, over their mint juleps, to hear this bright little daughter rattle off comments with considerable bite.

She was passionate in her views then, as in later years, and eager to express herself. The talk at this time sank deep into her consciousness. She could always interest and amuse Lincoln with her comments on the personalities who had passed her way in the Lexington days, and he liked to hear her talk about Clay.

Her boldness with this politician became legendary in her family, and her sisters recalled her riding a dashing new pony up the dusty road to show it off to her idol at Ashland. He was entertaining guests at the time and did not come out at once. Mary imperiously sent in word that Mary Todd was waiting and must see him. When he came out, she smiled radiantly at him and announced that the pony would dance for him. She raised her whip, the pony reared and pawed the air. Clay lifted Mary down and took her in to dinner.

This was the occasion on which she was quoted by members of her family as saying: "Mr. Clay, my father says you will be the next President of the United States. I wish I could go to Washington and live in the White House." After a pause she went on: "I begged my father to be President but he only laughed and said he would rather see you there than to be President himself. He must like you more than he does himself."

"Well," said Mr. Clay, "if I am ever President, I shall expect Mary Todd to be one of my first guests."

Lexington during these years had a woodland beauty that impressed visitors, who found its homes spacious and furnished with old-world elegance. Its trees and flowering shrubs seemed a miracle of well-ordered verdancy. One commentator viewed it as a "city that goes on wheels" because of all its gigs, barouches, coaches and assorted vehicles. To others it seemed quiet in comparison with the commercial furore of Cincinnati and Louisville. Its residents were people of substance, and its quiet streets, shaded by rows of locust trees, gave it a venerable air, unlike the bustling cities nearby that were growing fast on the wings of industry.

It was a scholarly center, with Transylvania University as a focal point. Pioneers in the arts and sciences converged in this setting, and professors, doctors, lawyers and preachers abounded. A number of excellent schools flourished in the region. From June to September its inns, boardinghouses and hotels were filled with visitors to the Bluegrass country, and politicians were always to be found at the Phoenix Hotel, which dated from the time of the Jefferson administration. Today a plaque attests to the role it has played in American history.

Many of Mrs. Lincoln's ideas for the elaborate feasts she served during her days in the White House went back to early impressions of Mathurin Giron's fascinating establishment around the corner from her father's shop. His historic confections included the castellated cake with the Stars and Stripes given by the people of Lexington to the Marquis de Lafayette in 1825, when Mary Todd was seven. His upstairs ballroom, with Etruscan pillars, lacy balconies and landscape murals, was the scene of many of Kentucky's great prewar parties. But his confectionery and catering shop downstairs was of more interest to Mary in her school years. She was a particular pet of rotund little M. Giron, who talked to her in his native language. Her cousin Elizabeth Humphreys wrote of his indulgences: "Mary and I could never pass the confectionery shop of Monsieur Giron. Most of our small allowance of pocket money went to swell his coffers, not so much for the pleasure of the palate as for the joy of filling our eyes with the beauty of his unique creations."

One of the deep traumas of these years was a cholera epidemic that swept Lexington and resulted in the deaths of Todd friends and relatives. The house reeked of burning tar. Fruits and vegetables were banned, and the fare consisted of boiled milk and boiled water, biscuits and eggs. When there were not enough coffins in town to bury the dead, Mary's father handed down trunks and boxes from the attic to help meet the desperate need.

The other dark aspect of her childhood, and one of which she was constantly aware, was the slave traffic. She had seen slaves being dragged to the block and had heard their cries and the sound of the lash. Although Lincoln saw little or nothing of slavery in his childhood, it was an omnipresent fact for Mary Todd. The city was in a state of turmoil on this issue because of Henry Clay and the emancipation society founded locally to back a bill that would stop the importation of slaves into Kentucky. Mary was well informed on the subject, for her father and two of his friends, Robert J. Breckinridge and the sturdy and belligerent Cassius Marcellus Clay, had spoken on behalf of the bill.

The leader of the opposition was Robert Wickliffe, one of the largest slaveholders in Kentucky, and two of his daughters, Margaret and Mary, were Mary Todd's closest girlhood friends. Thus she heard all sides discussed on the most personal basis. The Todds' own black house servants were in the old Southern tradition of being valued members of the family. They ruled their various domains with considerable authority, and Mammy Sally had more power over the children than their stepmother. She spoiled and scolded them all, but they loved her dearly. Her eerie stories frightened them at times, and Mary was the only one bold enough to challenge some of Mammy's farfetched tales. She had sworn Mary to secrecy on the fact that she had put a nick in the back fence to show fugitive slaves that she would feed and help them. In the war years Mary remembered the shadows that had passed in the night and gone on their way sustained by Todd food.

The jail where the fugitive slaves were kept when captured, the black locust whipping post identified with their flogging, and the auction block where they were displayed—all could be seen from the front porch of the Widow Parker's house on West Short Street, and Mary was not unfamiliar with the horrifying sights and sounds of the slave trade. She talked freely on the subject and echoed the view of Grandmother Humphreys that there should be gradual emancipation. Anything else was still unthinkable to the Todds in that particular region at that time. But Mary and her cousin, Elizabeth Humphreys, developed strong views on the subject when fresh evidence of cruelty reached their ears.

Early in 1837, before he knew Mary Todd, Lincoln had said at Vandalia that "slavery is founded on both injustice and bad policy," but it was his wife who would bring him the most enlightenment on the subject. It took time for her to shake off some of the inherited convictions of her upbringing, but after she had lived for a period in Washington, her horizons widened, so in the end she was more ardent in her defense of the black people than her husband. The storm was already on the horizon when Mary was graduated from Madame Mentelle's in the summer of 1837. The finishing process had turned her into a model of accomplishments and good manners, but it had not chastened her rebellious spirit, and her wit was now compared to a hornet's sting.

She was nineteen, and her well-stocked mind and haughty manner made her somewhat intimidating to the smooth young men in the Todd circle. Although a born coquette, she was as likely to snub a youth as to flatter him. The older men who came to her home liked to talk politics with Mary, now grown up, and she was at her best in company of this sort. Although by no means a beauty, she was always fashionably dressed, meticulously groomed, and spirited in her responses. There was nothing dreamy or slow-moving about Mary Todd. Sure of herself at all times, she had little patience with young men who were sheepish or slow thinkers.

Her student years had been the happiest of her life, and in a later era she would have been prime material for college. But, according to custom, the next move was to catch a suitable husband, and Mary was not at all averse to this idea. The problem was to find a man who really interested her, and it was soon clear to her family that this would not be easy in Mary's case. She was hard to please and knew what she wanted. Nineteen was getting to be old age for marriage in her particular set. Mrs. Edwards had succeeded in marrying off Frances to Dr. Wallace, and Mary's turn came next, so she was invited to Springfield to live at the Edwards' home. The year was 1837, and it took her one step on her way to meeting Abraham Lincoln.

When she became a national figure, the story persisted that the three older sisters had been desperate to get away from their stepmother and that Mary had left home because she could not get along with the second Mrs. Todd. Her grandmother Parker was as resentful as ever of the woman who had taken her daughter's place, and she was thought to have influenced the sisters in their attitude toward their stepmother. A lawsuit over the Parker estate later brought some of this animosity to light, but Mary was always discreet and polite in her references to her stepmother.

Whatever the immediate situation may have been when she left for Springfield, she was ready for travel and fresh adventure. A number of her friends and relatives had moved from Kentucky to fast-growing Springfield. She was worldly enough to know that in the Edwards' circle she would be meeting a new breed and a wide variety of men from the East and Middle West. But she was not to meet the man of her life on this occasion. Although balls and parties were given in her honor, the tall young lawyer from Sangamon County who had been taken into the law office of her cousins, John Todd Stuart and John J. Hardin, was not yet in the Edwards' social circle.

The three young men had served together in the Black Hawk War, and although Stuart and Hardin were already popular and important, Lincoln was still an outsider, watching with some amusement the brisk social life around him. He and Mary were heading toward each other, but after three months of intensive entertainment she decided to go back to Lexington and take more classes with Dr. Ward. Her reason for returning home so quickly has never been explained, but her passion for scholarship was unassuaged and she seemed to be groping for a wider range for her talents. Restless, discontented, ambitious, she might well have found her way to a career had she been a twentieth-century girl. As things were, two more years elapsed before she returned to Springfield and met Abraham Lincoln. In the meantime he had made great strides in legal and political affairs, and she had studied, flirted and grown more temperamental but without finding the goal she seemed to seek.

II

Across a Dance Floor

ABRAHAM LINCOLN FIRST saw Mary Todd across a dance floor in Springfield in 1839. It was not love at first sight, but by some magic a fire was lit that burned through a quarter of a century of love and sorrow. Each had heard of the other, so recognition was instantaneous. When Springfield took the place of Vandalia as the capital of Illinois, Lincoln, as a rising lawyer and a member of the firm of Stuart and Hardin, was coming into view as a young man of some consequence.

The youthful beauties of the region danced and flirted with the lawyers and scholars rapidly making headway in the city they were destined to put on the map. Mary Todd, back from Kentucky, older and wiser than on her first visit, stood out among them as a bright and brainy girl. While the older men liked to talk to her and listen to her political views, the younger ones preferred to dance with her and flatter her. Mary was highly susceptible to both approaches, but it was already well known that her coquettish ways and sparkling conversation could flash suddenly into an angry tirade or chill with an annihilating note of sarcasm. She evidently found the right approach to Mr. Lincoln, who wasted no time in getting to know her.

The likeliest version of this first encounter comes from Katherine Helm, who heard it from her mother, Emilie Todd Helm, half sister of Mary, and if it seems faintly romanticized, at least it stands as family legend. Lincoln is pictured as having worn a black satin waistcoat and high black satin stock on this occasion, while Mary, in a pink organdy and lace frock, with pink slippers and stockings, danced and swayed "as lightly and gayly as a branch of fragrant apple blossoms in a gentle spring breeze."

Lincoln may not have seen things in such a flowery way, but his attention unquestionably was focused on John Stuart's cousin, a small rounded girl in pink with vivacious manners and nimble feet. He moved across the room to her and remarked, according to Katherine Helm: "Miss Todd, I want to dance with you in the worst way." And it was indeed in the worst way, Mary later confessed to Emilie. Lincoln's great height and clumsy feet made a shambles of the dance. But she would not have been true to herself had she not gushed her opinions to this simple young man in whom her cousin, John Stuart, put such trust. When he told her that he was studying Euclid and could do with some help, Mary invited him to the Edwards' house for the following evening. He brought his textbook with him, and knowing the subject well, she applied her bright wits to elucidation, so Euclid was the earliest link between these two historic characters.

It seems likely, however, that Lincoln was more aware of Mary the girl than of Mary the scholar, for somewhere along the line the alchemy of love seemed to settle in their blood. For the next two years, in spite of a maze of contradictory events, they were inevitably drawn to each other. Mary played the coquette, Lincoln sometimes the fool, relatives pushed them around, obstacles intervened, politics made contact difficult, but the string of communication held except for one big break, and they could not escape their ultimate fate. Mary somehow knew that she had met the man she must marry; yet the course was so rocky that up to the moment of their marriage neither one was altogether sure of the other.

It seemed a desultory romance in the course it followed, and a number of historians have chosen to regard it as a marriage of convenience on both sides, rather than of deep-rooted love. William H. Herndon, Mary's bitterest enemy, bluntly called it a "policy marriage" for Lincoln. There is little doubt that his association with the Edwards family in Springfield helped him on his way up the ladder, both politically and socially. But this had its obverse side, too, for when he was defeated for reelection to Congress, he wrote to an old friend that Sangamon County had rejected him because it "had classed him as an aristocrat."

In marrying Lincoln, Mary had nothing to gain beyond her love for him and her faith in his future. Her letters to an intimate friend made it clear that she longed for the perfect man to come along but that, hard to please, she rejected one suitor after another. Lincoln seemed the most unlikely of all, with Stephen A. Douglas strongly in the picture at the same time. Katherine Helm came to the conclusion that Mary found in Lincoln the "most congenial mind she had come across." Ambitious though she was, it cannot be said that she made a worldly choice in Lincoln, but they had a strong link in their political understanding.

Mary had said all along that she would marry for love and not for gold. Young girls of the period were constantly marrying older men, often widowers with children, and she watched this custom with suspicion, remembering the havoc it had wrought in her own home. When a friend admitted marrying a withered old man for "houses and gold," Mary reacted sharply. "Is that true?" she said. "I would rather marry a good man, a man of mind, with a hope and bright prospects ahead for position, fame and power than to marry all the houses, gold and bones in the world."

In Lincoln she seemed to find the qualities of honesty and sincerity that she valued in men. She had already had plenty of the soft gallantry of the South, the courtly manners, the picturesque attire. In moving to Springfield she found mixed elements in a state of fusion as Southern and Eastern girls visited kinfolk on the frontier, married, and became part of the history of the Middle West. Mary was a prime example of the girl with good connections who responded to the vigorous men carving their way to fame in the harsh prairie setting.

Her own life was linked to both types, and although Lincoln was no longer the shabby, out-at-elbows youth who had arrived in Springfield from New Salem two years earlier, carrying all his possessions in two bags slung over the saddle of his horse, and had found a lodging over Joshua Speed's store on the town square, he was still the most unkempt and unworldly man Mary had ever known. John Stuart kept impressing on him the need to wear conventional attire in their law office and when he visited the Edwards' home.

After the cotillion he became a persistent caller there, when his legal work and political interests gave him a chance to climb the hill to the imposing house where Mary lived. He seemed to find in her wit and well-stocked mind stimulation of a heady kind. "Mary would make a bishop forget his prayers," said Ninian Edwards of his sister-in-law after watching her mimic Lincoln dancing the Virginia reel. Mrs. Edwards often found them seated together in one of her parlors, with Mary reading poetry or "leading the conversation" with the rapt young man while he gazed at her as if "irresistibly drawn by some superior power."

He had little to say, but Mary listened attentively to his slow sentences delivered in a high-pitched voice. Elizabeth Edwards thought him cold and dull, as well as gauche. She felt sure that Mary's sense of humor and her social ambitions would protect her from Lincoln. Frances Wallace was equally scornful, saying that they could lead him around but that he was "not much for society." Since she herself was reserved, this bothered her less than it did the worldly Elizabeth. Mary, on the other hand, was the "very creature of excitement . . . and never enjoyed herself more than when in society and surrounded by a company of merry friends," according to James C. Conkling, a handsome young lawyer fresh from Princeton, writing to his fiancée, Mercy Levering, who was one of Mary's closest friends.

The hidden thoughts of Mary Todd and Abraham Lincoln during their two years of intermittent courtship come to the surface in bright flashes and somber undertones through the correspondence of Lincoln and Joshua Speed and in Mary's animated letters to Mercy. They all belonged to a group known as the Coterie, dedicated to the cultivation of the arts, to political happenings in their fast-growing state, to the causes that excited the scholars of the day. They were conventional but avant-garde, and they went in for a round of parties, dances, sleigh rides, political rallies, picnics and other excursions. Lincoln was more at home swapping jokes and stories with his cronies around the stove in Speed's quarters, but John Stuart saw to it that he joined the Coterie gatherings and visited Mary.

Although he had thought himself in love several times and had recently been jilted by the highly intelligent if not beautiful Mary Owens, a Southern girl who had crossed his path, he had never met anyone quite like Mary Todd—so warm and beguiling in her ways, yet firm and original in her views. Clearly she was an exhibitionist, the opposite of everything he was. "He found in her," according to Katherine Helm, "a bubbling fun, an enthusiastic love of life. She in turn was intrigued by his moodiness, his sincerity and honesty, his freedom from the pretty flatteries and the conventional gallantries of the men in her social set."

Lincoln's uncouthness shocked Mary at times. His table manners were strange, and she did not always relish his broad jokes; yet his common sense and political understanding made her value his opinion on the issues. Mary was a clever girl, a thinking girl, a girl who understood politics, a girl who liked the poets, a girl with status and assurance. Did he see her as a wife who could help him on his way? The sharp wit and pedantic conversation that frightened off some of her more worldly suitors had a strong appeal for Lincoln. Yet he called her Puss or Molly and in his big, clumsy way treated her as gently as if she were a porcelain doll or an impulsive child who needed to be humored, an approach that was to be the right one for Mary in the future.

Herndon described her as being openly flirtatious, leading the young men of Springfield a merry dance. He was quite chagrined by her treatment of him on their first meeting. When Herndon asked her to dance with him at the home of Colonel Robert Allen, he felt that he had never before danced with anyone who moved with such grace and ease.

When promenading afterward through the hall, he complimented her on her grace and apologized for his own awkwardness, but his chance remark that she seemed to glide through the waltz with the "ease of a serpent" brought a quick retort from Mary. He saw at once that he had struck the wrong note. She drew back, her eyes flashing, and remarked: "Mr. Herndon, comparison to a serpent is rather severe irony, especially to a newcomer."

He soon found the quick retort to be typical of Mary Todd. They were never to like each other, and he wrote that although she had charming manners, when offended or antagonized, her "agreeable qualities instantly disappeared beneath a wave of stinging satire or sarcastic bitterness, and her entire better nature was submerged." He noted her appeal for older men and conceded that she was a shrewd observer and a sound critic. He thought that she wrote with wit and ability, although when she used a pen, "its point was sure to be sharp." Her bearing seemed to him proud and vivacious, and he admired her gifts as a conversationalist. But she struck him as being the exact reverse of Lincoln in all respects—in her physical proportions, education, bearing, temperament and background.

Lincoln's interest and perhaps his competitive sense were whetted by the presence of Stephen A. Douglas in Mary's circle. Here was a formidable rival, a poor boy from Vermont admitted to the bar of the State Supreme Court on the same day as Lincoln, and already meeting with spectacular success. He would serve in the Senate while Lincoln was a Congressman. They would meet in their historic debates and face each other again in the national counsels after Lincoln became President.

Douglas was little more than five feet, but his stocky frame and massive head gave an impression of dynamic strength, borne out by his strong jaw, his blazing blue eyes, and powerful oratory. Lincoln did not underestimate him either politically or as a suitor for Mary. He had great fascination for women, and Ninian Edwards and his wife saw him as a man who might well be on his way to the White House. They encouraged him as they became increasingly frosty to Lincoln, and Mary often chose his company in the two years that Lincoln was wooing her. In later years she was apt to say that she had never been in love with Douglas; but once she was quoted as confessing that she would have married him but for her feeling for Lincoln. In any event, tales of a romance between them flourished in Springfield and were recalled at the time of the Civil War, when Lincoln and Douglas were pitted against each other.

It was always easier to round up Douglas as an escort when Mary needed one, for Lincoln was apt to be away campaigning, or he forgot to show up, or he was not in the mood for party going. On these occasions she could rely on the Little Giant, whose legs were as short as Lincoln's were long, whose moods were as dynamic as Lincoln's were hesitant and low-key. Although Mary tried to brush off this romance when party differences set them worlds apart, in her days of mirth and frivolity they were often observed together. On one occasion Douglas strode along the street with her, a wreath of roses dangling rakishly on his massive head. He had found Mary sitting on the Edwards' porch weaving a wreath for a costume party. When he invited her to walk with him, she said she might if he would wear the wreath. Thus dared by impish Mary Todd, Douglas swung it into place and they promenaded with a dash of swagger.

Douglas called so often on Mary that when asked by a friend which man she intended to marry, Lincoln or Douglas, she retorted with an uncharacteristic lapse in grammar: "Him who has the best prospects of being President." Mrs. Edwards said on different occasions that Mary, who had often predicted when they lived in Lexington that she would be the wife of a President, said it in earnest after settling in Springfield. And with some reason.

Perhaps no one knew better than Mary the burning ambition that smoldered in her tall suitor, and it was in her power to open many doors for him. With thirteen years of intensive education behind her—an uncommon state of affairs for girls of her generation—she delighted in discussing philosophy, politics, history, languages and literature with Lincoln. Summing up their relationship in a letter to one of her cousins, she wrote: "I know his intellect, for I've helped to stock it with facts."

She read omnivorously, and the mutual exchange of ideas that began during their courtship in Springfield became a lifelong habit. In a memorandum Lincoln prepared anonymously for campaign purposes, he described his own educational background with total simplicity: "When I came of age I did not know much. Still, somehow, I could read, write, and cipher to the rule of three, but that was all. I have not been to school since. The little advance I now have upon this story of education, I have picked up from time to time under the pressure of necessity."

But in the year 1840, when he was thirty-one and wooing Mary, he was far from being the simple country bumpkin that history has made him. He was gaining stature in the political field. He was well liked by all manner of men. His friends included men of wealth and education, and he could hold his own with the tough-minded politicians who were shaping state affairs. There were many jests about his graceless ways and his great height. He was six feet four, and he and Ninian Edwards had been members of the "Long Nine," men over six feet tall from Sangamon County who sat in the legislature at Vandalia.

But the master hand at making fun of Abraham Lincoln was Lincoln himself. He liked to jest about his dark, unruly hair that had a "way of getting up as far as possible in the world." He spoke of his "poor, lank, lean face," and he had an awkward time disposing of his long legs when sitting on a slippery horsehair sofa at Mrs. Edwards', and listening to Mary recite from Shakespeare. His description of himself was typical in its definitive simplicity: "I am, in height, six feet four inches, nearly, less in flesh, weighing on an average of one hundred and eighty pounds, dark complexion, with scarce black hair and gray eyes." He walked slowly, pitching forward slightly, and he never seemed at ease in the Edwards' house, surrounded by bevies of girls in rustling dresses and handsome young men wearing long-tailed coats, high stocks and narrow trousers. It took Mary to shake him out of himself and to entice him to whirl her around in the rollicking dances of the day. He never knew what to expect from this vital, excitable girl—floods of tears welling from her big blue eyes, an angry flip of her fan, or a cold snub when someone offended her. She was a strange mixture of impatience, hauteur and elusive charm.

Mary was always kinder to Lincoln than she was to other members of the Coterie, perhaps because she detected a lonely spirit and a need for affection behind his unresponsive manner. He bore no resemblance to his friend Joshua Speed, a romantic figure, slightly Byronic in attire and bearing. Like Mary, Speed was a Kentuckian, and the *bons vivants*, wits and scholars of the group gathered at night above his store for discussion and conviviality. Lincoln virtually made this his home, but Stuart was always behind him, to ease him into the more fashionable areas of life in Springfield.

The most exuberant member of the Coterie was James Shields, a high-spirited Irishman in his early thirties. Mary was scornful of his overdone gallantry and pompous manner. She and her friends laughed at him, but she would meet him again as a general in the Civil War and as a United States Senator whose image would eventually find a place in Statuary Hall in the Capitol. At least three members of the group—Lincoln, Douglas and Shields—would travel far on the national scene. Most of the others were worldly, handsome, relatively well off, and thoroughly informed on political issues.

By all odds, the least promising of the Coterie members was Abraham Lincoln, and although he shared in many of their gatherings, he was noted chiefly for his jokes and stories, when he chanced to come out of his shell at all. Conkling and Mercy, who had come from Baltimore to visit her brother in Springfield for the winter of 1838–39, were close observers of the developing romance. Mercy lived next door to Mary Todd, and the two girls were inseparable at this time. When Mercy went home, they kept up a correspondence that was most revealing about Mary's feeling for Lincoln. She was suffering from her usual discontent, hankering for great things but never quite sure how to attain them. Meanwhile, her days were filled with parties and expeditions.

Mercy was of a different temperament, and she reproached Mary for her lightheartedness and for her love of excitement and parties. Her admonitory letter brought a characteristic answer from Mary: "Would it were in my power to follow your kind advice, my ever dear Merce, and turn my thoughts from earthly vanities, to one higher than us all. Every day proves the fallacy of our enjoyments, and that we are living for pleasures that do not recompense us for the pursuit."

But live for pleasure Mary did, even while her mind kept her deep in political affairs. During the summer of 1840 she went to Columbia, Missouri, to visit her Uncle David Todd and his daughter Ann. This meant going to St. Louis by stagecoach, taking a packet boat up the Mississippi, then on to Rocheport, and finishing the trip by horseback. On July 23, 1840, Mary wrote to Mercy that she and Ann had gone to Boonville for a week and had attended four parties. One in particular had impressed her with its "brilliancy & city like doings." They had danced all the traditional Virginia reels at top tempo until three in the morning, and she thought Mercy would have been amused could she have seen the "excitement of the dancing style." Boonville had an appeal for her, and she confided to Mercy: "A life on the river to me has always had a charm, so much excitement, and this *you* have deemed essential to my well-being. . . ."

There were suitors, too, an essential part of her life, but evidently she had not forgotten the tall man whom she and Mercy had seen so much of earlier in the year. Without mentioning Lincoln by name she wrote that she had been surprised by some letters she had received since leaving Springfield—"as I *must confess* they are entirely unlooked for. . . . Every day I am convinced this is a stranger world we live in, the *past* as the future is to me a mystery." But Mary failed to mention a meeting with Lincoln at Columbia that summer, chronicled by Katherine Helm from family letters.

According to this source, Lincoln, attending a political rally at Rocheport, visited Columbia and attended church with Mary, sitting in the Todd pew in the local Presbyterian Church. What this may have meant to the Lincoln courtship remains obscure, but there is no doubt that Mary at this time was assuring Mercy that she would never marry a man she did not love. The issue was clear-cut at the moment, for the grandson of Patrick Henry was a suitor, and Mary wrote: "There is *one* being here, who cannot brook the mention of my return, an agreeable lawyer & grandson of *Patrick Henry—what an honor*! I shall never survive it—I wish you could see him, the most perfect original I had ever met. My beaux have *always* been *hard bargains* at any rate."

This remark suggests Mary's dissatisfaction with her suitors. There was always something wrong with them, or she sought some quality they lacked. She was affectionate and emotional, but her intelligence kept her from committing herself when she was not deeply moved. Although her uncle told her that this young man surpassed his *"noble ancestor* in *talents,"* the thought of marrying him seemed impossible. In spite of all his virtues "yet Merce I love him not, & my hand will never be given where my heart is not," she wrote.

It was obvious that Mary's relatives all were anxious to get her married off, and since they abounded, she may have been conscious of family pressure. But she was not blind to the fact that there was nothing for a well-brought-up girl to do at that time but to get married as early as possible and to the best advantage. Mary was independent in this respect. She knew what she wanted, but she must have registered another failure when she returned to Springfield from Missouri. All her friends were struck by her air of blooming health after this change of scene. Her rounded figure was beginning to show the tendency that persisted throughout her lifetime, and Conkling wrote amusingly to Mercy about Mary's increase in girth.

The campaigning tradition was in Mary's blood from her Lexington days, and she threw herself into the local events with spirit, an early liberationist knowing quite well that it was considered déclassé to follow this course. Lincoln, Douglas, her cousins and nearly all the young lawyers she knew were deep in the struggle on behalf of William Henry Harrison. The Coterie members talked of little else. Mercy had not been able to resist the speechmaking either, although she wrote to Mary that she doubted that the "narrow capabilities" of her sex would permit her to understand much of what was said. Yet she believed that women should not be ignorant of the "great and important questions hanging upon the Government." Mary was not overawed, however. She listened attentively, expressed her views, and cheered the Tippecanoe Singing Club in the office of the Sangamon *Journal,* a familiar haunt of Lincoln's.

When the campaigning ended, he showed up more often at the Edwards' house, but a coolness developed when he made it clear to them that he was a suitor who could not be ignored. There was a political breach, too, when Lincoln was renominated for another term by the Sangamon County Whig convention and Edwards was not. Lincoln expressed regret, but starchy Ninian continued to discount him until his time of need arose. Meanwhile, he and his wife pushed the cause of Edwin B. Webb, a widower with two children, whom they now paraded as the "principal lion" in Mary's circle. She reminded Mercy that, although he had been regarded as an eligible of only modest merit the winter before, he was now rated one of the "marriageable gentlemen." It was clear that since Mary had returned from Missouri without getting herself suitably engaged, there had to be more drive on the part of her family. The golden days of her youth were passing and Mary was being difficult. Mercy had had no trouble whatever in landing the attractive Mr. Conkling, and all her friends were getting married and starting families. Yet in many ways Mary Todd seemed to be endowed with more of nature's gifts than the girls she knew who moved into the conventional marriage pattern with instinctive ease. Mrs. Edwards conceded that Mary loved glitter, show, pomp and power. She wrote that Lincoln was charmed with her "wit and fascinated with her quick sagacity, her will, her nature and culture," but she thought her much too lively, gay and frivolous to be well matched with the unworldly and sluggish Mr. Lincoln.

Yet Mr. and Mrs. Edwards approved the suit of the aging Webb, who wooed Mary with great persistence but whom she found wholly uncongenial. He was nearly twenty years her senior, small in stature, fussy and limited in his interests. She wrote to Mercy that she would not marry him, even though he might be "far too worthy for me, with his two *sweet little objections*." Fond though she was of children, her own recollections of a stepmother were not reassuring. And she regretted that Webb's constant visits and attention should have started gossip that she found offensive. Her heart would never be his, Mary wrote to Mercy with finality.

While she was still electioneering, eighteen-year-old Matilda Edwards, a cousin of Ninian's, arrived from Alton to stay at the mansion on the hill. She was an ethereal beauty and so deeply religious that she could not be persuaded to attend a ball they wished to give in her honor. Matilda primly wrote that she hoped to have strength "to resist these worldly fascinations which if indulged in bring a reproach upon the cause of religion." She found Mary Todd, who could enjoy going to church and be ecstatic over balls, too, a "very lovely and sprightly girl."

Joshua Speed, the susceptible Kentuckian, was immediately drawn to the beautiful Matilda, and Lincoln was dimly aware of her presence in the Edwards' house. Mary wrote at once to Mercy to let her know that she had found a congenial spirit in the new arrival. "I know you would be pleased with Matilda Edwards, a lovelier girl I never saw," she wrote. But Mary's spirits seemed to droop toward the end of 1840. The Edwards were doing everything they could to swing her away from her interest in Lincoln. They realized how serious things were when Ninian received a letter from Robert Smith Todd, Mary's father, asking for information about the character and ability of Abraham Lincoln. This communication persuaded the Edwards family that Lincoln had written formally to Todd, asking for Mary's hand in marriage, a convention of the era. It was clear from this that the young pair were making their own plans outside the periphery of Ninian's guardianship.

Lincoln was exhausted at this time from the hard campaign he had waged. Speed noticed that he was moping and that things did not seem to be going smoothly between the pair he assumed to be engaged. Mary, too, looked unhappy. She had lost eight pounds since returning from Missouri, although, in her own words, she was still a "ruddy pineknot." But it worried her when Lincoln made engagements and then forgot to keep them. On one of these occasions Mary lost patience and went off with Douglas. Lincoln arrived late at the Edwards' house, then hurried to the party, only to find Mary flirting with the irresistible Douglas. He left without a word, and the endless battle with his own uncertainty of purpose went on.

Speed was well aware of the turmoil his friend was in. Popular though he was with girls, Joshua had some of the same doubts and fears himself. Both young men were anxious to marry, but at this point they wavered, lacking confidence in their own capacity to make good husbands. Lincoln was doubly troubled because of the social gap between Mary and him and the outspoken criticism of her relatives. They made no secret of their disapproval of his presence.

One evening late in 1840 Lincoln showed Joshua a letter he had written to Mary. In it he said that he had thought things over with calmness and deliberation and had come to the conclusion that he did not love her enough to marry her. Speed advised him to burn it at once and instead to visit Mary and state his case to her in person. Lincoln returned at eleven that night, and according to the story that Joshua gave to Herndon on September 17, 1866, he told Mary that he did not love her. This version went on: "She burst into tears and almost springing from her chair and wringing her hands as if in agony, said something about the deceiver being himself deceived. . . . To tell you the truth, Speed, it was too much for me. I found the tears trickling down my own cheeks. I caught her in my arms and kissed her."

There was nothing left for proud Mary but to write Lincoln a letter releasing him from their engagement but making it clear that she had not changed her mind about him. Had Mary offended Lincoln by flirting so openly with Douglas? Had Lincoln fallen in love with the gentle Matilda Edwards, as Ninian Edwards insisted? But Matilda assured Herndon, when he asked her if Lincoln had ever mentioned the subject to her, that he had not, nor had he even "stooped to pay me a compliment." Mary's continuous friendship with Matilda, both at the time of the break and for years afterward, makes this romance seem unlikely.

The fact was that Lincoln was fatigued and close to collapse, torn by his doubts and uncertainty, and deep in melancholia. Mrs. Edwards gave Herndon two different versions of what had happened. She said that Lincoln "went crazy," not because he loved Matilda Edwards, as her husband believed, but because he wanted to marry and doubted his capacity to possess and support a wife. In a later interview she said that her sister had annoyed Lincoln by flirting openly with Douglas, but it was her own belief that in doing this Mary was merely trying to stir up laggardly Mr. Lincoln. In any event, after the break she and Ninian again advised Mary to give up all thought of marrying Lincoln. Their natures, education and upbringing were too unlike to ensure their happiness as husband and wife. His future was nebulous, said the pair who never gave Lincoln just recognition until he became a man of fame. Mrs. Edwards called it the year of the "crazy spell," and she vaguely lent countenance to the fantastic story spread on the record eventually by Herndon of a marriage date being set, of Mary waiting for the ceremony, of Lincoln backing out at the last moment and disappearing, only to be found the next day in a demoralized state.

In dissecting every angle of the confused wedding story, Ruth Painter Randall has dismissed it as a total distortion of events by a man who detested Mary Todd. According to Herndon, the marriage date had been set, an elaborate supper was ordered, the guests arrived, furniture was rearranged, flowers scented the air, and Mary was in an anteroom in gown and veil, waiting for the bridegroom, who failed to arrive. Messengers were finally sent out to find him, since he was known to be absentminded and late in keeping appointments. But time passed, the guests went home, Mary slipped out of her wedding gown, and darkness settled over the Edwards' house on the hill.

Such was Herndon's story, and it would shake the Lincoln worshipers when it finally reached the public. But Lincoln's breakdown was no myth. His friends found him the next day in a dangerous state of depression. They watched him closely, fearing that he might injure himself. He wrote to John Stuart: "I am now the most miserable man living, if what I feel were equally distributed to the whole human family, there would not be one cheerful face on the earth. . . . Whether I shall ever be better I can not tell. I awfully forbode I shall not. To remain as I am is impossible; I must die or be better, it appears to me."

Mercy and Conkling exchanged letters about Lincoln living in a lost world. On January 13, two weeks after his collapse, Conkling wrote: "Poor L! How are the mighty fallen! He was confined about a week, but though he now appears again he is reduced and emaciated in appearance and seems scarcely to possess strength enough to speak above a whisper." Mercy's answer was revealing: "Poor A—I fear his is a blighted heart! Perhaps if he was as persevering as Mr. W. [ebb] he might be successful."

Conkling felt sure that Mary had jilted him. Speed thought that it was the other way around, but all believed that the attitude of the Edwards family figured strongly in the broken engagement. Lincoln aimlessly walked the streets of Springfield and stayed away from Coterie members. He was said to be crazy, to be dying of love, to look like a wraith, and Matilda's name figured in much of the gossip. But Mary kept her counsel, held her head high, and did not lose interest in Mr. Lincoln, who by slow degrees recovered his balance. Matilda soon became Mrs. Newton Denning Strong, and "dear Molly" asked her to visit her in Springfield in the spring of 1842, indicating that she had never regarded this friend as a threat to her own happiness.

More menacing to Mary's reputation than the story of the broken engagement was Herndon's fantastic deduction that in the end she married Lincoln and treated him badly to get revenge for the slight she was supposed to have suffered. As one crisis after another developed in their married life, this outlandish theory was repeatedly applied to Mrs. Lincoln's history, distorting her image in an unjust way. "Herndon, self-convinced of his righteousness and omniscience, committed a terrible wrong," Mrs. Randall writes. "He was a lawyer and he framed her with a lawyer's skill. The greatest problem in telling Mary Lincoln's story is to remove the encrustations with which he has overlaid it."

Even her own family added to the confusion and contradictory evidence. Mrs. John Todd Stuart attributed the broken engagement directly to Mr. and Mrs. Edwards. She quoted Mary as saying that their opposition forced the issue, and this seems likely enough. Tall, dark Ninian, always a fashion plate in black broadcloth, with a gold-headed cane and high stock, was "naturally and constitutionally an aristocrat," wrote a legislative colleague, "and he hated democracy . . . as the devil is said to hate holy water." None of Mary's close relatives in Springfield, who would undoubtedly have been invited to her wedding, ever acknowledged the incident. Thus Herndon alone seems to bear the responsibility for having added this wounding story to Mary Lincoln's history.

Lincoln, who to Ninian Edwards at this time seemed "crazy as a loon," showed up intermittently in the legislature, and on January 20, 1841, his distraught frame of mind was mirrored in a letter he wrote to John Stuart, asking him to give the postmastership of Springfield to his friend, Dr. Anson G. Henry. "I have within the last few days, been making a most discreditable exhibition of myself in the way of hypochondriasis and thereby got an impression that Dr. Henry is necessary to my existence," Lincoln wrote. "Unless he gets that place he leaves Springfield. You therefore see how much I am interested in the matter. . . . I have not sufficient composure to write a long letter."

Dr. Henry was acting as Lincoln's physician, and hypochondriasis was medically defined at the time as a state of depression, low vitality and apprehensiveness. Lincoln qualified on all three counts. Two days later he was writing to Stuart that he was the most miserable man on earth, that he feared he could not attend to his business in Springfield, and that a change of scene might help him.

Mary worried about him, but they had no communication. In June she wrote to Mercy that the last two or three months had been of "*interminable* length." She added that she had lingering regrets over the past, which "time can alone overshadow with its healing balm." Summer had spread its beauty across the prairie, but something was missing. Without mentioning Lincoln by name she referred to Speed and went on: "*His* worthy friend, deems me unworthy of notice, as I have not met *him* in the gay world for months. With the usual comfort of misery (I) imagine that others were as seldom gladdened by his presence as my humble self, yet I would that the case were different, that he would once more resume his Station in Society, that 'Richard' should be himself again, much, much happiness would it afford me."

Mary showed strength and genuine sympathy in this time of

crisis. Lincoln seemed no longer to be a candidate for fame, but she was deeply committed to the steadfast love that proved to be unchanging with the years. She became more serious and thoughtful, and Sarah Edwards, of Alton, visiting the Edwards' home late in spring, wrote of the deep quiet that prevailed. She found Mary, or Molly, as she called her, as "lonesome as a gay company-loving girl, could be so situated." Mrs. Edwards had become deeply religious and there were few parties, but Mary declined an invitation to visit Sarah in Alton. She had no intention of leaving Springfield while Dr. Henry encouraged her with the thought that broken fences might be mended. It was his belief that Mary had overplayed her hand with Douglas.

In June, Lincoln was attending to his legal business, and later that summer he visited Joshua Speed, who had returned to live at his country estate near Louisville. On the well-stocked Speed farm, Lincoln was built up with good nourishment and the attentive care of Joshua's mother and sister. He was in better health when he returned to Springfield in September, and he and Joshua were soon exchanging letters that had close bearing on his own fate with Mary. Joshua had fallen in love with a girl named Fanny Henning and expected to marry her, but, like Lincoln with Mary, he was torn by doubts as to his capacity to make her happy.

Their cases seemed to be reversed, for Lincoln now became the adviser, encouraging Joshua, who confessed that he was afraid he did not love Fanny enough for marriage, and the mere thought of the wedding threw him into a panic. Joshua had been notorious in the Coterie for his many flirtations and his changing interests, but when it came to the final step, he was like a bashful stripling. Lincoln assured him that he did not feel his own sorrows any more keenly than he did Joshua's. For a time it seemed as if Mary's future depended on how things went with Joshua and Fanny, for Joshua was to report on developments when the dreaded step was taken. The pair of young men went in for extravagant soul-searching, and by 1842 it was Joshua who was having "melancholy forebodings" and was worrying about Sarah Rickard, a girl both had known and with whom Joshua had flirted.

The situation cleared when he married Fanny on February 15, 1842. Lincoln wrote to him that their mutual forebodings had been the worst sort of nonsense, since "it is the peculiar misfortune of both you and me to dream dreams of Elysium far exceeding all that anything earthly can realize." Within a month Speed had no doubt that he had found his own paradise and that he and Fanny were in perfect harmony. Lincoln was reassured about Speed, but he was still in some doubt about his own situation and was worrying about Mary. "Your last letter gave me more pleasure than the sum total of all I have enjoyed since that fatal first of January, 1841," he wrote to Speed. "Since then it seems to me that I should have been entirely happy, but for the absent idea that there is *one* still unhappy whom I have contributed to make so. That still kills my soul. I cannot but reproach myself for even wishing to be happy while she is otherwise."

This exchange of intimate letters between the two young men seems to have had a therapeutic effect on Lincoln, who was busy with legal matters and was beginning to show interest in the world again, in spite of fluctuating moods. He was evidently still deeply conscious of his incapacity to make a good living, a fact that the Edwards family had made amply clear to him. When Joshua invited Lincoln to visit Fanny and him that summer, he declined, writing on July 4, 1842, that he was so poor he seemed to be making little headway in the world and would "drop back in a month of idleness as much as I gain in a year's rowing."

God had made him one of the instruments of bringing Joshua and Fanny together, Lincoln wrote. "Whatever he designs, he will do for *me* yet. 'Stand *still* and see the salvation of the Lord' is my text just now." Hope was rising in him again, for there were indications that he and Mary would find each other once more. Their meeting, carefully planned by Dr. Henry and Mrs. Simeon Francis, wife of the editor of the Sangamon *Journal*, had the air of a casual encounter. Mrs. Francis and her husband were close friends of Lincoln's. He had passed much time in the office of the *Journal*, which later became the Illinois *State Journal*, ever since John Stuart had brought the gangling young Whig lawyer to meet them soon after his arrival in Springfield. They were close to the Edwards family, too, and were fond of Mary. Mrs. Francis' sister, Julia Jayne, was a friend of Mary's, so it seemed natural for her to be in the Francis' parlor the night that Lincoln appeared as if by chance.

It is legendary that Mrs. Francis said: "Be friends again!" when Lincoln saw Mary across the room. He moved toward her, took her hands gently in his, and soon they were discussing the resumption of their engagement. It was agreed that they would meet secretly at the Francis' home and that this time nothing would be said about a wedding date. But before long Mrs. Edwards heard what was going on and she asked Mary why she should be so secretive. Mary answered sharply that if "misfortune befell the engagement all knowledge of it would be hidden from the world."

The veil of silence did not cover them for long, however, for in September Mary inadvertently caused Lincoln one of the most serious embarrassments of his life when he was challenged to a duel over a senseless piece of tomfoolery that showed her at her most reckless. Mary liked to dash off verse, and she and Julia Jayne, thinking they would have a little fun at the expense of James Shields, the boastful gallant from Tyrone who had been one of Mary's suitors, satirized some of his follies in rhyme. This appeared in the Sangamon *Journal* as one of the four "Rebecca Letters," which caused a local stir. One reflected Lincoln's views on taxation and banking, in opposition to those held by Shields, who was State Auditor and a Democrat. The others, more personal in tone, were devastating in their satire. Years later Mary told Mrs. Gideon Welles that she was the author of all the offending letters but one, which Mr. Lincoln had written, but to protect her he had accepted responsibility for all four. Shields was furious and challenged him to a duel. Lincoln chose broadswords for the contest and practiced using the weapon. Because of his height he thought it likely that he could disarm Shields. "I didn't want the d—d fellow to kill me, which I rather think he would have done if we had selected pistols," Lincoln told a friend.

None of this was at all amusing to Lincoln, and Mary saw what a blunder she had made. "I doubtless trespassed, many times & oft, upon his great tenderness & amiability of character," she wrote to a friend long afterward in connection with this incident. It became a painful memory for both, although the issue was settled amicably without bloodshed when the principals finally met with much ceremony on Bloody Island opposite St. Louis.

"The occasion was so silly, that my husband was always so ashamed of it . . . we mutually agreed never to speak of it," Mary confessed to Mrs. Welles. And years later in the White House when a general jestingly referred to a duel for "the sake of the lady by your side," Lincoln, obviously annoyed, replied: "I do not deny it, but if you desire my friendship, you will never mention it again."

It was while Mary and Lincoln were embroiled in this absurd adventure that Lincoln wrote urgently to Speed. Apparently he wanted further reassurance that he would not be making a mistake in marrying Mary. Speed had now been married eight months and

Lincoln wrote: "Are you now, in feeling as well as judgment, glad you are married as you are? From anybody but me this would be an impudent question not to be tolerated, but I know you will pardon it in me. Please answer it quickly as I feel impatient to know." Speed answered at once, assuring Lincoln that his marriage had brought him great happiness.

The next step for Lincoln was marriage, and if he had some doubts and qualms, Mary had none. With pride and independence she had decided on a course of her own, knowing that it would mean estrangement from her family and a total change in her standard of living. From the start she never had any doubt that Lincoln was her man. Dr. Anson G. Henry, his physician and friend who had helped Mrs. Francis in bringing them together again, eventually wrote that Mary loved Lincoln as "women of her nervous sanguine temperament only can love." The seeds were deeply planted where she was concerned. All else had been flirtation; this was love.

III

Mary Todd Becomes Mrs. Lincoln

THE MARRIAGE OF Mary Todd and Abraham Lincoln was almost impromptu when it did come off as rain pelted the Edwards' house on the evening of November 4, 1842. Both had made sure that there would be no fuss, no ceremonial, no advance notice of their intention. When they stood in front of the fireplace, with astral lamps on the mantelpiece, and took their marriage vows, Lincoln was thirty-three and Mary was almost twenty-four.

Two years of love and hate, of delay and misunderstanding, of family pressure and political necessity had ended in a whirlwind of action, typical of Mary Todd's impulsive nature. She was consciously flouting tradition, her family and many of her friends to commit her life to a man who had recently undergone a breakdown and was still unsure of his wish to marry her.

Knowing how hostile the Edwards family was to the whole idea, Mary and Lincoln had planned to have Dr. Charles Dresser marry them in the Episcopal rectory that was later to become their home in Springfield. On the morning of the wedding Lincoln called on Dr. Dresser and told him that he needed his services that night. Meanwhile, Mary faced her sister Elizabeth with the news that she intended to marry Mr. Lincoln at Dr. Dresser's house. Mrs. Edwards reminded her that she was a Todd and that she was making a mistake in marrying a man so different from herself.

Mary was quiet and steadfast, instead of being her usual excitable self. She had been through it all before, and when Mrs. Edwards saw that nothing could stop her, she decided to make the best of things. Ninian, by accident or design, met Lincoln on the street and told him stiffly that since Mary was his ward, she would be married at his house and not at the rectory.

With this compromise accepted, Mary hurried to the home of Julia Jayne to ask her to be one of her bridesmaids. A cousin, Elizabeth Todd, also had to be rounded up, and she hurriedly washed and ironed her best white dress for the occasion. The third bridesmaid was Anna Caesaria Rodney, grandniece of Caesar Rodney of Delaware, a signer of the Declaration of Independence. According to Katherine Helm, Mary wore one of her "lovely embroidered white muslin dresses." Her sister, Mrs. Frances Wallace, recalled in later years that it was a delaine, and not the white satin dress that historians were disposed to link with Mary Todd. The chances are that she wore her best dress, whatever it was, and made herself as attractive as possible, since this was part of her nature.

It was not the kind of marriage that she had dreamed of in Lexington, nor were her father and stepmother present to see her become Mrs. Abraham Lincoln. But she was getting the man she wanted, and in her case at least the magic of love was there. It was Mary who had pushed the issue, with full belief in what she was doing. Lincoln arrived at the Edwards' mansion after a close inspection by the family of William Butler, where he boarded, to see that his attire was in order. Mrs. Butler tied his high stock, and her daughter Salome smoothed out a few wrinkles. One of the children, not in on the secret, asked: "Where are you going, Mr. Lincoln?"

"To the devil, I suppose," Lincoln answered, obviously striking a jesting note, but this was used later by Herndon against Mary as a serious statement of fact.

When he asked J. H. Matheny nearly a quarter of a century after the wedding how Lincoln had looked that night, the best man promptly recalled that he acted as if he were "going to the slaughter." Mrs. Wallace's recollection may have been closer to the mark. She thought that the bridegroom acted as he always did in company and was as cheerful "as he ever had been, for all we could see."

Thirty guests, mostly relatives, were present. The Edwards' house, where so many great parties had been staged by Elizabeth, acting as hostess for her widowed father-in-law, the governor, was well adapted to an occasion of this kind. Flowers scented the air. Supper was served on a long table with a linen cover embroidered with the turtledove design used for weddings. It was not a Giron feast, with spun-sugar confections. The arrangements had been so rushed that the wedding cake was still warm when it was served.

Dr. Dresser in his canonical robes performed the ceremony, and Lincoln's huge fingers fumbled with the plain gold band that was to become famous for its "Love is eternal" inscription. As he slipped it on Mary's hand, her sense of triumph was very apparent to her wondering sisters. The rain pelted down as it would on other unforgettable occasions in her life—on the day of Willie's funeral, on the day that her husband was elected for a second term, and on the morning he died. But the hailstones that fell did not dim the romantic aura of their wedding night as they slipped out after a few toasts to begin their married life at the Globe Tavern, where they occupied a $4-a-week room that Dr. Wallace had vacated when he married Frances.

Lincoln was almost penniless at the time, but Mary had made up her mind that she would share his poverty and live within his income. A hundred and thirty years later people still ask: "What did Mary Todd and Abraham Lincoln see in each other?" At the time they seemed to be incompatible in all respects—in looks, social background, training, education, outlook and habits. Was it love on both sides? Or did ambition enter into it? Did strong-willed Mary believe from the start that Mr. Lincoln was a man of stature who could fulfill himself with her help? And did Lincoln really believe that the Edwards family, who had treated him with open scorn, could contribute anything to his political advancement? It seems unlikely, although Herndon, who had viewed him as going to the slaughter when he married Mary, noted that it was natural that he "should seek by marriage in an influential family to establish strong connections and at the same time foster his political fortune."

Whatever the motivation in either case, physical harmony seemed to wipe out the complexities that had gone before. All of Lincoln's fears and uncertainties, expressed so freely to Joshua Speed, dissolved in his alliance with the deeply affectionate and emotional Mary Todd. Like his friend Speed with Fanny Henning, Lincoln had found the answer to his discontent in a responsive bride. John Nicolay later wrote with understanding of their union: "His marriage to Miss Todd ended all those mental perplexities and periods of despondency from which he suffered more or less during his several love affairs, extending over nearly a decade."

It seemed a miracle to Lincoln himself. Two weeks after his wedding day he wrote to a friend: "Nothing new here, except my marrying, which to me is a matter of profound wonder." It was to all his friends, too, but obviously a world of greater security than he had known, and some relaxation had opened up for him with Mary by his side. He took delight in her small curvaceous figure, her coquettish ways, and her bookish interests. He did not change overnight, and he was still subject to melancholy moods and periods of total silence, but Mary brought gaiety and laughter into his life with her thoroughly feminine ways that softened the sharp edges of some of her comments on political affairs.

Disparate though they were, the delight they found in each other from the start established a lasting family pattern that seemed to sustain them through stress, discord and disaster and to heighten their moments of triumph and success. The encompassing affection that Lincoln felt for his wife shows clearly in the letters they exchanged through the years. His have no words of love, but they mirror his constant concern for his wife and sons, his loneliness and longing when they were separated, and, most of all, the gentle and understanding way in which he coped with Mary's moods and tantrums.

Her pride was at stake from the moment she unpacked her things at the Globe. Her break with her family was self-evident when she no longer went up the hill or attended the parties where she had once played a stellar role. Mary neither forgot nor forgave the people who cold-shouldered her husband at this time, and there were many. As Lincoln grew in importance, Mr. and Mrs. Edwards tried to heal the breach, but the chill remained.

Since there was no housekeeping to be done at the hotel, Mary, no longer part of the social flow to which she had been accustomed, chose the solitary role and buried herself in books, for her bridegroom was traveling most of that first year. But when he returned and was joyfully welcomed, she studied him at close range to see where she could best help him. She was no amateur where men were concerned. From her earliest years she had associated with worldly and brilliant men, and her conversational powers were considerable. The bookish link between them that had been intermittent for two years flowered in the more intimate association of the married state. They had time to talk and be alone without having Coterie members always around them.

Mary was able to indulge her passion for reciting page after page of poetry. In commenting on this taste, her cousin, Mrs. Margaret Stuart Woodrow, wrote of the intensity with which she did everything. "She was very highly strung, nervous, impulsive, irritable, having an emotional temperament much like an April day, running all over with laughter one moment, at the next crying as though her heart would break."

Lincoln, who had already been indoctrinated in her swift changes of mood, treated them with indulgence and sometimes with amusement. He liked to hear her read, and sometimes he picked up the thread himself. He was proud of the fact that she could read both French and German poetry. With persistence and authority she took issue with the *Southern Literary Messenger*, a favorite publication of the Lincolns, on its translation of a speech by Victor Hugo on capital punishment. Convinced that the "true Hugo fire and force" were missing in this tepid version, she made one of her own from the original copy of the address. This was a miracle to Orville Hickman Browning, who commented on it, and no doubt it was to her husband, too.

Mr. Lincoln already knew that her energy was boundless, and he came to rely on the careful study she made of books and reports on political affairs while he was traveling the circuit. She was always ready for helpful discussion with him on his return, and she never showed in any way that she missed the old round of parties or the comings and goings of her more affluent friends. Years later, when her husband had gone all the way to the top, there were people in Springfield who believed that she had been a kingmaker from the start, and that much of her impatience with him was based on her passion to have him succeed. She was credited by some of his intimates with bringing fresh vigor into his life at this time. He had more assurance and his sluggish nature quickened in tempo. Herndon considered Mary a whiplash to her husband, rousing him from his lethargy and dreams. "Her pride was almost sinful in its intensity," he commented with some perception.

The first lesson she had to learn was frugality, a quality alien to her life in Lexington and in Springfield up to the time of her marriage. Lincoln's legal work brought him less than $2,000 a year in the early 1840's. He had to pay the bills he still owed in New Salem, and he contributed to the support of his paternal relatives. Mary soon found that he was haphazard about collecting his office fees and that he charged too little for his services. She applied her bright wits to improving this situation, and her parsimony amused her husband, who had never known what it was to have much money. It was as excessive as her extravagance in later years, for even in the White House Mary was apt to swing with pathological intensity between the two extremes. There was something desperately urgent in her nature, and she had to gratify each whim as it developed.

Something new and vital came into her life when her first son, Robert Todd Lincoln, was born on August 1, 1843, nine months after the rain-swept night on which she and Mr. Lincoln settled in the Globe Tavern. For one who reacted extravagantly to the major and minor crises of life, Mary seemed to be natural and happy in coping with childbirth. It was never easy for her, but she was motherly by nature, and she had repeatedly watched friends go through the experience. The baby was born at the Globe, and none of her sisters or relatives helped her at this time, but Mrs. Albert Taylor Bledsoe, a fellow guest at the Tavern, nursed her and attended to the baby. Bledsoe was a lawyer friend of Lincoln's, and his wife took charge until Mary was able to cope with matters herself.

Her father was touched that she should have named the baby for him, and he came from Lexington to see how Mary was getting along. He decided that she was faring badly, and he arranged to give her a cash advance of $120 a year until Lincoln was better established in his law practice. When he died, the final settlement of the Todd estate showed that he had given them $1,157.50 in this way over the years.

Soon after the baby's birth they began to feel the need for a home of their own. There were complaints at the Tavern about the infant's crying, and Mary had made no attempt to make friends in her new setting. The first year of her marriage might be said to have been the most unsocial period of her entire life until her last days, but it had been a year of development for both Lincolns.

In the autumn of 1843 they moved to a frame cottage with three rooms at 214 South Fourth Street, and that, too, was an obscure period in Mrs. Lincoln's life as she coped for the first time with serious housekeeping. But on a May day in 1844 they moved into the Dresser house, which is a historic landmark as the home of Abraham Lincoln in Springfield. Situated at Eighth and Jackson streets, it was close to Lincoln's law office. They had another bonanza from Mary's father at this time, when he gave her eighty acres of land three miles southwest of Springfield.

This was the true beginning of their family life; their way of living was typically mid-Victorian, so far as furniture, costume and the care of their children were concerned, but they were not in any sense an average pair. Lincoln, strange, kindly and a clever politician, had many friends, but Mary, ambitious, eager for fine clothes, fun and entertainment, baffled her new neighbors. She had always been identified with the aristocrats on the hill. Although she usually had a servant, her housekeeping was not greatly admired in her new milieu. She was used to being waited on, and now she had to learn to cope with every kind of household emergency. There was little time in which to read and dream.

Springfield did not have gas until the 1850's, so oil lamps had to be tended and candles made at home. Mary had an able woodchopper in Mr. Lincoln, who kept her supplied with logs to feed the fire. Water was drawn from a backyard pump, and bread had to be baked. Mary was a deplorable cook, but she was an accomplished seamstress, thanks to the instruction she had received at Madame Mentelle's. Even her most critical neighbors noticed that she spent hours sewing fine tucks in her husband's shirts. As the children arrived, she had to cope with sturdy garments for the cold prairie winters, and Mr. Lincoln was as used to seeing her with her sewing basket at her side as with the books that she loved to read. He had a special genius of his own for losing buttons, rumpling his attire, and turning a carefully pressed coat into a ragbag effect. There is no doubt that Mary nagged him unmercifully about his untidy ways as she tried to smarten him up.

This was a struggle that went on as long as he lived. Mary at all times was intensely conscious of appearances, and it worried her that clothes did not settle smoothly on her husband's ungainly figure, although in Washington he wore much the same garments as his fellow politicians. But nothing much could be done about his unruly hair, his disorderly stock, his unfurbished look in general. She treated him with motherly concern, as she did the sons who came along until there were four.

Convinced that he had tubercular tendencies at this time, she fretted about the need for overshoes and warm clothes to protect him on his circuit trips. She dosed him as she did the children with castor oil, calomel, ipecac, Box Ox Marrow and cough candy, in the fashion of the day. Lincoln's devotion to liver pills was thought to affect both his health and his moods, and it was not until his later years that he slackened up on his dosage of this potent medicine.

Their second son, Edward Baker Lincoln, was born on March 10,

1846, and a third boy, William Wallace Lincoln, arrived on December 21, 1850. Mary was so ill when Willie was born that Lincoln hesitated to leave home to visit his father, who was also in desperate straits at the time. On April 4, 1853, Thomas Lincoln was born, a child with spindly legs and a head so large that his father likened him to a tadpole. This boy would become the much-loved Tad of White House fame, but he almost cost his mother her life, and for twelve years after his birth she suffered from complications of this obstetrical ordeal. Both Lincolns had hoped for a girl this time, and in 1860 the President-elect wrote: "I regret the necessity of saying I have no daughter."

Herndon called Lincoln a good husband but only in his own peculiar way. He lacked the tender ways that pleased women, and "if his wife was happy, she was naturally happy, or made herself so in spite of countless drawbacks." But Mary's own testimony reveals more strongly than anyone else's that she found him a cheerful, funny, and also a tender man.

In describing him physically Herndon wrote that the "whole man, body and mind, worked slowly, creakingly, as if it needed oiling." He had a "woestruck" air, with his dark skin, dry and tough, crinkled and lying in flabby folds; a loose and leathery structure; and a body "all shrunk, cadaverous and shriveled." Herndon saw him as thin, wiry, sinewy and with heavy bones. When standing, he leaned forward and looked stoop-shouldered.

In the early years of their marriage, he spent three months in spring and three in autumn riding the circuit in fulfillment of his legal duties. Lincoln enjoyed this free existence, meeting men of diverse interests, traveling on horseback or in curious vehicles, staying at village inns and farmhouses, meeting the local lawyers and holding court in dim quarters, or sometimes out in the open under trees or in the street. He was in his element leading this rough existence, joining in the talk and conviviality of his fellow lawyers and judges, sharing quarters sometimes with eight in a room or two in a bed. They sat around the stove in inn parlors or in village stores when they were not being entertained by the town's best families.

The lawyers usually made frequent trips home, joining their families for weekends. Herndon made much of the fact that Lincoln did less of this than any of them because he had no peace at home, but the fact is that he covered more ground than most and was intent on saving as much as he could, for he was badly off. He was away for three months before Robert was born and Mary suffered over this. In her later years she said that she could have been a better wife to Lincoln had she seen more of him in these early days. She wrote regretfully of the loneliness of her married life at this time.

Fellow lawyers on the circuit remembered many strange things about his habits, and some of them realized that Mary's life with him could not have been easy. They found him alternately moody and silent or extravagantly loquacious, telling stories and making jokes. He was a restless sleeper with disturbing dreams, and he would wake up suddenly talking gibberish and seeming not to know where he was. Mary, too, had to cope with his midnight wanderings, his uneasy dreams, his early rising. Getting used to his habits must have been a long and painful process for her.

Fastidiously trained herself, she had to watch him wander about with a plate in his hand at mealtime, roughhouse the children at the table, and otherwise help in the general bedlam that seemed to characterize the Lincoln home after their sons were born. Perhaps because of his height he seemed to be most comfortable on the floor, and visitors were used to the sight of Mr. Lincoln jouncing his children from this stance or reading with his back resting against a turned-down chair. He liked to shuffle about in slippers or to poise his stockinged feet on a table or windowsill.

Mary could never forget her Kentucky training, and it made her angry when her husband answered the doorbell, although they had a maid at the time. Worse still was his cheerful greeting to a group of the town's more distinguished ladies that his wife would be down when she got her "trotting harness" on. On this occasion she did not wait for her guests to leave before giving Mr. Lincoln a tongue-lashing that persuaded them things were not going well with Mary Todd.

Early in their married life she came through as a strong and purposeful figure. There is no doubt that her tantrums did not begin in the White House, or even in Springfield, but dated back to her childhood days in Lexington. Her stormy moods, followed by periods of dazzling charm and gaiety, took on a certain stridency as she coped with household cares, tended sick children, tried to make ends meet, and came to grips with Mr. Lincoln's irregular hours. Mary's soft Kentucky accent took on a shrill emphasis as she harangued him, and an occasional scream might have been heard as her temper rose with sudden turbulence, beating against the steady front of Lincoln's strength and patience. Dr. W. A. Evans, with

Freudian foresight, suggested that she had a father fixation and longed to be treated like a child.

Mary had a well-developed sense of order that was shattered as the children ran wild and she never knew when her husband would arrive for his meals. Joshua Speed reported to Herndon that in all his habits of eating, sleeping, reading, conversation and study Lincoln was "regularly irregular," so how could Mrs. Lincoln be expected to have his meals on time? Her occasional failures in this respect bothered him little, since he was just as happy with a bag of crackers and cheese; he was not a gourmet either then or after he settled in Washington, where he was exposed to the best cuisine of the day.

Actually Mary was a conscientious housekeeper, and she had gone to great pains to furnish their new house with taste and some echoes of the life she had known in Lexington and in the Edwards' mansion. Her means were limited, but she never complained about the things she lacked. Her conviction that she had chosen the right course was unshakable. She shared with her neighbors the daily round of concern over their children's illnesses, of fashioning clothes in the manner decreed by Madame Godey, of exchanging recipes and helpful hints. It was characteristic of Mary that at a Fourth of July party she was more interested in a plumed pink velvet bonnet worn by one of her friends than she was in the state of the ice cream when no cornstarch was available. "Oh, use flour," said Mary cheerfully. "I always do, and you'll find it a great deal better."

Pink was one of her favorite colors, and she liked to point out that, although Mr. Lincoln did not know pink from blue when she first met him, he learned in time to compare the blue clusters of flowers on a dress to the blue of her eyes.

On the whole this was a period of comparative happiness for Mary, as one son followed another. Her maternal instincts were so strong that after Tad was born, she took on the added task of nursing a frail infant born to a neighbor, Mrs. Charles Dallman. Lincoln would knock gently at the mother's door so as not to disturb her and then pick up the child in his massive hands, bringing it across the road to Mary to feed. It did not survive for long, however.

Mary's anxiety when her children were ill was beyond all reason. Her neighbor James Gourley, to whom she often appealed for aid when her husband was away, found her most excitable, and he also seemed to sense the fact that she had hallucinations. Thunderstorms always threw her into a panic, and when Lincoln was in Springfield, he would hurry to the house from his office the instant a storm threatened.

Gourley saw Mrs. Lincoln at her worst and also at her best. He thought her too clever for her own good but intensely feminine in all her ways. He came to the conclusion that the Lincolns got on reasonably well, but only because the master of the house surrendered quietly when his wife lost all control, as she sometimes did. She suffered intensely from the headaches known today as migraine. From the start Lincoln seemed to accept this debility in his wife and to treat her with understanding and sympathy when her attacks came on. When she took to her bed or was having a tantrum, he would quietly say that his wife was not well that day. A century later Mrs. Lincoln's hormonal balance no doubt would have been called into question by the medical profession, for her letters contain references to her "female problems."

In any event neighbors seemed to understand when papers or small household objects came whizzing through the door, a sure sign of trouble inside. Occasionally Lincoln would carry a small desk stuffed with papers to a neighbor's house for safekeeping, saying that his wife had a severe headache.

Various neighbors noticed that when Mary went too far, Lincoln would pick up one of the children and go out with him until she recovered her poise. But before taking this measure, he would try to laugh her out of her rage. This rarely worked, but when she had had time to wear out her hysteria, she settled into gay spirits and all was forgotten—until the next outburst. Lincoln let the storm rage. He rarely crossed her on these occasions, and he knew that he could not reason with her. But he could always walk out and leave her alone.

When he showed up at his office at seven in the morning instead of the customary nine o'clock, Herndon would assume that he was having trouble at home, although there was no proof of this. He would throw himself on a lounge or double up in a chair and rest his feet on the sill of a back window. Herndon commented on the deep melancholy of his manner as he ate crackers and cheese and looked into space.

A light in the office after dark also informed the suspicious Herndon that Lincoln was fleeing from Mary, and a mutual friend assured him that Mary Todd, by her turbulent nature and unfortunate manner, prevented her husband from becoming a domestic man and kept him out in the world of business and politics, to his own political advantage. He frequently brought his boys to the office, and they infuriated Herndon. They ruffled papers, spilled ink, pulled down books and left things in a state of confusion. He wanted "to wring their necks and throw them out the window." But he dared not say a word in their father's presence, for he "worshipped his children and what they worshipped; he loved what they loved and hated what they hated."

Lincoln liked to take his boys into the country, to romp with them in the woods, to share in their childish sports. Sometimes he took them with some of the neighborhood boys for a drive deep into the country in the family calash, to fish, picnic and play games. They had no dogs, but Bob sometimes had the fun of harnessing the Gourley boy's dog and going with him to the woods for roots. Lincoln preferred cats.

The Gourleys were impressed with the ways in which Lincoln helped his wife, particularly with the children. He sometimes wheeled them while she was in church, and it became a family joke that one Sunday, while pushing the baby carriage with one hand and holding a book open in the other, the baby fell out and was left behind as Lincoln stalked on, unconscious of what had happened. This was one of the sins for which Mary was later held accountable.

Neighborhood boys did some baby sitting for the Lincolns at five cents a night. One named Howard M. Powel sometimes drove their carriage for the same fee. This youth liked to listen to Lincoln declining Latin nouns and conjugating verbs with Robert. He thought that Willie was the living image of his father, even in the way he tilted his head to the left. Albert S. Edwards, Mrs. Lincoln's nephew, who spent his weekends at their home, loyally insisted in later years that he had "never heard a harsh word or anything out of the way." He was always his Aunt Mary's champion and was convinced that his parents had done their best to prevent the Lincolns from marrying.

Mary had particularly good relationships with the Samuel H. Melvins and with Mrs. John Henry Shearer, keeping in touch with them after she went to the White House and inviting them to visit her. The Melvins had a large yard and an experienced nurse who was glad to keep an eye on the Lincoln children, too. Their father would often stop and pick them up on his way home from the office, for Mary was frequently out at church parties or other functions. She never missed a chance to socialize, and she had great charm for the little girls of the neighborhood because of her pretty dresses and fetching ways. Maggie Blaine, who later became Mrs. W. O. Wirt, of Council Bluffs, wrote years later that when she was attending a private school in Springfield, she loved to sit beside Mrs. Lincoln at the church parties. She remembered her in pale lilac, with ribbons and bows, and a lacy parasol, engaging in lively conversation.

If Mrs. Lincoln was at times a shrew with some of their elders, there is strong evidence that she was more than kind to children. She made them welcome at her house and gave them gingerbread and macaroons. She was interested in what they learned in school, and at times she rattled off French to them or read poetry. Everything she did made her a little different from her neighbors, even when she seemed anxious to conform to the standards of the community. The children saw nothing but indulgence in Mrs. Lincoln, and little Julia Isabelle Sprigg recalled how welcome she was made to feel when she stayed overnight in the Lincolns' home. She was tucked into a smothering pile of blankets, her ruffles were crisped, and she was conscious of the faint fragrance of lavender that drifted from Mrs. Lincoln as she moved about the room.

For someone with a temper as ungovernable as Mary's, it is difficult to believe that she never lost her poise with the children, but all evidence points to the fact that both parents were fantastically indulgent. Mary amazed some of her friends by insisting that her boys did not need punishment, an incredible thought to those who had to deal with them in the White House and also in Springfield. Lincoln had been severely whipped as a child; Mary had been pampered and no one had ever laid a hand on her. Sometimes Lincoln would make a switch from a tree branch and flourish it, but somehow he had difficulty applying it. Mrs. Wallace thought it absurd that he should carry Tad halfway to the office when he had reached an age to walk by himself, but Lincoln had special tenderness for his handicapped son, who was mentally retarded. "Oh, don't you think his little feet get too tired?" he answered. Willie thought he would like to be a preacher. Bob had a mania, sometimes fulfilled, for running away. Mary worked hard to train them well, in spite of the irregularity of her husband's comings and goings.

She read to them, dressed them in sturdy clothes, patched their baggy trousers, and bore down heavily on their manners at table. This must have often been amusing to her husband, who had table ways of his own. Herndon was scornful of Mary's efforts in this direction and wrote that when important visitors were coming to the house she would dress the children up and trot them into view "to monkey around—talk—dance—speak—quote poetry." There was nothing that Mary enjoyed more than a children's party, and as the years went by, she would draw in as many as fifty or sixty boys and girls, sending them carefully prepared invitations.

Maids came and went at the Lincoln home, but this was a common state of affairs at a time when it was difficult to get servants or to keep them. Many were intemperate, incompetent and hard to handle, but Herndon made much of the fact that Mrs. Lincoln could not keep a maid because of her temperamental furies. There was no doubt that she was a penny pincher at this time, and maids in general were paid only $1.50 a week. In one instance Lincoln paid one of their girls an extra dollar a month to make sure that she stayed. This was done without Mary's knowledge, for in her desire to husband the family finances at this time, she bargained over every box of berries and haggled over the cost of ribbons and muslins. A Portuguese maid and a black maid whom she had at different times were devoted to her, but Mary all her life would be the victim of backstairs gossip.

The Herndon digging into the ways of the Lincolns during these early years in Springfield took no account of the hours of love and peace that must have been theirs. In spite of all the jangling and the worries of the day they seem to have achieved a physical harmony that survived the years with a life-giving warmth. Mary read to her husband by lamplight—books, reports, verse, the classics and newspapers. Lincoln liked the sound of her voice as she read soothingly but with dramatic effect. Astronomy was a popular study at the time, and on a starry night Mary would sit with him on the porch, naming the planets and pointing out the constellations. It was sometimes hard to stir his interest in such things, but he knew he could count on her to understand fully the political issues that filled his thoughts. He was proud of the fact that his wife could read French classics in the original, but he preferred to hear her talk about Henry Clay and the rising tide of antislavery feeling in the South.

Herndon expressed the view that it was by dint of Mrs. Lincoln's untiring efforts and the recognition of influential friends that Lincoln managed to move ahead. "In his struggles, both in the law and for political advancement, his wife shared in his sacrifices," Herndon wrote, throwing her a bouquet instead of a brickbat when he added: "She was a plucky little woman, and in fact endowed with a more restless ambition than he. She was gifted with a rare insight into the motives that actuate mankind, and there is no doubt that much of Lincoln's success was in a measure attributable to her acuteness and the stimulus of her influence."

She greatly influenced his course up to the time he reached the White House; and the Springfield years, with Lincoln growing in political stature, seemed to Mary like a revival of her life in the Todd household, with political talk around the dinner table but from a vastly different point of view. Here Mary had full play with her varied knowledge of the nation's politicians, particularly those of the South. Politics was a game that she had always understood and delighted in, which made her different from many of the women of her time, although Springfield seethed with political feeling. She gave Lincoln much enlightenment about the South, and she was always ready with an acerbic or positive judgment. The one major crime in Mary's estimation was any attempt to hinder her husband's progress.

The strength of her ambition was made clear to Ward Hill Lamon in 1847 when he first met the Lincolns and dined at Mary's well-appointed table. This fashionable Virginian, with ruffled shirt and swallowtail frock coat, struck Lincoln as being a lightweight who would never understand working by the sweat of one's brow as long as there were slaves. Lamon, like Herndon, would tear Mary down in the future; he was conscious almost at once of her intense ambition. He mentioned the fact that her husband was a great favorite in the eastern part of the state, where he had been visiting.

"Yes," said Mrs. Lincoln quickly, "he is a great favorite everywhere. He is to be President of the United States some day; if I had not thought so I never would have married him, for you can see he is not pretty. But look at him! Doesn't he look as if he would make a magnificent President?"

Lamon chose to take Mary literally, although she was given to making jesting remarks of this kind. Her enthusiasm seemed excessive, and Lamon secretly thought Lincoln at that time about as unpromising a candidate as the American people would ever be likely to put forward. Later he would reverse this opinion. At the moment he smoothly agreed with Mrs. Lincoln to mollify her, and in telling this story in his book he wrote: "At that time I felt convinced that Mrs. Lincoln was running Abraham beyond his proper distance in that race. . . . Mrs. Lincoln, from that day to the day of his inauguration, never wavered in her faith that her hopes in this respect could be realized."

Mary spoke up repeatedly for her husband, surprising colleagues with her emphatic note of confidence and her fluent and aggressive magnification of Abraham Lincoln. Her own nature complemented many of his qualities, for she was pragmatic where he was impractical; she was orderly where he was slovenly; she moved quickly into action while he dreamed. Herndon wrote that when she visited their law office she seemed to be inordinately proud of Mr. Lincoln. "She saw in him bright prospects ahead, and his every move was watched by her with the closest interest. If to other persons he seemed homely, to her he was the embodiment of noble manhood, and each succeeding day impressed upon her the wisdom of her choice of Lincoln over Douglas—if in reality she ever seriously accepted the latter's attentions. 'Mr. Lincoln may not be as handsome a figure,' she said one day in the office when the conversation turned to Douglas, 'but the people are perhaps not aware that his heart is as large as his arms are long.' "

When Douglas defeated him in the Senate race and the word went forth that "Abe was through," Mary more emphatically than ever insisted that he would yet be President. But however effective her methods may have been, it was self-evident that Lincoln's own ambition was unquenchable. He could handle men and he was a master politician. His fortitude and persistence were in view long before Mary Todd came into his life, and she never at any time laid claim to having helped him on his way. Rather, in her later years she tortured herself over the hard times she had given him with her tempers and illnesses. Her remorse was as swift and extreme as the temper that ruled her.

It was not until Lincoln was dead and his wife's unpopularity was at its crest that these tales, carefully assembled by Herndon, became public. At the time the Lincolns were not considered remarkable, although it was an accepted fact that Mr. Lincoln was moving ahead fast in the political world and that his wife mingled charm, good manners and breeding with a maniacal temper. But did she chase him out of the house with a broomstick? Did she throw papers after him on a number of occasions? Did she toss a bucket of water on his head from an upstairs window as he tried to get into the house? Did she chase him with a knife? And did she dash a cup of coffee in his face?

Some of these incidents have been reliably documented by witnesses, but Herndon was prone to draw deductions based solely on his observations of Lincoln's moods. These were often tinctured with his detestation of Mrs. Lincoln, who had never invited him to their house for dinner and who disapproved of his drinking. When her husband took Herndon into partnership, Mary thought that he was making a mistake. But politically, Herndon was closer to the more radical faction of the Whig Party, numerically strong and alive with youthful insurgence as opposed to the conservative faction represented by John Todd Stuart, John J. Hardin and Stephen T. Logan, senior lawyers who had earlier taken Lincoln into their firm. Now he felt the need for someone without political ambitions, who would be a good office administrator and might bring him closer to this rapidly growing Whig constituency. Lincoln needed the support of both elements to shape his political destiny, and it had not helped him in some quarters to have been identified with the "pride, wealth, and aristocratic family distinction" that Mary Todd had brought into his life.

Lincoln characterized Herndon as one of the "shrewd boys" because of his political prescience, his wide acquaintance, and his sympathy with the lowlier Whigs as opposed to the aristocratic faction. Herndon's biographer, David Donald, called him a "child of the frontier," a man's man with the earthy flavor of the prairies. "He knew the talk of racing and cock-fights and horses and women; he liked ribald anecdotes and practical jokes. His was a horselaugh, not a titter." He was born in Kentucky on Christmas Day in the same year as Mary Todd. His parents were Virginians, and his father, a tavern keeper, had fought to make Illinois a slave state, but Herndon was bitterly opposed to the slave traffic.

He was a familiar figure in Mary's life but never a trusted one. She had never liked him, nor did she consider his influence on Lincoln good. He offended her in all respects, in spite of his wide learning and superficial sophistication. But knowing how her husband felt about him, she preserved civil relations with Herndon during the years in Springfield. His smashing attack on their love life in 1866, after her husband's death, was a mortal blow for Mary, from which she never wholly recovered.

IV

A Congressman's Wife

P OLITICAL AMBITION STIRRED strongly in Mary Lincoln when her husband was elected to Congress in 1847. This meant the widening of their horizons and the first step on the national scene. At the time she was merely another obscure frontier wife accompanying her husband to Washington, but this was never how Mary felt about herself. Her belief in Lincoln was too strong for that. She decided to make a family pilgrimage to Lexington on their way to the capital. This was her first chance to show off her able and ambitious husband and to revisit her early home.

They rented their Springfield house for a year at $90; then, with four-year-old Robert and nineteen-month-old Eddy, they went to St. Louis by stagecoach, traveling the rest of the way by steamboat and rail. Sailing on the Mississippi was high adventure for Bob, with the strumming of banjos on board and the excitement at the landings of a chattering assortment of people crowding around their boat.

Lexington had changed, but the brick mansion on Main Street had the old familiar air, with the Todds and their servants all lined up to greet Mary and her family. Emilie Todd, her half sister and eighteen years her junior, recalled later that she looked lovely and glowing that day, with Eddy in her arms and her blue eyes shining with excitement at the waiting group. Her white skin was delicately flushed, and her dark hair curled softly at her neck.

All eyes, however, were focused on Lincoln as he unbent from his great height and deposited Robert at the door. Although Mary's father had visited them in Springfield, her stepmother and her half brothers and half sisters had never set eyes on the extraordinary man whom she had married.

"So this is Little Sister," he said as he embraced Emilie, who would always be a favorite with Lincoln. His friendly, simple manner endeared him to the Todds once they had become used to his strange appearance and wry jests. In the three weeks they stayed, he came to know the verdant little city and its leading figures. He also had his first full-scale view of the slave traffic in action.

From the terrace of Mrs. Parker's lawn he could look over spiked palings into the grim structure that housed most of the runaway slaves. Strange cries and shouts came from behind its high walls. William Pullum, a leading slave dealer, was quartered only a few yards from Mrs. Parker's side porch, and around the corner on Broadway was the two-story brick house where trading was carried on. Pullum and his family lived upstairs, above the large double room with bars where dealers, drivers and others identified with the slave trade assembled to chaffer and drink. Here the slaves were exhibited to prospective buyers in cold weather. In the yard behind were rows of slave pens, vermin-infested, with damp brick floors lightly strewn with straw and small barred windows near the roof.

The black locust whipping post, put up in 1826, had decayed and been supplanted by a tall three-pronged poplar tree in the courthouse yard which served the same purpose. Slaves were sold almost every day, but Saturdays and court days were set aside for the auctioning of flesh and blood. At the same time junk, old horses and various commodities were bartered at Cheapside, the public meeting place since Lexington was founded. Groups of men discussed the slaves, the crops, politics and horses as they sat on low wooden benches close to the iron fence that enclosed the courthouse yard.

At the Todd home Lincoln saw the other side of the coin, with blacks apparently content with their situation. In many ways they seemed to run the household. Mary relaxed as the children were taken over completely by Mammy Sally and her assistants. At Mrs. Parker's the faithful trio, Ann, Prudence and Cyrus, who had served her for years, studied Lincoln with interest. Mrs. Parker was known to be against slavery, and she would free her slaves in her will.

All this was a new experience for Abraham Lincoln, and Robert Todd saw to it that he viewed the best as well as the worst of the town. He visited Henry Clay, then mourning the death of his son in the Mexican War, and he heard him speak before a large audience on November 13. Clay said the war was one of "unnecessary and offensive aggression." To take over Mexico would mean acquiring new territory into which slavery could spread.

The people of Lexington did not forget that Mrs. Lincoln was a Todd, and they were lavishly entertained. There was no visible friction between her and her stepmother on this visit, and her brother Levi Todd drove Lincoln to the village of Sandersville, where the cotton mills of Oldham, Todd & Company were in operation with slave labor. Mary knew that Levi ran this business himself.

Her father and Lincoln were already on congenial terms, and she did not need to draw her husband's attention to the fine library with which she had grown up. The silver, the crystal, the chandeliers, and graceful furniture all were too strong a reminder that life was sparse for Mary in Springfield. She made a point of seeing her friends and sought out the Wickliffe sisters at once, in spite of the strong feeling her father had about this powerful slaveholding family.

The substantial mansions and large estates of Lexington were thoughtfully studied by Lincoln, who took stock of their landscaped gardens and deep courtyards. He was well aware that something of this sort might have been Mary's fate had she not married him. The most spectacular were Babel, belonging to Leslie Combs; Joel Johnson's Castle Haggin; Elisha Warfield's Thorn Hill; and Chief Justice George Robertson's Rokeby Hall.

Mary felt refreshed and rejuvenated by a taste of the life she had once known so well, but five years of marriage had matured her and she was ready to move on to the capital, where she firmly believed her husband would have a chance to prove himself in the national spotlight. But as it turned out, the time for this had not arrived. The experience was deeply disappointing for Mary, since Lincoln made much less of an impression there than he did in his own Springfield.

They arrived in Washington on December 2, 1847, going first to Brown's Hotel and then settling in Mrs. Ann G. Sprigg's boardinghouse, where the Library of Congress now stands. She knew the ways of the legislators well, for many of the men on the Hill lived in her house and discussed the day's activities in Congress at her long dinner table, overlooking the Capitol grounds. Mary's first taste of Washington life had little savor. She made no attempt to make friends, and she was busy with Eddy and with Bob, who was being difficult in such confined quarters after his freedom at home and in Lexington. Wherever they went, observers commented on the fact that Lincoln's sons lacked discipline.

Mary both helped and hindered him that winter. She made many demands on his time where the children were concerned, but she also studied legislative reports as she watched the children and gave him a quick analysis of what she had read. He was often very fatigued at the end of the day, and her presence was comforting and reassuring. She stayed with him until spring and then took the children back to Lexington, where they could enjoy country life to the full, have servants to watch them, and cousins with whom to play. They went wild with joy as they frolicked at their grand-father's country place, Buena Vista, a quarter of a mile from the highway and situated above the Leestown Pike on a knoll heavily wooded at the foot with locust trees. It was a free and vigorous existence after the confinement of Mrs. Sprigg's boardinghouse and the strictures of Capitol Square.

But Lincoln, alone in Washington where one day he would cast a long shadow, felt lonely without Mary and the boys. It would be difficult to identify as love epistles the letters he sent her. At no time did he use the language of love, but his longing for Mary was evident in the letter he wrote to her on April 16, 1848: "In this troublesome world we are never quite satisfied. When you were here, I thought you hindered me some in attending to business but now, having nothing but business—no vanity—it has grown exceedingly tasteless to me. I hate to sit down and direct accounts and I hate to stay in the old room by myself. . . ."

Lincoln assured his wife that he had staged a hunt the day before for the "little plaid stockings" she wanted for Eddy. But not a single pair was to be had of the kind she preferred, and there was only one pair that he thought might fit Eddy's little feet. He would try again, however. And no doubt Mary would be glad to know that he had bought himself a pair of jet studs, set in gold and costing fifty cents each. Apparently Mr. Lincoln was giving thought to appearances, with the assortment of dudes as well as frontier types filling the seats of Congress.

His political instincts were well to the fore when he warned Mary in this same letter against associating with the Wickliffe girls. Since their father stood for the things that Henry Clay and Robert Todd most abhorred in their fight against slavery, did she not think there was danger of wounding her "good father" by being openly intimate with the Wickliffe family?

This letter also shows Lincoln's early understanding of Mary's recurrent headaches. "And you are entirely free from headache?" he wrote. "That is good—considering it is the first spring you have been free from it since we were acquainted—I am afraid you will get so well and fat and young as to be wanting to marry again. . . . Get weighed and write me how much you weigh."

He had had a bad dream about Bob and could not shake its impact until a reassuring letter arrived from Mary. His longing for his family welled up again. "What did he and Eddy think of the little letters father sent them?" he wrote. "Don't let the blessed fellows forget father. . . ." He signed this letter "Yours affectionately" and reminded frugal Mary not to use the title Hon. on his envelopes, although he knew her intention was to benefit from the government frank. Or possibly he felt that the Hon. was pretentious.

If Lincoln longed for Mary, there is little doubt that Mary felt lost without him. "How much I wish, instead of writing, we were together this evening. I feel very sad away from you," she wrote on a May evening as she sat by an open window with the fragrance of lilac rising from the bushes below. It was Saturday night. The boys were asleep, or the "codgers" as he liked to call them, and Eddy had recovered from a brief illness. He had found a lost kitten that day—"your hobby"—but Mrs. Todd, disliking the "whole cat race," ordered it thrown out, although Eddy staged a scene. Mary thought this act "most unfeeling."

She assured him that the children were not forgetting him and that Eddy's eyes brightened at the mere mention of his name. Mary's longing to travel and to be with her husband came to the surface with her jesting suggestion that she might take a trip with some friends who were going to Philadelphia. "You know I am so fond of *sight-seeing*, & I did not get to New York or Boston, or travel the lake route—but perhaps, dear husband . . . cannot do without his wife next winter, and must needs take her with him again."

The longing note continued to infuse their letters that spring, and on June 12 Lincoln wrote that he would welcome Mary in the East. "Will you be a *good* girl in all things, if I consent?" he wrote. "Then come along, and that as soon as possible. Having got the idea in my head, I shall be impatient till I see you. . . ."

Joyfully Mary began packing new dresses that had come her way in Lexington, and her husband sent her drafts for her expenses. He knew how irresponsible she could be about money and that she had left some unpaid bills in Washington without telling him about them. Her frugality was less marked when she traveled. With the draft he enclosed a copy of the last speech he had made in Congress, knowing that this would be of prime interest to his politically minded wife. Mary treasured every word he uttered in public but did not hesitate to make critical comments, with which he usually agreed.

She and the boys finally joined him as he campaigned in the East for Zachary Taylor. The highlight of their trip was a visit to Niagara Falls. Mary would return again, always with nostalgic memories of this particular visit. She was with him in Buffalo when he took the steamer *Globe* bound for Chicago. He had been busy all summer and autumn campaigning for Taylor. Lincoln's stand on the Mexican War was unpopular with many of his constituents, and Herndon reported defections in the Whig ranks. Lincoln suggested that all the "shrewd, wild boys about town," well known to Herndon, be organized into a "Rough and Ready Club" for General Taylor. Some were to speak, some were to dance, and all were "to holler," according to their capabilities.

Herndon was convinced that old fossils in the party were bent on keeping the young men down, but Lincoln assured him that the way for a young man to rise was to improve himself in every way he could, "never suspecting that anybody wishes to hinder him." But in spite of his valiant efforts, Illinois went for Lewis Cass, even though Zachary Taylor was elected President. This was profoundly depressing for Lincoln, who served out his time in Congress, the lone Whig who had not held his state. He had little to say while in the House, but he voted repeatedly for the Wilmot Proviso against slavery in any territory acquired from Mexico.

Mary had not rejoined him in the capital, and when the Thirtieth Congress adjourned in March, 1849, he returned to Springfield, where she and the boys greeted him with fervor. He was soon back in his cluttered office, his feet on his desk, old friends to be seen, new cases to be studied. At this point he was offered the governorship of Oregon, but Mary made up his mind for him and he said no. She was convinced that he would be burying himself politically. She may also have considered the loneliness and disadvantages of frontier life for herself and her children. Either way it was a fortunate decision, since Lincoln might have been lost to the political world at this point.

It seemed at the time as if his political career had come to an abrupt close. But he traveled the Eighth Circuit and kept in touch with the people. His uncommon appearance sank deep into the public consciousness, and he became a unique figure in the byways of Illinois. Meanwhile, Mary coped with the boys in Springfield and eagerly looked forward to his sporadic visits.

The years 1849 and 1850 were darkened for her by the deaths in quick succession of three of those she loved most. Her father died of cholera on July 16, 1849, and Mrs. Elizabeth P. Parker, who had outlived her husband by half a century, followed her son-in-law in January, 1850. Little Eddy was desperately ill with diphtheria at the time, and the Lincolns were in a feverish state of anxiety over their son when the news of Grandmother Parker's death reached them. The child grew steadily worse and died on February 1, 1850.

His mother sorrowed for him with all the intensity of her emotional nature, but not with the total abandonment she was to show later when Willie died in the White House. It was the common fate of families at this time to lose many of their children in their early years, and Mary's Springfield friends rallied around her with neighborly sympathy. The hurt for Lincoln was deep and enduring. His gloom was constant, and he talked of the "mystery of the hereafter and the improbability of immortality." He had found his greatest happiness up to that time in little Eddy. This child's death seemed to bring the Lincolns closer together.

While the lilacs bloomed and spring showers washed the Bluegrass country, they went south to Lexington. Lincoln hoped that a visit to her home might help assuage Mary's grief. There was also business to attend to in the settlement of the family estate. Robert Todd left the bulk of his fortune to his wife Elizabeth, with the remainder of his property to be divided equally among the children of his first and second wives. A great deal of litigation followed, and Lincoln represented the interests of Mary, Elizabeth (Mrs. Edwards), Frances (Mrs. Wallace), and Ann (Mrs. Clark Moulton Smith), the four daughters of the first Mrs. Todd.

When the court ruled that the estate must be distributed equally among the fourteen children, Elizabeth was upset, since this involved converting into cash her husband's holdings, including his interest in the firm of Oldham, Todd & Company, long a family standby. The hearings in the case brought to light the relationship of the second Mrs. Todd with Eliza's daughters. The tales of bad feeling that had freely circulated in Lexington and Springfield seemed to gain authority with the testimony brought into court.

Mary held her peace, no doubt on the advice of her lawyer husband, and maintained courteous if distant relations with her stepmother, but in a separate action her young brother, George R. C. Todd, charged that his father "was mortified that his last child by his first wife should be obliged, like all his first children, to abandon his house by the relentless persecution of a stepmother."

The amount that Todd had contributed to his daughters' support after they went to Springfield came under scrutiny, and except for random gifts to Mary, there was little evidence of largesse on his part except for the land he gave her. But she had never lacked for anything. Her grandmother Parker and Mrs. Edwards saw to it that she was well supplied with all she needed for clothes, travel, parties and education.

The litigation was painful and long drawn out, and it had many ramifications in Lexington, where the ownership of land was involved. The sisters said they had never consented to the sale of land left by their mother. Lincoln moved like an alien spirit among them, but he protected the interests of Mary and her sisters with persistence and success. There was no open breach with the second Mrs. Todd, for Mary wanted nothing to sully the reputation of her father.

Two years later, in 1852, the Lincolns returned to Lexington to settle fresh differences that had arisen over the disposition of the slaves of the Todd and Parker estates. This was a subject that had been growing in importance since Clay had made his compromise proposals in 1850, and Lincoln gave much thought to it. He was aware of a change for the worse on this trip to Lexington. During his brief stay more than 150 blacks went on the block and scores changed hands by private sale. Floggings at the poplar tree drew crowds, and Lincoln had formed some conclusions of his own after listening to Clay's last speech, with pandemonium breaking out around him. When Clay died in the summer of 1852, a special train bore his body back to Lexington. The great antislavery fighter of the South was gone, but his influence lived on in Lincoln.

When Emilie visited her sisters in Springfield in the summer of 1854, she saw a great deal of Mary and Mr. Lincoln, and in her diary she recorded her impressions of the happiness they shared. "Little Sister" was now eighteen, a beauty, and highly intelligent. She was impressed with Mary's constant efforts to look her best, and she swore that Lincoln's eyes lit up when he saw his wife waiting for him at the door on his return from the office. Sometimes she would meet him at the gate, and they would come in together, swinging hands.

"Oh, how she did love this man!" Emilie wrote, recalling Mary's lighthearted and joyous ways, and the tempers that blew up so fast and were quickly spent. "Her husband loved her none the less, perhaps all the more, for this human frailty which needed his love and patience to pet and coax the sunny smile to replace the sarcasm and tears. . . ."

Emilie took delight in the long country drives she had with the Lincolns, stopping to pick wild flowers along the way and to study the prairie land so different from the rich terrain of the Bluegrass country. With her unquenchable interest in appearances, Mary gave Emilie a plumed white velvet bonnet when she noticed that one of the Springfield girls wore a more fashionable bonnet to church than her exquisite half sister.

Lincoln liked Emilie and teased her at times, but she was aware that he was often silent and absentminded. When playing checkers with Bob, he would fall into a deep reverie until Mary laughingly reminded him that they were not yet ready for sleep. It was no surprise to Emilie to hear her half sister priming her husband on books she had been studying for his benefit. She noticed that he freely discussed his political affairs with Mary and listened attentively to what she had to say. When he received batches of books, she was apt to pounce on those that looked promising and read them far into the night.

Emilie came to the conclusion on this visit that Lincoln thoroughly understood the complex nature of his wife. Mary made no attempt to conceal her feelings. Her face showed every passing emotion, but she needed all the self-control she could muster when she went to the State House with Mrs. Edwards and Emilie on February 8, 1855, for the election of the Senator they felt sure could be none other than Abraham Lincoln.

The result was one of the great disappointments of Lincoln's career, and Mary was never to forget the special agony of his defeat by Lyman Trumbull, a member of the Coterie whom both knew well and whose wife, Julia Jayne, had been her bridesmaid and closest friend for years. Lincoln was ahead on the first ballot, but the tide turned as Shields and Trumbull cut in on him. He held out as long as he could before swinging his support to Trumbull.

Albert J. Beveridge, who shared Herndon's critical view of Mrs. Lincoln in many respects, attributed Lincoln's inexplicable holdout to the presence of his wife in the gallery and her determination that he should win. When Trumbull came out the victor, according to Beveridge, "her anger was so fierce, unreasoning, and permanent, that she refused then and forever to speak to the wife of the victor, Julia Jayne."

Emilie, sitting beside Mary, had an entirely different impression of her half sister's reaction. They all had feared that her husband's defeat would be a crushing blow for her, but she managed to conceal her disappointment, whatever she may have felt. Her pride no doubt was deeply involved at this crucial point in her idol's history. Lincoln had cared deeply, but he did not show his feelings and he managed to congratulate the victor at a reception held that night at the Edwards' house.

However, Lincoln's dejection was noticed when he went out on the circuit again, and although they had much to do with each other in the years that followed, there was never the same warmth between him and Trumbull, and Mary and Julia seemed to be worlds apart after years of intimate association. The feud continued through the Presidential years, and when Dr. Henry visited the White House in 1863, he wrote to his wife: "Mary & Julia have both made me their confidant telling me their grievances, and both think the other *all* to blame. I am trying to make peace between them."

It was another issue by then, but evidently the old wound had not healed. After his defeat by Trumbull, Lincoln gave careful thought to the next step he should take. He was irresistibly drawn to the party then taking shape to fight the extension of slavery in the territories. After the state convention at Bloomington at which the Republican Party in Illinois came into existence, the Lincolns ceased to be Whigs. In linking his fortune with the new party, Lincoln knew that he was closing the door on some of his Southern friends, like Joshua Speed. This was a serious matter for Mary, although on the slavery question her convictions sometimes seemed stronger than Lincoln's. In writing to Speed about the decision he had made, Lincoln pointed out: "On the leading subject of this letter, I have more of her sympathy than I have of yours. And yet let me say I am your friend forever."

At this time both of the Lincolns were for gradual emancipation with compensation to the slaveowners, a compromise that would haunt them later, but the label "abolitionist" was considered so extreme and subversive at the time that Mary feared for its effect on her husband's career. Yet in a sense, being Southern and related to prominent slaveholders, she herself was deeply involved in his early views on this subject.

When he campaigned for John C. Frémont after the newborn Republican Party had nominated this newcomer as a candidate for the Presidency, Mary's sympathies were not with her husband's choice. "My weak woman's heart was too Southern in feeling to sympathize with any but Fillmore," she wrote. "I have always been a great admirer of his, he made so good a President & is so just a man & feels the necessity of keeping foreigners within bounds."

This statement suggests her prejudice at that time about letting people from all lands pour into the United States. But her husband gave Frémont his support, and he was mentioned as a possible Vice Presidential choice, indicating his strength in the Republican Party. With the death pangs of the Whigs, new blood and a determined spirit were welcomed in the Middle West.

All through the 1850's the horizons of the Lincoln family widened. Lincoln was being cultivated as a political figure with an original turn of thought and a striking personality. They were better off financially, and Mary was back in the social swim as her family saw where they were heading. She appeared more often at the important parties in Springfield, and she entertained on a more elaborate scale.

Where she had bought mostly calico, Merino, delaine and Swiss muslin in the early years of her marriage, her bills showed that she now chose silks, ribbons, laces and fancy buttons for the dressmaking that went on constantly. Everything she owned had to have a distinctive, fashionable touch. Lincoln, too, was beginning to smarten up to some degree on Mary's urging as she studied the attire of the men with whom he associated. The politicians of the period were individualists. Some were dandies, but they were moving away from the stiff proprieties of the Whig exterior. Ninian Edwards was the epitome of starchy convention with the right clothes for every occasion; he and his wife found Lincoln's sloppy ways repugnant. But now Lincoln at times wore broadcloth pantaloons and a black coat, with a satin vest and tall black cravat. His towering moleskin hat and short circular blue coat were not unlike those worn by fellow members of the bar. His hat size was 7⅛, and Herndon noted that his hair, almost black, "lay floating where his fingers put it or the winds left it, piled up and tossed about at random."

Lincoln was incredulous when Edwards turned Democrat rather than Republican as the Whig Party dissolved. It had been suggested that Ninian thought he could get into Congress on the Locofoco side. But soon he would be a suppliant, begging favors of his despised brother-in-law. The Edwards' fortunes declined as the Lincolns' gained ground. With the Parker and Todd estates finally settled, Mary had a modest inheritance. And as Lincoln became prominent in the fast-developing Republican Party, he earned larger fees and retainers. They could now spend more on their home, their entertaining, their clothes and children.

Their neighbor Gourley helped Mary choose a new carriage when their old calash had had its day. She had become used to driving around in the McClernands' luxurious coach lined with orange and white brocade. John Alexander McClernand, a fellow lawyer and friend of Lincoln's who would become a general during the war, did not share his political views, but Mary and Mrs. McClernand had attended school together in Lexington, and they saw much of each other with no inkling of the breach to come. The carriage passed muster, but Mary's most ambitious extravagance took Lincoln by surprise. She conspired with Gourley to enlarge their home while her husband was in Chicago in 1856 on legal business. Erected in 1839, it had one and a half stories. With some careful planning it was raised to two stories. It was the only home that Lincoln ever actually owned, and he lived in it from May, 1844, to February, 1861, except for a brief period when Cornelius Ludlum rented it while he was in Washington. Three of his sons were born in this house, one died in it, and it was rich in associations for Mary. The original shingles were hand-split white oak, and much of the construction was done with wooden pegs and handmade nails. Native hardwoods and white pine were used throughout, although the framework and floors were of oak and the laths of hand-split hickory.

When Lincoln arrived home and saw that his house had risen in the world during his absence, he was quoted as saying: "Stranger, do you know where Lincoln lives? He used to live here." He was none too pleased about this change, particularly when he learned that it would cost $1,300. He scolded Mary for her extravagance. Her spending proclivities were beginning to show after years of extreme frugality. Soon she had squandered another $200 on a high-board fence running to the carriage house. Yet her guests noted the stinginess with which she ran her home. Fires were allowed to go out after a few chips had set up a preliminary blaze. Rooms were shut off to save fuel, not an uncommon frontier practice. Mrs. John Stuart Todd noted that "Mary seldom ever uses what she has," a perceptive comment at an early date on the woman who would amass piles of unused materials, dresses and possessions of one kind or another and then neither use them nor even look at them. The compulsion was merely to buy.

In 1857 Mary went in for a feverish round of buying wallpaper, a future mania of hers. She was refurbishing her house and planned to give a large party when it was finished. With quantities of buff linen and cotton damask she sewed the curtains herself. Mary was well indoctrinated in the importance of backing up political strategy with good entertaining. She had seen this in her own home in Lexington and again when she lived with Mr. and Mrs. Edwards. This time she was going to hold her own and enhance the image of her ambitious husband. The party she gave early in 1857 was pronounced a great success by Orville Browning and other guests.

She wrote to Emilie on February 16 that she was recovering from the effects of a "very large & I really believe a very handsome & agreeable entertainment, at least our friends flatter us by saying so." Five hundred had been invited, and three hundred had turned up in spite of torrential rains. It was not at all unusual for her at this time to entertain two hundred or more in an evening. According to Isaac N. Arnold, her table was famed for the "excellence of many rare Kentucky dishes, and in season, loaded with venison, wild turkeys, prairie chickens, quail and other game."

Parties aside, the fare was sparse at the Lincoln home, and Lincoln had to think twice and get Mary's consent before bringing guests home for dinner. Otherwise she would be driven into one of her rages. But Arnold remembered many delightful occasions when Mrs. Lincoln was at her animated best and the evenings were further enlivened by the "wit and humor, anecdotes and unrivalled conversation of the host."

Mary particularly liked the "strawberry parties" for old and young after church, when she would draw in as many as seventy guests at a time for berries and ice cream. Although the members of the Coterie had scattered, there were many pleasant gatherings of mature married friends in these surroundings. Mary in particular expressed herself quite frankly on the burning political issues then raging around them. She worked for the formation of a library association in 1856, and she and Lincoln were enthusiastic about the opening of a new theater in Springfield where Shakespearean productions were staged. Then, as later, they never failed to attend a good dramatic performance or other entertainment when it came within their range. Mary could never resist theatrical events of any kind. She observed each change as Springfield grew and flourished, and she loved to gossip over tea and macaroons. But Paul Angle has made the point that in spite of the enjoyment the Springfield people found in social activities, the "prevailing tone of society was one of moral and intellectual seriousness."

The Lincolns could remember the town when it was still in an abysmal state of mud and semidarkness, when it did not have one good sidewalk or a public lamp. Yet even then the houses were large and comfortable, with spacious grounds and fine gardens. Oil lamps finally shed their wavering light from lampposts around the square in 1853, and the next step was the illumination of the stores.

Mary Lincoln wrote to Emilie of the great changes that had taken place since she had been in Springfield. "Almost palaces of homes have been reared since you were here, and some of them very elegant," she wrote. The mansion finished in 1856 for Governor Joel A. Matteson opened with a great party for a thousand, with another the following day for the children of the community. The governor's administration was lively, and this party was the largest ever given in Springfield. A group of showy homes now stood on what was known as Aristocracy Hill.

Mary's own home was of the most modest dimensions, but it was the center of a rising tide of political activity. By the time she reached the White House she had been doubly trained in the traditional hospitality of the South and the fast-developing worldliness of the Middle West. Manners were less courtly, accents were more harshly pitched, weather conditions were severe, but the vigor and sincerity of the people who had settled in Springfield from many quarters generated an electric quality that stimulated Mary Lincoln.

When Lincoln sank into one of his depressions, Henry B. Rankin, who studied law with him in 1856, observed that his wife was never the cause but was invariably his comforter. He thought she was the only person who had the skill and tact to charm him out of these moods and shorten their duration. Mary was quick, volatile, her face mobile, her speech rapid and vivid, Rankin wrote. She reached conclusions quickly and was a fast thinker, but "without intending to wound she sometimes indulged in sarcastic or witty remarks."

This admirer of Mrs. Lincoln's insisted that she was wholly free of affectation and that she was always an inspiration and sometimes a prodding one to her husband's ambition because of her belief that "high national preferment awaited him politically, if she with others could only keep him steadily aspiring thereto."

Mary was most companionable when they traveled together, and there was laughter and fun when they took the children. She was so well read and well informed that there was instruction for all, as well as games and sight-seeing. Mary loved to don a wide-hooped dress, tie a plumed bonnet over her glossy dark hair, and twirl a dainty parasol as she walked beside her towering husband. There was never any doubt that he took pride in his attractive wife.

Life was good to them when they went east to New York in September, 1857. Mary looked fresh and young for thirty-nine. She toured the shops, drove up Broadway, and had her biggest thrill at the wharves watching steamers ready to leave for Europe. "I felt in my heart, inclined to sigh that poverty was my portion and how I long to go to Europe. . . . I often laugh & tell Mr. L.—that I am determined my next husband *shall be rich,*" Mary wrote lightheartedly on this occasion. They revisited Niagara, where they had been happy before, and after stopping at several other points in the East, returned to Springfield in a mood of having had a second honeymoon, or so Mary liked to regard it.

The year 1858 was a momentous one for them, since in June the state Republican convention chose Lincoln as its candidate for the United States Senate. That evening he made the speech in which he used the phrase "a house divided against itself cannot stand." The Todd, Stuart and Edwards families thought that this speech was too radical, but Mary kept assuring them that Mr. Lincoln was not an abolitionist.

His opponent was Stephen Douglas, now more prominent on the political horizon than her husband. His features, his dynamic presence, his oratory were formidable, and when he proposed a series of debates, Mary advised her husband to take up the challenge. This was the third time that she had cast a decisive vote. It was she who had made the final decision that Lincoln should not become territorial governor of Oregon. Again she had urged him to join the Republican Party, although this involved great risks at the time. Now she decreed that he should face Douglas in open debate. They were to meet between August 21 and October 15 in seven Illinois towns—Ottawa, Jonesboro, Freeport, Charleston, Galesburg, Alton and Quincy.

Political debate was a spectacular way for candidates to make themselves known to the people. There was no lack of din and nineteenth-century press agentry in the shows staged by both parties. Big issues were at stake, with slavery the leading point of discord. Torchlight parades and blaring bands kept the prospective voters entertained night and day. Bells rang. Processions moved through the streets, with wagons full of people in from the country for a day's fun and a dash of electioneering. Barbecues and ice-cream festivals kept the participants busy. Lincoln pungently summed it up as "fizzle-gigs and fire-works."

Crowds welcomed him at wharf or depot. Douglas arrived at each place with the air of a conquering hero. His beautiful wife, Adelaide, who was Dolley Madison's niece and probably the first candidate's wife in America to campaign for her husband, was always at his side. Her presence gave strength to his cause, for men and women alike admired her. Mary had heard so much of Adelaide's charm in public that she decided to go to Alton and watch her husband and Douglas battle it out. There was curiosity about her, since Lincoln's wife was still comparatively unknown.

Mary had one of her raging headaches, so it was anything but a joyous occasion for her. Robert accompanied her on the train as a member of the Springfield Cadets. The noise and confusion of bands and the Mabie and Crosby French and American Circus that preceded the debate created a state of bedlam. Lincoln was worried about his wife, and he discussed her condition with Gustave Koerner, the German-born politician who was rapidly climbing the political ladder in Illinois. He stayed close to Lincoln during the debates and was chosen by him at this point to go up to her room and reassure Mrs. Lincoln. "Tell Mary what you think of our chances," said Lincoln, always concerned about his wife's welfare. "She is rather dispirited."

This in itself was an unusual state of affairs, for her belief in his success was talismanic in its strength. To Mary her husband on the platform already seemed the giant figure that he later turned out to be, although her astute political sense told her that his chances of winning were slight. But the sight of the two men together drew from her the comment to a niece: "Mr. Douglas is a very little, *little* giant by the side of my tall Kentuckian, and intellectually my husband towers above Douglas just as he does physically."

She could scarcely listen without prejudice to the two men she knew so well. Again her husband said that a house divided against itself could not stand, that the government could not endure half slave and half free. He touched on the evils of slavery, explaining his position and seeking to convince his audience that he was not stirring up strife in taking this stand. Douglas had talked so much that he was hoarse that day, but the debate was stormy to the end. In the evening Mary dined at the hotel with her husband, Lyman Trumbull, Horace White and John and Robert Hitt, to whom she jestingly said that her prospects of living in the White House were poor. Her spirits always revived when she was entertaining, and on this occasion she chose to cover her husband's long silence with her own merry chatter. She could see that he was utterly exhausted and depressed from the long ordeal of the debates.

A riotous Republican rally in Springfield in October brought the campaign to an end, with one of Lincoln's most impressive speeches sounding only faintly through the enveloping uproar. The usual torchlight procession brought the day to a close, but in the end it was the Little Giant who won, and Lincoln was left in a disconsolate frame of mind. Again he felt that his political career had ended, but Mary did not share this conviction. It simply could not be.

When he had ceased to brood, Lincoln wrote to Dr. Henry a letter suggesting his farewell to public life. He was glad he had made the race because it had given him a hearing on the "great and durable question of the age," he wrote, adding: ". . . though I now sink out of view, and shall be forgotten, I believe I have made some marks which will tell for the cause of civil liberty long after I am gone."

His law practice needed immediate attention, for he had neglected it for nearly a year while he traveled 4,200 miles, paying his own expenses at hotels along the way. Mary had to face the fact at the end of 1858 that he had barely enough money to cover their household expenses, but she thought it all had been worthwhile. By spring both were again full of hope—or ambition.

The debates with Douglas had been so unique and powerful in their impact that Lincoln was being discussed as a nominee for the Presidency. Mary's friend Cassius Clay stumped central Kentucky in his behalf. But William H. Seward, with his strong following in the East, loomed up as the favorite candidate. "I must in candor say I do not think myself fit for the presidency," Lincoln wrote in a self-deprecatory way, but this was not how his wife felt. She studied every move he made and knew what he was saying. She longed to travel with him, but early in 1859 Tad was ill with an attack of "lung fever." Willie joined his father in Chicago during June, and they went to two theaters in one night, visited an exhibition, and admired the growing city strung out along the lake.

Willie made quaint diary notes on this adventure, commenting on his father's ways with the two little towels and the two little basins in their hotel room. Traveling with Father was more bewildering and also more thrilling than traveling with Mother, although Mother always had more to say about everything they saw. But Lincoln was alone on his February trip to New York in 1860, when overnight he was silhouetted in giant form across the nation with his Cooper Union Speech. Here was the prairie politician who had jousted with Douglas, a man with rumpled clothes and an uneasy manner, whose comments on slavery projected him to the forefront of the political battle.

He had so many invitations to speak on this trip that he wrote to Mary that he would not have traveled east had he known what lay ahead of him. But shrewd politician that he was, he was well aware that the Cooper Union Speech had done something vital to his political future. He went to Phillips Exeter to see Robert and he made a speech there. The boys caught his unique quality behind his rugged front, and they were impressed with the way in which he answered their questions. Stuffy Robert looked on in amazement.

Back in Springfield, Mary was missing her oldest son as well as her wandering husband. Robert's departure for prep school had been the first break in their family circle. Tad, now nine, had a servant who took good care of him, and for the first time she felt free to travel with her husband and to share in some of his political life away from home. They visited Columbus and Cincinnati, and wherever they went, she found old friends to visit.

Mary would never again be back in the same old domestic cage, but she could not follow Lincoln everywhere as he drew great crowds in Kansas, Indianapolis, Milwaukee and all through Ohio. He was already the dark horse of the coming convention; 1860 was the year of destiny for Abraham Lincoln—and for his wife, Mary.

V

Farewell to Springfield

Life changed dramatically for Mary Lincoln on the May day in 1860 when Abraham Lincoln was nominated the Republican candidate for President on the third ballot at the convention held in Chicago. The White House had been the dream of her life—a not impossible dream any longer. The firing of a hundred guns in Springfield proclaimed his victory, and Lincoln broke away from the jubilation at the State House with the quiet remark: "There's a little woman down at our house would like to hear this. I'll go down and tell her."

Mary was too wise to think that the fight was over; it had only just begun. But her confidence was apparent to the delegation assembled in her parlor for the official notification. Her house was in perfect order, and a suitable array of refreshments was on display. Her plan to serve champagne had been vetoed by Lincoln, since the official group included temperance advocates. Tad and Willie had been polished up for the occasion, and they larked about freely, with little awe for Father's role. The distinguished guests who filed in took note of some of their antics. The Springfield houses were illuminated for the occasion. Fireworks exploded. In the weeks that followed, the city was in a state of perpetual excitement, with political rallies, geysers of oratory, the roar of cannon, and visits by famous men.

The Lincoln house was the focus of attention, and the earliest image of Mary Lincoln took shape in the press. Her husband was unique—that was self-evident; her boys made lively copy; and she herself emerged as a charming hostess, a woman of wit and tart address. She was well aware of the importance of press comment on their homelife. They were plain people—she understood the national definition and did not quarrel with that—but she resented the implication that they were uncivilized boors. So it gave her some satisfaction to read in the New York *Herald*, a hostile paper, that the reporter who had visited them had found her "gracious and charming" in a joint interview with her husband. "The conversation was lively, and occasionally interspersed with some brilliant flashes of wit and good nature from the Kentucky lady, his wife," the dispatch read.

Many observers noted that Lincoln did not change in any respect. As soon as his official duties were out of the way, he fell into his easygoing way of telling jokes and stories. And he was only amused by Mary's efforts to keep him looking his best. This was an old story for her, but she worked harder at it now. Carl Schurz, one of their visitors, had already established his image. At Quincy he had noted Lincoln's battered stovepipe hat and his neck, long and sinewy, emerging from a white collar turned down over a thin black necktie. His "rusty black dress coat" had sleeves that needed to be longer. His black trousers gave a full view of his large feet, and on his left arm he carried a gray woolen shawl, which he threw around his shoulders like an overcoat in cold weather. In his left hand he held a bulging cotton umbrella, and his black satchel bore the marks of hard use. This portrait of Abraham Lincoln took a firm hold of the public's imagination and was one of the earliest impressions of him.

But blunt Carl Schurz, who had harbored Presidential aspirations of his own, took a second look when he had supper with the Lincolns while attending a political rally in Springfield after Lincoln's nomination. He found Mary more decorative than provincial and wrote to his wife about her: "His lady had decked herself out very prettily and already knows very well how to wave a fan. She chats quite nicely and will be able to adapt herself to the White House without difficulty."

Many nationally known politicians were entertained by the Lincolns at this time, and it was apparent to all that Mrs. Lincoln often spoke up brightly on public issues. She was her most effective self while she waited for the results of the election. Her political understanding did not fail her at this point, and she made plans for the course she would follow if her husband won. She also smiled on the press, for the visiting correspondents and sketch artists listened attentively to what she had to say, soon finding out that she was much more communicative than her husband. But she was already showing an aversion to photographs and caricatures, often most unflattering to her rough-hewn husband. He was genial about the "picture business," however, and would assume any pose they wished, making jokes and telling them stories as they worked. In time Lincoln would become one of the most photographed men in American history, and the record began during these first months in Springfield, between his nomination in May and his election in November.

The early pictorial effects were so grim that he was described in one instance as being "half alligator half horse in appearance." But as time went on, he became the perfect Uncle Sam. "I can't understand why the boys want such a homely face," he remarked when Alexander Hesler of Chicago took an early photograph in 1857. After the nomination Mary showed a personal interest in the matter. She suggested the clothes he should wear, his best angles for the camera, and she had the final say on the pictures Lincoln approved. He took her with him to the State House when Alban J. Conant painted him in Springfield. She liked this portrait, for Tad was jumping around while it was being done and she thought that her husband's love for his youngest son showed in his eyes. "That is the way he looks when he has friends about him," Mary commented.

Thomas Webster, a visiting politician, watched Mary as she studied the portrait of Lincoln done in November by George P. A. Healy. He commented on her "quiet, dignified, self-possessed, undemonstrative manners." He thought Lincoln "slouchy, ungraceful . . . lean and ugly in every way." There was a noticeable change in his appearance when he grew a beard. His first portrait with this adornment was taken in November, 1860, a month after he had received a letter from a little girl named Grace Bedell, of Westfield, New York, urging him to grow whiskers and wear standing collars. These changes would make him more appealing to the voters and women would urge their husbands to vote for him, in Grace's opinion.

Lincoln answered her in a jocular vein: "My dear little Miss . . . As to the whiskers, having never worn any, do you not think people would call it a piece of silly affectation if I were to begin it now?" But it seems likely that he must have talked it over with Mary, for he would never have made such a drastic change in his appearance without her approval. In any event, he became the first bearded

President, and his beard went through many variations in the years that followed. It was heavy and at its longest when he left Springfield. Washington barbers shaped and trimmed it in a variety of ways, and it was comparatively short at the time of his death. His pictures show that he parted his hair to the right until 1865, when a change was made to the left.

Mrs. Lincoln had not yet been compared to Queen Victoria, and so she and Lincoln were almost unaware of Baron Renfrew's passage through Springfield on September 26, 1860. The Prince of Wales, traveling incognito, was bound for St. Louis, and a great crowd assembled to see him during a ten-minute stop at the depot. His visit to Washington and his grand tour of the major cities in America had resulted in floods of publicity, but when asked about his failure to appear at the Springfield station, Mr. Lincoln said that his position did not permit him to take the initiative; otherwise he would have been glad to welcome the royal visitor. "I remained here at the State House, where I met so many sovereigns during the day that really the Prince had come and gone before I knew it," he said with a flash of wry wit.

A few days before the election Mary ran into Mrs. Conkling (her old friend Mercy Levering) and told her that she was quite confident her husband would win. But something went wrong between them on that crucial day, and the answer has never been made clear. Lincoln passed most of the day at the State House and voted during the afternoon. In the evening he followed the returns in the telegraph office with Lyman Trumbull and other friends. New York was the key state, and when the flash came in that it had gone to Lincoln, there was wild excitement. For hours the crowd shouted, yelled, danced. The winner ignored the cries for a speech and headed toward his home. According to Ruth Randall, Lincoln took Mary later that evening to attend a victory supper given by the Republican ladies at Watson's Confectionery.

But Herndon, twenty-nine years later, gave the public a strange view of the President-elect's arrival at his home, which was perpetuated in Robert Sherwood's *Abe Lincoln in Illinois,* written before the Herndon-Weik papers were made public and their contents studied. This widely heralded play that opened on Broadway in 1938 had Lincoln cursing his wife on election night after asking their guests to leave the room. Mrs. Randall, in her thorough research, concluded that this story was one of Herndon's many distortions, involving separate incidents that he had pieced together; that it was secondhand; and that it was most unlikely that Abraham Lincoln would have stepped out of character to damn his wife. There were few known occasions in his life when he spoke harshly to her. And surely he would have known how much his victory meant to her.

Yet this became one of the many tales, apocryphal or not, that traveled far as the years went by and helped cloud Mary's reputation. Henry C. Bowen, editor of the *Independent*, gave a different and very simple view of the night's events. Lincoln told him, he said, that he asked Mary not to wait up for him, as he would probably not be back before midnight. When he arrived, he found his wife sound asleep. He touched her shoulder gently and said: "Mary." When she did not respond, he tried again, this time more loudly: "Mary, Mary! *We are* elected."

Mrs. Judith A. Bradner in her old age told of calling on the Lincolns the day after the election. She found the President in high spirits, but Mary seemed annoyed when he jestingly said that she had locked him out the night before. She had warned him that if he were not home by ten o'clock she would lock the door, and lock the door she did. But when she "heard the music coming to her house she turned the key in a hurry," said Mr. Lincoln.

Evidently something unusual had taken place, aside from the undeniable fact that Mary's husband was now definitely on his way to the White House, where her tantrums and her triumphs from then on would be public knowledge. According to Rankin, Lincoln had one of his strange visions at this time. He had flung himself on a lounge, totally exhausted, and in the bureau mirror across the room he saw himself full length but with two faces. The illusion passed when he got up, but it returned when he lay down again. One face was deathly pale. A few days later the vision returned, and Mary told Rankin it meant that her husband would be elected for a second term but that the death pallor of one face meant he would not live through it.

To all outward appearances harmony prevailed in the Lincoln home, and Henry Villard reported that Mrs. Lincoln did not put on any airs but was as "pleasant and talkative and entertaining" as she could be. He had harsher things to say about her later, but for the moment he shared in the general adulation. This observant critic noticed that the elite of Springfield now poured into the house they had shunned and that Mrs. Lincoln held a court of her own.

Exhilarated by her new role, she sparkled and used her best arts as hostess. In her usual frank and realistic way she expressed herself on public issues.

The boys, well aware that something big had come into their lives, roistered and responded with yells to the cheering crowds outside. "The whole lower story of the building was filled all the evening with well dressed ladies and gentlemen, whose comfort was, however, greatly diminished by the constant influx of an ill-mannered Populace," Villard wrote disparagingly. On November 20, the date selected for the celebration of the Republican victory, it swelled to flood proportions at the State House. People had come in from the country to look at the man who would soon be in the White House. But the official celebration fell flat. There had been so many demonstrations during the campaign that people could shout no longer. The Lincolns themselves were only too glad to leave for Chicago, where they passed a week while Springfield drowsed like a deserted city.

The trip gave Mary a chance to see the Wigwam, where her husband had been nominated. They were feted for several days, and she had her first experience of an imposing receiving line at the public reception given the President-elect on this visit. Lincoln was very tired and showed it. The campaign had worn him down, and as she watched him shaking hands, Mary wondered how he could stand up to the coming strain. Donn Piatt, an Ohio newspaperman, took aim at both Lincolns while they were in Chicago. He found the President-elect's face "hard, angular and coarse" and he thought his nature might be unforgiving. Mrs. Lincoln affected him adversely by intruding on a conversation with more vehemence than logic. He was critical of a supper she had served him in Springfield, calling it an "old-fashioned mess of indigestion." The Lincoln boys annoyed him, too, but Donn Piatt, who would have much to say about Lincoln as time went on, was a political enemy.

These were springing from the woods in amazing numbers. The praise and good wishes that reached the Lincolns were more than balanced by the savage attacks made on them even before they got to Washington. Their hate mail was overwhelming, and Mary was startled early in January, 1861, to receive a painting from South Carolina showing her husband with chained feet, a rope around his neck, and a coating of tar and feathers on his long form. Immediately after the election he had been burned in effigy at Pensacola.

Lincoln was used to political abuse, but his wife had not yet become hardened to this kind of attack, and the threatening letters and savage ridicule touched her to the quick. Her husband laughed it off, and she tried to ignore it, devoting her energies to plans for the future. She was uplifted by a new sense of power, and it was soon evident to the politicians who visited them that she was playing the role of adviser. She made no secret of her views on her husband's projected appointments, and she was strongly opposed to the selection of Seward as Secretary of State. Mary called him a sneak and much too cool on the slavery issue. She considered her husband gullible with men of this type, and she sincerely felt she was helping him in suggesting certain appointees. But stories soon spread that her advocacy could be bought with a diamond bracelet. In her own eagerness for fast results she did not take into account her husband's political sagacity and his sense of caution.

Both were faced with antagonism in the North, as well as in the South. The abolitionists would have preferred Salmon Portland Chase as President and were impatient with Lincoln's temperate point of view. Mrs. Lincoln was misunderstood because of her genuine concern for the blacks, even though she came from Kentucky. Neither region accepted her without reservations. In the North she would always be regarded as having Southern sympathies. In the South she would be remembered as the First Lady who had rejected her own people. And in many ways she would suffer for the strange ways of Abraham Lincoln before his statesmanship commanded the respect of the entire nation. She was alive to this state of affairs, but her love for her husband and her faith in him were overwhelming factors in his favor. The ridicule and slander sharpened her perception of the man he was. She became his most tireless advocate.

At times she seemed to burn with elation, and she was in high spirits when she set off for New York in January on the first of the shopping expeditions that were to become notorious within the space of a year. Robert came down from Harvard to join her, and Villard noted that the young Prince of Nails, as he was now known, was dressed with an elegance in striking contrast to the "careless, awkward rigging of his Presidential father." Mary was proud to be seen with her fashionable son, and they went to the theater together and visited popular restaurants. The shops were paradise as leading merchants personally escorted Mrs. Lincoln from counter to counter, offering her the finest of their wares. Mary's buying mania took hold as she watched lustrous bolts of silk being unrolled and studied laces, shawls and jewels. She was demanding in her needs, and the prices appalled her as she took this first step into the ocean that would swamp her in the future.

Villard soon decided that she was reluctant to leave the winter gaieties of New York, but Mr. Lincoln was waiting patiently for her return and was not sure of what Mary might be saying. "He always enjoined upon me to be quiet," she admitted in one of her letters, but a persistent critic of her husband's wrote to a Chicago newspaperman while she was away that it was shocking for Mrs. Lincoln "to go kiting about the country and holding levees at which she indulges in a multitude of silly speeches."

Lincoln and his secretaries were well aware of the inflammatory possibilities of this situation while his Cabinet was still in the making. They knew that she said what she liked when she was deeply moved, and in New York she was in Seward's territory, where many of Lincoln's enemies were to be found. Her actions and her words were followed there more closely than she knew, since it was already apparent that she acted with total spontaneity and a lack of caution.

Robert returned to Springfield with his mother, but Lincoln had to meet the train from the East three nights in succession before they finally arrived, laden with bundles. They came in a heavy snowstorm, and Mary was wildly exhilarated, bubbling with news of her trip and eager to show off her purchases. She found her husband beset by the press, by politicians seeking office and by men asking for jobs. He was in a hurry to get things ready for their departure, and the house was in a state of confusion.

Lincoln had made up his mind to take John Hay and John G. Nicolay with him to Washington. Hay delighted him with his wit, scholarship and easy air of self-assurance. He was a young man destined to go far in life, and Lincoln found him a winning youth. He had been class poet at Brown University. He spoke French fluently, and Mary had observed how popular he was with the Springfield girls. While Hay studied law with his uncle Milton on the same floor as Lincoln and Herndon, the President-elect astutely saw that he might be a great help to him in Washington. "We can't take all Illinois with us down to Washington, but let Hay come," said Lincoln.

He was appointed assistant to Nicolay, the President-elect's regular secretary, a hard worker of Bavarian ancestry, whose boyish freckles and reddish hair belied his serious manner. Both men had much to do with Mrs. Lincoln during her first days in the White House, and sparks soon flew between them. But each was well geared to working with President Lincoln. Hay's social grace and Nicolay's steadfast support became part of the early history of the Civil War, but in their ten-volume record of the period Mrs. Lincoln's role was completely lost in the rich pattern of events. It was not until they reached the White House that the trouble began. Until then Mary had found Hay charming and Nicolay useful.

On February 6, 1861, the Lincolns gave a farewell reception in their home, inviting everyone who cared to come. The crush was continuous from seven o'clock until eleven as the "political elite of this state, and the beauty and fashion of this vicinity" streamed through the house. Lincoln stood near the door greeting each arrival, and Mrs. Lincoln was in the parlor with her sisters. She was wearing one of the dresses she had bought in New York, and Rankin recalled it as being most becoming, with a small lace collar, a string of pearls around her neck, and a headdress of trailing vine. "I thought I had never seen her fine figure appear more becomingly dressed and her countenance more expressive," he wrote, realizing how well suited she was to being mistress of the White House.

There was much interest in Robert's fine looks and fashionable grooming, and it was noticed that his father gave him a playful slap in the face when his son moved up to him and said with a grin, "Good evening, Mr. Lincoln." Tad and Willie were on their best behavior, and Mary had seen to it that her husband and small sons were properly dressed for this farewell party.

Their house was rented, and when their household furnishings were privately sold, she may have felt some pangs; but she was well aware that she was moving on to a new and better life, and she was already refurnishing the White House in her mind's eye. Historians have blessed her for saving some of her letters from Lincoln, particularly those of their early days of courtship and marriage. But she was busy burning others when Jared P. Irwin, a neighbor, asked if he might scrape around in the outdoor bonfire for some papers as souvenirs. He was lucky enough to find a few letters that this famous pair had exchanged.

Lincoln cleaned out files, disposed of rubbish, and gave Mrs. Elizabeth Grimsley, Mary's cousin, a carpetbag, which he called his "literary bureau." It contained old manuscripts and had a seedy air. He worked on his inaugural speech and the talks he would give on his way to Washington. He roped up the family boxes and trunks and wrote on Chenery House cards: "*A. Lincoln, White House, Washington, D.C.*" They had moved to that hotel for a few days of privacy before leaving. Lincoln made some familial visits to relatives with whom he had never been close. He was breaking with the past. A new life was beginning, and it was already clouded by threats. The indications of danger along the way mounted as the time of departure approached. When the suggestion was made that Mrs. Lincoln and the boys should travel separately, the New York *Herald* quoted Mary as saying that she would "see Mr. Lincoln on to Washington, danger or no danger."

One of the most damaging stories told about Mary Lincoln concerned her last hours in Springfield. Hermann Kreismann, a German-American politician who disliked her intensely, was supposed to have told it first, and Villard gave it to the public in his *Lincoln on the Eve of '61.*

The story was that when there was a delay about the Lincolns' departure for the depot, Kreismann was sent to their quarters, where he found the President-elect in a state of turmoil and Mrs. Lincoln lying on the floor, seemingly "quite beside herself." Lincoln, looking miserable, said: "Kreismann, she will not let me go until I promise her an office for one of her friends." Another variation of this story was that Kreismann and Norman B. Judd, counsel for the Rock Island Railroad and Republican state committee chairman, visited Lincoln soon after his election and on their arrival found Mary hysterically demanding that her husband make a certain appointment—a favor for which she had been promised a diamond brooch.

Mrs. Randall has dismissed both stories as being apocryphal, with differences in timing, detail and general plausibility. She could not believe that Lincoln would have invited Kreismann into their hotel room if his wife were on the floor in a disheveled state, making such demands. However, when Villard's book was published, it became another thorn for Mary's crown. He and others wrote of her susceptibility to gifts in exchange for favors, and this story may well have been the starting point of the tales of cupidity attached to Mrs. Lincoln's name. Goodwill offerings reached unprecedented proportions during the Lincoln administration, and all manner of gifts, from a pig's whistle to valuable jewelry, were received at the White House. Mary, childlike in her love for glittering baubles, was deluged with jewelry, enameled clocks, laces, shawls, and *objets d'art* from different parts of the world.

Whatever may have happened on the day of Lincoln's departure,

Mary, Tad and Willie left separately and joined his train at Indianapolis. This was explained at the time as being a precautionary measure taken because of the threats to his life. Robert went with his father and was with him as a cold drizzle dampened the scene at the depot. Crowds had turned out to wish Lincoln farewell and good luck. He had not intended to make a speech, but as he stood on the car platform and saw his fellow townsmen waiting for his final words, he doffed his hat with much feeling and said: "To this place, and the kindness of these people, I owe everything. Here I have lived a quarter of a century and have passed from a young to an old man. Here my children have been born, and one is buried. I now leave, not knowing when, or whether ever, I may return, with a task before me greater than that which rested upon Washington. Without the assistance of that Divine being, who ever attended him, I cannot succeed. With that assistance I cannot fail."

Then began the long, slow journey through five states, stopping at the larger cities, meeting governors, legislators and men of affairs at each place. There were receptions, parades, thousands of hands to shake, speeches to be made, and all the bright panoply of a triumphal processional. It was exhilarating for Mrs. Lincoln, but her husband looked wearier by the day. War was in the air, and his role was dimly sensed by the political hierarchy. Towns and hamlets were decorated with flags. Where there was human habitation, the tracks were lined with cheering crowds. The Republicans had used all possible resources to impress the people along the route. They were a new party and they were to be led by a most uncommon man.

All the Lincolns were on display, and there was constant excitement in the Presidential saloon car. Scrolls and tassels adorned the dark wood furniture. Crimson plush lined the walls, and the curtains were of blue silk with thirty-four silver stars. The national flags were impressively arranged at either end of the car. Flags and streamers were everywhere, reflecting the patriotic image, and the outside of the Presidential car had brightly varnished orange panels splashed with black and brown. Outside and in, the mood was one of jubilation, and Mary proved to be a good campaigner. Robert had Hay, Nicolay and young Elmer Ephraim Ellsworth for companions. Ellsworth, an eager youth who would soon be known to the country at large, was a favorite with both of the Lincolns. They regarded him almost as a son.

But the two men who hovered around the President were his trusted adviser, Judge David Davis of Bloomington, huge and rotund, and Ward Hill Lamon, on his way to becoming Marshal of the District of Columbia and already dedicated to guarding the person of Lincoln. Before the trip was over, the President-elect had made more than twenty speeches and been viewed by thousands who would come to know him well in the next four years.

Robert refused to speak when he was called on to say a few words in Indianapolis. Tad was impish and excited, thinking it funny to say to strangers: "Do you want to see Old Abe?" while he pointed to someone else in their party. He liked the plumed horses with flags waving from their harnesses that drew their equipages through city streets to the blare of bands and the shouts and cheers of bystanders. There were dark looks and imprecations, too. Their welcome in Ohio was thunderous, but Lincoln was so hoarse that he could scarcely be heard when he spoke in Columbus. Mary tried to save her husband by taking over the burden of the conversation when people crowded around them. Her animation and graceful ways were commented on favorably wherever they went. She smiled through it all, waved her dimpled arms, and gave every evidence of enjoyment as she talked to groups of women who obviously were weighing her in the balance as the next First Lady.

Lincoln never failed to make jesting remarks about Mrs. Lincoln in the course of his speeches, and at Ashtabula, Ohio, where the crowd called for her, he had his audience laughing when he said that he did not believe he could induce her to come out; in fact, he "never succeeded very well in getting her to do anything she didn't want to do." At a stop in Pennsylvania he brought Mary out on the platform "to show them the long and the short of it."

At Utica a black servant boarded the train with a handsome broadcloth coat and a new stovepipe hat in a box. Mary had become painfully aware of the shabbiness of her husband's attire after studying the well-groomed politicians they had met along the way. The word had gone forth that he must be smartened up before reaching New York, and the New York *Times* commented that he looked much better in his new coat and hat, adding: "If Mrs. Lincoln's advice is as near right as it was in this instance, the country may congratulate itself upon the fact that its President-elect is a man who does not reject, even in important matters, the advice and counsel of his wife."

Tad was tiring of the trip toward the end, and although he enjoyed watching the skaters on the Hudson, by the time they reached Poughkeepsie he lay down on the floor and said he would not make any more appearances. Robert alone responded when the window was opened to return salutations. But the crowd wanted to see the other boys, and finally Mrs. Lincoln appeared and apologetically explained that Tad was not in the mood to be shown off. Generally he was.

They all were in a state of exhaustion when they reached New York on February 19 and went straight to the Astor House. An elaborate welcome had been arranged for them, and Mrs. Lincoln now faced her most critical and sophisticated observers. Some were already well primed on her history and were prepared to snub her. The links between Springfield and New York had been close in the weeks since Lincoln's election, and her first shopping expedition had come under fire. The undertones of the approaching war already surrounded the Lincolns and the threats to their safety were not mythical.

Mrs. Lincoln gave a reception of her own on the day after their arrival at which she received with Mrs. James Watson Webb. There was nothing ostentatious about her manner or attire. Her high-necked gown of steel-colored silk was trimmed with plaited satin ribbon. A diamond brooch held her lace collar in place, and she wore diamond eardrops under a black chenille and gold headdress. She carried a nosegay and a small ivory fan, which she whisked restlessly as she chatted with her guests.

More than a hundred of New York's leading social figures paid their respects to Mrs. Lincoln that night, but one who was conspicuously absent was Mrs. August Belmont. The social freeze on the interloper from the Middle West became public chatter when *Leslie's Weekly* ran a revealing item: "We are requested to state that Mrs. August Belmont did not call upon Mrs. Lincoln during her stay at the Astor House."

An observer of Mary at this reception wrote to friends in the West that she was a "plump, amiable, modest, pleasant, round-faced, agreeable woman, with no silly airs, & they say is a pious woman." It is doubtful that this was the way in which Mary viewed herself, for she was uncommonly vain and understated her age without compunction. But comment came at her from all sides until she was hardened to being called stout, motherly, amiable and much else that implied the commonplace. She was definitely not that, for whatever the outer shell, Mrs. Lincoln was a dynamic woman who would soon make herself felt, for better or for worse. Hate her or love her, she was a personality, beneficent or destructive, as the case might be. Little was forgiven her as she lived in the lengthening shadow of Abraham Lincoln, soon to be the nation's most controversial man.

VI

Mrs. Lincoln in the White House

MARY LINCOLN ARRIVED in Washington to assume the role of First Lady with an outer show of confidence, but she felt more angry and upset than triumphant. She had expected a proud entry by her husband's side. Neither had anticipated the sudden change of plan when the threat of an assassination plot in Baltimore caused Allan Pinkerton, the Chicago detective who would loom large in the espionage activities of the Civil War, to bypass that city and get Lincoln into the capital secretly and ahead of the Presidential party.

In the end it proved to be an extravagant subterfuge, and the protective measures used seemed stealthy and humiliating to Mary. She alone was told of the change in plan and she became hysterical and defiant, for she had vowed to stay by her husband's side through every danger. War was in the air and passions blazed with primitive force. Fear and suspicion clouded the atmosphere, and General Winfield Scott, resplendent in full Army regalia and plumed hat, had felt the necessity of turning Washington into an armed city for the arrival of the Lincolns. The President-elect, still untried, had to deal with a nation torn by divisive forces without precedent since the days of the Revolution.

The journey east had been hectic and tiring, and Mrs. Lincoln's cold reception in New York had not been reassuring. She was Southern-born, obscure, and had come directly from the Middle West, which she knew would not endear her to the ruling establishment in Washington. Although she had carefully planned her course of action, she was fully aware of the obstacles she faced. But she held her head high and was brightly responsive as she was escorted on Seward's arm to the Presidential quarters at Willard's, where her husband was already established. The boys were ready for anything in this strange new world, but the confusion surrounding them was considerable at this point.

After a family reunion Mrs. Lincoln received guests in a parlor of her own. She found politicians, office seekers, correspondents and old friends crowded around her husband. He was already involved in all the formalities of an official call on President James Buchanan, a reception by Mayor James E. Berret, and a conference with John Tyler and Salmon Portland Chase, leaders of the Peace Convention, a futile gesture of hope that came to nothing.

Back in their quarters Mary saw at once that he was handling things in his usual casual way. He jested and told stories, but Seward quickly brushed off an attempt to be measured against the towering President—a favorite whim of Lincoln's when he saw a likely subject. Seward, who was not particularly tall, was taken aback by this sudden challenge. It seemed to him an inappropriate piece of buffoonery at a crucial moment in the nation's affairs, and he diplomatically remarked that it was a time for "uniting their fronts and not their backs."

Regardless of what went on around her husband, Mrs. Lincoln was careful to avoid gaffes as she greeted guests. Keen and attentive, she took in names and needed no cuing on their regional interests, for she had prepared herself with the zeal of a student tackling a stiff examination. She surprised some of the men with her free use of the Kentuckian "sir." Seward, Chase, Simon Cameron and Edward Bates, all of whom had been aspirants for the White House, were thoughtfully studied by Mrs. Lincoln. Seward, who had come closest to winning the nomination, and Chase, who would never cease to covet the Presidency, were the losers who concerned her most.

She had arrived with her own little coterie of relatives, attractive women fashionably dressed, and well able to hold their own in any company. Mrs. Elizabeth Edwards was an experienced hostess, used to official life. With her were her daughters, Elizabeth and Julia, who by this time had married Edward Lewis Baker, editor of the Illinois *State Journal*. The most vivacious member of the family group and the one who would later write graphically of these early days at the White House was Mary's cousin Elizabeth Todd Grimsley. She had been one of Mary's bridesmaids; now she would see her become First Lady. Margaret Todd Kellogg, one of Mary's half sisters, was also on hand to share in the great event, and Mrs. Grimsley wrote disapprovingly to her cousin John Todd Stuart that there were a hundred Todds on deck, all of them seeking appointments.

Mrs. Edwards' daughters and Robert brought a touch of youth to the Presidential party, and Hay, Nicolay and Ellsworth, the handsome young aide with black curly hair and eager manner, were in and out of Mrs. Lincoln's quarters, in addition to attending to the President's needs. They continued to function as they had in Springfield, except that they were now swept into the wider embrace of the State Department. There had been some doubt about Seward staying on, but Lincoln had finally persuaded him, and he became his most loyal supporter. Mary had disliked him from their first encounter, and he was one of several men around her husband whom she would never learn to trust. She voiced her feelings about him during her first days in Washington, but Seward was too smooth and experienced a politician to take her seriously at this point. Later he came to understand her power over Lincoln.

Inauguration morning was foggy and cold. Mary, always a prey to weather conditions, was not feeling her best. Her husband had read his inaugural address to her, but he had been upset over its temporary disappearance. He had given Bob the satchel in which he had put his speech. Before leaving Springfield, he had given an advance copy to William H. Bailhache, co-editor with Baker of the Illinois *State Journal*, to use immediately after his inauguration. Not conscious of its importance, Robert had allowed it to be swept into a pile of luggage at the hotel. For once Lincoln was angry, and he and his oldest son, never on the best terms, tangled sharply. He had a vision of his speech, the text of which he could not now remember, being published in Springfield. According to Nicolay, he went striding across the hotel lobby and dug out the oilcloth bag himself.

But he had calmed down by the time he drove to the Capitol with President Buchanan. Mrs. Lincoln was well aware of the green-uniformed sharpshooters watching from rooftops and of the armed guards posted at every street corner. Troops lined Pennsylvania Avenue, and there were imprecations as well as cheers when the tall-hatted Abraham Lincoln came into view. "There goes that

Illinois ape, the cursed Abolitionist. But he will never come back alive," sent a shiver through Julia Taft Bayne, an interested observer.

Mrs. Lincoln was studied closely as she sat in the diplomatic gallery with her sons and other relatives and watched Vice President Hannibal Hamlin being sworn in. The sun had come out, and it shone on a large concourse of people as the Lincolns appeared on the platform outside the east front of the Capitol. Mrs. Grimsley took note of the "sea of upturned faces, representing every shade of feeling, hatred, discontent, anxiety and admiration." But Mrs. Lincoln could think of nothing but her husband, about to take the oath from Chief Justice Roger Taney that would make him President. When this was done, Lincoln, addressing himself to the nation's divided forces in a high-pitched voice that carried to the outskirts of the appraising crowd, shot his bolt with: "Though passion may have strained, it must not break our bonds of affection. . . ." and on in thoughtful sequence until he had riveted the attention of his listeners.

The boom of cannon, soon to be an everyday occurrence, announced the fact that Abraham Lincoln was now President, and no one doubted that war was already at his doorstep in spite of his conciliatory words. A scattering of applause followed his course to the White House, and a bevy of girls representing the states of the Union stepped forth to kiss him. Mary was quiet and thoughtful as they drove up to the White House and were welcomed by Edward McManus, familiarly known as Old Ed, doorkeeper through five administrations.

Seventeen of Mary's relatives dined that night in historic surroundings and settled in their rooms to prepare for the inaugural ball, to be held a day later. In the morning the boys explored the mansion from roof to cellar and made friends with the staff. Mrs. Lincoln was up early and went straight into action, studying her new domain and mentally planning changes. Her first visitor was Mrs. Elizabeth Keckley, one of the capital's most treasured dressmakers, who told of the work she had done for Mrs. Jefferson Davis, Mrs. Stephen A. Douglas, Mrs. John McLean and other well-known customers.

Mrs. Keckley's first impression of Mrs. Lincoln was that she was noticeably stout in her cashmere wrapper. She seemed to be greatly concerned about costs and said at once: "I cannot afford to be extravagant. We are just from the West, and are poor. If you do not charge too much, I shall be able to give you all my work."

And that was how things turned out. Not only did Mrs. Lincoln give Mrs. Keckley all her work until she began buying imports from A. T. Stewart's, but she made her a close friend and confidante. With Lizzie's appearance on the scene, the stage was set for Mrs. Lincoln's plunge into an endless orgy of buying. It also opened the way for the publication of some of the most revealing information on the domestic habits and private thoughts of the Lincolns that ever reached the public. Mrs. Keckley was a mulatto from near Petersburg, handsome and articulate about the sorrows of her race. The fact that Southern-born Mrs. Lincoln chose a mulatto as a confidante and seemed to be influenced by her where the blacks were concerned was a matter of comment in Washington, which seethed with racial antagonism at this time.

From the start Mrs. Keckley realized that she was up against a disturbed and tortured woman, as she soothed Mrs. Lincoln in hours of anxiety and illness, and often helped look after Willie and Tad. Her observations about the President were quaint and perceptive. She saw that he was completely exhausted on the night of the inaugural ball. He had been through a strenuous experience since leaving Springfield, and the White House rooms and corridors were in a state of confusion. Office seekers and visitors wandered all over the place, and the Lincolns had no privacy.

Although five thousand attended the ball, which was held in a rambling plank building on Judiciary Square, Mrs. Lincoln soon learned that the Southerners had stayed away in spite of the emphasis on "union" and that old-guard Washingtonians had refused to turn out for the invaders from the Middle West. But Mary beamed and waved her fan as the gaslight from five chandeliers shed the glow of illusion over what came to be known as the White Muslin Palace of Aladdin. The two divisions, one for dancing, one for supper, seemed to sway and rock in their white muslin swathings.

At a preliminary reception the President shook hands with guests for two hours, his expression kind but absentminded, his white kid gloves getting dark and soggy in the process. When Scala's Marine Band played "Hail, Columbia" at eleven o'clock, the President led the grand march with Mayor Berret. Mrs. Lincoln, becomingly dressed in blue, with a feathered headdress and pearl and gold jewelry, followed on the arm of Stephen A. Douglas, who had wooed her before Abraham Lincoln had. They danced the quadrille of the evening together, and as they swung around the ballroom floor, it must have seemed like an old refrain to them. They had done it so often and so gracefully in the past. Mary had always been an accomplished dancer, and although she was heavier now, she was still quite equal to the schottische, polka, mazurka and waltz.

Mrs. Lincoln's animation was closely observed, and a few spectators, noticing how well they danced together and how much alike they were in height, thought they were better matched than Mary and Abraham. There was speculation as to what they might have discussed after all that had gone before—their early courtship, the debates, the defeat of the eloquent Senator, who was soon to die, or the fact that Mary had fulfilled her ambition. She was now the wife of a President.

"All eyes were turned on Mrs. Lincoln, whose exquisite toilet and admirable ease and grace, won compliments from thousands," according to Mrs. Elizabeth F. Ellet, a social commentator who observed the First Lady at close range. She noted that a fashion transition was under way as she studied the stiff brocades braided and trimmed lavishly with Honiton lace, after a period of ruffles and garlands. Now elaborate headdresses of feathers, flowers and illusion were an essential part of the formal costume, to balance the ever-widening hoops. Black velvet and diamonds, violet brocades, watered silks, flounced tarlatan and flashing jewels gave Aladdin's Palace a deceptive glamor, as the structure swayed, the skeleton showed, and a sense of impending disaster was the mood of many.

The President, central figure of the evening but obviously the most uncomfortable, left the ball before midnight. Mrs. Lincoln and her relatives stayed on. It was a night to remember, for it was her formal introduction to the social life of Washington, and for the time being she forgot the threatening shadows around her. In the warm glow of ambition achieved, she was in her element, as Mrs. Grimsley pointed out with scathing emphasis.

On March 8 the Lincolns gave the first of a series of levees at the White House, and Mary was chagrined when it wound up in a state of chaos, with such crowding that coats and hats were lost. The Washington *Star* noted that perhaps not one person in ten went home with all his own possessions. It was reminiscent of a Jackson jamboree.

The evening had begun with Mrs. Lincoln in a temper because Mrs. Keckley had been late in delivering her gown. She reached the

White House at the last moment with the rose moiré antique that Mrs. Lincoln had ordered and a blue watered-silk blouse for Mrs. Grimsley. Mary raged and said that there was no time for her to get dressed. She would stay where she was and let Mrs. Edwards and Mrs. Grimsley go downstairs with Mr. Lincoln. Both cousins worked hard to mollify Mary.

With skilled fingers Mrs. Keckley fitted the rose moiré with its point-lace flutings to Mrs. Lincoln's rounded figure, and the sight of herself in a mirror altered Mary's mood like magic. Invective changed to trilling laughter. The color was flattering, and the craftsmanship met her exacting standards. With swift touches she added a pearl necklace, pearl earrings and a pearl bracelet, modest jewelry compared with the flash of diamonds she would find down-stairs. Mrs. Keckley settled a cluster of red roses on her burnished hair. When the President came in and threw himself on a lounge to play with Tad and Willie, he complimented Lizzie on her work.

At last the family group was ready to face the critical audience waiting downstairs. Mrs. Julia Edwards Baker wore lemon silk, Mrs. Charles H. Kellogg was in ashes of roses, and Mrs. Ninian Edwards, slim and much taller than Mary, looked stately in brown and black silk. They all watched the President as he drew on white kid gloves, reciting poetry as he did so. He was more amused than angry when Tad hid his mother's lace handkerchief, which had to be found before the cavalcade could start. Then, according to Mrs. Keckley: "Mrs. Lincoln took the President's arm, and with smiling face led the train below. I was surprised at her grace and composure." After all the preliminary excitement she marveled that Mrs. Lincoln could have borne herself with such calm and dignity. Having passed this judgment, Mrs. Keckley never again underestimated Mary's capacity to preside at a reception, however doubtful she might be about her sanity behind the scenes. She made sixteen dresses for the First Lady that winter, and the impression quickly spread that Mrs. Lincoln was ostentatious and more concerned with show than with the subdued taste that wartime demanded. As time went on and she bought on an increasingly elaborate scale, her photographs invariably showed her tastefully dressed in the current fashion.

It was at this first reception that Mary Lincoln realized she had a powerful social rival in Kate Chase, the most discussed hostess in Washington at the time. Seasoned observers saw in Kate a lady of quality who had come from Ohio in time to take the place of the veterans from the South. With Mrs. Seward ill and out of the running, she automatically became the premier Cabinet hostess. Kate felt it was her function to represent the State Department and to entertain the diplomats and visiting celebrities from abroad. She had the triple endowment of beauty, style and brains and was one of the most interesting women ever to grace the Washington scene. Her proud bearing, her creamy skin and hazel eyes, her Titian hair, her intelligence and graceful manners made her a distinctive figure in the smartest circles.

Mrs. Lincoln noticed at her first reception that the dazzling daughter of the Secretary of the Treasury was holding a levee of her own, and she could not fail to recognize the impact of Kate's appeal. Before long she was complaining openly that Miss Chase made a habit of holding court at White House receptions. The strongest antislavery elements were behind her. Both women had come to Washington with parallel ambitions—one for her husband, the other for her father.

Kate had only to look around at Mrs. Lincoln's first reception to see that the Lincolns were being snubbed. The cream of the social crop was missing. The powerful dowagers of the South, already scattered, had left a vacuum, and she decided that the invasion of Todds from Kentucky did not adequately take their place. Top Army and Navy officials and old-guard conservatives of all types had decided to ignore the black-supporting Republicans. But Mary was the President's wife and so had the advantage in power. However, in battles of wit and social counterplay Kate took the honors easily and had no trouble deepening the social boycott of the Lincolns, yet without displaying malice or spreading gossip.

Kate was unconscious at first of Mrs. Lincoln's reaction to her social success, although she was soon to feel its menace. Driving home from the first levee with her father, she gave Mrs. Lincoln credit for more social skill than she had expected; for agreeable Kentucky speech; for passable, if not fluent, French; for unsophisticated but becoming attire; for being less the vulgarian than rumor had made her. But the levee, with its incredible cloakroom confusion, struck Kate as having been an untidy and undistinguished affair.

As time went on and she conducted a calculated social campaign of her own, Kate found it easy to put Mrs. Lincoln in the wrong. As an honored member of the Cabinet family she had ample opportunity to observe, and her own worldliness and assurance diminished Mrs. Lincoln's image and emphasized her effusive drive for success. Kate was hardheaded, cool and intelligent, while Mary's emotions ran riot and her moods were unpredictable. Mr. Lincoln was soon aware of the depth of her feeling where Kate Chase was concerned.

Since Miss Chase was part of his official family, this feud was more hurtful to Mrs. Lincoln than the ostracism traceable to the breach between North and South. Kate's subtle moves were graphically pinned down for the President by Mary, but without effect. He continued to honor her and to listen attentively to her sparkling conversation. Seward tried at first to control all state entertaining by the new Republican administration, thinking that Mrs. Lincoln might lose her way in the pitfalls of social custom in Washington. But she took a firm stand on this and made it clear to him that she would manage things herself, which she did and with some skill. "It is said that you are the power behind the throne—I'll show you that Mr. Lincoln is President yet," she told him bluntly on one occasion.

Worldly-wise Seward, eight years older than Lincoln, was a sumptuary in his way of living. His five-course dinners, noted for their style and charm, as well as for superb cuisine and rare wines, were assets on the diplomatic front. His Arabian horses were of interest to the sporting world, and he was one of the first of his generation to give up snuff for cigars. He was popular with women, but he soon learned to be wary of Mrs. Lincoln and not to impinge on what she thought to be her territory. The President found Seward a political wizard and helpful to him in many ways. He welcomed his social guidance, but Mary soon threw off this yoke and did what she wished. She knew that her own early training could be of help to her husband, surrounded by smooth politicians and business princes who thought his manners boorish. It did not make her happy to hear him referred to as Good Old Abe, even in the kindliest way, and he was always Mr. Lincoln or Father to her. The Cave Dwellers and the small group of Virginia hostesses who had long been dominant in the capital shrank from the buffoonery that sometimes went on around Mr. Lincoln. But his idiosyncracies in time became his virtues, whereas Mary's image as an autocratic and pretentious First Lady did not change.

The President might have been genial and humble in manner, but his wife was not, and she resented the efforts of some of the socially initiated who wished to help steer her course. After carefully studying the detailed memorandum prepared by the State Department to cover formal functions, the use of visiting cards, the order of precedence and the inviolable points of etiquette, she decided on a few innovations of her own.

The fact was that Mrs. Lincoln was better bred, better educated, better mannered than many of the women she faced in Washington. She was also more intelligent and perceptive in her judgment of men and situations. But her wit was sharp and her reactions so swift that she made no attempt to be conciliatory. Until the 1940's quiet women fared best at the White House, and Mary had never learned to hold her tongue under pressure. Every move she made was chronicled, often with scorn, for Washington was filled with secessionists who watched the Lincolns with unswerving attention. It became a habit to strike at the President through his vulnerable wife. Calumny smeared her at every turn as she floundered in a hostile atmosphere, gave her confidence indiscreetly, and made scenes that were duly reported by servants. Stories spread about her tempers, her extravagance, her tears, her vanity and her mania for clothes.

Criticism came from many quarters, but Mrs. Lincoln had her champions, too, and they made themselves heard in unmistakable terms. Visitors from abroad gave her credit for intelligence, grace and skill as a hostess. The diplomats found it a pleasant change to have a President's wife chat with them in French, although Mrs. James Monroe had been a jewel in this respect. But it surprised them in Mrs. Lincoln, for they had not known what to expect of the giant from the plains and his wife. Although she was known to be a scholar, she did not flaunt this in her everyday dealings with guests, but she used her knowledge to good advantage when intellectuals came her way. There were many literary visitors and distinguished scholars roaming the country in the Civil War era, and in spite of all the false stories they heard about her, some were disposed to admire her.

But the Adams' influence, still strong in Washington, was not helpful to Mrs. Lincoln. If the women of the Deep South ignored her, the women of New England appraised her coolly, and she had short shrift in Mrs. Charles Eames' literary salon. In his diary Charles Francis Adams, Jr., noted how badly the Lincolns had fared in this select set. "If the President caught it at dinner, his wife caught it at the reception," he wrote. "All manner of stories about her were flying around; she wanted to do the right thing but, not knowing how, was too weak and proud to ask; she was going to put the White House on an economical basis, and, to that end, was about to dismiss the 'help' (as she called the servants), some of whom, it was asserted, had already left because 'they must live with gentlefolks.' "

Adams added scornfully that she turned to reporters and railroad conductors for advice. Villard bolstered this charge by writing that Mrs. Lincoln "allowed herself to be approached and continuously surrounded by a common set of men and women whose bare-faced flattery easily gained controlling influence over her." It was a well-known fact that James Gordon Bennett had staff writers who alternately flattered and sniped at Mrs. Lincoln, endowing her with every grace and paradoxically picturing her as a pretentious fool. These men circulated around her in the same way as the gossip columnists a century later focused on White House doings. She was the first President's wife to undergo such scrutiny, such ceaseless attack.

Her husband alone made allowance for the fact that Mary was ill during most of her days in the White House. Her headaches were annihilating and frequent. In later years she said she scarcely knew what it was to feel well in the miasmic Washington air. But when things were going well, she could quickly swing from deep depression to exuberant spirits and the President was always responsive to her moods. He took great pride in her looks, her gowns, her skill as a hostess, and one sure way to hold his attention was to tell him how well and how handsome his wife was looking. Various guests commented on the admiring glances he cast in her direction across a ballroom floor, and on one occasion he said: "My wife is as handsome as when she was a girl, and I, a poor nobody then, fell in love with her, and what is more I have never fallen out."

The old social and journalistic alignments ceased to have meaning when war broke out. The business families of the industrial East and the slaveholding families of the South had found a common meeting ground in the drawing rooms of the capital, but now there was a great parting of the ways. Mrs. Levi Woodbury, Mrs. Sallie Ward Hunt, Mrs. Charles Carroll, Mrs. Samuel P. Lee, Mrs. George W. Riggs and Mrs. Clement Clay all were potent in the social firmament. Mrs. Rose O'Neal Greenhow and Mrs. Alexander Slidell spoke out openly for the South. The Ogle Tayloes had power and money.

The social commentators like Ben: Perley Poore, Mrs. Elizabeth F. Ellet, Laura C. Holloway, Edna Colman and Mary Clemmer

Ames, who chronicled the social life of the period, immediately applied the clinical touch to Mrs. Lincoln. They agreed that in another era she might have functioned brilliantly in the White House. She had all the social requirements but the wrong temperament for the stress and fury of a nation at war. Mrs. Colman observed that the social graces were highly developed in Mrs. Lincoln, but that from the beginning criticism and prejudice made her path a difficult one. She considered her high-spirited, independent and frank but she "failed to win the hearts of the people," for she was willful, impulsive, and quick-tempered.

Mrs. Holloway deplored her failure to be conciliatory when attacked. She was overly ambitious and in this writer's opinion seemed too conscious of the immense assistance she could give her husband. "She found herself surrounded on every side by people who were ready to exaggerate her shortcomings, find fault with her deportment on all occasions, and criticize her performance of all her official duties." Mrs. Holloway considered her a lonely and unhappy woman, friendless and misunderstood, fighting battles for her husband, not for herself.

Mrs. Lincoln's consistently low décolletage caused a great deal of talk. When she greeted Laura Catherine Redden Searing, a deaf, handicapped writer who used the pen name Howard Glyndon, her lilac dress evoked this comment: "It was made very décolleté as to the shoulders, bust, and arms; but she had a certain dimpled chubbiness, which justified the style." Her face, said Miss Searing, suggested someone who enjoyed life, a good joke, good food, fine clothes, fine horses and carriages, and luxurious surroundings. It was also the face, she added, of one whose affectionate nature predominated all else, and she could not doubt that Mr. Lincoln had found in Mary just what he needed—a most loyal wife and mother and a good woman, in spite of her foibles and "puerileness."

But her décolletage became a matter of adverse comment across the country, and a visitor from Oregon who attended one of her receptions wrote to his wife in 1862 that the "weak-minded Mrs. Lincoln had *her bosom* on exhibition, and a flower pot on her head, while there was a train of silk, or satin, dragging on the floor behind her of several yards length."

Most contemporary descriptions of Mrs. Lincoln suggest the amiable and rounded face much photographed and often touched up in the years to come. Her fine eyes and graceful shoulders and arms usually drew comment, and the New York *World* of November

13, 1860, described her as slightly above medium height, with brown (sic) eyes, "clearly cut features, delicate, mobile, expressive, rather distinguished in appearance than beautiful, conveying to the mind generally an impression of self-possession, stateliness and elegance."

Mary Clemmer Ames was less flattering. "Mrs. Lincoln is very dumpy, and very good-natured, and very gorgeous," she wrote. "She stuns me with her low-necked dresses and the flower beds which she carries on top of her head." Jane Swisshelm, working for the government and partial to Mrs. Lincoln, wrote enthusiastically: "Her complexion is fair as that of a young girl, her cheeks soft, plump and blooming and her expression tender and kindly. . . ."

Men on the whole had a kinder attitude toward Mrs. Lincoln. John Lothrop Motley, the historian who was appointed United States Minister to Austria in 1861, wrote to his wife that he found the new First Lady "youngish, with very round white arms, well dressed, chatty enough, and if she would not, like all the South and West, say 'Sir' to you every instant, as if you were a royal personage, she would be quite agreeable."

William Howard Russell, the cynical correspondent of the London *Times*, was also irritated by her constant use of the word "sir." When he first met her, he commented on her "*embonpoint*," her plain features, and a certain stiffness occasioned by the "consciousness that her position requires her to be something more than plain Mrs. Lincoln, the wife of the Illinois lawyer." But he thought that she tried hard to make herself agreeable, and he noticed that she "handled a fan with much energy, displaying a round, well-proportioned arm." The more he saw of Mrs. Lincoln, the better he liked her and he soon came to the conclusion that his secessionist friends had erred in emphasizing her vulgarity. He had been told that Varina Davis was a "lady at all events, not like the other," the "other" being the unfortunate Mrs. Lincoln. By the time he had studied both he was more impressed with Mrs. Davis, but he did not downgrade Mrs. Lincoln.

One of the sharpest pictures of Mary during her early days in the White House was drawn by Mrs. Rose O'Neal Greenhow. For obvious reasons this accomplished and beautiful spy for the Confederacy had no cause to be flattering about Mary Lincoln, but with more savagery than subtlety she described her as a "short, broad, flat figure, with a broad flat face, with sallow mottled complexion, light grey eyes, scant light eyelashes, and exceedingly thin pinched lips. Self-complacency, and a slightly scornful expression characterize her bearing, as if to rebuke one for passing between the 'wind and her nobility.' "

On a marketing expedition in 1861 Mrs. Greenhow had gone out of her way to follow Mrs. Lincoln into a shop when she saw the "imperial coach, with its purple hangings and tall footmen in white gloves" pulled up at the door. Inside she found a small woman bargaining for black cotton gloves; this was Mrs. Lincoln—much too pretentiously dressed for the occasion, Rose decided. Her gown was a rich silk embroidered with showy flowers. Her Point Venise collars and sleeves were edged with pink ribbons. Her white hat was decked with flowers, feathers and tinsel balls, and her white parasol had a pink lining. A supermantel of black lace and white gloves completed the effect. With such touches as these Mrs. Greenhow managed to spread the impression that Mrs. Lincoln was ridiculous in her pretensions and lack of taste.

Many of the tales of Mrs. Lincoln's treatment of servants, her so-called vulgarity, her extravagance and her tempers were whipped into brisk circulation by Mrs. Greenhow, who could be strikingly eloquent on any subject close to her heart. Much of her ammunition on the Lincolns reached Rose through the diplomatic set, since she was their particular darling. She was highly critical of Mary's handling of the first diplomatic reception, which she said should have been second only to a presentation at St. James's or at St. Cloud.

Rose quoted one diplomat as saying of the Lincolns: "He is better than she, for he seems by his manner to apologize for being there." She conceded that the President was a "little less bizarre in his ministerial reception," although it was noted that when asked which wine he would take at an official dinner, he turned to the attendant and with the "most touching simplicity said: 'I don't know. Which would you?' " His clumsiness when he spilled a cup of tea on a guest's dress was a tiny item that ran through the social circuit. Rose could forgive this but not Mrs. Lincoln's message to Madame Mercier, wife of the French Minister, that she was studying French and would be able to converse with her in her own language by winter.

The White House was now like a hotel "filled with a crowd of common people," said Rose, referring to the Lincoln ménage as "High Life Below Stairs." But she was not naïve. She knew better, for she had visited the White House in Jackson's time, when muddy boots and uncouth manners were not unknown in the East Room. Rose was merely turning the knife in the unfortunate Mrs. Lincoln.

With two women as clever and attractive as Mrs. Greenhow and Kate Chase on her trail, Mrs. Lincoln was at a great disadvantage, and some of the stories circulating about her came from Hay and Nicolay, who were in Kate Chase's camp. These young men, who had become an essential part of the White House entourage, developed an intense dislike for Mrs. Lincoln once they all were settled in Washington. They called her the "hellcat" and showed their dislike for her in a number of whimsical ways. Her insistence on having her own way proved equally difficult for them. When the time came to assemble their ten-volume record of the Lincoln regime and the Civil War, Mrs. Lincoln got no more than nine brief references, three as Mary Todd, six as First Lady.

She was treated with more understanding by William O. Stoddard when he took over the task of attending to her mail and handling various social matters that had been treated disdainfully by the blithe young men who admired her husband but had little use for her. Stoddard was the first of the men around the Lincolns to spot signs of insanity in Mary, and he had ample opportunity to observe her at close range. It seemed to him that something more than willfulness and a hot temper drove her to such excesses, and doubt arose in him when he heard the President scold her gently for allowing her prejudices and dislikes to warp her judgment of people. Stoddard was an old friend from Illinois, and in serving the President as secretary he caught the full impact of the abuse from which both he and Mrs. Lincoln suffered. Even before they left Springfield, Lincoln was being called an ape, a mulatto, a monster, a gorilla, an idiot, and Mary was stunned when the Kentucky *Statesman*, from their own region, in the spring of 1861 described him as the "miserable imbecile that now disgraces the Presidential chair." He was "raw-boned, shamble-gaited, bow-legged, knock-kneed, pigeon-toed, slob-sided, a shapeless skeleton in a very tough, very dirty, unwholesome skin," the *Statesman* went on.

"In a word," the polemic concluded, "Lincoln born and bred a railsplitter, is a railsplitter still. Bottom, the weaver, was not more out of place in the lap of Titania than he on the throne of the ex-republic."

"No satire was too pointed, no ridicule too coarse, no calumny too vile or vituperation too profane to be hurled at Lincoln," said Stoddard, and Mrs. Lincoln's own mail was so abusive that she finally told him not to show her anything until he had screened it.

But there was no killing the legend in the North that she was a

Southern spy, or in the South that she was a traitor to the region of her birth. She was accused of beating her children, of being unfaithful to her husband, of having Negro blood, of being illiterate, dishonest, crude, lazy and shiftless, of being a snob and an insane one at that, of making the President miserable, and of being wildly extravagant and selfish.

Stoddard marveled at Mrs. Lincoln's strength of will. From the very beginning, he commented. she "assumed and held her rightful position as lady of the mansion," but she failed to accept the fact that she no longer was a private citizen who could do as she liked. It was to her own surprise that she made history, aside from her husband, and figured in countless news items. The swarms of correspondents who arrived from all quarters to report the Civil War had a hand in this, because Mrs. Lincoln grew ever more controversial as her husband rose above the storm and stood on a peak of his own.

VII

A Nation Divided

T HE LONG-FORESEEN SPLIT between North and South became an
awesome reality almost as soon as the Lincolns settled in the
White House. The waiting had ended. The feeble gestures for peace
had collapsed. When Jefferson Davis took his departure from the
Senate on a January day in 1861, the hour of decision had been
reached. From then on, events moved inexorably toward war.

The dissenting states went their way dramatically, but Mrs. Lincoln's native state, Kentucky, was not among them. The diplomats
watching from the gallery were aware that they were looking in on
history—that the United States was on the brink of civil war. Tears
flowed down the cheeks of what Mrs. Jefferson Davis described as
the "bright faces of the ladies assembled together like a mosaic of
flowers in the doorway," with their crinolines collapsing like fallen
balloons when they could not find seats in the crowded chamber and
had to sink to the floor. It was the close of a flamboyant era as they
left the capital in their great coaches piled high with possessions.

In April the President's call for 75,000 troops after the historic
shot had been fired at Fort Sumter brought the North to life. Mrs.
Lincoln and her sons watched the first comers stream into
Washington. She was hostess to the Frontier Guard who camped
temporarily in the East Room and went clanking through the
corridors with their paraphernalia. In spite of the guards assigned to
protect the White House and other public buildings, the capital was
vulnerable after the Fort Sumter incident until the Seventh New

York Regiment marched along Pennsylvania Avenue, with Tad jumping to the excitement of the bands and flags. This was less harrowing than the earlier arrival of the wounded soldiers of the Sixth Massachusetts Regiment, brought in after the rioting in Baltimore. Washingtonians breathed more easily as troops were quartered in every available space.

Men rushed to the colors, with the fate of the country at stake. The same intensity of feeling drove the men of the North and the South, although in separate directions. As friends and relatives broke away, Mrs. Lincoln suffered acutely because of her family roots, and she was soon aware that, in spite of her passionate loyalty to her husband and the Northern cause, she was regarded as a traitor and a spy. The presence of the outspoken Mrs. Grimsley did not help matters in this respect.

There was danger in the air. One night when everyone in the White House but the servants became violently ill, rumors spread that they had been poisoned. It turned out that the severe intestinal upset they all experienced was caused by tainted shad roe. But illness persisted at the White House, with measles coming next. Mrs. Keckley was called in repeatedly to attend to the boys, since Mrs. Lincoln's devoted nursing was mixed with hysteria; she was far from well herself. It was a deflating experience after the high moments of inauguration, but as soon as she was able to, Mary adapted to the new routine of a nation at war. Soon she was visiting encampments, entertaining generals, and watching the mustering of a great army in tents across the Potomac. She was conscious of a sense of strain and was suffering from the general malaise that has since been identified in her case as malaria.

But emergencies had to be met, and she pulled herself together time and again to meet them. Plans changed constantly. An endless stream of unfamiliar faces flowed through the Executive Mansion, and William H. Russell commented on the hobnailed shoes of the soldiers who hesitated at the threshold of the state apartments, "alarmed at the lights and gilding or haply by the marabout feathers and finery of a few ladies who were in ball costume, till, assured by fellow citizens that there was nothing to fear, they plunged in to the dreadful revelry."

War songs rang out around the campfires that glowed across the Potomac. Through it all Mrs. Lincoln went ahead with a full social program and the redecoration of the White House. There had never been more need for diplomacy on the part of a President's wife than in the early days of the Civil War, when both Britain and France were being wooed by North and South as potential allies. Mrs. Lincoln was an effective aid to her husband in this respect, since she handled the diplomats and visiting celebrities with considerable skill. She was well informed on European affairs and could talk to the representatives of all the foreign countries with more than average understanding. The diplomats were used to meeting clever women in Washington, since Jessie Frémont, Varina Davis, Kate Chase, Rose O'Neal Greenhow and Mrs. Charles Eames all were dazzlers in this respect. But Mrs. Lincoln more than held her own, and she took lessons to improve her French, in addition to all her other duties. Never a negative presence, she functioned with pride and determination against adverse forces. Clearly, she viewed herself as a potent force in her husband's administration, although his closest advisers countered many of her moves and deplored her interference.

Yet she was scrupulous not to violate decorum where army maneuvers were concerned, and she refused to accept a military salute from a regiment in front of the White House as she drove out one day. The soldiers on the whole were friendlier to Mrs. Lincoln than the civilian population. Some wrote to their families about her with high praise, and one young cavalryman who had commented on the President's long nose added that "His Lady is charming enough to make up for all his deficiencies."

Mrs. Lincoln and her sons were invariably cheered when they visited the encampments. The soldiers liked to watch little Tad's antics, and they could report on Mrs. Lincoln's clothes to their wives and mothers. Occasionally she was called on to christen a new encampment, and it became a family joke that one was called Camp Mary Lincoln.

All Washington was startled when romantic young Elmer Ephraim Ellsworth, who had just been through a bout of measles with the Lincoln boys, was killed on May 24, 1861. Impetuous and fearless, he had led his Zouaves into Alexandria, Virginia, the first federal troops to invade the Old Dominion. The town was occupied and the pickets posted when he noticed a Confederate flag being hoisted on the Marshall house. He rushed to tear it down and was shot in the chest by James T. Jackson, its owner, who was instantly bayoneted by Ellsworth's comrades. This was the first blood of the Civil War shed on secession soil.

Mrs. Lincoln wept inconsolably for young Ellsworth, who had

been part of their family life, and the President was deeply moved. Together they went to the Navy Yard, where the youth's body had been brought from Alexandria. The Zouave Guards, by the President's order, bore him to the White House to lie in state in the East Room. Flags were flown at half mast. Bells tolled and crowds streamed past the bier.

Ellsworth's picture framed in a wax laurel wreath was placed on his coffin by Mrs. Lincoln. John Philip Sousa dedicated his newly composed "Colonel Ellsworth's Funeral March" to the President's wife. But she turned away from the bloodstained flag that he held when he was shot. The young Zouave became a legend, the symbol of gallantry and patriotism. The repercussions were felt across the country, and Ellsworth's name was enshrined as the first hero of the Civil War.

As Kentucky drifted toward secession, Lexington was under military rule and Mrs. Lincoln watched the course of events while the tide turned and the Stars and Stripes fluttered from flagstaffs. The President sent all possible aid to back the Unionists, and five thousand Lincoln guns reached them. Major Robert Anderson, of Fort Sumter fame, was a native Kentuckian sent south to recruit military companies in Lexington. Mary's native state was bitterly divided in its loyalties. The slayer of young Ellsworth was a brother of Dr. John Jackson, of Lexington. But in June Mary wrote to Captain John Fry, a Kentucky friend, saying it gave her great pleasure to be the medium of transmission of weapons to be used in "defense of national sovereignty upon the soil of Kentucky."

Expressing pride in her native state, Mary wrote that she rejoiced that Kentucky, "ever true and loyal furnishes to the insulted flag of the Union a guard of her best and bravest. On every field the prowess of Kentuckians has been manifested. In the holy cause of National Defense, they must be invincible."

At this time no one expected the war to last for any length of time. "On to Richmond" was the cheerful battle cry in army barracks. But the gathering tide grew stronger as the summer advanced, and women everywhere were sending their men to war and preparing for hospital work. The city was clamorous with rattling gun carriages and the steady tramp of marching feet. The white tents across the river sparkled eerily with flickering lights, but the soldiers still lacked the precision of a well-trained army.

Mrs. Lincoln warmly welcomed at her levees young recruits caked with mud and their bearded seniors, already weary from the strain of war. Her levees, or regular receptions, differed from her official receptions by invitation. Mary was at her best on the more formal occasions, but her husband felt more at home at the general levees. These tired Mary, who found she could not stand for long. She missed many, for she dared not appear when her headaches took possession, as they often did. But her absences usually caused her critics to suggest that she stayed away because she was a secessionist at heart.

The President called the levees his "public opinion bath." Flanked by Nicolay and Hay, he looked down from his great height at Americans of all degrees. For every spruced-up dandy in lavender gloves, there were twenty big-boned woodsmen, men from the mountains and men from the prairies, men wearing cowhide boots and hickory shirts, and always men in uniform. But brass-buttoned frock coats and white stocks abounded, and occasionally men with ruffled cuffs and long coifed hair bowed over Mary's hand. For the first time the Middle West was heavily represented in the receiving line.

Mrs. Lincoln stood a few paces away from her husband, with Stoddard at her side. Now and again the President would spontaneously lead a favored guest directly to his wife. But some of the visitors who marched past Mrs. Lincoln studied her with veiled hostility and less warmth than they directed at her husband. Through it all Stoddard found her "bright, cheerful, almost merry." He failed to understand why so many people disliked her, since she had done no harm to those who assailed her.

The levees were usually held on Friday nights and the receptions on Saturday afternoons. There were times when Mary deliberately invited someone who might prove useful to her husband, like William Howard Russell, whose dispatches to the London *Times* had great significance in the early days of the Civil War. As a frequent guest at Seward's perfectly appointed establishment, he was well aware that the Secretary of State deplored Mrs. Lincoln's determination to run the White House as if it were her own home and not a somewhat official institution.

She was disposed to give up the levees and concentrate on official receptions, and she also favored abandoning the state dinners that had been customary from the early days of the Republic. "Public receptions are more democratic than stupid dinners," Mary maintained, arguing at the same time that this change would be a sound economy measure. But the President was opposed to major upsets in established custom. However, nothing could stop her from initiating one change that was immediately interpreted by many Washingtonians as an indication that she was a jealous wife. She confided to Mrs. Keckley that she did not see why she should not promenade with her husband instead of with another distinguished guest. It was traditional for the President to lead a prominent lady around the East Room. Mary decided that this custom put her in a secondary position, so she ended it, leaving no ground for debate. From this time on she promenaded on the President's arm. If she were not present, he walked alone or with another man.

It was no secret from her earliest days in the White House that Mrs. Lincoln kept a watchful eye on the President and circumvented the enthusiasm of the women who crowded around him. Mrs. Keckley has left a revealing record of one evening's conversation between them as President and Mrs. Lincoln prepared to go downstairs for a reception.

"Well, Mother, who must I talk with tonight—shall it be Mrs. D.?"

"That deceitful woman! No, you shall not listen to her flattery."

"Well then, what do you say to Miss C.? She is too young and handsome to practise deceit."

"Young and handsome, you call her? You should not judge beauty for me. No, she is in league with Mrs. D. and you shall not talk with her."

"Well, Mother, I must talk with some one. Is there any one that you do not object to?"

"I don't know that it is necessary that you should talk to anybody in particular. You know well enough, Mr. Lincoln, that I do not approve of your flirtations with silly women, just as if you were a beardless boy, fresh from school."

"But, Mother, I insist that I must talk with somebody. I can't stand around like a simpleton, and say nothing. If you will not tell me who I may talk with, please tell me who I may *not* talk with?"

"There is Mrs. D. and Miss C. in particular. I detest them both. Mrs. B. also will come around you, but you need not listen to her flattery. These are the ones in particular."

"Very well, Mother; now that we have settled the question to your satisfaction, we will go down-stairs."

With stately dignity, in Mrs. Keckley's opinion, the President offered his arm to Mrs. Lincoln and led the way downstairs. The "Mrs. D." was Mrs. Douglas, and "Miss C." presumably was Miss

Chase. It would have been difficult to escape either one at a Lincoln party.

Aside from the official functions that were part of White House life, even in the hour of battle, Mary's immediate concern was the protection of her husband as he faced the awesome problems of civil war. While threatening letters poured in and the streets seemed full of menace, she concerned herself with his meals and his need for rest and sleep. She insisted on a daily drive at four o'clock, with occasional stops at hospitals to talk to wounded soldiers. She was quick to discern his moods, and she often subdued her own fears so as not to add to his. On the whole she tried to meet each day's needs as they arose. Instead of harassing him with her own problems, she was quick to give him sympathy when he came in from the War Office despondent, as on one occasion when she asked him if there were any news and he sadly replied: "Yes, plenty of news, but no good news. It is dark, dark everywhere."

Mrs. Keckley pictured him as coming into his wife's room, throwing himself on a lounge, and dropping his long arms in utter weariness. When not too tired, he might recite from Burns or Shakespeare, and he seemed to find relaxation in reading the Bible. The family dined between five and six o'clock, but Mr. Lincoln scarcely noticed what he ate. He had no taste for hard liquor, but an occasional glass of wine or beer accompanied a meal while the finest vintages came in as gifts for the White House table. His spartan existence involved working at his desk in the evenings when Mrs. Lincoln was not having guests, followed by a trip to the War Office for firsthand news. It was his custom to stay until early morning during a battle. As the months went by and storms of criticism raged around him, he had nights of broken sleep and days when he could neither eat nor rest. He usually rose early and breakfasted on coffee, eggs and toast. After going over the day's mail his official day started at ten o'clock. He finally had to limit visiting hours to from ten to one o'clock, but he thought nothing of breaking the regulations to see a visitor on a whim or because he had received a note from Mary drawing someone to his attention.

In the early days of the war she was adamant about not leaving her husband when General Scott suggested that she and the boys go north after the Battle of Bull Run, which had shocked and surprised Washingtonians, on July 21, 1861. When the wounded were brought in by ambulance, the mood of the capital changed to grief and mourning. It had been a shattering blow, disillusioning to those who believed that the war would soon be over. The Lincolns saw optimism turn to chaos. They decided against going to Soldiers Home, where President Buchanan had summered three miles from the White House. It would have been doubly difficult to guard the President in the heavily wooded area where it stood.

But as the summer wore on, Mary's health was precarious, and the President insisted that she, Mrs. Grimsley and Mrs. John Henry Shearer, a Springfield friend, go to Long Branch, New Jersey, for the sea air. This was then the fashionable watering place, founded in 1788 as a holiday resort for Philadelphians. Long noted for its blue laws and religious gatherings, it had turned into a worldly paradise, aping Sarotoga and Newport unsuccessfully but maintaining a dizzy pitch of its own behind its cast-iron trimmings and gingerbread fretwork. Racing and gambling, shooting galleries and billiard rooms, high living and segregated bathing for the sexes were components of the scene.

Mrs. Lincoln was not in quest of gaiety or entertainment, however. She was far from well and sought the rest and seclusion that she badly needed. The last thing she desired was publicity, but correspondents from the New York *Herald, Frank Leslie's* and other publications picked up her trail. "Let all of our best society prepare to follow in her train," said the *Herald.*

Robert Lincoln and John Hay had arrived in Long Branch first, to the delight of the more susceptible girls summering there. But they soon found that Robert was a solemn fellow, not much addicted to parties and good times. "He does everything very well, but avoids doing anything extraordinary," was the way the *Herald* put it. "He doesn't talk much; he doesn't dance differently from other people. He isn't odd, outré nor strange in any way. . . . In short, he is only Mr. Robert Lincoln. . . . He does nothing whatever to attract attention, and shows by every gentlemanly way how much he dislikes this fulsome sort of admiration. . . ."

However successful Robert was in eluding public notice, his mother reaped a harvest that sometimes pleased but more often angered her. A group of thirty-four little girls dressed in white had been assigned to meet her on her arrival, but only twenty-seven were rounded up in time. She was smothered in flowers and followed with cheers, but the tide turned against her before her stay had ended, and on the last day of August, 1861, the Chicago *Daily Tribune* shouted HOLD, ENOUGH in a headline. Things had gone too far. "If Mrs. Lincoln were a prizefighter, a foreign danseuse or a condemned convict on the way to execution, she could not be treated more indecently than she is by a portion of the New York press. . . ." The Philadelphia *Bulletin* and other papers came to her defense.

The New York *Herald* had been printing two and three columns a day about her gowns, her companions, her amusements and her jewels. She was described as holding court like a queen at a notable ball at the Mansion House. Her own sister Ann was responsible for this comparison, which made Mary very angry. But the occasion had a certain degree of pomp that offended the public in time of war. Wearing a long-trained white grenadine dress, with satin quilling puffing her skirt at the hem, she was escorted by Governor William A. Newell of New Jersey. Once more she wore her necklace and bracelets of pearls, and she waved a pearl fan in her usual vivacious fashion. Wild white roses rested in a coronet on her dark hair, and she was a decorative picture as she stood in the center of the ballroom, surrounded by a "brilliant suite, bowing as the ladies were presented to her." A semicircle of men, attired in high fashion and deferential to the First Lady, gave the scene a somewhat European air. It took Mary Clemmer Ames to point up the fact that while this was going on, men were dying in the field. Fresh floods of criticism swept over Mrs. Lincoln from different parts of the country.

Before the ball she had made an inspection tour of the lifesaving stations along the Jersey shore with Governor Newell, who had masterminded this innovation and was proud of it. When President Lincoln subsequently appointed him superintendent of the lifesaving service in New Jersey, Mary was credited with having inspired the move. Newell was one of her particular favorites.

The sea air did Tad little good, and he was ill most of the time he was at Long Branch. In September they moved on to Niagara Falls, sight-seeing along the way. They stayed at the International Hotel and had another look at the Falls. To the public Mrs. Lincoln seemed always to be in transit, visiting Saratoga Springs, Boston, New York, Philadelphia, the White Mountains and the seashore. Tired of the ceaseless press coverage, she appealed to James Gordon Bennett for peace, writing him that she did not want notoriety and that her nature was sensitive. She thanked him for all the times he had defended her against charges made in other publications.

Mary was not misinterpreting her nature when she referred to her sensitivity, although this was the quality that her critics thought she lacked to a singular degree. She was vulnerable because of the instability of her moods, and almost inevitably she incurred the ill will of the women in the political set, even while she inwardly longed for their approval. Her feuds were closely tied to their husbands' attitudes toward Mr. Lincoln. The friends closest to her in Washington at this time were Mrs. Gideon Welles; Mrs. Elizabeth Blair Lee, wife of Rear Admiral Samuel P. Lee and sister of Montgomery Blair, her husband's Postmaster General; Mrs. James W. White, wife of an Irish immigrant who had become a Supreme Court Justice in New York; and Mrs. James H. Orne, a Philadelphian, whose husband, a carpet manufacturer, was an affluent and active Republican, and whose brother, Charles O'Neill, was a member of the House of Representatives.

In many respects she felt more comfortable with her old Springfield friends, and she installed Mrs. Shearer and her boys in handsome quarters at Long Branch. Mary was always generous with gestures of this kind, and she seemed to have a deep need for the companionship of her family and her earlier female friends.

Her stay in Long Branch did her little good. By October 6, 1861, she was back in Washington and was writing to Mrs. Shearer about how ill she felt again, with the customary chills that had been plaguing her for ten days. The weather was still quite warm on her return to the dusty city. The diplomatic corps had returned, and the Blue Room in the evenings was alive with what Mary called the "beau monde." General George McClellan had sent her great bunches of choice grapes, but he had not been making headway on the military front. "We are as far removed, as ever on this eastern shore, it appears, from war— If we could accomplish our purpose without resorting to arms & bloodshed how comfortable, it would be— But that is impossible."

The same month both the President and Mrs. Lincoln sorrowed over the death of Colonel E. D. Baker, the popular young Senator from Oregon who died at the battle of Ball's Bluff while leading a detachment across the river. He had breakfasted at the White House and played on the lawn with Willie before setting out on his fatal expedition, and when the news reached McClellan's headquarters, the President was moved to tears.

The colonel's friends viewed his death as a needless sacrifice and a prime example of the military bungling that beset Lincoln's army. Like young Ellsworth he was canonized as a symbol of the cost of war, but deaths were now mounting in massive numbers and in an indistinguishable pattern. Colonel Baker, too, would have lain in state in the East Room had not Mrs. Lincoln's upholsterers turned things upside down at the time of the ceremonies.

Since none of her acts escaped attention, she came under fire for wearing a lilac costume at the Baker funeral. It happened to be one of her favorite colors, and she considered it half mourning, but Mrs. John Crittenden of Kentucky said flatly that black would have been more suitable, particularly while a great war was being fought. Mrs. Lincoln was tart and impulsive in her comment on this reproach. Did the women of Washington expect her to muffle herself in mourning for every soldier killed in the war? she exclaimed. "I want the women to mind their own business. I intend to wear what I please," she added defiantly.

Crittenden, who had fought in the War of 1812 and had once been her father's close friend, was now at odds with her husband, although as one of the veteran statesmen of the South, he had helped keep Kentucky in line for the Union. But he had backed Stephen Douglas rather than Abraham Lincoln, and Mary could never forgive him for that. His son, George, fought in the Confederate Army, and a grandson died fighting for the North.

Elizabeth Ashley was a widow with three children when she became the third wife of Crittenden in 1853. An attractive and accomplished woman, she had much in common with Mary, but as the breach widened between Lincoln and Crittenden, their wives reflected their divergent viewpoints. Washington hostesses were well aware that in spite of the Kentucky tie Mrs. Lincoln and Mrs. Crittenden regarded each other coldly.

Insensitive though it seemed, Mary's lightning reaction to the criticism of her funeral attire was in no way typical of her feeling for the men who died in battle. When Mrs. Keckley lost her only son, Wilberforce, at the Battle of Lexington, Mrs. Lincoln was "all heart" and wrote what Lizzie described as a "kind womanly letter . . . full of golden words of comfort." Her inconsistencies were as characteristic as her love for Abraham Lincoln.

VIII

Spendthrift First Lady

Mrs. Lincoln refurbished the White House with speed, grace and strict attention to the best standards of the day during her husband's first year in office, but because of her extravagance and the fact that the country was involved in the bitterest war, this became the first major disaster in her troubled history. She failed to appreciate the Monroe furniture that some of her successors would resurrect when time had given it a halo. At first glance she was conscious chiefly of the lack of paint and varnish, the broken-down chairs, the sagging beds.

In another era she might have been applauded for the china and glass she chose, for the satin brocatelles, the specially woven carpet and the French wallpaper that she ordered for the East Room. Although the prices were reasonable by later standards, she ran up bills that were to haunt her as long as her husband lived. She was accused of the misuse of funds as well as of the wildest extravagance; in carrying out her plans, she became involved with shady characters, to the dismay of the President and the men close to him.

Mrs. Lincoln's first view of the White House with Mrs. Grimsley convinced her that everything needed to be redone, and by the end of February, 1861, she was badgering officials about the size of the appropriation that would be at her disposal. John A. Briggs, to whom she suavely outlined her plans, wrote of her "cultivated taste and refinement" and her desire to have her home adorned as became the residence of the President.

The appropriation allowed was $20,000, but between the purchases she charged to the Commissioner of Public Works and bills paid by her husband, the ultimate cost rocketed sky-high. The New York merchants were all too keen on catering to the taste of the First Lady, and her shopping trips for furniture, as for clothes, were soon discussed across the country. It was during this period that her reputation as an insatiable shopper was established. Her multiple orders set the pattern for later years and became an obsession as time went on.

Mrs. Lincoln was not unused to mansions furnished in the best tradition. She had been in and out of Henry Clay's beautiful home in her childhood, and she was quite conversant with the period style in furniture, crystal, silver and china of her own. During her early months of buying she had the help and support of the bluff and kindly Benjamin Brown French, who had been appointed Commissioner of Public Buildings by President Lincoln. His letters to his family, now in the Library of Congress, reveal a great deal about Mrs. Lincoln's character and operations. He had held a variety of government posts from the eighteen thirties on and was no novice in this field. By the end of 1861, after he had seen Mrs. Lincoln through several of her shopping crises, he wrote to his sister-in-law, Pamela: "They tell a great many stories about Mrs. Lincoln but I do not believe them—indeed I *know* many of them are false—and I am not certain that we may not apply the old law maxim *falsus in uno, falsus in omnibus*. She is a very imprudent woman, in many things, as I do know, and taking advantage of this the world delights to add in a compound ratio, to the reality."

Major French acknowledged that she was unlike any other human being he had ever known and was not easy to get along with, but he managed better than most. He was well aware of Mrs. Lincoln's flattering and wheedling tactics, but he was also impressed with her knowledge and intelligence, however unreasonable he found her on the emotional side.

Her first important purchase—a treasure that dignified the dinner table of a succession of Presidents—was a set of Haviland china in solferino and gold, with the American coat of arms on each piece. This turned out so well that she decided to have another set made for the family's private use, with her initials in place of the coat of arms. According to Mrs. Grimsley, the President paid $1,106.73 for this set out of his own pocket after the story spread that it had been purchased with government funds. It was common gossip in

Washington that guests at the White House dinner table cast disdainful looks at Mrs. Lincoln's beautiful but costly plates.

Her Dorflinger glass, the finest Bohemian ware of the day and another treasure for the White House that would be appreciated at a later date, led to more ugly stories concerning Mrs. Lincoln's purchases. But she was not shaken in her conviction that everything she bought for the White House should be the best of its kind available. Her 700-piece set of Bohemian cut glass was a glittering household adjunct during the war years. But the trouble was that these *were* the war years, and while others cut down on lavish display, she set a new standard of magnificence and then wondered why no one seemed to approve.

Mary repeatedly made trips to New York and Philadelphia to order damask, wallpaper, carpets and curtain materials, most of which were brought over from Europe. One of her most criticized purchases was the French wallpaper she ordered for the East Room. This involved 221 sections of a heavy velvet paper patterned in crimson, garnet and gold. The carpet for the East Room, which would be endlessly trodden on by spurred and booted warriors, was specially woven in Glasgow. Its wreaths, bouquets, and fruits and flowers in vases caused Mary Clemmer Ames to rhapsodize about the "pale green velvet carpet looking as if the Ocean, in gleaming and transparent waves, were tossing roses at your feet." By the end of the Lincoln administration it was torn to shreds, like much else in the vandalized mansion.

The East Room hangings, suspended from gilt cornices, were of crimson brocatelle with heavy gold fringes and tassels. The curtains were of white needle-wrought lace from Switzerland. Crimson satin brocatelle was used throughout for chairs and sofas, which were tufted in the approved Victorian manner. The same crimson brocatelle, along with gold damask, was used in the Red Room, which was Mrs. Lincoln's favorite sitting room from the start. With its gilded cornices and ormolu vases imported by President Monroe, it made a handsome setting for informal entertaining in the four years that followed. Here the Lincolns spent many quiet evenings with special friends. It was carpeted with a hardy Wilton that suffered less from the mud-caked boots of soldiers. Mary decided that the piano, and the painting of George Washington on one of the walls should stay where they were. In the general freshening up she elected to have Andrew Jackson's portrait varnished. She was always interested in this President, although he had fallen from grace in her estimation. She bought massive ornaments for the mantelpieces of the Green Room and the Blue Room and an assortment of vases that were disposed to the best advantage.

The state guest room had the royal touch, with a combination of purple and gold. A gold rose tree pattern veined the pale-purple wallpaper. The huge bed was cushioned and canopied in figured purple satin, ornately trimmed with gold lace. Mrs. Grimsley found it awesome, unsuitable and uncomfortable when Mary assigned it to her. Actually, President Buchanan had introduced the gold-and-purple note for Baron Renfrew's visit.

But Mary brought the White House up to date with gaslight, the primitive plumbing of the era, and heating by furnace.

The family quarters were done in Victorian fashion, with velvet hassocks, an abundance of lounges and chairs, and patent spring mattresses as well as new beds. The President used a small southwest bedroom, and Mrs. Lincoln a larger adjoining chamber. Their sons slept across the hall from their parents, and the guest rooms were part of this wing. There were footbaths and a generous assortment of flowered ewers and basins. As an experienced housekeeper Mrs. Lincoln overlooked nothing in the way of creature comfort. She made life more pleasant for the Marine Band by ordering five hundred yards of blue and white duck for a tent shelter when they played on the grounds. The Wednesday and Saturday concerts outdoors made for peaceful promenading and brief respite from the miseries of war.

The President's office and the secretarial quarters were on the second floor over the East Room and not far from the family quarters in the west hall. A big rack held war maps, which the amateur strategists of the government studied in earnest perplexity, according to a *Herald* reporter, who thought that in spite of all the new trimmings the shabby old chairs and desks in the office were "too rickety to venerate."

Nothing pleased Mrs. Lincoln more in her new environment than the wealth of flowers at her command. She had always delighted in gardens, and now she had endless resources on which to draw. John Watt, head gardener, was a protégé of Andrew J. Downing, the horticulturist who helped design Central Park in New York. Watt was expert in his field, but his record was otherwise shady, and during the Pierce administration he had been caught tampering with payrolls. He was pardoned on the ground of inexperience, and he remained through the Buchanan administration and then became the confidant of Mrs. Lincoln.

She gave careful thought to the flower arrangements of the White House. Like Mrs. John F. Kennedy long after her, she preferred assorted flowers casually arranged to the stiff effects that had become traditional along with the stately White House furniture. The family quarters were invariably scented with blooms straight from the gardens. Mrs. Lincoln was more lavish than any other President's wife with the bouquets she sent to friends, both men and women, on every possible occasion. Senator Charles Sumner and General McClellan were often the recipients, sometimes as she was about to ask a favor or when they had done something she requested. But usually she scattered flowers because she loved them and because she was as generous in some respects as she was parsimonious in others.

It was an era when fresh flowers were freely used as fashion adjuncts—in the hair, on gowns, in tiny frilled nosegays that Mrs. Lincoln, like the other fashionables of the Civil War years, carried in her hand to balls and receptions. There were many things about her early life in Washington that she greatly enjoyed, and she wrote enthusiastically to Mrs. Hannah Shearer about such perquisites as the flowers, the gardens, the carriages, the White House notepaper, the railroad passes, the scene in the Blue Room when visitors came. She wanted to share her pleasures with Mrs. Shearer, and she wrote on July 11, 1861: "We have the most beautiful flowers & grounds imaginable, and company & excitement enough, to turn a wiser head than my own. . . . There are so many lovely drives around W. and we have only *three* carriages, at our command."

The White House conservatory gave Mrs. Lincoln endless pleasure. Her favorite guests were always given a tour to admire the exotic blooms that flourished in its steamy interior. Sometimes she guided them herself, particularly if they came from Springfield or home territory, but she usually assigned Major French or Stoddard to this task. Like many women of her generation she was well versed in botany, a subject taught at most schools, and with her sharp mind she had specific knowledge to impart.

Mary had never been without books, and she saw to it that well-bound classics found their place in the White House. The President liked to pull out his Bible, one of the Waverley Novels, or a shabby old collection of Shakespearean plays that he treasured, when he felt in the mood to recite. But Mary insisted on handsome new sets of James Fenimore Cooper, Elizabeth Barrett Browning, Longfellow, Spenser, Bryant, Goldsmith, Hood and other favorites. Charles Sumner often gave her books, just as she gave him bouquets from the White House gardens, for busy though she was, she always found time to read. She was keenly aware of possessions and commented freely on the wedding gifts, the table arrangements, and the parties given by acquaintances. Not since the time of Dolley Madison had anyone presiding at the White House had such intimate knowledge of the lavish tables of the South, and she was not going to let the diplomats think that because she came from the Middle West she was ignorant of French cuisine and fine wines.

But late in 1861 Mrs. Lincoln was suddenly confronted with the consequences of her extravagance. Major French had a startling view of the President's reaction to this situation. He learned that, however mandatory Mrs. Lincoln might be with others, she could not budge Mr. Lincoln when his convictions were deeply involved, as they were in this case.

Busy all year with momentous affairs, he had paid little attention to his wife's frequent shopping excursions. He had great faith in her judgment in household matters, and from what he heard and saw, she seemed to be refurnishing the White House with good sense and good taste. He was stunned when confronted with the fact that she was being dunned for payment of bills and that she had overspent the government appropriation. A Philadelphia decorator named James Carryl, of the firm of William H. Carryl & Bros., had gone to Paris for the French wallpaper for the East Room and was now demanding payment of a bill for $6,700. He had advanced the money himself, paying $800 for the East Room paper alone.

The President flatly told Mary that he would never approve the bill, so she decided on other tactics when she observed his look of cold determination. She sent for Major French, who found her in the library at nine in the morning, in her wrapper, quite distraught, and imploring him to go to the President and make him understand the situation. He must not let Mr. Lincoln know that she had called him in, said Mary tearfully. He must show her husband that it was not at all unusual to overrun appropriations. "Tell him how *much* it costs to refurnish. He does not know much about it, he says he will pay it out of his own pocket. You know, Major, he cannot afford that; he ought not to do it."

Mary added docilely that henceforth she would always be

governed by the major and would not spend a cent without consulting him. French took his usual soothing line with her and told her that he would see the President. But when he reached him, Lincoln was ready for trouble. He brought the question up himself as he studied the various items on Carryl's bill. It was not his intention ever to approve it, he said. He would pay it out of his own pocket first, for it would stink in the nostrils of the American people to have it said that the President of the United States "had approved a bill overrunning an appropriation of $20,000 for *flub dubs* for this damned old house, when the soldiers cannot have blankets."

"Who employed Carryl?" the President asked. "Nicolay?"

"Mrs. Lincoln, I suppose," said the flustered major.

"Mrs. Lincoln—well I suppose Mrs. Lincoln *must* bear the blame, let her *bear* it. I swear I won't!"

Few of his associates ever heard Lincoln assail his wife, but on this occasion French felt he could never repeat, even to his sister-in-law Pamela, some of the things that had been said. Cooling off as he paced, the President finished more mildly with: "It was all wrong to spend one cent at such a time, and I never ought to have had a cent expended; the house was furnished well enough, better than any one we ever lived in, & if I had not been overwhelmed with other business I would not have had any of the appropriations expended, but what could I do? I could not attend to everything."

Major French was well aware that his predecessor, W. S. Wood, had authorized the purchase of the wallpaper on a trip to New York with Mrs. Lincoln. It was charged to an annual appropriation of $6,000 used by the Commission of Public Buildings for repairs on the Executive Mansion. When this sum was used up for outside painting and necessary repairs, the major urged Mrs. Lincoln to postpone papering the rooms for another year, but she went ahead without a pause, in her anxiety to have the White House in perfect shape by the end of 1861. Eventually the East Room carpet, the wallpaper and the silver, which Mrs. Lincoln had bought without authorization from anyone, were included by Major French in an appropriation for sundry civil expenses. But the echoes lingered on and came back to plague Mrs. Lincoln at various times in her history.

For the time being she looked with satisfaction on the miracle she had wrought at the White House. At the first levee of the winter season in December, 1861, her guests marveled at the style of the handsome rooms, conscious though they were of the storms behind the scenes. Mary was graceful in a figured silk brocade with a bright wreath of flowers on her hair. Robert had arrived from Harvard for his first Christmas in the White House, and it was clear to him, as to his mother, that the "flub dubs" had done much to improve its appearance. Mrs. Lincoln had silenced her critics for the time being with the effective results she had achieved in spite of wartime shortages. The White House had rarely shown such freshness and style, and its mistress had established herself as a personality not to be ignored. None but Mrs. Keckley knew the seething unrest that troubled her nights and days, with the secret knowledge of her mounting debts and the compulsion to buy and buy.

As time went on, even good-natured Major French grew impatient with her constant drive for possessions. "She plagued me half to death with wants with which it was impossible to comply," he commented. With the White House so effectively redone, she next wanted to spruce up the Soldiers Home, a dreary summer residence at best, and to get all possible perquisites for the Presidential family. Since his scene with the President over the Carryl bills, the major had been doing his best to curb Mrs. Lincoln's impulsive expenditures. But after a lively battle of wits he would find himself giving in when she turned angelic.

Major French had ample opportunity to observe Mrs. Lincoln in her best social moments, for it was his role to stand beside her at White House receptions, presenting visitors as they passed along the line. It was clear to him that she could never be a nonentity and that she had no intention of being the forgotten woman in the White House. Strongly silhouetted against the somber background of the Civil War, Mary had a well-defined public image, more controversial than benign, by the end of her husband's first year in office.

IX

Adviser to the President

T HE MEN WHO GATHERED around President Lincoln were soon aware that they must reckon with his wife. Some went so far as to call her Madam President when she showed clearly that she intended to uphold her end of the hierarchy. She was more approachable and quicker to respond than Lincoln, and it was soon known that he kept her well informed and trusted her with military secrets. This was only in the early days of his administration, however. A series of indiscretions by Mary and the deepening of his own responsibilities broke this close line of communication.

But Mary continued to dig out information where she could and to interfere without her husband's knowledge. She was desperately anxious to help him, but her efforts to play the same role in the national government that she had in Springfield soon became an embarrassment to the President. Her dislikes and prejudices were intense and often unreasonable, and the strange company she kept was harmful to her reputation.

As his first year in office neared a close, a dispatch on October 15, 1861, credited to the Washington correspondent of the Springfield *Republican*, was revealing: "We have for the first time in the history of presidents a president's wife who seems to be ambitious of having a finger in the government pie. Her friends compare Mrs. Lincoln to Queen Elizabeth in her statesmanlike tastes and capabilities. She is by no means a simple, domestic woman, but was evidently intended by nature to aid somewhat in politics."

The editorial continued that this was an undesirable state of affairs and that she had already made and unmade the political fortunes of men. She had been in close conversation with Cabinet members and had corresponded with them on political issues. "Some go so far as to suggest that the President is indebted to her for some of his ideas and projects," the writer added.

Gideon Welles credited Mrs. Lincoln with having Norman B. Judd, who had placed Lincoln's name in nomination for the Presidency, excluded from the Cabinet. Dr. James G. Randall, the historian, conceded that she intervened against Judd, but that this did not necessarily mean that "petticoat influence was actually the factor that controlled Lincoln's decision."

Mary was on a pedestal by virtue of being First Lady, but her tacit assumption of power was out of key with the times. Public opinion was against a woman in any way influencing the destiny of the nation, and the fires that Mrs. Lincoln lit of her own accord burned so savagely that she was seared in the process. Americans were not prepared to accept this situation, particularly in time of war. There were many clever women at work backing up both sides, but they did not let their methods show. This left Mrs. Lincoln in a class by herself, with a large segment of the public swallowing every slur that clouded her history. Although she made many mistakes, some of which she freely admitted as time went on, she was victimized as being an easy target through which the President could be hurt. Both acted on the assumption that nepotism was an accepted fact of political life, as indeed it was at that time.

Early in his administration she got into serious trouble through the men with whom she associated. Her choice of companions and advisers was incomprehensible, and through them she wandered into a tangle of debt and scandal. Astute in many respects, she was singularly bungling in her business operations and the public reacted with wholesale condemnation. In one crucial episode her honor and that of the President were at stake, and the three men who figured in a succession of dubious incidents involving charges of treason and misuse of public funds were Chevalier Henry Wikoff, a continental adventurer, John Watt, the gardener, and William S. Wood, who was party to her buying sprees for the White House.

Mrs. Lincoln had always been highly susceptible to flattery, which was indulged in to the full when she became mistress of the White House. She could scarcely have been exposed to a more seasoned practitioner of this art than Henry Wikoff, an adventurer who had gained a reputation in Europe before showing up in Washington before the Civil War and working secretly for the New York *Herald*. He posed as a guest at the top parties of the day and came away with a rich harvest of gossip. His particular anchorage was the White House, and Mrs. Lincoln was an easy quarry for one who had charmed some of the leading hostesses in Europe.

Wikoff was a chevalier by virtue of a decoration he received from Queen Isabella of Spain. He had inherited a fortune and roamed at will among the notables of France and England. Lord Palmerston was so impressed by this polished adventurer that he offered him a link with the British Foreign Office, and Wikoff served for a year as a secret agent in Paris for the British. He was close to several members of the French imperial family and earned the gratitude of Joseph Bonaparte by bringing some of Napoleon I's possessions back across the Channel to him from London. The prince gave him a silver drinking cup in appreciation. Soon Wikoff landed in a dungeon in Genoa after following an American woman to Italy and trying to abduct her. He believed that the British had arranged his imprisonment, and after being freed, he came to America and wormed his way into the inner social sanctums of wartime Washington.

Mrs. Lincoln was won by his habit of talking to her in French. She was anxious to perfect herself in the language, and his polished accent was just what she needed for easy conversation with the diplomats. Villard was scathing over Wikoff's flattery of the First Lady and wrote: "I myself heard him compliment her upon her looks and dress in so fulsome a way that she ought to have blushed and banished the impertinent fellow from her presence. She accepted Wikoff as a major domo in general and in special as a guide in matters of social etiquette, domestic arrangements, and personal requirements, including her toilette, and as always welcome company for visitors in her salon and on her drives."

Others besides Villard noticed how often Wikoff accompanied Mrs. Lincoln to the encampments. He was at the White House early and late, and there is no doubt that he helped her with her party plans. His knowledge of European court life made his suggestions irresistible to Mrs. Lincoln, and he was deeply involved in the arrangements for the state dinner given for Prince Napoleon Jerome Bonaparte on August 8, 1861. The *Herald* must have dismayed the old guard in Washington with its description of this function, presumably written by Wikoff himself:

The President's lady received and entertained the most polished diplomats and the most fastidious courtiers of Europe with an ease and elegance which made republican simplicity seem almost regal. Her state dinner to the Prince, on Saturday last, was a model of completeness, taste, and geniality; and altogether this Kentucky girl, this Western matron, this republican queen, puts to the blush and entirely eclipses the first ladies of Europe—the excellent Victoria, the pensive Eugenie and the brilliant Isabella.

With all her intelligence Mrs. Lincoln swallowed this sort of adulation, but before long she disowned her crown and deplored the prevailing impression that she thought of herself in queenly terms. If Mr. Lincoln did not tell her, the daily press unquestionably did. The President went his own unruffled way and coped amiably with every aspect of Prince Napoleon's official visit to the United States. But the White House dinner was the most sparkling social event of Mrs. Lincoln's first year as the nation's premier hostess. It was discussed at length both at home and abroad.

Like other visiting celebrities at this time, the prince planned to visit both the federal and Confederate encampments, preserving the image of neutrality. Princess Clotilde stayed on their yacht in New York harbor, so Mrs. Lincoln and Mrs. Grimsley were the only women at the dinner. Mary carried off her end of things with style. She had been well primed by Wikoff, who was thoroughly familiar with the etiquette of the French court. Beyond that, she had an inexhaustible range of interests and was instinctively friendly and articulate.

Because of the prince's status Seward tried to take over the arrangements, but Mrs. Lincoln held her ground, with Wikoff in the background, and gave her own orders. She looked her best that night in a white silk and grenadine gown with a long train. Mrs. Grimsley, seated at the President's right, wore a salmon tulle dress with fresh flowers. General Scott, blazing with decorations, sat to the left of the President, and Mrs. Lincoln had the prince at her right and Chase at her left. There were twenty-seven guests but Kate Chase was not among them. Lord Lyons, M. Mercier, William H. Seward, his son, Frederick Seward, and General McClellan all were in attendance, and after dinner Mrs. Lincoln stood slightly behind Prince Napoleon on the balcony as the crowd below cheered him, and the Marine Band played the "Marseillaise."

One day, when she was in deep financial trouble, she would have to account for the cost of this historic party, but it remained one of the great social events of her days in the White House. And Ben: Perley Poore wrote of her at this time: "I am sure that since the time that Mrs. Madison presided at the White House, it has not been graced by a lady so well fitted by nature and by education to dispense its hospitalities as Mrs. Lincoln. Her hospitality is only equaled by her charity, and her graceful deportment by her goodness of heart."

Russell noted that "few women not to the manner born there are whose heads would not be disordered, and circulation disturbed by a rapid transition, almost instantaneous, from a condition of obscurity in a country town to be mistress of the White House." He was conscious of Mrs. Lincoln's capacity as well as her vanity, and both were in full flower during Napoleon's visit.

When she went on her shopping trips to New York, Wikoff was on hand to pay tribute through the *Herald* to her "exquisite taste in the selection of the materials she desired, and of the fashion of their make." But while this was going on in the *Herald*, Joseph Medill, editor of the Chicago *Tribune*, got another view of the situation from a hostile observer writing from Washington: "Mrs. L. is making herself both a fool & a nuisance—Wikoff is her gallant, and I have within the week seen two notes signed by him in her name, sending compliments and invitations to parties addressed."

John W. Forney, publisher of the Washington *Chronicle* and Philadelphia *Press*, knew Wikoff well and understood the appeal he had for Mrs. Lincoln. He was extraordinarily versatile in his interests and could talk of Dickens and Thackeray as well as of love, law, war, commerce and the church. He knew the gossip of courts and cabinets, of the opera and the theater, and Mary had a well-developed taste for gossip.

Until Stoddard came to her rescue, she had been using Wikoff freely in sending out her invitations. Then out of the blue this association, which had been gossiped about in White House circles, became a public scandal after the *Herald*, in December, 1861, printed extracts from the President's message to Congress ahead of the official release date.

Where had it come from? Wikoff was known to correspond for the *Herald*, and he was called before the House Judiciary Committee on February 10, 1862. He admitted having telegraphed the material to the *Herald*, but he refused to tell how he had obtained it. He was jailed for several days in Old Capitol Prison and was freed on

February 14 after he had answered some questions and implicated John Watt, the gardener who worked so closely with Mrs. Lincoln. Watt did not deny the accusation and said that he had read the message in the White House library and had given Wikoff parts of it from memory.

Stories soon spread like wildfire that the President's wife had been the betrayer who had given Wikoff the speech. Deeply embarrassed, Lincoln went to the Capitol and appealed to the Republicans on the committee to spare him from disgrace; thereupon Watt's story, which exonerated Mrs. Lincoln, was accepted as the truth. Dan Sickles defended Wikoff, but according to Ben: Perley Poore, he was so excitable that he almost landed in jail himself.

The President never disclosed what he thought about the theft of this private document, but he turned his attention to Wikoff, whom he had not taken seriously up to this time. The *Herald* took the stand that it was a ruse by the antislavery forces to cause a breach in the Lincoln ménage. Wikoff continued to visit the White House until the President personally told him to leave, after he had studied the results of an investigation of the history of the chevalier. Among other things, it was recalled that in the first summer of the war he had asked Mrs. Greenhow to help him get to Richmond so that he could send a "peace letter" from there to the capital. According to Wikoff, he assured Mrs. Greenhow that he had Seward's approval for this action.

Mrs. Augusta Heath Morris, one of Mrs. Greenhow's fellow internees in Old Capitol Prison and anxious to get out, wrote to Colonel Thomas Jordan after the Judiciary hearing that Mrs. Lincoln was the person who had given Wikoff the President's message. The ladies in this historic prison were noisy about their grievances, and Mrs. Lincoln's name was soon being bandied about among them, tying her up once more with the Confederacy. Her loyalty to the Union had again come into doubt.

Mrs. Morris, an ingratiating captive and much more popular with her jailers than Mrs. Greenhow was, insisted that President Lincoln would let her out when she appeared before General John Dix's commission on a charge of smuggling letters south, including the one she said was from Seward.

"Perhaps Mrs. Lincoln would help you," a commission member suggested. Mrs. Morris appeared dubious about that, although she felt she had a link with the President's wife because she had had some dealings of her own with Wikoff. Gossip raged over this incident and reached such proportions that the question of disloyalty in the White House came up before the Committee on the Conduct of the War, whose members were predisposed to find fault with everything President Lincoln did. It has become legendary that when he heard what was afoot, he walked alone to the Capitol and appeared suddenly before the committee. His towering figure at the foot of the table brought everyone to attention, and his expression was later described as suggesting "almost inhuman sadness."

Abashed by his presence, the committee members listened attentively while he made his extraordinary statement in sorrowful tones: "I, Abraham Lincoln, President of the United States, appear of my own volition before this Committee of the Senate to say that, I, of my own knowledge, know that it is untrue that any of my family held treasonable communication with the enemy." Without another word the President turned away and left as silently as he had arrived. Stunned by this unexpected confrontation, the committee decided to go no further into the persistent reports that Mrs. Lincoln was a spy.

But the shadow lingered on. It clouded her reputation during the rest of her time in the White House, and it followed her to the grave. The committee was composed of members of the Senate and House led by the radicals who were bent on thwarting the President. After this Mr. Lincoln was more tender than ever to the suffering Mary. He felt the injustice of the charges, and he understood how muddled she was in some of her acts. But he realized to the full that she had been tarred with the charge of treason—an unheard of situation for the wife of a President—and in time of war. She would never live it down. No First Lady ever caused more commotion in Cabinet and military circles than the unfortunate Mrs. Lincoln.

Watt, the gardener, who was one of her favorites, was under the blight of being a secessionist in Washington. He had voiced the opinion after the First Battle of Bull Run that the South could never be conquered. George Bancroft, the historian, was scathing when he learned that Watt had been commissioned a lieutenant in the regular army. The story was that "Madame wished a rogue who had cheated the government made a lieutenant and that the President forced the reluctant Cabinet to approve" after Mrs. Lincoln had for three nights slept in a separate apartment. This bit of gossip spread far, but it was soon dismissed as another canard. In relaying it to his wife in a letter Bancroft added: "She is better in manners and in spirit than we have generally heard; is friendly and not in the least arrogant." As usual, Mrs. Lincoln sent him flowers, her favorite gesture when she wished to placate or honor someone.

Watt's army commission was revoked after he testified that he had given Wikoff the President's message to Congress. His name was dropped from Major French's payroll, but he continued to work around the White House.

Noah Brooks, who corresponded for the Sacramento *Daily Union* and was grieving over the loss of his wife and baby son, brought some consolation into the Lincoln ménage with his gentle understanding of the savage attacks being made on them. He had known them in Springfield, and now his daily visits to the White House gave them some sympathetic press coverage. He gave Mary credit for causing a "terrible scattering of ancient abuses which once accumulated below stairs," and he wrote of the "suckers who grew rich on the pickings and stealings from the kitchen garden and conservatory and who had spies in every room in the house."

But a turnover of this kind resulted in waves of backstairs gossip from the culprits, and many of the legends about Mrs. Lincoln that spread across the country came from this source, particularly where the secessionists were concerned. Her impulsive indiscretions in this shake-up and her support of Watt led to serious embarrassment for the President, who had neither the time nor the inclination for kitchen politics. Every hour of every day was filled with concern for the vast issues he faced.

When rumors spread that Watt, after all these complications, was attempting to blackmail the President, demanding $20,000 for three letters supposed to have been written by Mrs. Lincoln, firm measures were taken to quiet this dangerous murmur. Isaac Newton, who had been appointed Minister of Agriculture by the President, instructed a New York politician to visit Watt at the greenhouse he then had in New York and threaten him with imprisonment at Fort Lafayette if he did not desist. According to John Hay, Watt backed down, owned up to a conspiracy to embarrass the President, gave up the letters, and the matter was settled, but it never was wholly explained. It further clouded the reputation of Mrs. Lincoln, who was being battered almost into insensibility by gossip as she tried to fulfill her responsibilities.

Hay and Nicolay had been suspicious of Watt from the beginning and were at a loss to understand the influence he had over Mrs.

Lincoln. Even before the storm broke over the theft of the President's speech, these two young men were exchanging blithe but concerned notes about this inexplicable friendship.

"Hell is to pay about Watt's affairs," Hay wrote to his colleague late in 1861. "I think the Tycoon [President Lincoln] begins to suspect him. I wish he could be struck with lightning. He . . . has his eye peeled for a pop at me, because I won't let Madam have our stationery fund. They have gone off to New York together." A few days later he wrote again in the same vein: "Things go on here about as usual. There is no fun at all. The Hell-cat is getting more Hell-cattical day by day."

In his correspondence with Nicolay Mrs. Lincoln was always Madam or the Hell-cat, and the President was the Ancient or the Tycoon. She had caused Hay so much trouble on the financial end that he had little sympathy for her. He was aghast when she proposed the sale of the manure of the White House grounds as a source of revenue. But things were never dull when Mary was in action, and sometimes there were sighs of relief when word spread through the White House that she had gone to New York or been felled by one of her recurrent headaches.

Her relatives came under fire, too, and Hay wrote to Nicolay in March, 1862, that Mrs. Lincoln was "rapidly being reinforced from Springfield. A dozen Todds of the Edwards breed in the house." Hay had been a popular member of the younger set in the prairie city, but he was now headed for the larger world.

Ward Hill Lamon, the huge and commanding-looking Virginian who was one of Lincoln's most devoted friends, persisted in the belief that Mrs. Lincoln was a pawn in the hands of her husband's enemies, and he felt that the radical members of his own party were doing their best to undermine him. He did not underestimate Mrs. Lincoln, although he would shock her after her husband's death with his backward view of these days. At the time he found her "high bred, proud, brilliant, witty, and with a will that bent every one else to her purpose. She took Mr. Lincoln captive at the very moment she considered it expedient to do so."

Although the President gave no visible sign of his concern over the constant newspaper attacks, the echoes left by Wikoff, Wood and Watt were lasting, and they sank deep into the public consciousness. Less was heard of Mrs. Lincoln's kindness and the favors she did for all manner of people. Stoddard attributed her acquiescence to requests of many kinds as sheer good-heartedness rather than a desire for power and influence. She broke the official rules "all to slivers in her desire to oblige a persistent stream of applicants who appealed to her personal friendship for them."

Great care was exercised in Springfield matters, where one paper zealously championed Lincoln and the other assailed him constantly and tore Mrs. Lincoln to shreds. But it was always difficult for Mary to ignore a plea from the prairie state. Some of her relatives complicated matters for her in this respect. But she and Mrs. Grimsley conspired happily to persuade the President to appoint their old friend and minister, the Reverend James Smith, to serve as consul at Dundee in his native Scotland. In matters of this kind Mr. Lincoln was always ready to humor his wife, and in Smith's case he felt that he was making the right appointment.

But when Mary went further and expressed herself freely on Cabinet affairs in a letter to the unpredictable and often mischief-making James Gordon Bennett, she was on dangerous ground. Bennett veered with the wind, and he declined Lincoln's offer to serve as Ambassador to France. When he wrote to Mrs. Lincoln about the need for Cabinet changes, she answered him on October 4, 1862: "From *all parties* the cry, for a 'change of Cabinet' comes. Doubtless, if my good, patient Husband were here, instead of being with the Army of the Potomac, both of these missives would be placed before him, accompanied by my *womanly* suggestions, proceeding from a heart so deeply interested, for our distracted country. I have a great terror of *strong-minded* Ladies, yet if a word fitly spoken and in due season, can be urged, in a time like this, we should not withhold it."

The other missive mentioned by Mary was from Governor William Sprague, a particular favorite of hers, who was becoming the *enfant terrible* of the party with his controversial speeches attacking the rich and defending the poor.

The *Herald*'s treatment of Mrs. Lincoln, always attentive, sometimes flattering, occasionally slyly destructive, did much to influence public thinking about her. It reached the rich and the powerful at home and abroad, and its championship could at times be as dangerous as its attacks. Her public image suffered from this constant exposure. The range of her influence was apparent as she visited battlefields and expressed her views on her husband's generals. Everyone knew what she thought of the high command that passed through her receiving line, and all too many knew what they thought of her, because it had become a popular pastime in Washington to take potshots at Mrs. Lincoln.

The quest for Presidential favors never seemed to end, and a note from Mrs. Lincoln usually got attention from Mr. Lincoln. In small matters he would back her up; in large ones he would listen and weigh matters for himself. There were West Point cadetships, post-masterships, commissions and the routine patronage that went with political power, and Mrs. Lincoln's name showed up remarkably often in this respect. She was given to writing notes, and it was easy to convince Gideon Welles, who liked her, that one of her protégés would make a good watchman, but it was quite impossible to persuade Edwin M. Stanton, Secretary of War, who did not, that a note from her ensured leniency for a defector.

Her pleas were often on humanitarian grounds and she was disposed to help the young. She begged Stanton to give a second chance to a youth who had got into trouble at West Point, saying that he should have six more months in which to redeem himself.

Secessionist pleas were a problem for both of the Lincolns, and Mary was torn by appeals from the relatives of prisoners of war. They often tried to get at the President through her. Frank P. Carpenter, the artist who spent six months at the White House while he made his famous painting of the signing of the Emancipation Proclamation, had many opportunities to observe Mary's influence with her husband. He was struck by the President's caution when a woman, seeking an audience, arrived with two men, one of whom said he was a friend of Mrs. Lincoln's. This had been tried before. Lincoln pulled the bell rope and asked the attendant who answered to take the visitor's name to Mrs. Lincoln and ask her if she knew him. She promptly sent word that she had no knowledge of him at all. The President firmly declined to release the prisoner in this case, even though the man was prepared to take the oath of allegiance.

Mrs. Lincoln took special interest, however, in the case of a young soldier who had been sentenced to face a firing squad because he had gone to sleep while on picket duty. On a September day in 1861, General McClellan, who had received a bouquet of flowers from Mrs. Lincoln a few hours earlier, had a talk with the President about the errant youth. The death sentence was canceled when Mr. Lincoln said that this "was by request of the 'Lady President.'" The general then wrote to Mrs. McClellan that it had pleased him to grant a request from the "Lady President."

Those who sought favors and did not receive them were apt to be chagrined and malicious. When Murat Halstead, the powerful editor of the Cincinnati *Commercial Gazette*, failed to get an office for a friend, he had the means to reply—and did—in his newspaper: "I use the mildest phrase when I say Lincoln is a weak, miserably weak man; the wife is a fool—the laughing stock of the town, her vulgarity only the more conspicuous in consequence of her fine carriage and horses and servants in livery and fine dresses and her damnable airs."

X

Accused of Treason

O NE OF THE UNANSWERABLE realities of Mrs. Lincoln's unhappy
years in the White House was the extent of her family's
involvement in the Southern cause. The Todds were a large and
spreading clan in Kentucky, and with two exceptions her close kin
supported the Confederacy. Mary's youngest brother, Dr. George R.
C. Todd, and her three half brothers, Samuel, David and Alexander,
were in the forces opposing her husband. Her half sisters Emilie
Helm, Martha White and Elodie Dawson were the wives of Confederate officers. Her oldest brother, Levi, and her half sister Margaret Todd Kellogg sympathized with the Union.

It was Mary's fate to present a stolid front in public when some of
them died in battle and to hide her tears for their wives and children.
It was equally her fate to read of the "cruelty" of her kin to prisoners
of war and to be linked with them in charges of treason. Inevitably,
appeals for help from stranded widows and the close family feeling
of the South brought the situation directly into the White House, to
the embarrassment of President Lincoln at times. He was touched
by their plight but had to preserve the balance between the
demands of humanity and his responsibility as President and
Commander of the Union forces.

Mary stood solidly behind him on every issue, but it is fair to
assume that she sorrowed in private over the death of the men who
had been part of her youth. To solidify her public position, she chose
to emphasize the fact that they were half brothers, not blood kin,

and that she had seen little of them because she had been in boarding school and had left Lexington early for Springfield.

Aside from the fact that she was the President's wife, her situation was not unique. Torn relationships and family schisms were inherent in civil war. James B. Clay, one of the three sons of Mary's early idol, Henry Clay, donned the blue uniform of the North. Two sons of Robert Jefferson Breckinridge, a stalwart supporter of President Lincoln, allied themselves with the Southern cause. His nephew, John C. Breckinridge, who had been a Senator and nominee for President before he was forty, threw away a brilliant political career to become a Confederate major general.

But his wife's family presented many problems for President Lincoln, and when charges of treason came close to his own fireside, he had to use the utmost diplomacy to allay suspicion. The Confederacy had a successful spy ring operating in Washington, and Rose O'Neal Greenhow had taken full credit for getting information to General Pierre Beauregard on troop movements before the First Battle of Bull Run. The noisy presence of Rose and other women agents when they were finally lodged in the Old Capitol Prison had repercussions in the White House, but Mary stood firm as a rock behind her husband where the secessionists were concerned.

Yet she was wholly vulnerable because of the deep involvement of her relatives in the Southern cause and the fact that at times some of them reached the White House and many begged for favors. The most painful case to the President as well as to his wife was that of her half sister Emilie's husband, handsome Ben Hardin Helm, a West Pointer whose father, a Democrat, had served as governor of Kentucky. President Lincoln invited him to the White House as soon as war broke out. He seemed an ideal candidate for high-ranking service in the Union Army. Like Robert E. Lee, young Helm fought an inner battle before deciding to break away from the North and to back the Southern cause. The West Pointers were moving in two directions at this time. Some were packing to go south. Others were flocking to Washington.

President Lincoln had a warm personal liking for able young Ben Helm. Aside from the fact that he was Emilie's husband, he was obviously excellent officer material. After some persuasive discussion at the White House he was still undecided. As he left, Lincoln handed him an envelope containing a major's commission in the United States Army. "Ben, here is something for you," he said. "Think it over for yourself and let me know what you will do." Mary kissed him and said: "Good-bye. We hope to see you both very soon in Washington."

The President gripped his hand; then Helm walked thoughtfully down the stairs and out of the lives of the Lincolns. He had made his decision, and the President was saddened when he learned what it was. But Lincoln was soon aware of the mounting tide of suspicion that enveloped his wife because of her army connections. Stoddard broke the force of the attacks on Mary by keeping the more venomous letters away from her and ridiculing the absurd charges made against her. Nothing could stop the whirlwind however, and her extravagances, her pretensions, and her tart observations paled before the terrible charge of treason laid at her door. She would never wholly shed this burden.

The false evidence that had accumulated during the war years caught up with her even in Europe after her husband's assassination and enmeshed her as long as she lived. Beyond doubt it was a major factor in the public denunciation and hatred of Mary Lincoln; it must also have figured in her ultimate mental collapse. She was caught in the middle of a national catastrophe. In the South she was regarded as a traitor in reverse, heedless of the sorrow and suffering of her family and hostile to the Confederate Army.

Reports of the appointments and doings of Mrs. Lincoln's relatives came from all parts of the South, and some were plainly intended to embarrass the President through her. There was an uproar when Mary's brother, Dr. George Todd, was jailer at Richmond to the federal soldiers captured at Bull Run. "He was tall, fat and savage against the Yankees," said one newspaper report, "and so brutal that he would kick the dead bodies of Union soldiers, calling them d— abolitionists." When charges were brought against him by fellow officers, Jefferson Davis had him detailed to other duty.

Mrs. Lincoln suffered when the newspapers drew attention to the fact that she had eleven second cousins in the Carolina Light Dragoons of the Confederate forces. She did not know them; she had never seen them, but there they were, looming across her path. Once when a paper alluded to three of her brothers being in the Confederate Army, she exploded, telling Mrs. Keckley that at least it might have been pointed out that they were only half brothers. "I have not seen them since they were infants," she said. "My early home was truly a boarding school."

Mrs. Keckley was on her way to the White House when she heard that Captain Alexander Todd had fallen at Baton Rouge. She hesitated to convey this news to Mrs. Lincoln, but she saw at once that she already knew. Her manner was perhaps deliberately casual when she remarked: "Lizzie, I have just heard that one of my brothers has been killed in the war."

There were no tears this time, just a calm acceptance of a hard blow. She seemed to be keeping up a front when she told Lizzie that she need have no fear of discussing the subject with her. It was natural, she said, that she should feel for one so closely related to her, but he had made his choice long ago and "Since he chose to be our deadly enemy, I see no special reason why I should bitterly mourn his death."

It was clear to those who knew her best that Mary went out of her way to prove that she was not Southern in feeling, and she was much less tolerant than the President in her comments. "Why should I sympathize with the rebels?" she said to Mrs. Keckley in one of their boudoir conversations. "They would hang my husband tomorrow if it was in their power, and perhaps gibbet me with him. How then can I sympathize with a people at war with me and mine?"

The President took a loftier view and gave the enemy credit for gallantry. He spoke with admiration of the soldierly qualities of Robert E. Lee, Joseph E. Johnston and Stonewall Jackson, who was his ideal of a soldier. But the generals of the North were as bad as the generals of the South, in Mary's estimation. And in spite of her stoical attitude both she and Mr. Lincoln suffered acutely when Ben Helm fell in battle.

"I feel as David of old did when he was told of the death of Absalom," said the President when word reached him that Ben, aged thirty-two, had died at Chickamauga. He was leading John Breckinridge's division in a furious assault against Major General William S. Rosecrans' forces when he was stricken. Mrs. Lincoln was at the Fifth Avenue Hotel in New York when her husband telegraphed her the news on September 24, 1863. The Union Army had been worsted mainly in yielding ground, he said. The rebels had lost one major general and five brigadiers, "including your brother-in-law Helm."

His widow, Emilie, was dear to both of the Lincolns, and the President immediately sent an order to her mother, Mrs. Robert S. Todd, to go south and bring Mrs. Helm and her children back to Lexington. This was the start of a difficult family situation for the Lincolns. On her way from Alabama to Kentucky Mrs. Helm was stopped at Fort Monroe because of her refusal to take the oath of allegiance. The President telegraphed the military authorities to send her to Washington. She had a tearful reunion with Mary, and Lincoln embraced her and expressed the hope that she felt no bitterness toward him. The sisters found it hard to communicate without stirring up patriotic issues. "Allusion to the present is like tearing open a fresh and bleeding wound and the pain is too great for self-control," Emilie wrote in her diary. ". . . we weep over our dead together and express through our clasped hands the sympathy we feel for each other in our mutual grief."

Emilie had aged and was the picture of dejection and sorrow as she settled briefly in the White House. It was a delicate situation with servants talking and the story circulating that a rebel was being harbored by Mrs. Lincoln. Emilie usually kept out of sight when callers came, but when she saw them, she was bitter, and fiercely loyal to the South.

Like his mother Tad flared up when Emilie's little daughter shouted "Hurrah for Jeff Davis," strange words to be heard in the White House at that time. Tad gravely informed her that *his* father, Mr. Lincoln, was President of the United States. Stories like this circulated freely in the capital, but a true crisis developed when Senator Ira Harris of New York and General Dan Sickles called to see Emilie and to inquire about John Breckinridge. They had not counted on the militancy of Mary's half sister. General Sickles had lost a leg at Gettysburg, and he was not disposed to favor rebel talk. Emilie would tell them nothing about Breckinridge, and she showed a hostile spirit with her evasive answers.

"We have whipped the rebels at Chattanooga," Senator Harris announced, "and I hear, madam, that the scoundrels ran like scared rabbits."

Emilie, suffering from the loss of Ben, startled both men with her quick retort: "It was the example you set them at Bull Run and Manassas."

Mrs. Lincoln tried to smooth things over, but Senator Harris, whose only son was in service, turned on her suddenly and asked: "Why isn't Robert in the army?"

Shaking with distress, Mary hastily explained that Robert was anxious to enlist but the fault was hers, because she wanted him to graduate from college. The Senator promptly told her that if he had twenty sons, they all would be fighting the rebels.

Emilie cut in sharply: "And if I had twenty sons, they would all be opposing you."

She left the room in tears, and General Sickles hobbled upstairs on crutches to see the President, who was in bed convalescing from a mild case of smallpox. "You should not have that rebel in your house," he exclaimed, after repeating everything that Emilie had said.

Lincoln was amused by her audacity, but this incident persuaded her that her presence in the White House was embarrassing to Mary and the President. Convinced that she must leave before the gossip became any more pronounced, she and her daughter said good-bye on December 14, 1863. The President put his arms around her and said: "I tried to have Ben come with me." He gave her a pass that would get her to Kentucky and wrote out the oath of allegiance and a Presidential pardon, should she decide to concede. Emilie proudly stood her ground and remained a Confederate, believing that anything else would be treachery to her husband's memory and to the South.

But this was not the end of the story. In 1864 she returned to visit the Lincolns at Soldiers Home, and she made a request that the President felt he could not honor. She wanted to get her cotton out of the South so that she could meet their desperate family needs by selling it. She had asked for the same favor on her earlier visit, and the President had told her that he could help her only if she signed the oath of allegiance. Now for the second time Emilie refused to make this concession, and the President denied her request—not an easy decision for him or for Mary.

Cotton deals were among the scandals of the period, and his enemies would have pounced at once on President Lincoln had he shown any leniency to Mary's half sister. But Emilie sent him a cold and bitter letter on her return home, addressing him merely as "Mr. Lincoln." She wrote that she had found her half brother Levi Todd dead from want and destitution. He was "another sad victim to the prowess of more favored relatives." Again she begged for permission to go south and have her cotton shipped, asking only for the "*right* which humanity and justice always gives to widows and orphans." She finished half apologetically: "If you think I give way to excess of feeling, I beg you will make some excuse for a woman almost crazed with misfortune." She had used all that was left of her money for her "long tedious unproductive and sorrowful visit" to the White

House, she wrote, and now her mother was ill over Levi's death. Levi, she thought, might have been saved had he had proper food and medical attention. The once-proud Todds were at a low ebb, as Emilie pictured their plight, and Mary must have suffered over this, shiftless and difficult though Levi had been.

She felt great sympathy for Emilie, but not for Martha Todd White of Selma, a half sister who made impossible demands and was vengeful when they were not met. Stirring up clouds of scandal, she did more than anyone else to give reality to the tales of favored Southern relatives at the White House, yet Gideon Welles sought to prove how slight the connection had been.

On December 19, 1863, Mrs. Clement White wrote to the President asking for permission to buy articles of clothing not then available in the South and for an order that would permit her to take them through the lines. According to Gideon Welles, the President told him that Mrs. White had come to the White House and sent in her card to Mrs. Lincoln, who had refused to see her. Martha still persisted in her efforts to see Mary or the President, with the same result. But the President sent her a pass that would take her south. She returned it with a request that her trunks should go through without examination. When the answer was no, she talked "secesh" loudly at her hotel and asked Congressman Brutus Clay, a brother of Cassius Clay, for help. The President told Clay that if she did not leave the capital at once, she would find herself in Old Capitol Prison.

This was the skeletonized version as told by Gideon Welles, but the story persisted and circulated widely in the papers that Martha White was a frequent visitor at the White House, that she got through the lines with three trunks of medicine and clothing, that she had quinine hidden in her petticoats, and that federal inspectors had found a rebel's uniform with gold buttons and an accompanying sword. Mrs. White explained that Baltimore friends had put the uniform and sword in her luggage without her knowledge, but it became a Todd legend that she went south with this contraband and ultimately presented the sword to General Lee. To many she was a heroine and a woman of considerable charm.

Mary suffered over Martha Todd White, since she was accused of using this half sister to send information to the enemy. Her story was that she had steadfastly refused to see Mrs. White, in spite of her persistence and the pressure brought by friends. Martha showed up again at Willard's just before the President's assassination in the spring of 1865. With the war almost won, she asked for a permit to get cotton out of the South. She complained about the treatment she had received from the officers at Fort Monroe. At this point the President gave her a permit to go south, but not one that would enable her to have her cotton shipped to the north. Like Emilie and Martha, other Southerners were trying frantically at this time to have their cotton freed and to recoup their lost fortunes.

The Lincolns were bombarded with requests from old friends and from strangers trying to regain their possessions. Mrs. Sallie Ward Hunt, a Kentucky beauty well known to Mrs. Lincoln, was anxious to recover her piano, some chairs upholstered with white satin, and other treasured pieces being held by the federal authorities in New Orleans.

Mrs. Hunt's appeal brought an unusual response from President Lincoln, who had learned that she had been friendly to the Union since the outbreak of the war and that she was separating from her husband, who was one of General John Hunt Morgan's raiders in Kentucky. "I would not offer her, or any wife, a temptation to a permanent separation from her husband," the President wrote, "but if she shall avow that her mind is already independent and fully made up to such separation, I shall be glad for the property sought by her to be delivered to her, upon her taking the oath on December 8, 1863."

When Margaret Wickliffe Preston, who had been one of Mary's girlhood friends, wrote directly to her, asking for a pass through the Union lines to see her husband, General William C. Preston, of the Confederate Army, the President replied, explaining that Mary was ill. "Owing to her early and strong friendship for you, I would gladly oblige you, but I cannot absolutely do it. If General Boyle and Hon. James Guthrie, one or both, in their discretion, see fit to give you the passes, this is my authority to them for doing so."

Family relationships were vital to Mrs. Lincoln, yet she did not get on particularly well with her sisters in the Middle West, and she was unable to maintain communication with those in the South. Mrs. Edwards was her anchor through the years. There were times when she and Elizabeth were deeply critical of each other; yet as the oldest sister, who had followed her course with concern and authority, she had more understanding of Mary's nature and instability than anyone but the President. She was a practical, accomplished woman and had little patience with her sister's incalculable moods, nor did she approve of Mary's pretensions during her troubled years in the White House.

The President implored Mrs. Edwards to make long stays with Mary, feeling that she had the power and influence necessary to control matters when she became unbalanced. But for a long time there was a serious breach between them involving a letter Mary had opened that contained the frank opinion of Mrs. Edwards' daughter Julia about the mistress of the White House. Elizabeth was outraged that the letter had been opened, and she refused to speak to Mary for a long time after that. She would return her letters without comment.

Yet Mary felt that Mrs. Edwards was the only one of her sisters who rejoiced in what she called her "advancement" when she reached the White House. The others were hostile or indifferent, and she was deeply hurt by the begrudging spirit and venomous comments of her sister Ann, who was Mrs. C. M. Smith. It pained her also that Frances, who was married to Dr. Wallace, should ignore her completely and fail to show gratitude when the President appointed her husband Paymaster of Volunteers. But there were no sharp flare-ups with Frances as there were with Mrs. Edwards from time to time—just a lasting coolness.

The President was kind and courteous to all his wife's relatives. He saw for himself that there was much squabbling among them, but they backed each other in public, however much they might wrangle when together. All the sisters recognized the fact that, although hot-tempered, impulsive and unreasonable at times, Mary at heart was generous and responsive to their needs. The touch of nepotism was inevitable, the custom of the day. With vast sums of money at the President's command and patronage to be dispensed on a wartime scale, it was not surprising that Mary should plead for her relatives.

In time even proud Ninian Edwards was involved, when he lost his fortune and Judge Davis recommended him for a position in the Commissary Corps. Lincoln invited him to the White House and told him that he would try to help him, but Republicans in Springfield opposed the appointment of a Democrat to this post. Judge Davis pushed the matter, and the President finally appointed Ninian Captain and Commissary of Subsistence. When he felt he could, Mr. Lincoln backed Mary's maneuvers on behalf of her

relatives, but her family, like his own, added to his worries during
the war years.

Between the time of Lincoln's inauguration and the outbreak of
the war there were links with Lexington, too, and late in March
Mary's cousin, Dr. Lyman Beecher Todd, visited the capital and
without any trouble was appointed postmaster of Lexington.
Although Cassius M. Clay and other friends of the President's
backed another applicant, Mary's kin won in this particular case,
and one might assume that she had had something to do with it.

One relative who was always welcomed by the President was
Mary's cousin, Mrs. Elizabeth Todd Grimsley, a widow who spent
six months in the White House during the first year and has left
spirited comments on day-to-day occurrences. She was in some
respects Mary's most scathing critic, for she was realistic and perceptive. At times her tart manner was a tonic for her cousin, but like
other members of the family, she was inclined to scoff at Mary's love
of show and entertainment.

At first she found all the fuss about clothes and parties quite to her
liking, and she wrote to her cousin John T. Stuart on March 20, 1861,
that Mary had been uniformly kind and polite to her and evidently
wanted her to enjoy her visit. The rush for office continued unabat-
ed, Mrs. Grimsley wrote, with the papers announcing the presence
of one hundred Todds, all seeking office. She made no secret of the
fact that she sought a postmistress-ship for herself, but she vowed
that she had said nothing at all about this to Mr. Lincoln, and Mary
"could have no influence with him in regard to her friends and of
course I would expect nothing."

Mrs. Grimsley did not altogether enjoy the shopping expeditions
with Mary during the early months of extravagant buying. She was
inclined to share the view of the public that her cousin lacked
judgment when her eyes focused on something she liked. But she also
insisted that the tales of their purchases were wildly exaggerated.
They had only to drive past a shop to have it said that they had been
squandering government funds inside. She quickly denied the story
that Mrs. Lincoln had paid three thousand dollars for a point-lace
shawl and that she, Lizzie Grimsley, had bought one at the same
time for a thousand dollars.

Mary kept telling her that she had to use the most costly
materials, since people studied everything she wore with critical
attention and the fact that she had come from the Middle West

exposed her to the scorn of the fashionable ladies who bought their clothes in London, Paris and Berlin. The staff at the Astor Hotel in New York was baffled by a President's wife who insisted on carrying her own parcels, however large, instead of having her purchases delivered. This was a whim of Mary's that seemed to be linked to her insistence on getting things the minute she wanted them. The more charitable decided that it was a wartime measure taken because of the scarcity of help.

Mrs. Lincoln's bonnets were as much discussed as the President's stovepipe hats. "I want a lovely affair—the velvet gracefully twisted," she told one milliner. The silk velvet strings were to be trimmed with heartsease in the best of taste. It was to be finished in three days and it must not cost more than five dollars. But there were plumed bonnets that cost a good deal more.

Mr. and Mrs. Lincoln shared some fun over his hats and her bonnets. In February, 1861, a group of New York women gave her a costly bonnet with a likeness of "Old Abe" on the strings. His homely face was surrounded by a wreath topped with the national emblem. "Burleigh," a syndicated newspaper columnist, wrote that various cities were "contending for the honor of furnishing a hat for the head that rested on Abraham's bosom." From Philadelphia to Bangor the milliners fashioned Mrs. Lincoln bonnets, won her approval for their enterprise, and were allowed to display their models and use her name. Crowds gathered at shops displaying the Lincoln bonnets, all the way from Canal to Fourteenth streets in New York, and studied them with the same interest shown more than a century later in Mrs. Kennedy's pillbox hats.

Mrs. Lincoln understood the uses of publicity; already a practiced politician, she recognized the fact that her husband's hat had become a symbol to the public. Topping his enormous height, it made him seem like a giant as he ambled about. Hats rained down on him, as bonnets did on his wife. Lincoln was amused by all this, and studying a hat sent to him by a Brooklyn haberdasher, he remarked: "Well, wife, if nothing else comes out of this scrape, we are going to have some new clothes."

The perquisites of office were considerable. On February 25, 1861, the New York *Tribune* reported that a group of New York men had given the President an elegant Brewster carriage with a maroon hammercloth front and handsome carved stands behind. It was lined with crimson brocatelle and had a speaking tube and folding step. This was high style for 1861, and Mary studied it with approval. With the spotlight constantly on her husband and the comments on his appearance and attire a blinding revelation, she did her best to smarten him up. She had always been a critic in this respect, but now it was apparent that something more must be done. Seward and Chase were fastidious dressers, and no doubt this fact had its effect on Mrs. Lincoln, too. In any event, his frock coats were now more skillfully cut, his tie was in order when the day started if not when it ended, his hats were new and glossy, and he shoved his huge fingers into white kid gloves for state occasions. He still had his shambling air and was untidy in his ways, but his tailoring had improved.

Every move that the Lincolns made was closely and sometimes critically observed by visitors from Springfield, already familiar with their ways. "Only think of me writing to her *royal highness*," her old friend Mercy commented when her husband, James Conkling, was invited to a reception at the White House. Mary was astute enough to keep the Springfield links alive; besides, some of her old friends there were much closer to her than anyone she had found in the great loneliness of wartime Washington.

Mary made no secret of the fact that the fears she had harbored for her husband's safety were intensified after they reached the White House. Mrs. Keckley commented that she "seemed to read impending danger in every rustling leaf, in every whisper of the wind." She persuaded him to carry a heavy walking stick on his night trips to the War Office, and Mr. Lincoln "with a confident unsuspecting air would close the door behind him, descend the stairs and pass out to his lonely walk," Mrs. Keckley observed.

The President's own fatalistic attitude in this respect was not soothing to Mary, who was more suspicious and excitable by nature. It was never easy for her to ignore a threat, however irrational, and the menacing letters that got through to her kept her in a state of real anxiety. Her husband took it all serenely and told Noah Brooks: "If they kill me, the next man will be just as bad for them; and in a country like this, where our habits are simple, and must be, assassination is always possible, and will come, if they are determined upon it."

The President thought it a joke when a bullet whistled through his high hat one August night as he jogged along in the dark. Next morning he guffawed as he told Lamon of the speed with which his horse had raced home, leaving his eight-dollar plug hat behind him. In the summer months he made a habit of riding alone the three miles between the White House and Soldiers Home, often late at night, but after the shot in the dark Lamon, who was responsible for his safety, persuaded him to stay at his house while Mrs. Lincoln was away. The President also consented at last to the military escort that his staff had been urging. He disliked this intensely and criticized the clatter the small detachment of cavalry made with their sabers and spurs. He complained that he and Mrs. Lincoln could scarcely hear themselves talk, and some of the newcomers seemed so inept with their arms that he jestingly remarked he was more in danger from them than from Jeb Stuart's cavalry.

Mrs. Lincoln was never opposed to panoply, but the President considered military show unbecoming to the Chief Executive of a democracy. There was enough of that without applying it to his personal safety.

XI

Four Young Lincolns

THE FAMILY LIFE of the Lincolns was tempestuous and complex, laced with sorrow as well as with deep love and happy companionship. In the darkest hours of the Civil War Lincoln found comfort and relaxation in his wife and children. No young occupants of the White House were ever more closely observed and commented on than the Lincoln boys, and in the abundant records of the period they live on, caught from every angle in relation to their world-famous parents. They remain an inseparable part of the Lincoln tradition, with Tad in particular a living legend pictured in crucial moments at his father's side.

Young though they were, they were caught in the whirlwind of conflicting passions between North and South. They were criticized; they were loved. They were berated as undisciplined brats; they were praised for their brains and charm; they were deplored for their rudeness and stupidity. All factions agreed that they were woefully indulged, spoiled, and allowed to run wild. Their parents' obsessive love for them was discussed across the nation, and Washington matrons with Victorian instincts about the way in which children should behave were highly critical of Mrs. Lincoln's handling of her sons.

She really did not care. This was criticism that did not sting. Love meant everything to her where her husband and children were concerned. Family came first. The boys fulfilled her strong motherly instincts and gave her some of her happiest moments, as well as causing her the deepest grief of her life. Before she died, she said that the death of Tad had hurt her even more than the assassination of her husband. By that time her hold on life was weakening, and Tad's death was fresh in her mind. Death and disaster had followed her with cumulative effect, and this was the final blow.

Although Edward and Willie died in their early years and Mary's heart turned icy toward Robert when he had her committed for insanity, Tad at the end, as in the beginning, was the core of their family life, the pet of the President, idolized by his mother, the focus of many happy hours in the White House and in the dwindling years of her life. Tad had the special appeal of the handicapped child. Today he would be regarded as mentally retarded, with his defective palate, his thick, slurred speech and grunting syllables, his inability to read and write in his early years, his tempestuous moods and tantrums, resembling those of his mother. But she never despaired of Tad's ultimate capacity to learn and to study, and she saw this dream fulfilled to some extent during the years they passed abroad after the President's death.

In the White House days Tad demanded attention wherever he chanced to be, often to the confusion and despair of the anxious politicians and generals trying to hold Lincoln's attention while he listened to the boy in his lap. John Hay made no secret of the fact that he thought the boys a hellish nuisance and that he longed to kick them on the shins, but all recognized that Tad's handicap called for special consideration and understanding. Actually he was dearly loved by the White House staff and by most of the men and women close to his father. He was known at the army camps as the little soldier who liked to flourish guns. He was kind, like his mother, and eager to help those in need. Like her, he was demonstrative, extroverted, and prone to impose his will on those around him.

Some of the Cabinet members were apt to be impatient with the small fry at the White House. They had children of their own, and they did not think that the Lincoln boys should be so omnipresent when important issues were at stake, but there were no rules where Tad was concerned. Charles A. Dana told of giving the President an important report and having him read it carefully with his small son squirming like a tadpole in his lap.

Tad would rush into the room and hurl himself into the President's arms like a small fury. An attempt by his father to check these invasions had little effect. Father and son agreed to use the telegraph code that Tad had picked up in the War Office—three quick taps and then two slow ones. This became a game between them, but it did not keep the invader in his own quarters. His mother came under severe criticism when he went tearing through the East Room driving two goats hitched to a kitchen chair and cracking a whip over them as a group of visitors from New England were admiring the stately decor. This was registered as one more black mark against Mary Lincoln, but in later years the sons of Theodore Roosevelt and William Howard Taft also made a playground of the East Room.

Pets for White House children have been traditional and the Lincoln boys were no exceptions, but the goats had special appeal for Tad and they amused his father. He liked to watch them jumping on the lawn, and they received special mention in telegraph messages exchanged by the President and Mrs. Lincoln when she was away on shopping trips or at spas. "Tell Tad the goats and father are very well, especially the goats," he telegraphed, and again, in August, 1863, he asked her to tell "dear Tad" that his nanny goat was lost. Nanko had disappeared from its quarters in the stables after infuriating the gardener by crashing through his flower beds. That was the last heard of the goat, which may have vanished forcibly or perhaps by its own will.

This was one of the minor tragedies of Tad's life, but a greater one was the fire that burned the stables early in the Lincoln administration. Two of the ponies were burned to death. One belonged to Tad, and the other to Willie. When he heard what had happened, Tad flung himself on the floor and was inconsolable. His hysterics matched his mother's in one of her worst moments. But there were other ponies to cheer him after that, and dogs, including Jip, his father's dog, which liked to jump on his lap at mealtime and be fed by hand.

One of Mary's constant problems was keeping a tutor who could handle Tad. Her scholarly instincts persisted where her sons were concerned, and she did not always approve of the President's insistence that Tad should be free to run and play. "There's time enough yet for him to learn his letters and get poky. Bob was just such a little rascal and now he is a very decent boy," was the way he put it.

When Mary, with her strong academic sense, decided to have a small school run by a tutor for the boys, it broke up almost at once. One tutor after another abandoned hope and left. John Hay, involved in the selection of these men, was at his wits' end, and he noted bitterly that Tad would soon find means of getting rid of any tutor with "obstinate ideas of the superiority of grammar to kite-flying as an intellectual employment."

Between Mary's absences, illnesses and whims, it was almost impossible to pin anyone down for action, but one young Scot, Alexander Williamson, made such an impression that Mary corresponded with him in the years after her husband's assassination. Remembering his solicitude for Tad, she consulted him about her debts and financial worries.

The baffled scholars who were flattered at first to be drawn into the Lincoln nimbus came and went with regularity. If they did not leave of their own accord, they were dropped when Tad made clear to his parents that he disliked them. The boys responded well, however, to Mrs. Keckley and to Julia Taft, a slim girl of sixteen who looked after them for a year. Two of her brothers, Bud and Holly, matched Willie and Tad in age and lived across the street from the White House. They were the children of Judge Horatio N. Taft, and their family was socially prominent in Washington.

Since she had grown up with a large family, Julia was well used to the interplay of the young. It did not bother her when Tad decided to scramble the White House bell system to have the fun of seeing the staff run in all directions. Nor could she share the gardener's rage when the strawberry beds were stripped by Tad on the day of a state function. But Mrs. Taft was censorious of some of the boys' doings, and she thought it absurd of Mrs. Lincoln to have all four attend a state dinner when Bud and Holly could not get home on a stormy night.

Julia coached the boys on Saturdays in their Bible lessons and went to church with them on Sundays, but Tad's pranks extended to the family pew. When restless, he would sit squirming on the floor, and on one occasion Julia had to bind up his bleeding hand when he cut himself by accident with a pocketknife. She adored Tad's mother and remembered her as looking lovely in summer organzas of lilac and other pastel shades. Mary made an indelible impression also by treating her with great sympathy and understanding when she was afraid to attend her first formal dance. In later years Julia could never reconcile the Mrs. Lincoln she had known with the Mrs. Lincoln of legend and ill fame.

In her diary Julia described Abraham Lincoln as a "good, uncle-like person, smiling and kind." He liked to tease her and call her a flibbertigibbet, and she would always remember seeing him sprawled on the floor, with the four boys trying to hold him down.

They urged her to sit on his stomach, but Julia continued to watch the tussle with some alarm as Lincoln's long legs waved in the air and he bounced the boys around with his huge hands. "Jew-ly," the President called her, and she joined the family group when he read pioneer tales to the boys. "He always called me Julie—not the French 'Julie' but 'Jewly,' " she wrote.

Julia was well aware that some of her mother's friends thought the Lincoln boys untidy and badly dressed. It was a period of much primping, and small boys suffered from an excess of fine feathers. Mrs. Lincoln at all times kept the boys well scrubbed and neatly attired in sturdy clothes, but Tad sometimes looked odd in baggy trapdoor pants buttoned to the waist.

Like all children in wartime, they played army games. Their most ambitious game was staged on the roof, where "Mrs. Lincoln's Zouaves" had damaged old guns poised for action should the White House be attacked. A log was used for a cannon, and the roof was alternately a fort or a ship's deck, depending on whether it was army or navy day. Willie was colonel, Bud was major, Holly was captain and Tad was the noisy drum major. But when they fired a real gun from an upstairs window of the Taft home, the war games were suspended. And after letting Tad have a pistol of his own, his father had a dream that caused him to send a message to Mary: "Think you better put Tad's pistol away. I had an ugly dream about him."

The tall President often led tiny Tad by the hand to a toy shop close to the White House, where a French soldier named Joseph Shuntz displayed the little wooden soldiers that he carved. The public liked to see Tad being gently led around by his father, and his visits to the forts and army camps were always of great interest and commented on by the war correspondents, who welcomed a light touch in the midst of so much suffering and horror.

It was inevitable that the Lincoln boys should have been stirred by the military operations going on around them, the tales of battles lost and won, the excitement of their trips with the President and the stirring reviews of troops. Tad was always excited by visits to the encampments. The soldiers seemed to enjoy watching him playing the military game and riding a small horse close to his father's side. They were always ready to salute and humor him, although he created many complications for them.

One of the few occasions on which Tad really angered his father was when he discovered that the boy was waving a Confederate flag behind him as he reviewed troops from the White House portico.

Evidently Tad thought that this was funny, but the crowd reacted strangely. His father seized him roughly for once and swung him over to an aide. Another of his pranks was to play the role of the corporal of the guard, who blew a whistle every half hour at the White House to signal the step-up of the sentries' horses for a miniature changing of the guard. Tad badgered the corporal to give him his whistle, and he promptly caused chaos with mixed signals, which led to the thundering of horses' hooves outside the White House.

Tad was such a chatterbox, making sounds few could understand, that his father tried to silence him on one of their many trips together down the Potomac. They were heading for Fort Monroe, and Tad was bothering everyone. Finally his father said he would give him a dollar if he kept quiet until they reached the fort. Tad was silent briefly, but soon exploded again. When he asked for his dollar on their arrival at the fort, the President asked him if he thought he had earned it. Tad said that he had.

His father studied him with baffled amusement and took a dollar note from his pocket book. "Well, my son," he said, "at any rate, I will keep *my* part of the bargain."

On another occasion when the President was on his way to Fort Monroe, he asked Rear Admiral David D. Porter to let him go ashore in a boat with a couple of sailors so that he could pick some of the spring flowers carpeting the riverbank. "Tad is very fond of flowers," he remarked, as his tall form doubled up and he groped for the wild blossoms that his wife had so often arranged in small bouquets, one of Mary's many gestures to please with small graces.

The President saw to it that Tad's varied requests were filled. The Secretary of War was instructed to let him have all the flags he wanted, and more often than not, Tad showed up with a flag in his hand. Both parents encouraged him to send gifts to the soldiers, and he collected books, flowers, fruit and sweets for this purpose. His father told him to mark the box of comforts he was sending to some "lonesome soldiers" he had seen in camp as coming from Tad Lincoln. Every effort was made by his parents to give importance to Tad's kindly impulses. But he frequently embarrassed the White House ushers by leading waiting suppliants into his father's presence and demanding that they be heard. However, Old Edward, the veteran doorkeeper, was devoted to Tad and never failed to help him out of scrapes.

Like his mother, Tad liked to hoard things, as well as being a spendthrift. During a National Fast Day he stored a supply of food under a coach seat in the carriage house. When this was drawn to his father's attention, President Lincoln remarked: "If he grows to be a man, Tad will be what the women all dote on—a good provider."

Carpenter observed with a degree of wonder the President's adoration of Tad and wrote: "It was an impressive and affecting sight to me to see the burdened President lost for the time being in the affectionate parent, as he would take the little fellow in his arms upon the withdrawal of visitors, and caress him with all the fondness of a mother for the babe upon her bosom."

The photographers all made an effort to catch them together, and one of Tad's stormiest scenes with his father involved the picture taking that had become routine at the White House. He flew into a rage when he found that photographers from Mathew Brady's Gallery, who had come to the White House to do stereoscopic studies of the President's office for Carpenter, were allotted a dark room for development that Tad considered his own. He intended to use it as a theater, and the staff had helped him install such props as curtains and seats.

His father, posing nearby in a chair, heard Tad railing at Carpenter, whom he considered the culprit in the matter. He locked the door to keep the invaders out, and his father told him gently to return the key at once. Tad paid no attention but rushed off to his mother in the family quarters. Carpenter hurried after him but had to report back to the President that his son refused to give up the key.

At this point Lincoln's slack lips came together firmly, a gesture that his wife had found meant that no further argument was possible. Whatever the issue, she knew it was decided and that he could not be budged. He soon returned with the key and let the photographers in. Then he said to Carpenter: "Tad is a peculiar child. He was violently excited when I went to him. I said, 'Tad, do you know you are making your father a great deal of trouble?' He burst into tears, instantly giving up the key."

Tad disliked photographers from that time on, but he was no more averse to them than his mother was. Although many of her early White House pictures were attractive and flattering, she hated to pose. She was too restless to sit reposefully for any length of time, and apparently she did not always like what she saw, for on one occasion she asked that all her pictures be destroyed. Her own awkward comment on her portraits was simply: "My hands are always *made* in *them*, very large and I look too stern." She was right about the effect created by her gloved hands, and since she had passed her prime by the time she reached the White House, the effect was not always flattering.

The only pleasure she took in her portraits lay in her stately gowns, and she could see the value of this for historical purposes. She liked a picture that Brady took of her in February, 1861, but here her vanity showed, for it was painted over to give a more slimming effect and showed her attractively gowned in plain black velvet. She was fond of the early daguerreotypes by N. H. Shepherd of Springfield, given to the Library of Congress. "They are very precious to me, taken when we were young and so desperately in love," she said on one occasion.

In 1963 Alvin S. Keys, a grandson of Levi Todd, Mrs. Lincoln's brother, gave the Illinois State Historical Library a delicately embroidered gown, with scattered clusters of leaves and fruit in lavender, green and gold on black taffeta. This is of great interest today to visitors who stroll over from the Lincoln house to view some of her possessions.

It was always difficult to get her to pose with Lincoln. She was sensitive about the difference in their heights. And much as she loved her boys, she was rarely photographed with them, although Preston Butler caught her with Willie and Tad late in 1860. Unlike Lincoln, she did not inscribe her photographs, but she wrote "Our Willie" under a picture of the son who was soon to die, and on a *carte de visite* of Tad she wrote in her neat script: "Taddie Lincoln, May 20th, 1864." Katherine Helm, who lived to be ninety-four, inherited some of the most intimate family portraits of the young Mary, of Elizabeth Edwards, and of her own parents, Mr. and Mrs. Ben Hardin Helm.

Both parents had trouble getting Tad to pose, and he gave considerable ground for chatter with his quaint and disorderly ways. Mrs. Grimsley considered him quick and impulsive, like his mother, and she remarked that he was the worry, as well as the life, of his parents. But she found him a merry, spontaneous boy "bubbling over with innocent fun, whose laugh rang through the house, when not moved to tears."

Tad was conspicuously unlike his oldest brother, Robert, who was a quiet, aloof young man during the White House days, the only smoothly tailored member of the family. Mrs. Lincoln was proud of her oldest son for his worldly ease and his steady application to his studies. All this was in keeping with the tradition in which she had grown up, but there was little real warmth between her and Robert, who was destined to play a sad role in her life.

He had been a cross-eyed, difficult child and had repeatedly run away from home. In 1846 his father had pronounced him mischievous and all too smart, but both parents had to agree that prep school and college had smoothed Robert out. In his father's estimation school had also made him a snob, but he was popular in Washington, and he inevitably came in for close observation. No matter what occurred at the White House, criticism or approval rained down on its occupants. Robert was expert on the dance floor, and he had all the cachet accorded a President's son. But he suffered considerably for being one of the few eligible young men not in uniform as the war raged. His mother was blocking him in this respect, and he suffered in silence, chalking out a quiet and dignified course for himself.

When he told his father that he intended to study law at Harvard, the President remarked: "If you do, you should learn more than I ever did, but you will never have so good a time."

However, as the loveliest girls in Washington circled around Robert and he attended all the best parties of the period, he managed to enjoy himself, although he did not have the exuberance of his mother or of little Tad. Friends from Springfield were amazed to see the change in Robert, whom they had regarded as a solemn and unsocial young man. Now Mary wrote home proudly that he had "grown and improved more than anyone you ever saw," and his father conceded that his alien son was doing very well, "considering we never controlled him much."

There was little understanding between Robert and his father, and they argued constantly over Tad. Robert told Carpenter that he did not think his small brother should be allowed to behave so outrageously and to upset the established order. One time, flushed and angry, he came from an interview with the President in which he had protested Stanton's action in naming Tad a lieutenant and letting him drill the servants, arming them like soldiers. According to Carpenter, Robert insisted that Tad be disciplined, but the President refused to take the matter seriously.

Willie was little affected by his surroundings. Mrs. Keckley perceptively wrote that he was "bravely and beautifully *himself*—and that like a wild flower transplanted from the prairie to the hot-house, he retained his prairie habits, unalterably pure and simple, till he died." Orville H. Browning noted in his diary that Willie made one think of Abraham Lincoln in the backwoods as his step-mother had described him—eager for knowledge and books and the "best boy" she ever saw. He was simple and kind and he gave his parents no trouble. His tranquility offset Tad's overwhelming restlessness, although he tussled with his small brother over war maps.

To Mary, Willie was a "peculiarly religious child with great amiability and cheerfulness of character." It was his custom to make careful notes on the great events to which he was party. He kept lists of battle dates, national events and the deaths of famous people. His essays, verse and letters delighted his mother, who never lost interest in literary matters. His poem to Colonel E. D. Baker, the family friend whom he had seen ride off to die at Ball's Bluff, was often quoted as a boy's hymn to patriotism.

On the more practical side Willie was known for the facility with which he rattled off the names of all the railroad stations from New York to Chicago. He had a passion for timetables and an unusual way of doing things. He seemed to be as much like his father as Tad was like his mother.

Attorney General Edward Bates thought that Willie was over-idolized by his parents. Julia Taft called him the most lovable boy she had ever known—"bright, sensible, sweet-tempered and gentle-mannered." But he had the aura of an early death, which would affect his mother's equilibrium beyond repair.

XII

Mater Dolorosa

L IFE IN THE White House dimmed for Mary Lincoln and her entire future was affected when Willie sickened on the eve of an elaborate party she was giving early in 1862. His death two weeks later and the storm of criticism that followed caused a trauma from which she never fully recovered

The echoes of the Marine Band—"like the wild faint sobbing of far-off spirits" to the sick boy upstairs, in the words of Mrs. Keckley—were to reverberate through the nation and doom Mrs. Lincoln to further ostracism as a heartless mother, on top of all her other failings.

The truth was that she was deeply distressed that evening and was meeting a difficult situation with all the pride and spirit that she could muster. Neither she nor the President knew how dangerously ill Willie was, but they were worried about him. At the last minute they considered calling off the party, until they were assured by their son's doctor that there was no need for this. It would have created endless confusion. But the President's concern was evident to his guests, and during the evening he and Mrs. Lincoln slipped away separately from the glittering assemblage several times to look in on Willie.

Mary was breaking ground with this particular party. It was her most ambitious social affair since becoming First Lady, and she had planned it with care and forethought. Five hundred invitations went out, a breach in established custom. Good form at the White House meant private dinner parties with selected lists or huge receptions for the rank and file. Mary was trying something of a throwback to Dolley Madison's expansive hospitality. Stung by the snubbing she had received on all sides, she decided to give a party where wit, intelligence and spirit would prevail over the established political and social forces then dominating the scene in Washington.

The departure of the worldly and wealthy Southern hostesses with their husbands had changed the social structure, but at the end of her first year in the capital Mrs. Lincoln was still an outsider as she sought to establish a court of her own. On one occasion every woman stayed away from a reception except the generous-hearted Mrs. Stephen Douglas. Kate Chase pleaded a headache. When her father apologized for her absence, Mrs. Lincoln tartly told him that Miss Kate would undoubtedly hear all about the party. "She's fortunate in having so many admirers among the gentlemen who are here," Mary added.

Washington's Cave Dwellers stayed aloof from it all, scornful of Mrs. Lincoln's ways and of her break with established custom. But Seward had suggested a dignified function by invitation. President Lincoln was not altogether at peace over his wife's innovation, and so many complaints came from the forgotten that extra invitations had to be sent out at the last minute. In excluding the press at first, Mary raised a storm of protest that was stilled only by what her husband called the "pass" business.

However, *Leslie's Weekly* of February 5, 1862, came through handsomely in its tribute to the "distinguished, beautiful, brilliant people representing intellect, attainment, position, elegance" who were Mrs. Lincoln's guests. It was suggested that she was trying to gild the White House image by ignoring some of the wilder radical types close to her husband. In worldly terms there had been criticism of the mien and manners of some of the long-haired, tobacco-chewing abolitionists, but it happened that among the most elegant of her guests were Sumner and Chase, both deeply committed to the antislavery cause. They were men of grace, sophistication and worldly assurance. Although random spitting and tobacco chewing were common to all political parties, these men were the dandies and scholars in the group close to the President.

The invitations called it a "dancing party," so the guests arrived in their best ballroom attire, but at the last moment dancing was ruled out. Willie's illness and an acid note from Senator Benjamin Wade rejecting his invitation pointed up the unsuitability of dancing at the White House in time of war. "Are the President and Mrs. Lincoln aware there is a Civil War?" asked the hostile Senator Wade, a fighter who had been a day laborer on the Erie Canal, a farmhand, cattle driver, schoolteacher and prosecuting attorney. "If they are not, Mr. and Mrs. Wade are, and for that reason decline to participate in feasting and dancing."

In the end it proved to be a party of some magnificence, and if there was no dancing, the feasting, gaiety and music were defined as roistering in the midst of war. The press later compared this function to the Duchess of Richmond's ball in Brussels on the night before Waterloo. In stiff silks and rich brocades, trailing garlands of flowers and wearing their finest jewels, the guests moved in their bumping hoops through the Blue Room and on into the East Room, where they were received by the Lincolns. Mary, promenading around the East Room on the President's arm, wore a low-cut gown of white satin, with a train swathed in black Chantilly lace. A wreath of black-and-white crepe myrtle rested becomingly on her dark hair, and a garland of myrtle trailed down her gown. Her jewelry was simple—a pearl necklace, inconspicuous against the blaze of diamonds, emeralds and rubies and the opaque glow of turquoise and coral that gave warmth and glitter to the crinolined figures moving past her.

Mrs. Lincoln was believed to have chosen black and white as half mourning for Prince Albert, a gesture aimed at Lord Lyons. The President had looked somewhat dubiously at his wife's costume before going downstairs for the promenade. He had wandered into her bedroom as Mrs. Keckley was dressing her. Standing in front of the fireplace, he studied Mary with some surprise. She had learned long before reaching the White House that low décolletage showed off one of her best features to advantage—her fine shoulders and arms.

"Whew!" commented the President. "Our cat has a long tail tonight. Mother, it is my opinion if some of that tail was nearer the head, it would be in better style."

But her guests did not seem to think that Mrs. Lincoln lacked style that night. There were more comments on the clumsy fit of the President's white kid gloves than on his wife's revealing décolletage. Few realized that the night that was to have been one of triumph for the much abused Mrs. Lincoln was a nightmare for both parents. The band played softly, flowers scented the air, the lights threw a glow over some of the nation's best-known faces, but there was no denying the conflicting sentiments of a nation at war—and civil war at that. The feeling of death and disaster was in the air like some mystic force, with the battlefield and the White House closely linked. The President's face was a study in fatigue and melancholy, but since it was his custom to look abstracted in a good-natured way at parties, no one thought his manner strained until he mentioned Willie's illness to several guests. He told General Frémont, who was sunk in gloom over the loss of his command in the West, that he was apprehensive about his sick son, and he talked to Dorothea Dix about assigning a military nurse to Willie.

Mrs. Lincoln, always an effusive and attentive hostess, covered up her anxiety with vivacious conversation and quick, nervous gestures. Friend and foe watched her attentively, including Kate Chase and Jessie Frémont, two worldly-wise and brilliant women who had no reason to love the Lincolns at the moment.

Kate, a vision in café au lait lace, unbent for the time being as she passed along the receiving line. She inquired with warmth about Willie's condition, and for a moment a flash of sympathy passed between the two women in common concern for the sick child. Chase and Sumner moved among the crinolined beauties with majestic calm, observing the assortment of legislators on Mary's invitation list. Only top Army brass had been invited, but the clank of war was observable everywhere. The diplomatic corps blazed with gold lace, feathers and decorations, and Mrs. Lincoln gave special attention to M. Mercier, the French ambassador, and to Lord Lyons, who had come to Washington prepared to dislike her but had been won over by this time. The goodwill of Britain and France was of paramount importance at the moment, since the tide seemed to be swinging in favor of the Confederacy.

Remembering the feasts of Kentucky rather than her spartan fare in Springfield, Mary had ordered a lavish banquet, catered by Maillard's. This was a sphere in which she was not to be outdone, and the New York *Tribune* of February 6, 1862, described it as "one of the finest displays of gastronomic art ever seen in this country." The confectionery conceits set the pattern for all the more elaborate functions of the Civil War period.

Robert Lincoln, grave in demeanor but sporting in his fashionable attire, led the younger guests to the tables, where the decorative theme was war. There was strain here, too, since many wondered why the President's son was not in uniform. It was later reported that nearly a ton of turkey, duck, venison, pheasant, partridge and ham had been ordered for the feast, and much of the dressed game surrounded a sugar model of Fort Sumter, the starting point of the war.

The frigate *Union* was in full sail on a stand supported by cherubs, and water nymphs made of nougat supported a fountain that sprayed spun sugar. Plumes of spun sugar waved from a war helmet, and sugar beehives foamed with charlotte russe. A Chinese pagoda, a Swiss chalet, and a cornucopia overflowing with candied fruits reminded Mary of M. Giron's confections. She studied the tables with quiet satisfaction, knowing that the champagne punch in the Japanese punch bowl and the carefully chosen wines were the best that any hostess could provide.

Her quick trips up to Willie's room were reassuring as she mopped his brow and was told by Mrs. Keckley that his fever had dropped. The night passed at last, but he was worse in the morning. While flattering comments appeared in the papers about Mrs. Lincoln's party for five hundred, he became dangerously ill. What had been diagnosed first as a cold, then as bilious fever developed into typhoid, and soon the Lincolns knew that their son would die. For the next two weeks Mary hung over his bed in anguish as she watched him struggle for breath. Torn by official demands, the President was in and out of the sickroom, but by February 17 he had given up hope.

Willie had asked for Bud Taft, who refused to leave his bedside lest his friend slip away. The President, finding the faithful and exhausted Bud asleep by his son early one morning, carried him off to his room. On February 20 Willie, with a sudden burst of animation, clutched Bud's hand and revived briefly, but this created false hope. It merely signaled the end.

Exhausted with her constant care of Willie, Mrs. Keckley was not with him when he died, but she was sent for at once and she helped prepare his body for burial. She recalled the President coming in and lifting the cover from his son's face. "It is hard, hard to have him die!" he said, burying his face in his hands. Mrs. Keckley, watching him from the foot of the bed, wrote later that she had not dreamed his rugged nature could be so affected.

Mrs. Lincoln alternated between bouts of convulsive weeping and total prostration. The funeral arrangements moved ahead almost without her knowledge. She could never again bear to look at Willie's picture, nor could she enter the purple and gold guest room where he died or the Green Room where he was embalmed. The mere mention of his name years after his death brought tears to her eyes. His father rarely spoke of him in the brief span of his life that followed. It seemed at the time that the wound both suffered would never heal.

They had accepted Edward's death in Springfield as an experience common to families in an age when children died as often as they lived. Mary was younger then, and she had not been subjected to the stress of war, to the waves of criticism and slander that now enveloped her, or indeed to the constant menace to life itself. Moreover, she was fresh from a taste of the social triumph for which she had fought so hard. The combination of circumstances rocked her unstable nature, and a sense of guilt must have been added to her misery as a fresh storm of criticism broke around her after Willie's death. It scarred Mary, a conscientious mother, to be accused of being heedless and unfeeling, putting her social ambitions ahead of her child's well-being.

The Orville Brownings stayed most of the time at the White House until the funeral was over. The Senator went to Georgetown to see the vault where Willie's body would be placed until he was taken to Springfield. Many of the men who had attended Mrs. Lincoln's party two weeks earlier gathered in the East Room and watched the suffering President with sympathy as a simple service was held in the presence of Cabinet members, diplomats, soldiers and friends. The only person missing was Mrs. Lincoln, lost upstairs in convulsive grief.

The day of the funeral was wild and gusty, with flags being torn to ribbons and roofs being blown off houses. Trees were uprooted, and nature was in turmoil. Death in the White House impressed itself on both the North and South in a moment of great national emergency. Crepe hung in somber folds on the building, and the black horses and huge hearse with funeral plumes that drew up at the entrance added to the gloom of the capital. The Washington Day illuminations were canceled, but colored lanterns hung from many houses and busts of George Washington were decked with flowers as the cortege moved slowly through the streets, with the black servants, all of whom had been devoted to Willie, in the rear carriage. Robert drove with his father, who had Senator Trumbull and Senator Browning, two old friends from Illinois, in his carriage.

Mrs. Keckley, who had lost her son, Wilberforce, in battle, did her best to comfort Mrs. Lincoln, and Dorothea Dix, at the President's request, had assigned Mrs. Rebecca R. Pomroy, a military nurse, to look after Tad and his mother. Few were aware of the depth of the President's suffering as he coped with this personal emergency while being battered on all sides by the problems of war. Moving through a cloud of worry and grief, he could do little to allay his wife's hysteria. Mrs. Keckley watched him lead her gently to a window one day and point toward an asylum for the insane in the distance. "Mother," he told her sorrowfully, "do you see that large white building on the hill yonder: Try and control your grief, or it will drive you mad, and we may have to send you there."

He had besought Mrs. Edwards to stay as long as she could with his wife, but she had come reluctantly from Springfield to the White House, and she was eager to get back to see her new grandson, Edward Lewis Baker, who would grow up to be a comfort to Mrs. Lincoln in the last days of her life. Mrs. Edwards wrote with cool realism about her distraught sister. Her presence had tended to soothe the "excessive grief that natures such as your Aunt's, experience," she wrote to her daughter, Mrs. Julia Edwards Baker. She felt she had also been able to help Tad, who was not well and seemed to be suffering acutely from the loss of Willie. He would let no one talk to him about the disaster that had come into his life, and his mother had been kept away from him as much as possible lest she upset him further with her grief.

In spite of the tension between the two sisters the President felt that Mrs. Edwards was needed at the White House because she had "such a power & control, such an influence over Mary." She was more disciplined in spirit than her younger sister, and she thought such manifestations of grief excessive and unnecessary. Having little interest now in society, she did not enjoy the official air of the White House, and she wrote that she would have been happier in a small simple room than in the chamber with gold and purple hangings where Willie died. But she accepted the fact that Mary wished her to have the best and anything that suited her—"from the least to the greatest."

Finallly, on March 2, Mrs. Edwards got her up and into one of her black silk dresses. Studying her sister knowingly as she dressed, she cynically reflected that such was Mary's nature that she did not think she would "long forego" all her pleasures. And sure enough, Mary was soon preoccupied with the outward trappings of mourning, extravagantly overdone in the Victorian era. Queen Victoria was fostering this cult in Britain, and there was nothing out of character for Mrs. Lincoln to dress herself in rich black fabrics and to wear the jet jewelry that went with them, or to order notepaper with the deepest black border to be had. This was the custom of the era, but her critics jeered at what seemed to be an excess of sorrow at a time when countless mothers and wives were losing their men in battle. Her sorrow was not unique, but her impulsive ban on the Marine Band playing on the White House grounds caused a great deal of resentment. The music had been diversion for the crowd who sauntered there, seeking relief from their troubles. When Gideon Welles made it clear to the President that the public was incensed over this whim of Mrs. Lincoln's, arrangements were made for the band to play in Lafayette Square.

During her brief stay at the White House after Willie's death Mrs. Emilie Todd Helm noted that Mary had hallucinations and that her behavior seemed beyond control. Mary urged Emilie to try to communicate with her dead husband, Ben, saying that she was deriving great comfort from nightly "visitations" with Willie and Eddy. Willie, she said, let her know that he was in touch with her brother Alexander, recently killed in battle.

The supernatural entered so strongly into the picture that Emilie gave the President a few blunt truths about his wife. She had been shocked by the changes she saw in her, even though Mr. Lincoln had warned her that Mary was in a highly nervous state. But the frightened look in her sister's once lustrous eyes at times appalled her. Every sound made Mary jump with fright, and she seemed to have lost all self-control, but Emilie noticed that she pulled herself together when Mr. Lincoln came into the room.

Robert was worrying both parents at this time. His relations with his family had become strained and intermittent. The Prince of Nails came down from Harvard from time to time, usually during vacations; he was a model of quiet propriety but never spent himself on trivial duties. He disliked his mother's exaggerated reactions to simple things, and he had little opportunity to talk to his hard-pressed father. Actually he was seething inwardly all summer because he wanted to be in the Army and his mother was moving heaven and earth to prevent this from happening.

Mary was intensely proud of her oldest son with his worldly assurance, but she strongly opposed his wish to leave Harvard and don uniform, as the other young men of the North and South continued to do. She used Willie's death as an excuse for her reluctance to let him go. "We have lost one son, and his loss is as much as

I can bear, without being called upon to make another sacrifice," she said to friends.

President Lincoln felt that his son should serve, like countless other young Americans across the country. He reminded Mary that their boy was no more dear to them than other sons were to their parents and that many mothers had given up all their sons. But Mary was so utterly absorbed in her own family that she was blind to this self-evident fact. Emilie recorded in her diary one conversation she heard between the Lincolns on this subject. Mary said to her husband, who was reading across the room, "I know that Robert's plea to go into the army is manly and noble and I want him to go, but oh! I am so frightened he may never come back to us."

Mary's rising dementia became as clear to her sister Emilie at this time as it had long been to her husband and to Stoddard. The President's hesitation over backing up Robert in his wish to join the Army rested wholly on his conviction that Mary would have a total collapse if her son went to war. In his posthumous study of Mrs. Lincoln's history Dr. Evans categorized the death of Willie as one of the great destructive forces of her lifetime. He theorized that her mental and nervous disintegration was more noticeable and rapid after this shock.

In the months that followed, Mary had to live through one of the most searing attacks of all, based on the party that had begun so brilliantly and ended in disaster. The costs were discussed in detail, the venison weighed, the liquor appraised, until Major French, writing to his brother about the "magnificent affair," added that the President would pay for it *"out of his own purse."* He was one of the few who understood Mrs. Lincoln's inner motivation and the way in which the party had been planned. He was sympathetic and thought that she was most unjustly abused. No mother, he wrote, could have done more than she had done for Willie, staying constantly at his bedside after they knew that his illness was critical, wearing herself out with vigilance and mourning as "no one but a mother can at her son's death."

But the papers continued to pound away at her in the excessive language of the period. One called her a "Delilah." Another wrote of the "disgraceful frivolity, hilarity and gluttony" of the party. The *Liberator* cut deep with the charge that Mrs. Lincoln's party was just what might have been expected from a woman "whose sympathies are with slavery and with those who are waging war."

This was crucifying to her nervous system, but she was shaken out of her self-absorption with a poem by Eleanor G. Donelly that was widely distributed soon after Willie's death. It was called "The Lady-President's Ball," and its special sting lay in the fact that it was presented as the message of a dying soldier who had watched the lights of the White House on the night of the famous party.

It mentioned the jellies, the fruits and ices, the fountains that flashed as they fell, the satins, jewels and wine, and the French dishes consumed by Mrs. Lincoln's guests while the soldier sickened on his black broth and cried:

> *O God! for a cup of cold water*
> *From the Lady President's Ball.*

Mary Clemmer Ames fed this fire by writing that while her "sister-women sewed, scraped lint, made bandages and gave their all to country and to death, the wife of the President spent her time rolling to and fro between Washington and New York, intent on extravagant purchases for herself and the White House." Mrs. Ames considered her much publicized purchases "vulgar and sensational in the extreme."

By June Mrs. Lincoln had pulled herself together and was seen driving through Washington, a drooping figure with the luster gone from her eyes. She had had enough of the gibes about the women who tramped the hospital wards and brought comforts to soldiers. Her spirit was chastened, and she fell in with the fashion of the hour. All Washington women were doing it, some with more concentration than others. Clara Barton was in and out of the battlefields. Kate Chase was visiting the encampments, attending the best parties, but keeping clear of the hospitals. Kate was fragile and her father feared for her health. Her work was political and tangential, and no one was more adept at playing hostess to visiting celebrities from abroad.

Soon Mrs. Lincoln was distributing more fruit, flowers and comforts at the hospitals than anyone else in Washington—a thousand pounds of grapes in one week, strawberries from the White House beds, flowers from the greenhouses, wines and gourmet foods sent to the Lincolns as gifts. She would drive up with her carriage filled with delicacies for the wounded, and her bouquets scented the grim wards. Occasionally she was accompanied by Mrs. Ann Stephens, the novelist, who helped her lay flowers on pillows and write letters to soldiers' families. One signed "Mrs. Abraham Lincoln" reached the mother of James Agen in Eagle, N.Y., assuring her that her son was getting on well and would be all right.

Usually she walked alone through crowded rows of cots, ignoring the stench of gangrene and the frightful wounds of the amputees. It was a severe indoctrination for a woman with shattered nerves, but she told Mrs. Stephens that it was easing her pain and enabling her to face the world again. Mrs. Lincoln's good deeds in this field were noticed chiefly by the soldiers themselves, and the Southern papers were apt to refer to her with scorn as the Yankee Nurse. Stoddard considered it a great mistake that she did not take newspaper correspondents with her and let them see what she was doing. He believed that this "would sweeten the contents of many journals and of the secretaries' waste-baskets." The opposite course that she had pursued had not been successful, he pointed out, although she could have had the benefit of good public relations.

Mrs. H. C. Ingersoll, who worked with her in the hospitals, wrote a defense of Mrs. Lincoln that was not made public until ten years after the President's death. When she urged Mary to deny the disloyalty and other serious charges made against her, she was told that this would be futile and would lead only to fresh attacks. Although she would go into hysterics defending her husband, she never attempted to exculpate herself. "I do not belong to the public, my character is wholly domestic, and the public have nothing to do with it," she quietly told Mrs. Ingersoll.

Mrs. Lincoln had a staunch friend in Mrs. Jane Grey Swisshelm, the first newspaperwoman to get a seat in the Press Gallery in Washington. Jane was a fighter, an agitator, an abolitionist to the core, and until she met the Lincolns, she was disposed to think that they were not sufficiently committed to this cause. In fact, she had thought of Mrs. Lincoln as being a Southern sympathizer.

Mary was well aware of Mrs. Swisshelm's reputation as a tartar, but her work in the hospitals, her crusading paper, the Pittsburgh *Saturday Visiter,* and her friendship with Sumner had their own appeal for the President's wife, who was soon helping her in her drive to round up lemons for the hospitals. The need for citrus fruits was desparate with so much gangrene in the wards. Jane did full justice to the horrors of the wartime hospitals and the treatment of the soldiers when she came to write her autobiography.

When she went to her first White House reception, Mrs. Swisshelm was disposed to show contempt for the whole entourage.

She watched the scene from the sidelines, then strode toward the President, who recognized her at once, and said: "May the Lord have mercy on you, poor man, for the people have none."

Mr. Lincoln passed her along to his wife, and Jane reported that a "sudden glow of pleasure lit her face, as she held out her hand, and said how very glad she was to see me." Jane said she must not shake hands with her, for her black gloves would soil Mrs. Lincoln's white ones, but Mary laughed and said with one of her spontaneous bursts of warmth that she would keep the glove, for she had long wished to meet Mrs. Swisshelm. Lemons were soon being rounded up at the White House for the citrus campaign.

But there were complications for Mrs. Lincoln as the wife of the President. The medical and military officials were increasingly averse to the well-meant efforts of philanthropic women, and the accredited nurses found them an embarrassment in the crowded wards. Some fainted; others had to be led away from sights of horror. The presence of the President's wife was a matter of some concern, and Mary found as the summer wore on that it was better to deliver her delicacies and drive on.

She did her best to cheer and comfort the President when they settled at Soldiers Home. "When we are in sorrow, quiet is very necessary to us," said Mary, who felt that they would be more inaccessible at their summer retreat. But she could no longer control her emotions in public, and when Howard Glyndon rode out for an interview, Mrs. Lincoln burst into tears and talked of nothing but her lost Willie.

It was a bad summer for the Union. Criticism of McClellan was mounting, and in the midst of his sorrow over Willie the President finally ordered a military advance in April. Shiloh that month was a deadly blow, and attention swung from McClellan to Grant, who came out of this battle with his prestige temporarily damaged. When the Confederates evacuated Manassas, the fiasco of the Quaker guns and weak fortifications jolted the North and shook the President's faith in some of his generals. The romance, the chivalry, the medieval conception of war were turning as cold as ashes now. The patriotic spirit still blazed high, but it was a fight to the death, and Mary could not fail to feel that her husband was at the very core of the tragedy. She knew that the loss of Willie was a constant dark undercurrent in his thoughts, but he had little time to brood over his own problems with all the pressure around him and the public demand for action by McClellan.

Mary was relieved when the President moved at last with decision on the larger front and put General Henry W. Halleck, lawyer and businessman from the West, in charge of all the Union armies. McClellan was ordered to give up his position south of Richmond and unite with the federal forces in northern Virginia, under the command of Major General John Pope. Halleck was soon bogged down in red tape and became a mere administrator. Pope headed into defeat when he pursued Stonewall Jackson and found himself confronted by Lee's army.

The miasmic Washington summer, the constant clash of war, and the sad associations of the White House distracted Mary so much that by August it was suggested that she leave the city for her health. Many Washingtonians were taking the Saratoga waters, although the glories of the spa were somewhat dimmed by the absence of the Southern women who had given it such éclat. It still reflected the style of the period, however.

The President missed Mary and Tad as he passed the hot summer nights at Soldiers Home, with a housekeeper and maid looking after him. His daily drives in to Washington gave him time to think and plan before hearing the latest bad news from the War Office. Messages passed regularly between him and Mary, who was closely following the war news. When she visited General Scott in New York, "all the distinguished in the land" made her welcome, and many told her they would worship him "if you would put a fighting General, in the place of McClellan."

It had become a habit with Mary to nip at the slow-moving McClellan, and her opinion may have influenced Lincoln to some extent when he demoted the general momentarily. But then in a swift move he reinstated him, and by the end of summer Lincoln's new Army of 200,000 was being trained at a heightened tempo. On a golden September day Antietam was fought, to be followed by Lincoln's long-awaited announcement that he was ready to issue the Emancipation Proclamation. Mary was in New York when Antietam was fought, and she asked Mrs. Keckley to follow her there. She wanted to help Lizzie, a former slave herself, get support for the blacks, who would need it when they were freed without resources. She introduced her to abolitionists and philanthropists who were interested in the newly formed Contraband Relief Association, and she gave her loans to help with this work.

When Mrs. Lincoln went to Boston to visit Robert at Harvard, Mrs. Keckley went with her and had a chance to meet some of the more noted abolitionists, such as Wendell Phillips. A mass meeting was held at the Colored Baptist Church in Boston, where a branch of the society was formed.

The Emancipation Proclamation was welcomed by Mrs. Lincoln. Although her life began with the slaveholding tradition, she had felt its injustices even as a child. The course her life took in Springfield tended to strengthen her convictions, and by her second year in the White House she was more articulate on the subject than her husband. With Mrs. Keckley at her side, she was reminded constantly of the needs of the blacks and was always ready to plead their cause. One of the White House parties to which she gave the most attention was the opening of the grounds for a black picnic. On this occasion she made special arrangements to have everything done in the grand style. Later she and the President treasured the Bible bound in violet velvet and edged with gold that the blacks of Baltimore gave to Mr. Lincoln on July 4, 1864. The cover showed him knocking the shackles off a slave.

Sumner influenced Mary profoundly in her thinking on the black question and what should be done about the freed slaves when the war ended. Both he and Chase deplored Lincoln's delays in issuing the proclamation. But Mrs. Lincoln's views on the subject were well known, and the blacks honored and praised her, even when others were tearing her apart.

XIII

The Bible and the Occult

W HILE MARY SOUGHT escape from her sorrows in hospital
work, the Lincolns' inner lives were undergoing a tremendous upheaval. The President turned more and more to the Bible for
consolation, while his wife veered off into the eerie world of spiritualism involving him in it to some extent.

At heart the President was more superstitious than Mary and had
long been subject to dreams and visions. When Mary took up the
occult, nothing could stop her in her quest to reach beyond the veil
to her lost Willie. She was greatly influenced in this by Mrs. Keckley,
who knew the practicing mediums of the day, but a variety of
experiences with charlatans diminished Mrs. Lincoln's interest until
the last days of her life.

Although she was a natural target for spiritualists at this time,
there was nothing strange in the fact that both she and the President
showed interest in the occult manifestations of the period. The
movement was so strong in Europe that some of the best scientific
minds were concentrating on the extrasensory world. And in
America spiritualism flourished throughout the Civil War, as in all
wars. Mediums held séances all over the country, and fascinated
devotees played planchette, studied astrology and tinkered with
psychic phenomena. Tables flew into space, spirit voices were heard,
tambourines were shaken, and stringed instruments were plucked.
Semiluminous figures draped in veiling and carrying bunches of
roses flickered through darkened rooms, and phosphorescent lights
wavered in the air.

In the 1850's Margaret and Kate Fox of Rochester had moved in White House circles and created a furore with strange rappings, mirror writings and mythical messages from the other world. Mrs. Franklin Pierce, sorrowing over the death of her son in a railroad accident, had consulted them. Horace Greeley backed them and held séances at his house attended by William Cullen Bryant, George Bancroft, James Fenimore Cooper, Nathaniel P. Willis and John Bigelow. Sir William Crookes, the British physicist, and Camille Flammarion, the French astronomer, studied their effects and they were the rage on both sides of the Atlantic until they finally recanted and pronounced themselves frauds. The strange rappings that had baffled scientists were made by their toe joints.

In Europe, Franz Mesmer had developed the theory of animal magnetism. In Germany Andreas Justinus Kerner combined poetry and occult study at the Swabian School in Weinsberg. In the United States Andrew Jackson Davis, a clairvoyant cattle herder from Hyde Park, New York, was an articulate guru and advocate of the animal magnetism cult in America. But Washington became a mecca for mediums of all kinds as war casualties kept the country in a state of continuous bereavement.

Many women took doses of paregoric, morphine or laudanum to assuage the sorrows and pains of wartime. Small electrical charges from magnetic equipment helped them face the strain of their hospital work or the big parties that were as characteristic of the period as its hardships. After studying Mrs. Lincoln's history, Dr. Evans came to the conclusion that there was no evidence that she was addicted to any of the drugs, bromides and opiates that were widely used and tended to produce hallucinations. He was convinced that her mental illness manifested itself strongly in 1862 after Willie's death, again in 1865 after her husband's assassination, and definitely from 1875 until she died.

Her dabblings in the occult ranged widely, for she consulted mediums in Chicago, Batavia, Springfield, Washington and Europe. At times she shrank with fear and revulsion from the whole idea, particularly when she was with friends who were unbelievers. In 1869 she wrote to Mrs. Welles that she was not a spiritualist but that she sincerely believed the loved ones "who have only 'gone before,' are permitted to watch over those who were dearer to them than life."

Mary's "visitations" weighed heavily against her during her

sanity trial in 1875. The theory projected by Dr. W. D. Hammond, one of her medical judges, that spiritualism was both a cause of insanity and a manifestation of mental instability bordering on the pathological strengthened the case against her.

The President accompanied Mary to some of the séances, and others were held in the White House. He was never a scoffer, although he was skeptical of some of the charlatans who circulated in Washington and he laughed heartily over the more fantastic posturings of the mediums. But all who knew him intimately believed that he had a strong mystical sense and was susceptible to occult manifestations. In his childhood he had listened to the folklore of the period, and during his deep depression before he married Mary he had felt as if he were outside himself, a disembodied spirit. But it was not until Willie died that Mary sought desperately to break through the veil and have what she called "visitations."

The White House séances and some of the absurd antics of the poltergeist gave the papers a chance to make fun of the President and his wife, but the ringing of bells, the twanging of banjos, the linked hands around a table, and the jumping Ouija board were prevalent in many homes, so nothing much was thought of the custom. Too many people were suffering for this mounting passion for communication to be dismissed as hokum.

When Mrs. Lincoln was driving with Orville Browning on New Year's Day, 1863, she told him that she had gone the night before to visit a medium in Georgetown. This was Mrs. Cranston Laurie, who not only established communication with Willie for her that night, according to Mary, but told her that all the Cabinet members were Mr. Lincoln's enemies and that they would have to be replaced if he were to succeed.

In her book about the Lincolns Mrs. Nettie Colburn Maynard, a medium of some reputation, told of a séance held in the Red Room with Mr. Lincoln present and of another in Georgetown attended by him and Mary. According to her story, the President suddenly decided to accompany his wife when she told him that she was going to a "circle" in Georgetown. Mrs. Maynard was to be put to a test that night, for Mrs. Lincoln was skeptical of her powers. The plan was to challenge her to identify a military figure wearing a long all-enveloping cloak. Mrs. Maynard's control, supposedly an Indian maid named Pinkie, said the cloaked soldier was "Crooked Knife."

Since the sickle resembled a crooked knife, it took no stretch of the imagination to conclude that the disguised subject was General Sickles.

There was a strong need for the skeptical spirit in this world of shadows, and Mrs. Lincoln, always suggestible, ran into serious trouble with one of the handsomest and most popular mediums of the period. "Lord" Colchester was an Englishman who posed as being the illegitimate son of a British duke. He was a fluent talker and a man who inspired confidence with his assured ways. He was received at the White House and held several séances at Soldiers Home in the summer of 1862, after Willie's death.

Mrs. Lincoln was persuaded that she was receiving messages from her lost boy, and this gave her comfort, but the President was not convinced that Colchester was anything more than an accomplished charlatan. He asked Dr. Joseph Henry, superintendent of the Smithsonian Institution, to call for a séance and study his methods. The scientist soon found that the sounds coming from various parts of the room, like those evoked by the Fox sisters, were created by Colchester himself. He had an instrument strapped around his arm; when he contracted or flexed his muscles, tappings could be heard. It was almost impossible to detect the ruse even when his hands were held by others.

Noah Brooks went further than Dr. Henry in exposing his methods. With a friend he attended one of Colchester's séances and listened attentively to the customary ringing of bells. A banjo twanged and a tub was thumped monotonously. Brooks suddenly broke the circle of linked hands and groped around until he was able to seize a hand beating a bell on the drumhead. As he ordered his friend to strike a light, he was hit hard on the forehead with the drum. With blood streaming down his face, he hung on to Colchester, and the séance broke up with people running in all directions.

Immediately after this Mrs. Lincoln received a note from Colchester demanding a pass to New York. His tone was threatening, and he intimated that if she refused, he might have some unpleasant things to say to her. Brooks studied the note and persuaded Mrs. Lincoln to invite Colchester to the White House the next day. She left the two men alone together. They regarded each other angrily, and then Brooks pushed back his hair and showed the scar on his forehead, which was only half healed.

Brooks tore loose and accused the handsome Englishman of being a swindler and a humbug. He ordered him to leave the city at once or he would be confined in Old Capitol Prison. But Colchester was not intimidated. He stayed on in Washington and continued to fascinate the women who attended his gatherings. Mrs. Lincoln no longer was one of them, and this incident shook her faith in some of the psychic manifestations and hocus-pocus to which she had been exposed since Willie's death.

Although the President kept a close eye on the men and women involved in séances attended by his wife, most of those close to him were well aware of his own fatalistic and superstitious strain. Herndon pictured him as a "blind intellectual Samson, struggling and fighting in the dark against the fates" and never shaking off the feeling that he would have a violent end.

Mary tried to make light of her husband's dreams, but they affected him intensely, and when he wakened and spoke of them, it was as if a misty veil hung in the room. According to Lamon, the most explicit historian on Lincoln's dreams, she chilled with fear. But the President had cheerful and good dreams, too, and he foresaw Antietam, Gettysburg and other notable victories. On the day of his assassination General Grant, attending a Cabinet meeting, reported that he was awaiting a dispatch from Sherman, who was then confronting Johnston.

"We shall hear very soon, and the news will be important," the President announced. "I had a dream last night; and ever since this war began I have had the same dream just before every event of great importance."

But the dream he had that was closely fashioned to the ultimate reality of his assassination disturbed Mary and rocked Lamon, who jotted down the President's account of it. Before telling it he spoke of the dreams in the Bible and in particular of Jacob's dream. He looked so grave that Mary teased him lightly, but when she realized how deeply affected he was, she exclaimed: "You frighten me. What is the matter?"

According to Lamon, he saw that he had startled his wife and regretted having brought up the subject at all, but somehow it had taken possession of him, and "like Banquo's ghost, it will not down."

The President said that ten days earlier he had gone to bed very late after waiting up for war dispatches. He had fallen asleep at once and had dreamed of a deathlike stillness around him, broken by subdued sobs, as if a number of people were weeping. He thought that he had left his bed and wandered through the White House, going from room to room but without seeing a living person. All the rooms were lighted and every object was familiar to him. Again he heard the sobbing and wondered where it originated.

When he reached the East Room, he saw a catafalque on which a corpse wrapped in funeral vestments rested. Soldiers surrounded it, acting as guards, and a throng of people passed, some weeping, others staring at the catafalque.

"Who is dead in the White House?" Lincoln said to one of the soldiers, according to Lamon's version of the President's dream.

"The President," was the answer. "He was killed by an assassin."

This was followed by a burst of grief from the crowd, and the President woke up at that point. Ever since, he had felt strangely upset by the vivid nature of this dream. Mrs. Lincoln regretted that she had insisted on his telling it. "I am glad I don't believe in dreams, or I should be in terror from this time forth," she commented.

"Well," said the President, according to Lamon, "it is only a dream, Mary. Let us say no more about it, and try to forget it."

Lamon was struck by Lincoln's pallor and solemnity as he talked. But his mood changed quickly and he jested with his guardian about fears for his safety. Then, grave again, he added: "Well, let it go. I think the Lord in His own good time may well work this out all right. God knows what is best."

There is no evidence that Mary, unlike her husband, was ever a Bible reader, but she had grown up with the conventional sense of reverence for religious observances, and much of her social life in Springfield was tied to church affairs. In her letters she often apostrophized God, like most women of her era in times of stress. But, more surprising to some, her favorite exclamation was "Oh, God!" tossed off without irreverence. She used it as freely in the presence of the lordly Salmon Portland Chase as she did in front of Mrs. Keckley.

The question of Lincoln's religious faith was to be debated through the years, and nothing in Herndon's revelations would worry Mary more than the misinterpretation of some of her own words suggesting that the President was something of an infidel. He had always engaged in discussion of the fundamentals of faith with his agnostic friends, such as Herndon and Joshua Speed. His interest in the subject had been strongly piqued by the Reverend James Smith, a witty raconteur with much appeal for fun-loving Mr. Lincoln. During country drives and evenings by the fireside they discussed *The Christian's Defense,* his book addressed to infidels and atheists. Watching Mrs. Lincoln in her home setting, he came to admire her for her intelligence, kindness and social grace. When she came under heavy attack after her husband's death, the Reverend Mr. Smith was one of the first to defend her.

Whatever Lincoln's earlier beliefs, his outlook changed during he agonizing period after Willie's death. He slipped briefly into the kind of melancholy that had beset him before his marriage. He was visited by ministers who prayed with him. One tried to stir him by reminding him that as head of the nation he could not afford to indulge in excessive mourning for the dead. Lincoln seemed to find his own consolation in the Bible, and soon he was caught up in such cataclysmic moments of decision that he recovered his balance immediately and went on a stronger man, while Mary became more erratic and unpredictable.

In spite of her adherence to tradition no one ever thought of her as being deeply religious, even in the days of her greatest anguish. Born into a Presbyterian family in Lexington, she swung to the Episcopalian church when she moved to Springfield and lived with the Edwards family. It was mere chance that her rector, the Reverend Charles Dresser, was out of town when Eddy died and that the Reverend James Smith officiated. They became such good friends that she joined the First Presbyterian Church on April 13, 1852. Although Mary took the sacrament, her husband never did, nor did he become a member of the church, yet he paid annual dues for the family pew. To the end of her life, Mary observed the religious customs of the period. When abroad after her husband's assassination, she wrote to a friend that she never traveled on Sunday—"that sacred day."

For years Mary and her sons occupied this pew in the fifth row of the building that preceded the one that is today known as Lincoln's church in Springfield. They seemed to be the convential family so far as churchgoing was concerned, except that tall and craggy Mr. Lincoln was more apt to be wheeling the youngest child along the street on Sunday morning than disposing of his long legs in the narrow pew.

There were many occasions during his years in the White House when church ceremonial was inescapable, and Mary was always punctilious in this respect. Lincoln made the traditional gesture of going to St. John's on his first Sunday in Washington before inauguration. After his assassination Mary clung desperately to the belief that the husband and sons she had lost were near at hand and that she would join them in a better world. She chose to think that her severe afflictions had been visited on her because of her worldliness and her absorption in her husband's political advancement. A dash of penitence, or perhaps a sense of guilt, ran like a thread through her endless sufferings. In today's terminology Mrs. Lincoln might qualify as a masochist. She was never religious in the sense that Abraham Lincoln was.

Carl Sandburg has pointed out that Lincoln knew the Bible from cover to cover—"its famous texts, stories and psalms; he quoted it in talks to juries, in speeches, in letters. There were evangelical Christian church members who saw him as solemn, reverent, truly religious." As in all else about Mr. Lincoln, he chose to be religious in his own way.

XIV

From Darkness into Light

M RS. LINCOLN EMERGED from her long siege of mourning early in 1863, the year of reviews and shifting command, of extravagant parties and insensate carnage, the year of Gettysburg, and the emergence of General Grant as the man who would lead the federal army to victory.

Ten months had passed since Willie's death when she finally stood shakily beside her husband at the New Year's Day reception. Her history during this dark period was well known to the public, and the passing crowd studied her attentively. Groomed to perfection, her mourning attire was fashionable in all respects, but it gave her a lugubrious air. She had visibly changed. Her hand shook; her naturally lustrous eyes were clouded with fear; and Major French had to support her as she greeted a long parade of callers.

Mary left before the reception ended, but it was her first step back into the social world where she must again preside. Before leaving, she reminded Major French of her crushing sorrow since they had last stood together receiving guests, and in a soft voice added: "The world has lost so much of its charm. My position requires my presence, where my heart, is *so far* from being."

In the midst of death and disaster the party spirit prevailed and elaborately gowned women sparkling with jewels drove with their escorts from one mansion to another in a single evening. Sometimes they took in as many functions as five, and the most high-paced parties were those given by Seward, who was apt to have Charlotte

Cushman or other theatrical stars staying at his house; by Schuyler Colfax, Speaker of the House, whose bounty at this point knew no limits; and by Kate Chase, the capital charmer. Even Mrs. Lincoln had to bow to this necessity, and on March 4, 1863, she sent out an invitation to Mrs. Charles Heard, the wife of a New York dry goods merchant, to visit her "sans ceremonie" at half past eight and added a postscript: "If you attend the party at Mr. Chase's this eve, we will excuse you at a suitable hour."

The official set, the parvenus who were growing rich on the war, the visitors from all parts of the country and abroad, moved through waves of spending, feasting and dancing. Gambling flourished, and the ladies of the night abounded. The concert saloons with girl waiters seductively attired were a preview of the bunnies of the 1960's. The theater flourished, and Ford's and Grover's were packed for every performance. The city's population had swelled from 60,000 to 200,000. Houses went up overnight, and the hotels were so crowded that guests slept in the corridors. Restaurants did a thriving business, and women who worked by day in hospitals danced by night, easing the tensions that had everyone strung up to a reckless pitch.

The Sanitary Fairs brought the cream of the entertainment world into Washington, and while ambulances and gun carriages rattled through the streets, the day's agony could end with Christy's Minstrels, the Hutchinson singers, or the great stars of the era in Shakespearean productions.

One of Mrs. Lincoln's first receptions after her re-emergence into the limelight was for two tiny guests of unique interest to the public. When Miss Lavinia Warren and Charles Sherwood Stratton were married in Grace Church, New York, on February 10, 1863, the legend of Mr. and Mrs. Tom Thumb was born, well press-agented by P. T. Barnum. On their wedding trip they stayed at Willard's and were received at the White House by the Lincolns. Tom Thumb's brother, a soldier in the Fortieth Massachusetts Regiment, served as one of the defenders of Washington.

Cabinet members, Senators, generals with their families and children were fascinated observers as tall Abraham Lincoln bent to take Mrs. Tom Thumb's tiny hand. Grace Greenwood later wrote of the "pigeon-like stateliness" with which they walked up almost to the President's feet. "With profound respect they looked up, up, to his kindly face," she added. "It was pleasant to see their tall host bend, and bend, to take their little hands in his great palm, holding

Madame's with special chariness, as though it were a robin's egg, and he were afraid of breaking it."

The President presented them "very courteously and soberly to Mrs. Lincoln," who greeted them warmly. Mrs. Tom Thumb sparkled with diamonds. Her heavy white satin dress, made by Madame Demorest, the New York fashion arbiter of the day, was looped with carnation buds and green leaves. Tom Thumb shone and glittered, too, with sparkling breastpins, shiny patent-leather shoes and white kid gloves of infinitesimal size. They were an endearing pair as their wizened featutes crinkled up in smiles and laughter.

But Bob Lincoln did not think so, and to his mother's annoyance he refused to come downstairs to meet Mr. and Mrs. Tom Thumb. This was the sort of thing that dignified Robert did not like about White House life. It might be fun for Tad but not for him. "No, mother, I do not propose to assist in entertaining Tom Thumb," said Robert firmly. "My notions of duty, perhaps, are somewhat different from yours." His father had a pleasant sense of humor about it all.

The pair were mobbed at a hop in Willard's, and Mrs. Lincoln's Saturday reception after their visit to the White House the previous day was what Major French called a "crusher." "I never saw such a crowd in the reception room before," he wrote to Pamela. "When we had gotten about half way through Mrs. Lincoln remarked, 'I believe these people came expecting to see Tom Thumb and his wife.' I guess she was right."

Mrs. Lincoln was older, sadder, wiser now. In spite of all the work she had done on the White House decor, it was lapsing back into shabbiness. Vandals were already doing their work. The brocatelle was fading and some of it was in tatters. Designs had been neatly cut from lace curtains and the damask hangings looked bedraggled. Pieces of carpet had been carried away. Mary's tired eyes caught the picture, but her days were filled with military events and official duties. She was glad when the President could join her for the simple family dinners they had at half past six.

The burdens of war grew heavier by the day. Dissatisfaction spread through the land as shifts in command added to the confusion of the war effort. The President rode the storm impassively; only Mary knew the toll it was taking on both of them. Chase wrote of Lincoln's incessant trips to the War Department to communicate with his generals by telegraph. The bearded Stanton, restless and abrupt, kept up a running fire of comment that cut into the President's homely jests and stories. Chase, joining them at times, was amazed at the ease he showed under stress. But both men caught another view of him when he flung himself on a lounge and slept from utter exhaustion. Stanton fussed, Chase sat with monumental detachment, and Lincoln's face told nothing as he absorbed portentous dispatches.

Although outwardly Mrs. Lincoln seemed to have recovered her poise, those who knew her best realized how badly shaken she was. She continued to shop, always for the finest materials, although they were invariably mourning and half mourning now. She held her own at public functions, but fresh tales came from the White House of her temper and erratic behavior. She was thought to be linked too closely to the Copperheads of New York. This group made a fuss about her on her shopping trips to the metropolis. Mrs. Keckley alone realized how heavily she was in debt; how profoundly she still mourned Willie; how much she worried about the health and safety of her husband.

The full panoply of war surrounded them now, and all that year they were drawn into a succession of parades, reviews, and visits to the encampments. When Ambrose Burnside resigned, Joseph Hooker, who had been one of his most persistent critics, took charge. Like the handsome McClellan, he made an impression at first with his blond and handsome presence, riding a white horse with considerable swagger. It was to visit his headquarters that the Lincolns set off early in April, traveling through countryside that should have been in full flower, but instead was deep in snow. Mary had proposed this trip as a morale builder in the face of growing dissatisfaction with the conduct of the war. She also thought that the change might be as salutary for her depressed and tired husband as for the soldiers, and there was nothing that Tad preferred to a stirring military event. Dr. A. G. Henry, Noah Brooks and Attorney General Edward Bates, all good friends, accompanied them.

Their dispatch boat, the *Carrie Martin,* anchored for a night in the Potomac because of a blinding snowstorm. In the morning they moved on to Aquia Creek, where Tad reacted excitedly to the complex operation of an army base of supplies. They had a brief run to Falmouth sitting on rough plank benches in a freight car draped with bunting because the President was on board. A detachment of cavalry met them at Falmouth, and they were driven in ambulances to General Hooker's headquarters.

Tad had his greatest hour as a small soldier in the review there. The President, described by Noah Brooks as "wearing a high hat and riding like a veteran," headed the column with General Hooker. Various branches of the army were reviewed in turn, while bands played, flags waved, and the cavalry made its own particular clatter. The President doffed his hat to the men in the ranks and touched it lightly in saluting their officers. Tad was described as riding close to his father with his "grey cloak flying in the gusty wind like the plume of Henry of Navarre." His spidery legs straddled his horse and his brown eyes shone with excitement.

Mary felt a brief exhilaration as the patriotic tempo rose, but the President was weary when the day ended. "It is a great relief to get away from Washington and the politicians, but nothing touches the tired spot," he remarked after touring the hospital tents and feeling how little the pageantry meant by comparison. They were quartered in hospital tents during their stay at General Hooker's headquarters.

Some of the camps were more remarkable for their luxury than others; General Sickles in particular was a high flyer in this respect. He had European ideas about setting up a court for Mrs. Lincoln, and he brought catering aides, provisions, silver and crystal when he gave a party for the Lincolns. More than a dozen hospital tents had been joined to hold two hundred guests. Chinese lamps gave an exotic glow to the interior, and garlands and flowers were intertwined with the bunting.

It was at General Sickles' camp that Princess Salm-Salm of Prussia rushed at the President and kissed him. Although Mrs. Lincoln was in camp, she did not see this occur, but when Tad told her about it, she gave the President a "long curtain lecture" in their tent, according to General Sickles. Prince Felix Salm-Salm had come to America in 1861 with letters from the Crown Prince of Prussia to Baron Friedrich von Gerolt, Prussian minister in Washington. He met the princess at General Louis Blenker's camp and married her on August 30, 1862. She was something of an adventuress, and Mrs. Lincoln had many chances to observe her. But the Lincolns were well used to European nobility, and Mary liked to practice her French on the young princes of the House of Orléans, who invariably attended her receptions.

McClellan welcomed the titled volunteers from Europe who attached themselves to his staff and delighted the hostesses of Washington. The comte de Paris, pretender to the throne of France, moved about the capital with considerable dash. The duc de

Chartres was a lean youth with a sense of humor and great zest for army life. Both young men, exiled during the regime of Napoleon III, were unpretentious and popular, and their fellow officers knew them as Captain Perry and Captain Chatters.

Their deaf and solemn uncle, the prince de Joinville, supervised the captains who had their own house in Washington. President Lincoln always greeted them with a kindly air, and Mary practiced her French on them. She liked their continental manners. It was instinctive with her to respond coquettishly to the "courtiers" who were always at her command. One of her favorites was Nathaniel Parker Willis, the editor and poet who wrote for his magazine, the *Home Journal,* a piece on Willie's death that she found unforgettable. Dan Sickles was another of her favorites, but Sumner rated top place among her escorts. She valued him for his cultivation and scholarly interests, and they shared a common cause in their strong abolitionist sentiments. He and Mrs. Keckley led Mrs. Lincoln faster along that road than her husband, who was slow to issue the Proclamation.

No sooner had the President moved to Soldiers Home that summer than Mary made one of her trips east with Tad. He reported to her on June 15 that he was faring "tolerably well" on his own but had not done much driving without her. It meant little to him when she was not in the carriage beside him.

She was anxious about his health and sent him three messages in succession before a reply on June 11 assured her that he was well, and he was relieved to get news of her and Tad. They were soon back and the daily drives were resumed, but on July 2 Mrs. Lincoln, going to Washington from Soldiers Home, had a serious accident. The coachman's seat collapsed. He was thrown to the ground and the horses bolted in fright.

Mrs. Lincoln fell or jumped out, landing hard on the ground and gashing the back of her head on a sharp rock. She was taken to a hospital to have the wound dressed, and Mrs. Pomroy, by this time a familiar figure in the Lincoln ménage, went back to Soldiers Home with her and nursed her through the three-week illness that followed. Her wound became infected and had to be reopened. The President telegraphed to Robert at Harvard: "Don't be uneasy. Your mother very slightly hurt by fall." But two years later Robert told his Aunt Emilie that he thought his mother never had fully recovered from the fall. Because of the manner in which the driver's seat had detached itself from its moorings, there was some speculation as to whether it had been intended as a plot against the President.

Later in the summer of 1863 Mrs. Lincoln's carriage ran over a little boy and broke his leg. She took him to his home and showered his family with fruit, flowers and gifts of all kinds. But her nights became increasingly restless, and at times she fancied that she saw Willie smiling at her from the foot of her bed.

Mrs. Lincoln was so adversely affected by these carriage accidents that she left the President again during the first week of August and took Tad and Robert to the White Mountains. Tad had been ailing, too, and when the temperature in Washington touched 104, Mary decided that they must get away from the humidity that always felled her in the capital. Moreover, she was suffering acutely from the hate and hostility that still seemed to dog her everywhere.

The mountain air did her good, and Tad began to run about with more of his customary spirit. But the President, coping with Gettysburg and the mounting problems of war, longed for his family. On September 20, 1863, he sent out a feeler for his wife's return: "I neither see nor hear anything of sickness now; though there may be much without my knowing it. I wish you to stay, or come just as is most agreeable to yourself."

A day later his message was slightly more urgent. "The air is so clear and cool, and apparently healthy, that I would be glad for you to come. Nothing very particular but I would be glad to see you and Tad."

By this time Mary was in New York and back in the shops, greatly refreshed from her stay in the mountains. When she received a message from Mr. Lincoln on September 22, saying, "I really wish to see you—Answer this on receipt," she responded at once, assuring him that she had answered his earlier message, but there had been some confusion. Taddie was well, but she had been suffering from a severe cold, said Mary, with a suggestion of apology for her prolonged absence.

Tad was usually the focus of these exchanges; both parents worried about him constantly, and with some reason, for he no sooner recovered from one illness than he developed another. Mary was at home, worrying over her sick son, who had scarlatina, when the President made his Gettysburg Address. She was unconscious of the fact that he was making history that day with a few lines of commanding oratory. At times she was inclined to be critical of her husband's speeches, and he had not given her any inkling of what he intended to say that day. He had left home anxious about Tad, but just as he was about to speak a telegram from Stanton reported that the boy was better. At the Gettysburg ceremonies Major French introduced Edward Everett, and the Baltimore Glee Club sang an ode written for the occasion by French. When Lincoln, a somber figure all in black, rose to his great height he was introduced by Ward Hill Lamon. In one hand he held two sheets of paper and glanced at them through his steel-bowed glasses as he spoke in a high-pitched voice that reached thousands gathered on Cemetery Hill.

It took him only three minutes to say what he had to say, and few caught the ring of history at first, although Hay wrote briefly in his diary: "The President, in a firm free way, with more grace than is his wont, said his half dozen words of consecration." *Harper's Weekly* was impressed, and *The Lounger* wrote: "The creation by Mr. Everett was smooth and cold. The few words of the President were from the heart to the heart. . . . It was as simple and felicitous and earnest a word as was ever spoken." Everett, whose speech had filled several newspaper columns and lasted for two hours, wrote humbly to the President: "I should be glad if I could flatter myself that I came as near to the central idea of the occasion in two hours as you did in two minutes."

The Gettysburg Address was recognized abroad as superb oratory before it attracted much attention in America. The London *Spectator* and *Edinburgh Review* called it a classical production and a masterpiece. Mrs. Lincoln's opinion of the Gettysburg Address is not on record. Although she did not think that oratory was her husband's special gift, he had so many other virtues in her eyes that he was Mr. Lincoln the Incomparable in whatever he did. Because of her well-known loyalty to her husband, Richard J. Oglesby, later governor of Illinois, was all the more shocked to hear her exclaim in public after one of his less inspired addresses that it was the worst speech she had ever heard. "I wanted the earth to sink and let me through," Mrs. Lincoln said within the hearing of many. The President was paying a tribute to the women who were active in war relief. But there are few recorded instances of this kind in her history. Whatever she may have said to her husband privately, she rarely criticized him to others.

Just before delivering the Gettysburg Address, the President attended the marriage of Kate Chase and Senator William Sprague of Rhode Island. From his great height he bent to kiss the bride, who then, as always, was scheming to have her father take his place in the

White House. Mrs. Lincoln deliberately stayed away from the wedding, which was held in the Chase mansion on November 12, 1863, and the New York *Herald* maliciously suggested that she should have invited Kate to hold her wedding reception in the East Room so that she might have had a chance to judge "how its associations suit her."

The President looked sorrowful as he entered the Chase home. He was not in the mood for merriment. The dead of Gettysburg weighed on his spirit. The end of the war was not yet in sight. People everywhere suffered, and Lincoln's sympathies blanketed both the North and South. He was weary from lack of sleep, from studying maps, from hearing bad news, from conciliating generals and Cabinet members. Not the least of his worries was Salmon Portland Chase, who greeted him at the entrance as if he were God himself. The President had arrived unattended, but a burst of cheering from the crowd heralded his presence.

Deep though they were in the woes of war, spectators jammed the street and carriages had difficulty moving through. The gowns, laces, jewels and feathers were the most extravagant of the day. Kate looked dazzling as she walked in a golden glow of gaslight, with the President, the Cabinet, diplomats, Senators and generals looking on. The official set was present without a break in the ranks, save for the generals in the field and Mrs. Lincoln, whose excuse was that she was still in half mourning.

The President watched Kate with kindly interest as she marched in on her father's arm. They made an impressive pair. Her skin was as white and smooth as the long velvet train of her gown. Her lace veil was held in place by a parure of pearls and diamonds in orange blossom design, the gift of the bridegroom. Bishop William Newton Clarke had come from Rhode Island to perform the ceremony. Forty guests from Rhode Island were present, and champagne flowed freely for another five hundred, most of whose names were well known across the country. The Marine Band played the "Kate Chase Wedding March," composed by Joel Benton, a young protégé of Horace Greeley.

President Lincoln gave Kate a fan, one of the simplest of her wedding gifts. He had never shared his wife's dislike of her, in spite of her undeniable machinations against him. The wedding cost $4,000 and Chase was already deep in debt. In this respect he shared some of the worries of Mrs. Lincoln, although he was Secretary of the Treasury and she was the President's wife.

XV

A Second Term

WITH SENATOR SPRAGUE's millions behind her, Kate Chase had become more formidable than ever on Mrs. Lincoln's horizon. An election year had dawned, and the beauty from Ohio was entertaining lavishly. Her drive for the White House had reached its climax, and she was as determined that her father should be the Presidential nominee as Mary was that Mr. Lincoln should be returned to office.

Witty John Hay and dependable freckle-faced John Nicolay were at times indomitable in their efforts to keep Mrs. Lincoln from stirring up social tempests, particularly where Kate was concerned. A circular sent out by Senator Samuel C. Pomeroy of Kansas under Congressional frank early in the year, urging thousands of voters to promote Chase for the Presidency, caused consternation in the Lincoln camp. Kate was believed to have figured in the initiation of the circular, but President Lincoln took it in stride. After a face-to-face talk with Chase he accepted without question the sincerity of his Secretary of the Treasury when Chase wrote a letter withdrawing from the race.

But Mrs. Lincoln did not forget. She was so angry that she decided not to invite Chase or the Spragues to the next Cabinet dinner. Nicolay, who had charge of the seating arrangements, saw at once that this was a serious tactical blunder. Chase must not be openly insulted, and Kate was a formidable character to snub. He practically "ordered" Rhode Island and Ohio to be included in the list. This was followed by "such a rampage as the House hadn't seen for a year," but Nicolay won his point and, in his own words, compelled "Her Satanic Majesty to invite the Spragues." No doubt Lincoln or Seward had been the adjudicator in this important matter, but Mary had her revenge by dropping Nicolay's name from the seating list. He responded by refusing to help her any further with her dinner arrangements, and this left her stranded. When she calmed down, she called him in on the day of the dinner and accepted his much-needed help. Nicolay wrote to John Hay, who was away at the time that he thought she felt happier "since she cast out that devil of stubbornness."

Many sympathized with Mrs. Lincoln in her burning indignation over the Pomeroy circular, an open attempt to undermine the President at a crucial moment in the nation's history. She found in it justification for her constant warnings to her husband about the ambitions of Chase and his daughter. Vigilant at the dinner table that night, she resented the fact that Mr. Lincoln treated them as if nothing so malign had occurred. Mary was even haughtier than usual with Kate, whose manners were quite equal to this or any other occasion. Sprague who, from being the "Boy Governor," was now a Senator, endeared himself to Mrs. Lincoln, however, with his genial ways. She considered him the generous and unfortunate victim of a scheming pair, and she felt he was truly her husband's friend. Sprague was a man of riches who spoke constantly for the people.

Mrs. Lincoln was anxious at this time to entertain on a broader scale than the tight little circle of officialdom. Her worldly sense informed her that she must work personally for her husband's renomination, a debatable issue in a year of such crucial combat. His own weariness as he coped with disaster, defeat, warfare in the military command and in his own Cabinet was such that he exclaimed one day: "I feel as though I shall never be glad again."

Outwardly Mrs. Lincoln had shed her mourning and was coping with life again. A large crowd turned out to see the revived First Lady at the New Year's Day reception of 1864. It was a day of sunshine and high wind. She was her most animated self as she received her guests, wearing a purple silk dress trimmed with lace and black velvet. They passed over a miniature bridge extending from the window of the East Room to the sidewalk, and it was noted that four blacks "of genteel exterior and with the manners of gentlemen" passed in the line and shook hands with the President, a milestone in White House history. Frederick Douglass, Sojourner Truth and other noted fighters for abolition were soon honored guests of the Lincolns.

Receptions were regularly resumed after this beginning in 1864. Mrs. Lincoln, shopping again with her old enthusiasm, appeared in a succession of costumes in half-mourning colors, ranging through all the shades of lavender, lilac and purple or making effective use of black and white. With white flowers in her hair and black lace shawls draping her handsome shoulders, she was the old Mrs. Lincoln, richly attired and anxious to please.

Her long period of grief and immolation had sobered and chastened her. She had learned the danger of her own impulsive actions, but she was still unable to control her rages when she felt her husband was being abused. None but Mrs. Keckley knew how desperately worried she was about her mounting debts, even as she added to them with abandon.

Madame Ruth Harris, who had a shop on Broadway, was always on call for another bonnet for Mrs. Lincoln, who knew exactly what she wanted and sometimes made little sketches to illustrate her point. "My strings must be one yard long each— Do have my bonnet got up in exquisite taste," Mary wrote. "It is a bonnet for *grand occasions* & I want it to be particularly stylish & rich . . . the feather must be long & beautiful—lace trimmings *very* rich & full . . ."

A black velvet headdress was to have velvet bows and strings and a bow on the top. It was to be made in Madame Harris's "handsomest style" with a bunch of black berries—"your richest berries—without they are of the best & most stylish, I do not want them." After Willie's death she wrote to Madame Harris that she needed a mourning bonnet, but it must be "exceedingly plain & genteel. I want one made of crape with folds, bonnet of blk [*sic*] crape—that is trimmed with it. I want the crape to be the *finest jet black* English crape—white & black face trimmings— Could you obtain any black & white crape flowers? small delicate ones." Mary would have nothing but the "genteelest and tastiest" undersleeves and collars in white and black, with cuffs to match, and only the "finest, and blackest and lightest crape" would suit her for her mourning garments. She wanted all her bonnets to be lightweight.

It was a wild and rainy winter, and torrents seemed to come down on most of her reception days, making it difficult for her guests to find their way to the White House through mud and hail. Mrs. Lincoln was irked when they failed to show up after elaborate preparations had been made to receive them, but Major French reported cheerfully to Pamela that the reception of April 10 was well attended, even though it poured—"and still they came & would come if a Sodomitic shower were in full progress."

Mrs. Lincoln had not expected anyone to show up that day, and when he found "my good friend Madame L—seated in the servants room in full rig," she apologized for not letting him have the day off. They were having a "cozy talk" when Sumner arrived and they all moved into the Blue Room. The Secretary soon left, and Mrs. Lincoln and Major French sat on a sofa and chatted until a quarter to two, when the President joined them and was "as pleasant and funny as could be. Pleased, I flatter myself, to find his better half in such excellent company," Major French jested.

To their surprise Edward arrived to announce that the hall was filled with people. Outside a pair of troopers had directed the line of carriages with brandished swords. When the doors were opened, the crowd that streamed through resembled a New Year's Day reception. Generals flashed their stars and privates clumped through in muddy boots. Many wore traveling costume and backwoods fashions. But French bonnets, ermine muffs and exaggerated bustles abounded, for now that the Union forces were making headway, Mrs. Lincoln's receptions drew the fashionables for the first time since she had been in the White House.

In spite of the state of tension in which he lived, Lincoln took time to jest and tell stories, according to the observant Carpenter, who found his laughter like the "neigh of a wild horse on his native prairie." This artist observed that his bluish-gray eyes were constantly shadowed by heavy upper lids and his expression was "remarkably pensive and tender, often inexpressibly sad, as if the reservoir of tears lay very near the surface."

Carpenter's studio while he did his famous painting of the signing of the Emancipation Proclamation was the State Dining Room, and after nightfall he worked on the huge canvas by the light of a chandelier. He observed the Lincolns closely during this period of intimacy, and in his book he described the interplay of emotion between them and commented on their literary interests. At times the President read Shakespearean passages, usually reciting from *Hamlet* or discussing *Richard II.* He had no taste for fiction and bogged down on *Ivanhoe,* the current craze in the North and South. He liked poetry and commented on Oliver Wendell Holmes' "quaint, queer verse."

When Stephen Massett, the Western poet, visited the White House and read some of his sketches, *Drifting About by Jeems Pipes of Pipesville,* Carpenter could hear the President's laughter coming from the Red Room, where he sat with his wife. "The foremost funny men of the age, the leading American comics, understood Lincoln," Carl Sandburg wrote. "They shaded their foolery and colored their jests as if in the White House was one of their own." Lincoln's fondness for Artemus Ward helped make him a best seller.

It was in 1864 that Walt Whitman, living across from the Chase mansion and picking up odd sums writing for the papers and copying in the Paymaster General's office, had glimpses of the Lincolns as they drove past. They usually appeared in the late afternoon in a plain equipage but with a guard on whom Mrs. Lincoln insisted. Whitman noticed that she was "dressed in complete black, with a long crape veil." Once when their carriage passed close to him, his burly florid figure with bushy beard and wide sombrero caught the President's attention. He greeted Whitman, and the poet noted in his diary the depth of sorrow he saw in Lincoln's eyes at close range.

When Harriet Beecher Stowe called at the White House, the President welcomed her with outstretched hands and said: "So you're the little woman who wrote the book that made this great war." They talked together by the fireside, and she detected in Lincoln a "dry, weary, patient pain, that many mistook for insensibility." He said to her, prophetically enough: "I shall never live to see peace. This war is killing me."

Lincoln was well aware that he was pleasing no one and was losing too many men. His wife often reminded him of that. Mary had always been outspoken about the generals and their wives, and they did what they could to conciliate so formidable a First Lady. As early as 1861 General George Meade was assuring his wife, Margaretta, daughter of a well-known Philadelphia lawyer named John Sergeant, that he was trying to make himself agreeable to Mrs. Lincoln, who seemed to be an "amiable sort of personage."

Mrs. McClellan was young, modest and pretty, and Mary was disposed to like her, but when the generals themselves were not pleasing her or were letting her husband down in their operations, their wives also fell from favor. Mary was frank in her condemnation of the errant command. Every stage in the shuffling of generals was agonizing for her, as for her husband, and she blew hot and cold according to their failures or accomplishments. In the beginning she had deluged McClellan with flowers and invitations. She had liked his flattering manner and social flair, but she chilled to him during the long days when the Army of the Potomac seemed to be standing still. Mary thought entirely in terms of the effect his controversial command had on her husband and on the course of the war. Fast thinking and quick moving herself, she reacted instantly to the public criticism of McClellan, while her husband moved at a slow pace, thoughtful, sometimes bemused, but always conscious of the tremendous responsibility he bore.

Mary, distrusting his advisers, was dubious when Chase backed Hooker. The Secretary of the Treasury had not considered Chancellorsville the end of this general, and he was surprised when Hooker asked to be relieved and Meade succeeded him. Chase also pushed General Halleck, believing that he had "large capacity." Mary resented Chase's constant interference in Army affairs, which she thought were none of his business. She interpreted his zeal in this respect as one way of improving his chances of becoming President, and she told Lincoln that if Chase could make anything by it, he "would betray you tomorrow."

But Grant was the general Mrs. Lincoln could not stand, even when one victory for the North followed another and he became a public idol. She preserved the outward civilities but was unrelenting. "He is a butcher," she said on many occasions, "and is not fit to be at the head of an army."

When the President pointed out mildly that Grant had been highly successful in the field, Mary's response was quick and encompassing: "Yes, he generally manages to claim victory, but such a victory! He loses two men to the enemy's one. He has no management, no regard for life. If the war should continue four years longer, and he should remain in power, he would depopulate the North. Grant, I repeat, is an obstinate fool and a butcher."

Lincoln answered gently, with a trace of irony: "Well, Mother, supposing that we give you command of the army. No doubt you would do much better than any general that has been tried."

During April the war went into a new phase, terrifying in the magnitude of its casualties. In May the fields ran red with blood as the battles of the Wilderness, Spotsylvania and North Anna were fought in quick succession. Six thousand Union soldiers died in the space of an hour at the Battle of Cold Harbor in June. At that time General Sherman wrote to his wife: "It is enough to make the whole world start at the awful amount of death and destruction that now stalks abroad."

Nowhere was the holocaust felt more directly than in the White House, where the President had sleepless nights and was haunted by visions and dreams. His health seemed to be failing, and he grew more gaunt by the day. He had severe headaches and ate so little that Mrs. Keckley told of his wife's efforts to tempt him with dishes that she thought he might like. She sent trays to his office, but still he could not eat, and his deep-set eyes were dense with weariness. Tad alone could cheer him up. As the summer advanced, Mary was having acute headaches and "bilious fever," her usual malarial reaction to the changing seasons. In breaking a hospital appointment with Mrs. Welles, she wrote of the "prolonged pain and dreadful nausea" from which she suffered.

The tide of battle had turned in favor of the North since Gettysburg, but behind the bloody victories of the summer of 1864 Lincoln saw the dead—both of the North and South. "How much more of this killing have we got to stand!" he exclaimed after Gettysburg.

Now the name that resounded through the North was that of Ulysses S. Grant. He was summoned to Washington early in March, 1864, to meet President Lincoln for the first time. With military and political alignments changing almost overnight, it was a relief to Lincoln to have a general with a winning touch. Grant's young son Fred arrived with him and they registered at Willard's as "U. S. Grant and son, Galena, Ill." General Sherman took charge of Grant, awkward and diffident in a shabby uniform, and he was soon being mobbed in the dining room and lobby.

When presented to President Lincoln at the White House, he clutched the lapels of his coat in a characteristic gesture and looked up into the face of the towering figure whom he had never met but already seemed to know. Mrs. Lincoln looked with interest at these two significant Civil War figures together. Later she paraded with Grant. There was so much clamor to get a good look at him at the levee that Seward jumped up on a sofa and drew Grant with him. The general responded to a tumultuous welcome with a quick bow and a puzzled air.

Next day he visited the Army of the Potomac with General Halleck. The President commissioned him a lieutenant general, and Grant responded hesitantly from notes written in pencil on a scrap of paper. He was informed that Mrs. Lincoln had planned a dinner in his honor with twelve generals for that night, but he declined, since he was heading for Nashville to sever his relations with the troops he had led to victory.

"But we can't excuse you," said the President. "It would be the play of *Hamlet* with Hamlet left out."

Grant mumbled that he appreciated the honor Mrs. Lincoln was paying him, but time was precious and he thought he had had enough "of the show business." He also excused himself from attending a gala performance of *Richard III* at Grover's with Edwin Booth playing. The names of Grant's victories adorned the boxes, and a huge banner inscribed *Unconditional Surrender* ran across the front of the stage. The Lincolns sat in a flag-draped box, but Grant was missing.

He learned while on his way west that the President had made him supreme commander of all the armies. This meant moving east to head the Army of the Potomac and concentrate on Lee. His friend Sherman, supreme in Mississippi, would cope with Joseph E. Johnston. From the field Grant made a succession of trips to Washington to confer with the President and the War Department. On each occasion he was mobbed and serenaded, with crowds following him everywhere, to his intense annoyance and embarrassment.

With these developments Julia Dent Grant moved to Washington and settled at Willard's. It was her first glimpse of the muddy, frenetic capital. She had bought some elaborate gowns in Philadelphia, knowing that she would be meeting Mrs. Lincoln and the ladies of the court.

When she was first received at the White House she moved so modestly in the line that the President failed to catch her name until Adam Badeau, her husband's military secretary, repeated: "Mrs. *General* Grant, Mr. President." Badeau noted that the "tall, ungainly man looked down upon his visitor with infinite kindness" as he clasped her hand in both of his. Mrs. Lincoln welcomed Mrs. Grant with spontaneous warmth and in her most charming manner. Like Mary, she was from a Border State. Like Mary, she was an adoring wife. The two women chatted amiably, and Mrs. Lincoln suggested that Badeau show her the conservatory, knowing Mrs. Grant to be a lover of flowers, like herself.

Through all the worry of that crucial year in the war the Lincolns went to the theater. They took their daily drives. They entertained, and Mary did what she could to assuage her husband's anxiety, although there were times when she added to his worries. Mrs. Keckley saw how bitterly she regretted each outburst, and she heard Mrs. Lincoln many times exculpate herself after she had wounded someone, particularly the President, who was wholly unselfish in all his dealing with her. "He asked nothing but affection from her, but did not always receive it," Mrs. Keckley noted. "When in one of her wayward impulsive moods, she was apt to say and do things that wounded him deeply . . . but calm reflection never failed to bring regret."

Late in April Mrs. Lincoln went to New York with Tad, and she was soon dragging him through the shops. She told Mrs. Keckley that she had to assemble a suitable wardrobe for the coming election and inauguration. She was completely confident that Mr. Lincoln would be returned to office, although doubters abounded. As always when she was away, messages passed back and forth between them, with solicitous questions about each other's health. Even in the midst of his greatest worries the President gave thought to the needs of Mary and Tad, and responded at once when she asked for money, as she often did.

The shopping expeditions were so tiring for Tad that he stayed with his father when Mary went briefly to Boston in June. He much preferred the drills, reviews and expeditions down the river to the tedium of Mary's quest for silks and laces.

Although she passed a restless summer doing much shopping in Philadelphia and New York, she was with her husband during the crucial days in June when Lieutenant General Jubal A. Early made his spectacular raid down the Shenandoah Valley and Washington was in peril. This foray was humiliating to Grant, who was blamed by Stanton for having moved great numbers of troops away from Washington. The President immediately toured the fort and outworks, and Mrs. Lincoln went with him to Fort Stevens, the capital's only defense at the time. It was lightly manned, and when the Lincolns were there, a stray rifle ball hit a doctor standing close to the President. Carpenter, then working at the White House, reported that no one took the incident more to heart than Mrs. Lincoln, who laid responsibility at the door of the Secretary of War.

One of Mary's real diplomatic coups was the way in which she conciliated Sumner as the breach widened between him and the President. As the election drew near, it was vital not to alienate the handsome radical Senator from Massachusetts. But he and Lincoln were instinctively antipathetic, and the President's temperate feeling about the South angered the strong and unforgiving radical who had been whipped in the Senate for his antislavery views.

Sumner had only a dim appreciation of Lincoln's sense of humor. He thought him crass and coarse and a bore when he should be talking business. He understood and was sympathetic to the magnitude of Lincoln's task, but as a snob, a dandy and a scholar he deplored the earthy quality that made President Lincoln unique. It was observed that when Sumner walked in, the President was disposed to take his feet off his desk and curb his stories.

But Mrs. Lincoln served as a catalyst between the two men. In Sumner she had found someone who was convinced that she suffered great injustice. He was always ready to defend her, and he gave her the highest accolade when he told her that he wished her husband were as ardent an abolitionist as she was. A few years earlier she had thought it important to keep her husband's name from being linked with the antislavery cause.

The cynical saw in the way Mrs. Lincoln cultivated Sumner a campaign to head off Chase and Frémont, who were looming as possible contenders for the Presidency in the winter of 1863–64. But she genuinely liked him, and was glad to have so cultivated a man in her husband's circle and to be treated herself as something more than a hysterical ignoramus. She was tired of being fawned on for favors or being pushed aside as a meddler. Although Mary took pride in improving the relations between these two formidable men, she was not altogether convincing when she said that Sumner "appreciated my noble husband."

The choicest bouquets from the White House Conservatory were sent to Senator Sumner, and the invitations became so numerous that the President stepped in with a semi-apology for his wife's persistence. He wrote on her behalf: "Mrs. L. is embarrassed a little. She would be pleased to have your company again this evening at the Opera, but she fears she may be taxing you. I have undertaken to clear up the little difficulty. If, for any reason, it will tax you, decline, without any hesitation, but if it will not, consider yourself already invited and drop me a note."

The Senator was one of the best conversational outlets she had during her years in the White House. He shared with her some of his correspondence with celebrities abroad. He was better known in the drawing rooms of British peers than he was in his own country. During his years abroad after his caning in the Senate he was a popular figure at the British court, and he worked hard to keep Britain from backing the Confederacy. Thanks to Mrs. Lincoln, he was able to say: "This is the first administration in which I have ever felt disposed to visit *the house* and I consider it a privilege."

Mary showed herself at her best in her letters to Sumner, covering a wide range of subjects, from their mutual abolition interests to music, books, poets, artists, and the conduct of the war. "And that cold & haughty looking man of the world would insist upon my telling him all the news & we would have such frequent & delightful conversations & often late in the evening—my darling husband would join us & they would laugh together, like *two* school boys," Mary wrote.

Few who knew Lincoln and Sumner well could imagine them in this hilarious juxtaposition, but at least some sympathy had been created between them by Mary. Sumner was the epitome of style in attire and looks. Women liked to have him in their drawing rooms but they did not warm to him. His *objets d'art* and fine cuisine made an evening at his house a notable event, but the lavish ease and more relaxed spirit at Seward's were preferred by the truly worldly.

Even with Sumner Mary got into a tangle when she sought his influence to keep General Nathaniel P. Banks from landing a Cabinet post. The likelihood of this appointment was most remote, she wrote, but her "true friends" kept writing to her deploring the possibility. General Banks was not one of the most ardent abolitionists, and she felt that he might be of more use in the battlefield. As soon as she had written the letter, Mary realized that she had made a serious mistake, and she followed it with another, apologizing for having written "so candid & as it now appears, so unnecessary a letter, as I did."

General Banks was returned to his command at New Orleans, and Mary calmed down. There was no question how she felt about him. Her attitude toward the President's generals and aides was well known in gossip-ridden Washington during wartime. At first she had many sharp exchanges with Stanton, but he never truckled to her and he won her respect in the end. She knew that he was apt to be as explosive with her husband as he was with her. He consistently refused to show favors to Mary's protégés. One time a man arrived with a card which he felt sure would get him an appointment because it was signed by Mrs. Lincoln. Stanton bluntly told him that he had found the right way to have his card torn up.

She was chagrined. It was a small favor and she felt that as the wife of the President she had the right to ask it. Stanton at this point gave her a severe dressing down, saying that if he were to make such appointments he would be striking at the "very root of confidence of the people in the government, in your husband, and you and me."

There were many later exchanges between Stanton and Mrs. Lincoln, and she felt that all too often he used a rough hand with her husband. But by 1864 she was trying to be the diplomat, and when Stanton died just after being confirmed for the Supreme Court in 1869, she wrote to a friend that she had dearly loved him and greatly appreciated the services "he rendered his country, our loved, bleeding land, during the trying rebellion."

As the summer of 1864 wore on and Mary added to her purchases on each trip to New York, her worries about the war and her family were augmented by her growing anxiety about her debts. She kept on spending at a mad rate, until finally she told Mrs. Keckley that she owed $27,000, and that if her husband did not win the election, she did not know what she would do. In addition to the furs, laces, silks, brocades and anything else that caught her fancy she had a monomania for buying expensive gloves, and one bill recorded a multiple order of eighty-four pairs. She paid $3,000 for earrings and $5,000 for a lace shawl. Friendly as she was with A. T. Stewart, he threatened at one point to sue her for her unpaid bills.

When Mrs. Keckley asked her if the President knew how much she owed, Mary exclaimed: "God, no." She explained that he knew nothing whatever about her debts, that he glanced at her rich dresses and believed that the few hundred dollars she got from him were enough to pay for them. "I must have money," she added, according to Mrs. Keckley, "more than Mr. Lincoln can spare for me. He is too honest to make a penny outside of his salary; consequently I had, and still have, no alternative but to run into debt. . . . I value his happiness too much to allow him to know anything. That is what troubles me so much. If he is re-elected, I can keep him in ignorance of my affairs; but if he is defeated, then the bills will be sent in, and he will know all."

Mrs. Lincoln collapsed in hysteria at this point in their conversation, but Mrs. Keckley was already very familiar with her *mea culpa* moods. At heart Mary seemed to feel that Republican friends would find a way out for her, but as election time approached, she had reason to believe that her husband's enemies were going to use this weapon against him. Major French wrote to Pamela on September 4, 1864, that the Democrats were "getting up something in which they intend to show up Madame Lincoln." The major added that he was glad he knew no more of her doings than anyone else, and he thought that an appeal to the people to frown upon "such ungallant and mean conduct as an attack on a woman to injure her husband" would be met with a curse on the "movers and dogetters up of the *vile slander....*"

Major French was not wrong in his apprehension. The *Illinois State Register* of October 30, 1864, ran an article "All About the Domestic Economy of the White House," in which she was described as the most talked-about woman in America because of her ostentatious buying—the best Inverness tapestries, the handsomest barouche and ponies, the best furniture and upholstery, and "clothing herself in the rich material of the country."

It hurt Mary to the quick to be described as a "coarse, vain, unamiable woman," tolerated only as the wife of the Chief Magistrate, and with less taste than any other woman in the land, one who failed to distinguish the *grand monde* from the *demimonde*, who had no conception of dignity and had all the peevishness of a baseless parvenu.

The attack went on without abatement. She had established the barefaced adventurer Chevalier Wikoff as the first gentleman of the nation. The wives of certain journalists, "not in the best esteem," had become her "gossipists" and companions. "She introduced sensationalism into the White House economy; courted low company in her innocence of what was superior, and forgetting that her husband's rank made her the head of her sex, desired more tangible token that this was so."

The writer accused her of trying to eclipse the great dinners given by Kate Chase, forgetting that the President's wife should acknowledge no rivals. Anyone visiting Washington could see her "seven times a day on Pennsylvania Avenue," and those who didn't had easy access to a photograph showing a "sallow, fleshy, uninteresting woman in white laces, & wearing a band of white flowers about her forehead, like some overgrown Ophelia."

The final wound was that she had "shamed the country" with her famous ball in the midst of battle anguish. "Only the death of her little boy could bring this vain and foolish woman to her senses; for a time she scandalized the nation no longer."

This was an attack without parallel in the history of presidents' wives—even more cruel and far-reaching than the defamation of Rachel Jackson. The heat intensified before the President's renomination. Early in 1864 Dr. Henry, traveling in the far West, learned that a program had been planned by Chase supporters and the most radical abolitionists to disparage Lincoln by the "circulation of scandalous libels over the Country against him and his accomplished Lady." Leaflets had been distributed by special agents to tie in with the fierce attacks on Mrs. Lincoln in the press. In this connection Dr. Henry gave his own estimate of Mary: "I have known Mrs. Lincoln since her childhood up, and I can truly say that I regard it as an outrage upon all propriety and common decency to continue men in office who use their position and influence continually to depreciate the President and his family."

Making all allowance for Dr. Henry's personal devotion and indebtedness to the Lincolns, others shared his views, and Major French believed that some of the leading ladies in the Republican Party were directly responsible for the attacks on Mrs. Lincoln. Mary had no doubt of this herself, and five years later, in a letter to Mrs. James Orne, she wrote: "All that I ever did was actuated by the purest motives, but where there are designing wicked men & I truly may say women—such acts are so often misinterpreted—a Deep interest in my idolized husband & Country alone caused me—ever to trouble myself, about other than womanly matters."

When Mary spoke of the women who had harmed her, she was well aware of the degree to which they had been the scandal mongers and gossips. The New York *Herald* again came to her defense, as it had at the time of the Wikoff scandal, when it charged that the "abolitionist party, unable to offset the permanent dissolution of the Union, or to mould the President to their detestable purposes, deliberately heaped insults upon the President's wife."

Lincoln had moved too slowly for their taste in issuing the Emancipation Proclamation. And Mrs. Swisshelm pointed out that Mrs. Lincoln "urged him to Emancipation, as a matter of right, long before he saw it as a matter of necessity." But the sum of her sins seemed to have reached its peak in the year her husband came up for reelection, and the fusillade continued, helped along by Mrs. Lincoln's ill-judged indiscretions on her shopping trips to New York. There she was exposed to the Copperheads who were powerful in the city government, and she had inexplicable dealings with Abram Wakeman, whom President Lincoln had appointed Postmaster and Surveyor of the Port of New York. He was a devoted follower of the powerful Republican politician and publisher, Thurlow Weed, and since he had worked for her husband's reelection, he was in high favor with Mrs. Lincoln. With her passion for correspondence she wrote him some letters with cryptic political allusions that were to prove intensely embarrassing to her after the President's assassination.

Welles expressed distrust of Wakeman in his diary, commenting that he was affable, insinuating and pleasant but not reliable, a politician who thought that the end justified the means, and Mary apparently made use of him to further her husband's interests. He had ingratiating manners and was one of the flatterers who had succeeded in making an impression on her.

The New York politicians who always welcomed her on her trips East not only showered gifts on her but helped her pay some of her debts, even before the President's death. Most of her wild buying had been done in New York, and she was frank in her admission to Mrs. Keckley that she had used some unscrupulous characters to work for Mr. Lincoln's reelection but that she had fully intended to drop them afterward.

The degree of Mary's culpability was never made clear. The President's expedient when the situation thickened around him was to say in a quiet tone that his wife was ill. None knew better than he how true this was, and how much it explained. Dr. Evans concluded years later that the constant character destruction and abuse were major factors in Mrs. Lincoln's collapse. They were more than her unstable nature could absorb. The President, subjected constantly to attack, let it roll off his back while he concentrated on the great business of the hour. But to Mary it was daily death, and she was deeply anxious when election day arrived. "I don't know how I would bear up under defeat," she wrote to Mrs. Shearer.

November 9, 1864, was a gray rainy day, and Noah Brooks found Lincoln all by himself at noon and the mansion quiet and deserted. At seven in the evening the President and John Hay crossed the White House grounds in a downpour to follow the election returns in the telegraph office of the War Department. The early reports were sent back to Mary, who, according to Lincoln, was more anxious than he was. By midnight the outcome seemed assured. At two in the morning a crowd gathered outside to serenade Mr. Lincoln.

The night had been one of anxiety and depression for Mary, but she did not lose hope that her husband would be reelected. She listened thoughtfully when he spoke briefly from a White House window, but after she had heard him giving thanks to the Almighty for "this evidence of the people's resolution to stand by free government and the rights of humanity," she said to Mrs. Keckley: "Poor Mr. Lincoln is looking so broken-hearted, so completely worn out, I fear he will not last through the next four years."

But this mood passed, and her husband's victory made all the difference to Mary. She came out of the doldrums and was her old spirited self as she wrote to Springfield friends that the White House had become a mecca again. She felt she could smile and be cheerful over the triumph of their party, and she assured them that, notwithstanding the great distinction conferred on Mr. Lincoln, he would "ever remain true to his friends and interested in all that concerns them."

There was still much to be done. The war had yet to be won. It was usually eleven in the evening before the President came in, weary and preoccupied. Whatever his thoughts, Mary had a renewed consciousness of the power and the glory that might still be hers. She had learned much in the preceding four years, and she planned to do better and to function with more diplomacy in the term to come. Her dread of exposure over her debts had subsided, and she ordered a $2,000 gown for the second inaugural ball.

XVI

Peace at Last

A T FORTY-SIX Mrs. Lincoln radiated some of her early vivacity in public as 1865 dawned and the end of the war seemed to be in sight. The effect was forced, however, and her laughter had lost its gaiety, for, like her husband, she had aged and changed during the four years of war and both were profoundly tired. The final move had yet to be made. The South fought desperately on, but Grant was closing in on Richmond.

Mary looked more matronly than ever, and her features sagged in the downward droop of suffering. The flicker of fear that had come and gone in her eyes since Willie's death was now as evident as her husband's well-known look of abstraction. But she waved her fan and showed a gushing air of interest as she coped with the generals, admirals, diplomats, war correspondents and other guests who gathered at the White House on New Year's Day. Their attention now was focused on the tall and weary man of fifty-six who was so closely linked to the sufferings they had endured, to the loss of men, and the agony of civil war.

Where he had once seemed a stranger out of the Middle West, awkward, boorish, unique in looks and attire, they now regarded him with liking and respect, except for the dissident elements that still abounded. In slow and difficult ways he had wrought a miracle, and even his wife's oddities were forgiven in the glow of hope and goodwill. She had learned a lesson in these bitter years and she met them all with a more conciliatory air. There were a few now who gave her credit for her well-established loyalty to her husband's cause in spite of her Southern ties. And there were many who sympathized with her over her family sorrows. Mourning and suffering had become a way of life that they all understood as the war neared its end. Their emptied homes, their wounded survivors, their broken lives had changed the face of the world for many.

However they felt, they all knew now that they would have four more years of Mary Lincoln. On the whole, men showed more gallantry and forbearance with her than the members of her own sex. Time and again they made excuses for her fluctuating moods, while their women were disposed to scorn and snub her. Lincoln's attitude toward his wife impressed itself on his closest associates. It was clear to them that he felt she was sick and needed help and support. Beyond that, they recognized her as a positive force in his life, not to be ignored, for she had the tenacity that went with her unreasonability.

The year opened with a series of entertainments, and Mrs. Lincoln appeared at each in full panoply. No one sneered any longer at her "provincialism," a false conception from the start, or at her clothes, which turned out, as photographs show, to have been the most tasteful for that era. It was true that her gowns were made of the richest silks, her laces were the best to be had, her shawls were of gossamer texture, but there was nothing strange about this. The women of the Civil War era were richly garlanded as if to offset their sorrows. Actually, most of Mrs. Lincoln's effects were comparatively modest, and her jewels were inconspicuous.

When she ordered a bonnet early in December, 1864, that was to be for "grand occasions, and I want it to be particularly stylish & rich," she was probably doing what most Presidents' wives would have done with a new term of office beginning. But every berry and leaf, every bow, loop and twist of ribbon got full press exposure.

Since these were not ordinary times, many thought that a better example might have been set at the White House. Senator Zachariah Chandler, the millionaire dry-goods merchant and landowner who was always a foe of the Lincolns, deplored the economy cuts that Mrs. Lincoln had made in the White House fare while still insisting on full-dress receptions. He wrote to his wife three times in January, 1865, saying that he was shunning Mrs. Lincoln's receptions. "If she will prepare refreshments I have no objection to a dress parade, but to fix up for nothing is in my judgment a humbug," he wrote. She was receiving in the morning and also in the afternoon, but the Lucullan repasts that had been so criticized in the days of desperate fighting were no more, and there was frank comment on the meager fare being offered at the White House. It was all in the sacrificial mood of a ravaged nation, but Elizabeth Cady Stanton wrote after a visit to the White House in 1863: "They say Abraham's shrivelled appearance & poor health is owing to being underfed. Madame is an economist & the supplies at the White House are limited."

The Marquis de Chambrun, grandson of Lafayette, writing to his mother, Marthe de Corcelle, compared Mrs. Lincoln after attending one of her receptions in the winter of 1864 to Madame Pierre de Ségur but "with this difference; she must have been pretty when young. She wore an ample silk gown. You have one very much like it. Not a single necklace, not a bracelet."

The Marquis' view of the White House entertaining in the closing days of the war was one of wonderment over the simplicity and spartan quality of the arrangements. He noticed that the small conservatory personally taken care of by Mrs. Lincoln was "simple and unpretentious like the rest." She seemed to understand his English very well and "looked pleased at what I tried to express." He commented on the regimental band playing in the "third parlor" and the simple arrangements of the Chief Executive's domain. He told Mary that he rejoiced in the success of Mr. Lincoln and the United States—"of which, at heart at least, I felt myself a citizen."

Another interested observer at the New Year's Day reception of 1865 was a visiting Briton named Edward Dicey, who was struck by the bright show of costumes that livened up the tired faces of women who had wept too much, worked too hard in hospitals, and suffered for four years. He commented on Southern wives by the side of men who were fighting the battles of the North, like the Virginia-born wife of Admiral David Farragut. He did not single out Mary Lincoln as a parallel case, but he was struck by the humility of Lincoln's manner and his courtesy to people of all kinds. His mournful expression seemed at odds with the "sparkle of dry humor in his eyes," and his smile was soft.

He found that Lincoln's "large rugged hands" had grasped his like a vine, and his "rheumy eyes beneath bushy eyebrows" seemed to go through him, yet without actually looking at him. His rough, lank, dark hair framed a wrinkled and indented face, with a stern mouth, close-set and thin-lipped and an uncommonly large nose and ears. This was how Lincoln looked to Dicey three months before his death, wearing gloves too large for him, a tall hat fluffed up with crepe, but with an air of strength, physical as well as moral, and a "strange look of dignity, coupled with all this grotesqueness."

Dicey had found the President's suit puckered up at every strategic point. It was long, tight and ill-fitting. But how did Mary view her extraordinary husband? She was constantly being reminded in cartoons and newspaper comments that he was a baboon, an ape, a gorilla, but his clumsiness had never been anything but endearing to her. His eyes rested on her with kindness or humor when they were not altogether blank and distant. His touch was as gentle with her as it was with the children when he roughed them up. He was often compared to a clumsy bear. Mary made few public comments on his appearance. To her he was always Mr. Lincoln, spoken of with respect and often with reverence, particularly after his death. She was intensely loyal to him, according to her fashion.

A painful situation developed for her early in 1865, when in the midst of festivities President Lincoln appealed to General Grant in scrupulous but unmistakable terms to find a place for Robert. Mrs. Lincoln's determined stand that he could not join the army because he must finish college carried no further weight since Robert had graduated. Criticism of the fact that he had never worn the uniform of the Union Army had embarrassed his father and hurt Robert deeply. The crisis had to be met, although everyone knew that the war was nearly over.

On January 10, 1865, the President wrote to his winning general, asking if his oldest son, without embarrassment to Grant or a detriment to the service, could go into your "military family with some nominal rank, I, and not the public, furnishing his necessary means?" He urged General Grant to refuse without the slightest hesitation if this should prove embarrassing to him. He wished him to answer the letter as though it were not from the President but from a friend. "I do not wish to put him in the ranks, nor yet to give him a commission, to which those who have already served long are better entitled, and better qualified to hold."

The President knew the criticism that a safe berth for Robert would involve. He had temporized with the issue, believing that the thought of Robert's being exposed to battle would be the last straw for Mary, who was already in the midst of a breakdown. He may or may not have had her consent when he wrote to General Grant that Robert, twenty-two and a graduate of Harvard, wished to see something of the war before it ended.

Grant took up the issue with goodwill, but he pointed out that it was only fair to Robert that he should be regularly commissioned and put on an equal footing with other officers of the same grade. He was appointed a captain and adjutant general and was attatched to General Grant's staff. Robert fitted in well and was popular with his fellow officers, never at any point expecting preferential treatment as the son of the President. But his mother chose to see mortal danger for Robert in this connection and wrote to Sumner somewhat unrealistically that "our own son, is daily participating or exposed in the battles. . . ."

He was also rapidly falling victim to the charms of Mary Eunice Harlan, daughter of Senator and Mrs. James Harlan of Iowa, who happened to be the girl he most wanted as well as the girl whom his mother had picked out for him. Stanton had made it clear to the President, if he did not already know it, that Mrs. Lincoln favored Mary above all the girls who hankered after Robert, and there were plenty. Many soon noticed that they appeared together at the crowded events of the weeks before the fall of Richmond and that they were inseparable at the time of the inauguration.

Lincoln's second inauguration bore little resemblance to the first. The clatter remained, but the glitter was gone. The nation was still at war, and men in blue and gray were dying as he took his vows. Grant was storming Petersburg. Thomas was severing Confederate communications in the West. Sheridan was riding up the Valley of the Shenandoah for the last time. Everyone wanted it to end. The mood was one of utter fatigue, and it was hard for families who had lost their men to cheer the tall, uncanny man who was still the War President. Even in the North he reminded them of pain, despair, ruined lives and amputated bodies.

The crowd that turned out was neither large nor enthusiastic. It was a pale carbon copy of the first inauguration when hopes were high. Four years of suffering and battles lost and won had tarnished the picture. Lincoln's grave face throughout the ceremonies told its own story. The day was cold and gusty, and he went alone to the Capitol to sign bills and await the moment of consecration.

Dr. Anson G. Henry, her old family friend from Springfield, rode to the Capitol with Mrs. Lincoln for the joint meeting of both houses of Congress. Senator Henry B. Anthony of Rhode Island escorted her to her place in the Diplomatic Gallery, which was rapidly filling with crinolined figures bumping their way to their seats. In spite of the rain there was a blaze of color as their glistening silks and nodding plumes made a flower garden of the dingy chamber. Some stared in Mary's direction and saw that she was becomingly gowned in blue.

She watched the parade of officialdom with an attentive eye—the Justices, governors, gold-laced diplomats with feathers, decorations and white pantaloons, and the soberly attired Cabinet members half lost in the crowded chamber. All was quiet until Andrew Johnson, pushed from behind by Hannibal Hamlin, reeled forward to be sworn in as Vice President. Startled, Mrs. Lincoln sat frozen with horror and listened to gasps going up as the ceremony proceeded. One by one, the Senators realized that Johnson was drunk. Seward gave no sign of concern, but Chase had a thunderous look of disapproval as he swore him in. Later he said that the Vice President was ill, not drunk. There was some truth in this, for he had come north from Nashville before recovering from an illness and he had taken three stiff drinks of whiskey to carry him through the ceremony. The stuffiness of the Senate Chamber had knocked him out. President Lincoln listened attentively while Johnson ranted through a speech that made no sense and finished in a loud voice: "I kiss this Book, in the face of my nation of the United States."

Characteristically, the President dismissed the incident with a kindly interpretation: "I know Andy—he'll be all right—he's no drunkard." But this scene by Johnson made a lasting impression on Mary, who was never to forget his grotesque behavior at this solemn moment in her husband's life. He had done the unforgivable in her eyes, and she was to be a bitter enemy from this time on. After this scene they all were glad to get out in the open air and to take their places on the stand at the east front of the Capitol.

A crowd fanned out into the distance and welcomed the appearance of the President with tempered applause. By chance the clouds rolled back and the sun shone on his furrowed and careworn face. Once again Kate Chase Sprague watched Lincoln being sworn in as President, this time by her father. Once again she saw Mrs. Lincoln reap the laurels. Kate watched her father, and Mary watched Lincoln as he voiced another of his brief and memorable speeches: "With malice toward none; with charity for all; with firmness in the right, as God gives us to see the right, let us strive on to finish the work we are in; to bind up the nation's wounds, to care for him who shall have borne the battle, and for his widow, and his orphan—to do all which may achieve and cherish a just and a lasting peace, among ourselves, and with all nations."

This time there was a more immediate response than to his address at Gettysburg. Even Chase conceded its strength, and Charles Francis Adams wrote to his father: "That rail-splitting lawyer is one of the wonders of the day. Not a prince or minister in all Europe could have risen to such an equality with the occasion."

As the crowd broke up, a handsome saunterer disappeared with Walter Burton, night clerk at the National and a friend of Lincoln's. This was none other than John Wilkes Booth, who had been close to the iron stand where the President took the oath and had listened thoughtfully to Lincoln's words. He had obtained a ticket to the platform through his sweetheart, Bessie Hale, and he was close enough to the President to shoot him, had this been the chosen time.

Tad sat beside his father as they drove to the White House through a straggling line of spectators. Flags whipped into strange shapes with the high gusts of wind, and Marshal Lamon had thirteen citizen aides and thirteen uniformed marshals accompany the President's carriage. Mrs. Lincoln's carriage had an escort, too, and she returned to the mansion that held no novelty for her now. It had become a house of suffering as well as of stirring events.

Chase sent her the Bible on which her husband had taken the oath, marking the page that his lips had touched, an extract from the fifth chapter of Isaiah, dealing with the wastage and desolation of war and warning against relaxing—appropriate to the moment, with the end yet to come: "None shall be weary nor stumble among them; none shall slumber nor sleep . . . whose arrows are sharp, and all their bows bent; their horses' hoofs shall be accounted as flint, and their wheels as a whirlwind."

A reception at the White House followed the inauguration, and the grounds were jammed with well-wishers. With icy hands and glazed eyes the President stood in the Blue Room, greeting his guests from eight to eleven o'clock. The Army and Navy brass not engaged in the field moved past with a quiet air of jubilation. Mrs. Lincoln put up a show of high spirits, but she watched her husband with apprehension, knowing that, ill and exhausted though he was, his thoughts were with the generals closing in from different directions on rebel forces.

The vandalism of that night reached new heights as visitors from out of town made off with souvenirs. The crimson brocade curtains of the East Room were robbed of large swatches and flower designs were meticulously cut from lace curtains. William Crook, the President's bodyguard, wrote that after the reception the White House looked as if a "regiment of rebel troops had been quartered there—with permission to forage." Crook heard the President say: "Why should they do it? How can they?"

Two nights later the inaugural ball was held—Mrs. Lincoln's last conspicuous stand on the Washington social scene. It was held in the rambling Patent Office, and four thousand guests had bought ten-dollar tickets to aid the soldiers' families. They came from all parts of the North, and as the evening wore on, there was a reckless jubilation that lasted long after the Lincolns had returned to the White House.

Mary looked her best for the ball in the white moiré gown trimmed with lace that the gossips said had cost $2,000. Her flowers were white jessamine and purple violets, and she waved a silver-spangled fan edged with ermine. The general effect was harmonious and simpler than the elaborate flower headdresses and sparkling jewels worn by many of the guests. They whirled around in waves of rustling silks, with ruches, flounces and streaming garlands. Tarlatans and delicate pastel chiffons were worn by the young, who were matronized by mature beauties with ornate coiffures, sparkling in some cases with silver and gold dust.

Sumner had been chosen to be Mrs. Lincoln's partner that night. He had decided to spurn the ball to show his disapproval of the President's reconstruction plans. But Mary had done her work well in healing the breach, and the ticket sent to him personally by the President was virtually a command to be on view. A good many eyes watched with interest the moves made by the President and Sumner on the night of the ball. Much had been made of the fact that they were on the verge of an open break, but Sumner's attitude that night fortified the impression that in spite of his opposition to Lincoln's postwar plans their personal relationship would hold firm. Sumner advocated full Congressional control in the reorganization of the South. The President stood for provisional regimes set up by the Army with humane measures in view. Sumner considered a government based on military power to be unconstitutional and not republican in form. Mrs. Lincoln thought that whatever her husband willed was right.

She looked happy and full of assurance as she marched in on the arm of the handsome Senator, immediately after the somber-faced

President, walking with Speaker Schuyler Colfax. The military bands had quieted the four thousand guests with "Hail Columbia" as they appeared and the way was cleared for them. After the promenade the Lincolns were led to the dais, where they sat on a blue and gold sofa in the great hall that had served as a hospital two years earlier and now reflected the spirit of victory, with flags and insignia that transformed its bleak interior.

Kate Chase Sprague, *enceinte* and feeling ill, did not dance that night, but the handsomest men gathered around her as she watched Mrs. Lincoln presiding on the dais. Chase, a majestic presence at all of Mary's receptions, was still the enemy, although his bland face and noble features gave no clue to what he might have been thinking. His manners to Mrs. Lincoln were always as flawless as they were to Mrs. Stephen Douglas and other favorites in the President's circle.

Mary, looking at slim, wiry Seward, was not unaware of the prestige that he had brought to her husband's administration abroad; nevertheless she hoped that he was on his way out. He had been much less her friend than Sumner, who, after accompanying her in the promenade, decided to leave when they reached the dais, until the President urged him to stay. Sumner, with an uncharacteristic touch of modesty, said that the crowds were interested in seeing only Mr. Lincoln. He escorted Mrs. Lincoln in to supper, and the four stayed until shortly after midnight.

There were many commentators on hand that night to observe what happened in the crowded corridors, in the supper room, and on the ballroom floor. Mrs. E. F. Ellet and Ben: Perley Poore found their way through swaying crinolines and battle-seasoned swords to take notes on the Cabinet members, Justices, generals, diplomats and plain citizens from different states who promenaded in the corridors. Robert Lincoln had arrived from Petersburg in uniform, and there was free comment that at last he was a soldier, even though he was attached only to General Grant's staff. He looked at ease in the blue of the Union Army as he danced most of the evening with Mary Harlan, leading her smoothly through the schottische, lancers and polka.

The banquet ordered for the ball was not on the magnificent scale of four years earlier. Too much hardship, deprivation and suffering had intervened, but Balzer, the confectioner, provided some spun-sugar conceits involving frigates and forts, admiral's hats and ironclads. Tables holding three hundred at a sitting were lavishly

Courtesy, Parks Department of Kentucky

The Mary Todd house on West Main Street, Lexington, Kentucky, as it looks today. Although run-down and neglected for many years, it has come under consideration recently as a possible historical landmark. It was a social center in the time of Robert Smith Todd, Mary's father, and after her marriage Abraham Lincoln visited it on three separate occasions. Although Mary was born in a house on West Short Street, no longer standing, her childhood and most of her teen-age years were spent at this house on West Main Street. A plaque in front of the house and a marker draw attention today to the fact that this was the early home of Mary Todd Lincoln. In her time the L-shaped house, more spacious than it looks, had a garden, a meandering stream and stables in the rear.

Century Magazine *1887*

Ninian W. Edwards' mansion in Springfield, Illinois, where Mary Todd and Abraham Lincoln were married in November, 1842. Torrential rains pelted the house, where she had been a belle at countless parties. The chill air of her family's disapproval did not discourage Mary as Lincoln fumblingly slipped on her finger the wedding ring inscribed "Love Is Eternal."

Harper's Weekly, *November 26, 1864*

Lincoln's house in Springfield as it looked at the time of the Civil War.

Mary Todd Lincoln and Abraham Lincoln in the early days of their marriage. These are the earliest known pictures of this famous pair, and Mrs. Charles Isham, granddaughter of President Lincoln, gave them to the Library of Congress in 1937. The daguerreotype of Mrs. Lincoln has since been given to the White House. Lloyd Ostendorf, in *The Photographs of Mary Todd Lincoln,* credits these two daguerreotypes to Nicholas H. Shepherd of Springfield. He gives their likely date as 1846, when Mary was twenty-eight and the mother of two sons. Robert Lincoln recalled that they always hung in his home. Mary was heard to say of them in 1860: "They are very precious to me, taken when we were young and so desperately in love."

Mrs. Lincoln in 1861 as her reign in the White House began. This was one of two poses for Mathew Brady, and she is wearing one of her most elaborate gowns, now on view in the Illinois State Historical Library in Springfield.

Mary Todd Lincoln in January, 1862. Another pose by Mathew B. Brady, showing one of the nosegays she invariably carried, and her love of stripes. She was wearing a black-and-white striped dress in the theater box at Ford's on the night the President was assassinated.

Mary Lincoln [signature]

National Life Foundation,
Fort Wayne, Indiana

One of Mrs. Lincoln's favorite pictures because it was much touched up and it slimmed her considerably. Mathew B. Brady took it, possibly in February, 1861. It is one of the rare instances in which she signed a picture.

This picture of Mary Lincoln is supposed to have been taken at the time her husband became President. The name of the photographer is unknown, but the simple collar and headdress correspond with the costume she was described as wearing at the notification ceremonies in Springfield before the Lincolns left for Washington.

National Life Foundation,
Fort Wayne, Indiana

Tad Lincoln, who liked to play soldier, in the uniform Secretary of War Edwin M. Stanton permitted him to wear.

Robert T. Lincoln, Mary Lincoln's oldest son, at the time of his father's inauguration as President of the United States.

Mrs. Lincoln with her sons, Willie and Tad, as they prepared to go to Washington and the White House. Lloyd Ostendorf credits this photograph, which is in the Illinois State Historical Library, to Preston Butler and deduces that it was probably taken in November, 1860.

Emilie Todd after the death of her husband, Ben Hardin Helm, at Chickamauga. The President gave her shelter at the White House, but her presence there led to stories that Mrs. Lincoln was harboring rebels. She refused to take the oath of allegiance and returned to the South, but she and Mary were always devoted half sisters.

Young Ben Hardin Helm, a West Pointer who refused Abraham Lincoln's offer of a commission to fight for the North, casting his lot with the Confederate forces and dying a brigadier general at Chickamauga. His wife, Emilie, Mary Todd Lincoln's favorite half sister, was immovable in her allegiance to the South and turned against the President, to whom she had been devoted.

Major General Edward O. Ord with his wife and daught Mrs. Ord inadvertently arous Mrs. Lincoln's jealousy wh Mary thought that she was ridi by the President's side at a m itary review of the Army of t James in March, 1865. M Lincoln created a public sce using such abusive language t Mrs. Ord burst into tears. La Mary tried to persuade the Pr dent to remove General C from his command, and s sulked for days until the sto died down.

National Archives

Mrs. Elizabeth Keckley, the n latto who was Mrs. Lincol seamstress, friend and confidar during the Civil War years. former slave, she influenced M Lincoln in the antislavery bat but lost her friendship forev when she wrote *Behind t Scenes,* a book filled with st tling revelations about the Li coln family.

Daguerreotype by
Nicholas H. Shepherd
Lloyd Ostendorf Collection
Dayton, Ohio

Mrs. Mary Todd Lincoln in January, 1862, just before the death of her son Willie. The low décolletage, the ruffles and flowers all are characteristic of the First Lady's attire.

By Mathew B. Brady.
Print from National Life Foundation,
Fort Wayne Indiana

Mrs. Lincoln in 1863, now saddened and in mourning for Willie, who died in 1862. She is wearing the typical mourning jewelry of the era, and she insisted on the finest and richest silks in all her mourning attire.

National Life Foundation,
Fort Wayne, Indiana

Emilie Todd (Mrs. Ben Hardin Helm), half sister of Mary Todd Lincoln and a favorite of Abraham Lincoln, who called her Little Sister. Spirited and intelligent, she discerned Mary's rising dementia after Willie's death.

Courtesy, Mrs. Joseph H. Murphy, from William Townsend's collection of family pictures

Mrs. Jefferson Davis, whose characteristics and sorrows paralleled Mrs. Lincoln's in some respects. Both were ambitious women, criticized for pretension, extravagance and interfering in political affairs in the struggle between North and South. Both lost young sons while the war was in progress. When Mrs. Lincoln entered Richmond as the war ended, she visited the Jefferson Davis house and saw where Varina had given her famous parties.

From author's collection

Mrs. Ulysses S. Grant found it difficult to maintain friendly relations with Mrs. Lincoln, who considered her husband a "butcher" and constantly assailed him for the heavy death toll of the battles he fought. Mrs. Grant witnessed some of Mrs. Lincoln's most hysterical scenes in the closing days of the war, and she considered her a sick woman.

Engraving by Samuel Sartain

Mrs. Lincoln to Mrs. James W. (Rhoda) White, Altoona, Pennsylvania, August 19, 1868

In this partial letter Mrs. Lincoln tells of her intention to attend Robert's wedding (the son who had her declared insane) and her dread of paying her first visit to Washington since the

Kate Chase (Mrs. William Sprague), daughter of Salmon Portland Chase, Secretary of the Treasury in Lincoln's Cabinet. She and Mrs. Lincoln had one of the most sustained and discussed feuds in White House social history. The beautiful Kate schemed constantly to have her father become President. Mrs. Lincoln snubbed her openly and all Washington discussed this situation, but Lincoln attended Kate's marriage alone, just before he made his Gettysburg speech in 1863.

Book Buyer, *1867 Picture Collection New York Public Library*

Charles Sumner, the Senator from Massachusetts who campaigned ceaselessly for abolition, was the man most admired by Mary Todd Lincoln aside from her husband. He shared her cultural interests, influenced her political views, and was one of the favored "courtiers" at the White House during the war years. After her husband's assassination he led the fight in the Senate for a pension for Mrs. Lincoln, defending and championing her. They corresponded, exchanged books and flowers and had much in common.

Harper's Black and White Prints, *1882*

Mary Todd Lincoln around 1869, showing the change in her after the President's assassination. Herndon's revelations had just shaken her, and she was about to escape to Europe.

This curious picture of Mrs. Lincoln is believed to have been taken in 1872. One of the spiritualists whose séances she attended is thought to have had a hand in its production, since there is a shadowy image (supposedly of Lincoln) in the background, with a hand on Mary's shoulder. She was ill and distraught at the time, and no one could persuade her that the picture was a fake.

stocked with beef, veal, game, poultry, smoked meats, oysters, terrapin, salads, jellies, ices, tarts, cakes, fruits, nuts, coffee and chocolate. A sugar model of the Capitol with a historical panorama from 1776 to Fort Sumter featuring both Army and Navy, was much admired until it began to dissolve on its pedestal in the shambles that ensued.

Instead of going to the tables in sequence, the crowd literally charged at the refreshments, wolfing down food, carrying off legs of lamb to be eaten in alcoves, nibbling at the sugar horse and throwing the admiral's hat in the air. The Ship of State vanished inch by inch, but the Capitol held its own. Glasses were smashed. The marble floor was littered with pulp and debris. The hilarity grew as the night wore on, and some of the inebriates lay down to sleep it off. Laces and silks were torn in the free-for-all, and mild Noah Brooks, who wrote that the ball was a handsome affair, added that its "beauty was marred by the extraordinary rush of hungry people, who fairly mobbed the supper-tables, and enacted a scene of confusion whose wildness was similiar to some of the antics of the Paris Commune."

The Lincolns wakened to another day of stress and strain. Mary was worried about her husband's fatigue, and she was determined to get him away for a change of scene before he collapsed altogether. On March 23 she wrote to Sumner, saying that they were leaving for City Point, Virginia. She hoped that rest and a change of air would benefit her "good Husband's health." But the fact was that Mrs. Lincoln herself was in a deeply disturbed state and the public scenes she made between inauguration day and her husband's assassination were the most exaggerated in her history. To some of them there were witnesses, including General Sherman, who would be slow to speak ill of Mary Lincoln.

Much of it was rooted in jealousy, and it was all part of her neurotic, possessive nature. It seemed absurd to those who knew the Lincolns, since no wife ever had less need for concern on the subject of her husband's faithfulness. Women flocked around him at army encampments and public functions in the tradition of the Civil War era, and many beauties did their flattering best to engage his interest. But being flirtatious with Abraham Lincoln was a task at which Mary alone was successful: He was not averse to giving a casual kiss to a girl who dashed at him in a crowd. He could roughhouse and tease, but he was not like the gallants around him—Seward, Sumner and Chase—all of whom knew how to interest and flatter women. He had no small talk, his height and manner could be forbidding, and he was so absorbed in the problems of war that the only women he studied with real affection were Mary and some of her relatives. The intense desire for warm relationships with women that he had shown before his marriage had diminished in the long years of affection that she had lavished on him.

But Mary's pride was involved in the outbursts of March and April, when she and her husband were on display on several trips they took to City Point on the *River Queen*. Tad enjoyed the excitement of these river trips. Their boat was anchored under the bluff where General Grant had his headquarters. The President went ashore frequently and walked up the hill to headquarters, sometimes picking flowers for Tad on the way and once swinging an ax. Jesse Grant, the rebel son of the famed Ulysses, usually played host to Tad, but he deplored Tad's poor horsemanship when he refused to ride a horse named Jeff. The general then decreed that Jesse should ride the horse while Tad was mounted on Rebbie. Jeff bolted, and both Grant and Lincoln went in pursuit of the boys, whose horses wound up in the corral.

While her men went up the hill, Mrs. Lincoln usually stayed on the *River Queen,* but Tad was kept busy running back and forth with messages between the President and his wife. Mrs. Grant called on Mrs. Lincoln on her first visit to City Point, but the two women were discordant from the start. Mrs. Lincoln was in one of her depressed moods, and the story spread rapidly that when Mrs. Grant sat beside her on a sofa, she said: "How dare you?"

In later years Mrs. Grant brushed off this incident by explaining that she had risen of her own accord when she felt that she was crowding Mrs. Lincoln. But Mrs. Emma Dent Casey, Mrs. Grant's sister, would not hold her peace and often said that Julia was outraged because Mrs. Lincoln had expected her to back out of the room and to treat her like royalty. This seems unlikely, since Mrs. Lincoln had long been hostess to the wives of generals, and at no time had this been true, in spite of the sneering references to the First Lady's Court.

Adam Badeau, a Huguenot still limping from his war wounds, felt that the ladies around Mrs. Lincoln were disposed to patronize modest Mrs. Grant. But no one could go far with that, since her retiring manner was deceptive. She was schooled in all the social usages and held her own in an inconspicuous way. Her intimates knew that she had a sprightly wit and was shrewd, particularly where her husband's interests were concerned. Although Mrs. Lincoln never warmed to her, most of the other women in the official circle were impressed with her candor and goodwill. Since she was cross-eyed and had become dumpy in middle age, she was too plain to arouse envy, too devoted to her family to incur gossip, and her comments were never stinging or hurtful.

There is a great deal of evidence, however, that Mrs. Lincoln was haughty with Mrs. Grant and openly showed her dislike of the general's wife. Two incidents in March, 1865, fanned the blaze, and Julia witnessed the most appalling public incidents in Mrs. Lincoln's wartime history. In later years she always spoke kindly of the President's wife as a sick woman, but Mary was unrelenting.

The first outburst came on March 23 when the President planned a visit to the front, but General Grant thought this too dangerous. As the fighting subsided, however, a special train was prepared and the wives had their closest glimpse of war. Colonel Horace Porter, who was with them, described the roadbed as being like a corrugated washboard. The wounded and the dead lay along the tracks in the vicinity of Fort Stedman, and gray and blue uniforms were tangled together in a gory glimpse of war.

The sight upset Mrs. Lincoln, who was out of sorts that day. This was war at firsthand. Since the military railroad went only partway, the men mounted horses and rode the rest of the way. Mrs. Lincoln and Mrs. Grant traveled in a converted ambulance that was like a half-open carriage. They bumped along over a road rough with the uneven trunks of small trees. Mrs. Lincoln grew impatient, fearing they would be late for the review they planned to attend. She urged Colonel Porter to speed things up, but this resulted in gobbets of mud being flung on them, while they were jolted from their seats. Their heads hit the top of the ambulance, and Mrs. Lincoln seemed slightly dazed.

Colonel Porter chose to think that what happened after that was due to the bump she had received. He decided that it had probably triggered off one of her devastating headaches. Adam Badeau, who also rode with them, took a more critical view of things. He sat on the front seat facing Mrs. Lincoln and Mrs. Grant, and he started the rumpus by announcing that all officers' wives had been ordered to the rear except the wife of General Charles Griffin, who had obtained a special permit from the President to remain.

"What do you mean by that, sir?" Mrs. Lincoln exclaimed excitedly. "Do you mean to say that she saw the President alone? Do you know that I never allow the President to see any woman alone?"

Mrs. Lincoln was so distraught that she insisted on getting out of the carriage immediately. When the driver did not stop, she leaned forward and pinioned his arms, with Mrs. Grant and Badeau trying to calm her. Finally Julia persuaded her to settle down, and they bounced along unhappily to their destination. They were met by General Meade, who took charge with instinctive diplomacy when he saw that the President's wife was upset.

By the time she returned to the carriage she had recovered her poise, and she explained that she had been assured that the Secretary of War and not Mr. Lincoln had given the permit. Mrs. Griffin, one of the great beauties of Washington, was a Carroll, who would eventually become Countess Esterhazy, well-known on both sides of the Atlantic.

Mrs. Grant was so concerned about the day's events and the unreasonability shown by Mrs. Lincoln that she urged Badeau that night to say nothing to anyone about the incident. She said she would keep quiet about it, too, except to tell General Grant what had happened. But Badeau felt released from his vow when a second and more public row developed almost immediately afterward, this time at a review of the segment of the Army of the James commanded by Major General Edward O. C. Ord.

The headquarters party set out from City Point early in the morning for the event, and on landing, Lincoln, Grant and Ord rode several miles to the reviewing grounds. Again the two women rode by ambulance, with Porter and Badeau. They crawled along because of the muddy, bumpy road and various delays along the way. Mrs. Lincoln again showed mounting worry about being late and she wanted the horses to speed up, but she was persuaded that this would do little good under such conditions.

The review was already in progress when they reached the field. The men had been held past their dinner hour, so orders had been given for the bands to play and the cavalcade to move. Mrs. Ord, a beauty and a notable horsewoman, had been assigned to wait for Mrs. Lincoln and Mrs. Grant. When they failed to appear, she asked a staff officer if she should accompany the cavalcade and he said: "Of course, come along." Mrs. Ord took her place in the reviewing column, and from a distance it looked as if she were riding with the President, or so Mrs. Lincoln thought when the ambulance arrived as the reviewing party was halfway down the line. Major Seward, a nephew of the Secretary of State, did not help matters when he rode up to the carriage and remarked jestingly, "The President's horse is very gallant, Mrs. Lincoln. He insists on riding by the side of Mrs. Ord."

"What do you mean by that, sir?" she demanded, and the young officer rode off hastily after catching the look of angry terror in Mary's eyes.

Mrs. Ord's warm greeting to the two women when she was able to join them was met with a storm of abuse by Mrs. Lincoln. According to Badeau, she "called her vile names in the presence of a crowd of officers, and asked her what she meant by following up the President."

Stunned by the attack, Mrs. Ord burst into tears, but Mrs. Lincoln ranted on. Mrs. Grant, who happened to be fond of the commanding officer's wife, defended her as well as she could and tried to stop Mrs. Lincoln's outburst. Mary promptly turned on her and remarked sarcastically: "I suppose you think you'll get to the White House yourself, don't you?"

Badeau described Mrs. Grant as taking it all with quiet dignity saying only that she was quite satisfied with her position and that it was more than she had ever expected to attain. Mrs. Lincoln had the last word: "Oh, you had better take it if you can get it. 'Tis very nice."

She was in such a state of excitement that the men feared she would jump out of the ambulance and interrupt the cavalcade. Mrs. Grant finally froze into silence. It was a painful situation, with Mrs. Lincoln believing that some of the troops might have mistaken Mrs. Ord for her. Actually, they were quite unconscious of the fierce battle raging around the ambulance, but it was overheard by a number of officers and the word spread quickly that the President's wife was on a rampage. Her ill humor continued through the day. Mrs. Ord rode back to headquarters at City Point with Captain John S. Barnes, commander of the *Bat,* and some fellow officers.

The Grants were hosts to the Lincolns on the *River Queen* that night, and at dinner Mrs. Lincoln peremptorily told General Grant that he should remove General Ord. The general defended Ord and looked with some concern at the President's wife. He realized that something was desperately wrong with her. Captain Barnes was sure of it when he was summoned to the upper saloon after dinner, where the Lincolns were discussing the incident. He was asked to give his view of what had happened. The President was assuring his wife that he had scarcely noticed Mrs. Ord, but Mrs. Lincoln turned to

Barnes to support her story. He promptly gave a firsthand account of what he had seen and heard, without taking sides.

Mrs. Grant had a way of pretending that she was jealous when women fluttered around Ulysses at camp, but it was pure badinage with Julia and had none of the pathological aspects of Mrs. Lincoln's possessive frenzy. Mrs. Stanton had flatly announced that she would not visit the White House or have anything to do with Mrs. Lincoln, but Mrs. Grant was sage enough to keep the peace. Both she and her husband could see from the President's stricken face when he talked of his sick wife how deep the tragedy was. It seemed to the idolatrous Badeau that Lincoln "bore it as Christ might have done, with an expression of pain and sadness that cut one to the heart."

But Army life moved on, and the disordered fancies of an ailing wife were lost in the excitement of General Sherman's arrival at City Point fresh from his victory in the South. Grant had invited several top officers to meet him, and they all listened attentively to his report of the famous march through Georgia. He described himself unabashedly as the "vandal chief" and thought the parallel just that the people of the South should regard him "as the Romans did the Goths."

Grant and Sherman paid a formal call on President Lincoln, and on their return Mrs. Grant asked him how Mrs. Lincoln was. Neither one had thought to inquire, and Sherman had not even known that she was on the boat with the President. They said they would do better when they called the next day, but again she was not on view. Lincoln went to her stateroom to see if she would receive them, but he came back with an air of failure and regret. He asked them to excuse her, for she was feeling far from well.

But her feud with Mrs. Grant went on, and Barnes was involved in it again when Robert Lincoln invited him to accompany them on an excursion to Point of Rocks. He found Julia sitting alone in the forward cabin while Mrs. Lincoln stood on the uncovered deck, close to the pilot house. When Mrs. Grant suggested that he push an upholstered chair through the cabin door so that Mary could sit down and rest, the distraught woman ignored his good morning and refused the chair.

A few minutes later she summoned Mrs. Grant to her side and told her that Barnes must be asked to leave the boat. When the Lincolns landed at Point of Rocks and went rambling in the woods, picking flowers, Mrs. Grant stayed behind and helped Barnes get off on the other side of the river. He galloped back to City Point from there, and Robert's scheme to bring peace between his mother and Barnes had failed.

But this did not ease the situation between two of America's most notable ladies as the day of victory approached. From this point on, the *River Queen* and the *Martin* came to be known respectively as Mrs. Lincoln's boat and Mrs. Grant's boat. The captains had a hard time maneuvering their craft to suit everyone involved. Orders crisscrossed, and Mrs. Lincoln had her husband's support in believing that the President's boat should be closest to the dock. She would not go ashore if she had to cross the *Martin* to get off. This meant that at times the Grant boat had to be shoved out into the river so that Mrs. Lincoln could be sure of the inside track.

The observant Barnes said that the President and General Grant ignored their wives' silly antics, which went on until Mrs. Lincoln left suddenly for Washington. Tad stayed with his father at City Point. No reason was given at the time for her departure, but she later said that the President had had a dream that Washington had burned up and it had so disturbed him that he wanted her to go up the river and see that things were all right. There was speculation that he was trying to ease an impossible situation, but his tendency to have strange dreams was a well-known fact, and his worries at the moment were intense.

He telegraphed Stanton to have the coachman meet her at the wharf on April 2, and Major General Carl Schurz, who by chance traveled on the boat with her, found her in a perfectly normal mood. Unconscious of the storm she had just been through, he wrote to his wife: "The first lady was overwhelmingly charming to me; she chided me for not visiting her, overpowered me with invitations, and finally had me driven to my hotel in her own state carriage." He had found her an "astounding person," he wrote, and had learned more state secrets from her in a few hours than he could otherwise have done in a year.

Mrs. Lincoln seemed to be herself again when she telegraphed her husband that she had landed safely and that all was well. She was already anxious to get back to City Point, and her message was as loving as usual: "Miss Taddie & yourself very much—perhaps, may return with a little party on Wednesday—give me all the news."

The news that came through was stupendous. The President had already sent her two telegrams that told her of Grant's envelopment of Petersburg. Clearly the end was at hand. He assured her that he would be glad to see her on her return and that he and Tad were well.

Mary's spirits soared in their volatile way, and she rounded up friends to accompany her back to City Point. Sumner was one, and she assured him that a proclamation might be issued within the next two weeks. "There is no such word as fail *now!*" she added. The Harlans were in the group so that Mary could be close to Robert in the final hours of the war. And Lizzie Keckley, who came from near Petersburg, asked to be with Mrs. Lincoln on the day of victory. On the way Mary sent a message to the President from Fort Monroe urging him to stay at City Point until they arrived. "We have several friends & would prefer seeing you & returning in your boat, as we are not comfortable here," she telegraphed.

When a message came that Seward had been seriously injured in a carriage accident, Mrs. Lincoln considered turning back, but Sumner decided against this when word came that, although badly hurt, he would recover. On their arrival at City Point Mrs. Lincoln was very upset to find that the President and Tad had entered Richmond without her.

It was a quiet arrival through a veil of smoke. The day was warm, the streets were dusty, the air was acrid and choking. The President, holding Tad by the hand, fanned his sweating face as he looked around the conquered capital and saw that the streets were filled with blacks. Few white people were in sight. Both the North and the South had suffered too much for jubilation or demonstration at this particular moment.

The President went straight to the Executive Mansion and seated himself at Jefferson Davis's desk. Within a matter of hours this historic house had become the headquarters of General Godfrey Weitzel, in command of the federal troops. The Davises were already fugitives heading for nowhere, half forgotten in the crash of their empire. Varina Davis was traveling along the back roads of Georgia with her children, including Winnie, later to be known as the Daughter of the Confederacy, who was born as the guns pounded at Petersburg.

Mrs. Lincoln was not to be denied an entry of her own, so the entire party from the *River Queen* proceeded to Richmond, with Mary still showing signs of distress that her husband had not waited for her. Her anger flashed when a young officer jestingly told her that some "pretty young ladies" had made a fuss over him in

Richmond. Her arrival on the scene was wholly different from the President's first entrance. She and her party had a cavalry escort, and the blacks clustered in the streets looked with interest at their savior's wife. They had heard much of her zeal in their cause, and Sumner was their ally. As the day wore on, gloom turned to revelry and Mrs. Lincoln noted that "even our stately, dignified Mr. Sumner acknowledged himself transformed into a lad of sixteen."

Mary took stock of the "banquet halls of Jeff Davis" which now looked "sad and deserted." She expressed the hope that the traitors would meet the doom "which a just Heaven ever awards the transgressor," but she must have viewed Varina Davis' surroundings with some curiosity. Both were highly intelligent women, deeply devoted to their husbands and children. They shared many characteristics and mutual history. The sum of Varina's woes had almost equaled Mary's and in a sense resembled them. But both had the inestimable gift of tenderness and understanding from the men to whom they were married. When Mary Lincoln lost this enveloping support, her life collapsed. Varina, stronger and more resilient by nature, had a quarter of a century more to pass with Jefferson Davis.

Mary, moving through the stately rooms in which so many Confederate parties had been staged, must have felt the echoes, for she was well aware that Mrs. Davis had suffered from much the same kind of criticism that she had endured. Varina was frank in her estimate of the Confederate generals and was feared by many of them. She was accused of being friendly to the North, of harboring spies in her home, of feasting while others starved, of pretentious ways, of nepotism, of extravagant entertaining and of meddling in political and military affairs.

She was disliked by many of the Confederate women and admired by their men for her intelligence and political understanding. Some of the stories told about her were true; many were not. But, like Mary Lincoln, she generated heat lightning and on one occasion sadly observed that she brought tragedy to those she loved.

Mrs. Lincoln studied the spot where little Joseph Emory Davis, aged five, fell from the piazza outside the servants' quarters and was killed on the last day of April, 1864. He was clambering up the railing when he plunged headlong to the pavement. Mrs. Davis had gone to her husband's office with a basket lunch, and the child died a few minutes after they got back to him. Like Lincoln, Davis could not sleep and had no appetite, so his wife was in the habit of going to his office every day with tempting meals when this accident occurred. The death of little Joseph had created some sympathy for Varina, just as the death of Willie Lincoln had softened some of Mrs. Lincoln's critics.

After Mary had viewed it all and had taken in the dim echoes that remained of crinolined beauties whirling around with Jeb Stuart and Southern heroes living it up before going out to battle to die, they all proceeded to the Capitol, where Sumner inquired about the fate of the Southern archives. They went on to Petersburg, where the President visited the hospitals and Mrs. Keckley took notes on the familiar scene. Everywhere they went they were conscious of the hurt of the vanquished, the bitter dregs of defeat, the terrible fatigue and grief of a lost generation of men, and a lost cause.

They returned from the South with mixed feelings. While driving from the wharf to the White House, Mrs. Lincoln turned suddenly somber and said to the Marquis de Chambrun, "That city is filled with our enemies." But Lincoln soothed her at once. "Enemies! We must never speak of that," he said.

Her depression turned to high excitement with the news she soon got from the President and on April 10 she sent Sumner a note, along with an uncommonly large arrangement of flowers: "Mr. L—told me the news, last night at ten o'clock, that Lee & his Army, were in our hands & it would have been my delight, to have been able to send you the communication to all of our recent companions, well knowing how much sweeter your dreams would have been."

She wrote of the rejoicing over the fall of Richmond. The capital had gone wild when operators shouted the message from windows. Guns roared. Bells rang. People dashed into the streets to dance, to embrace, to shake hands, to toss their hats. But remembering the other side of the coin, Mary concluded her letter to Sumner with a personal touch: "If the close of this terrible war, has left, some of our hearthstones, very, very desolate, God has been as ever kind & merciful, in the midst of our heavy afflictions as nations, & as individuals."

The Grants were momentarily out of sight in the moment of victory. The headquarters boat still floated on the James when Lincoln, first alone and then with his wife, visited Richmond. The general saw no reason for extravagant jubilation. He had been too potent a force at the heart of the struggle. After the historic encounter at Appomattox, when Lee surrendered with calm and dignity, Grant hurried back to Washington to countermand orders for supplies and reinforcements and to communicate with the generals still in the field. The shattered fragments of the great struggle had to be drawn together on the military end, and he had no wish to excite demonstrations. What the nation needed was *quiet,* but that, too, for the time being was a lost cause.

XVII

One Final Day Together

T HE FALL OF Richmond had been celebrated so riotously in Washington that the final gesture at Appomattox was more quietly received, but the city was ablaze with lights while flags, bands, crowds and all the outward symbols of victory abounded.

Mrs. Lincoln showed her joy and relief by sending lavish bouquets in all directions—to Sumner, to the Stantons, to the Marquis de Chambrun, to friends and even to foes. She invited Sumner and the marquis to join her in a celebration on April 11, suggesting that they drive around with her and another lady for half an hour to see the illuminations. She knew that her husband and Sumner must now work together, and she was determined that he should hear the President speak that night but he chose not to accept. He later told Chase that he was unwilling to give symbolic approval with his presence. Nor did he wish "to put himself in the position of opposing" the President on the White House balcony.

Mary's invitation to De Chambrun was coquettish in tone: "It does not appear to me, that this *womanly* curiosity will be undignified or indiscreet, *qu'en pensez-vous?*" De Chambrun would later recall the evening with keen appreciation of Mrs. Lincoln's reactions to what she saw. Her erratic conduct at City Point, her deep depression and uncontrollable outbursts were forgotten as she settled in the carriage and studied the scene around her. She was her most engaging self and gave no hint of the high tension behind her vivacity. De Chambrun wrote to his mother that the city was wild with joy, explosively manifested with a vigor he had never seen before. The cheers, the shouts, the hurrahs were deafening. "To those who know what the people have suffered, such outbursts are incomprehensible," he wrote.

The Capitol was illumined from dome to portico, with a faint mist enveloping it in a romantic glow and a gaslit transparency with huge lettering strung across the front. The White House glitter was partly veiled, and its myriad flags hung limp in the still air. The Treasury Building, sacred to Mr. Chase, had a fifty-dollar bond pricked out in lights, and Jay Cooke's banking house, which had helped him finance the war, signaled *Glory to God* in gold stars. Government buildings, hotels, restaurants, shops, homes, all signaled victory in lights. Even the prisons and the insane asylum flashed the joyous message. Fireworks went off over the Potomac and rockets exploded. General Lee's mansion blazed with light, and freedmen marched up and down on the lawn chanting "The Year of Jubilee." By Lincoln's wish the bands kept playing "Dixie" as well as "Yankee Doodle."

A great crowd had gathered on the White House grounds to hear the President. It was his last speech, and it encompassed his hopes for the future as he outlined his views on reconstruction and suggested practical measures for their fulfilment. It was not a speech that caught or held the crowd assembled that night. There were scattered cheers, but most of the serenaders heard it in silence. Some considered it a noble speech, but the radicals deplored its temperate tone on the black issue.

The most significant theater party in America's history was in danger of collapsing when Mrs. Lincoln had trouble finding anyone to go with them to see *Our American Cousin* on April 14. The President, worn and tired, was not keen on going himself, although he usually enjoyed a play. But he told his bodyguard, Crook, that their appearance at the theater had been advertised, and they must not disappoint the public. Grant had told him he would go, and he knew that the combined presence of Lincoln and Grant would fill the theater.

But when Mrs. Grant heard that her husband had rashly promised to go, she said no, and the man who had worsted the South had to back down before her protests. The excuse was that they had to join their children in Burlington, New Jersey. The war had interfered considerably with their family life. And neither wanted any more ovations. There had been enough of that. Mrs. Lincoln alone seemed to enjoy seeing her husband the idol of the crowds.

The Stantons had been invited, too. Mrs. Stanton, who consulted Mrs. Grant about it, said firmly that she would not go unless Julia also went. "I will not sit without you in the box with Mrs. Lincoln," said the wife of the Secretary of War, who had been constantly feuding with the President's wife. A Grant family legend handed down by Mrs. Emma Dent Casey was that her sister Julia also had had a premonitory dream of disaster on that night. When she had one of those, she was difficult to budge. Dreams seemed to be in the air, but whatever the true motive for their failure to go to Ford's Theater with the Lincolns, they were having supper in a hotel room in Philadelphia on their way to Burlington when word reached them that the President had been shot and might not live.

Had the Grants gone to the theater that night, it is probable that the general would have died with the President, for he was on the assassins' list. On the other hand, he sometimes voiced his regret in later years that he had not been there. His own stalwart presence and a military guard might have made a difference to the defenseless President. He had shaken hands with Lincoln and had said good-bye to him that afternoon, not knowing that it was forever. They had known each other for little more than a year, yet their history would be intertwined for all time. They understood and liked each other, and nothing that Mary had said about Grant ever shook her husband's confidence in him as a soldier. The results were now apparent.

The President seemed relaxed on the last day of his life. Crook noticed this at the Cabinet meeting, and his "intense seriousness" had turned to his more bantering style after he had had a brief talk with Stanton. Back at the White House with Mrs. Lincoln, Colfax and Noah Brooks, he was unusually cheerful, although he showed clearly that he was not anxious to go to the play that night.

His last country drive with Mary was like a return to the better days of the past. He had written her an affectionate note two days earlier suggesting the drive late on Friday and naming the hour. After his death she recalled that it was "playfully, tenderly, worded," and she chose to interpret it as having a loverlike quality. At last they were being freed from their terrible cares. At last they could look forward to some measure of peace and the resumption of a normal family life.

Mary had asked him if he wished to have company on their drive and he said: "No; I prefer to ride by ourselves today." She later revealed the nature of his mood on the drive and the reassuring things that had been said as they passed through the flowering April countryside. In retrospect—and perhaps because she wished it to be so—she said that she had never seen him so supremely happy as he was that afternoon. When she pointed this out to him, he said: "And well I may feel so, Mary, for I consider *this day* the war has come to a close."

He looked at the tired face of his wife of twenty-three years, who at the moment was developing another of her headaches. "We must both be more cheerful in the future. Between the war & the loss of our darling Willie—we have both been very miserable," he said.

Mary responded in her warmest and most attentive manner. She, too, felt that their lives might change with the terrible responsibility that had haunted their days and nights no longer dogging them. The President had a full term to run, but she believed that his days would now be filled with revival rather than destruction. She must have felt more certainy about her husband's future than he could have felt about hers after the public scenes of the preceding weeks and the vigilance needed to spare her aggravation. But both were close to collapse. In retrospect it is conceivable that Mary's wavering reason may have been further weakened by her acute anxiety over her husband's depression, his uncanny dreams, the feverish look in his eyes from lack of food and sleep. Her letters at this time strongly indicate her awareness of his condition. It also seems likely that her wild moods during the war years may have been tied to her worries about her husband's success in all things. Ambition and pride were her dominant qualities; she could not cope with failure.

Now with a fresh life ahead of them and the hope that they might at last be moving from darkness into light, they chose to talk of the future and of what they might do when the President's term ended. It had been an old dream to take the children to Europe, and this seemed possible, for Tad at least. Robert was already on his own, and they hoped he would soon be marrying Mary Harlan. More imminently, Mr. Lincoln considered a trip to California and a study of prospectors' claims for soldiers. Mary found him both "funny" and "cheery" on this subject. His face relaxed when he said that the soldiers might help pay the national debt by digging gold in the West. But the President had no illusions about the problems he faced in getting the country unified after the bitter struggle he had led.

It was with a deep sense of relief that the Lincolns talked of the more distant future and where they might settle. Their views on this had changed. The President's earlier plan to return to Springfield and practice law there was no longer the final goal. Other vistas stretched before them and Mary's ambition for her husband was not yet dead, but at the moment they longed above all for peace.

Both seemed soothed and contented when they returned to the White House from the drive, although neither one was eager for the night's performance. Mary's dull headache persisted, but she knew that if they did not go, her husband would be exposed to another tiring round of visitors. They were getting ready to leave for the theater when a note was handed to him from Senator William M. Stewart, of Nevada, asking if he might see him. The Senator was involved in the mining operations of the West and was in a good position to discuss the soldiers' prospects as gold diggers.

The usher returned with a card on which the President had written: "I am engaged to go to the theater with Mrs. Lincoln. It is the kind of an engagement I never break. Come with your friend tomorrow at ten and I shall be glad to see you."

The armed guard assigned that night to protect the President was John F. Parker, a member of the Metropolitan Police who, ironically enough, had been certified for duty at the White House by Mrs. Lincoln on April 3. She often made her own selections, but in this instance there had not been time for a full investigation of his history. The closing days of the war were overwhelming in the demands made on Mary's time.

It crushed her to learn in the blaze of publicity following the assassination that Parker's past record was poor. He had not changed. In the moment when he was most needed in the theater he was missing from the box. He had failed to notice the tiny hole that had been bored in the loge door for observation, and the play was only partway through when he left his chair in the passageway to seek refreshment away from the theater.

Stanton had sternly advised the President not to go to the theater that night. He did not think it safe for him to make this public appearance in the first flush of victory, yet his unescorted entrance into Richmond had entailed even greater risk. In the end the Secretary of War assigned Major Henry Reed Rathbone, a trusted attaché on his staff, to accompany the Lincolns. With him was his fiancée, who was also his cousin, Miss Clara Harris, daughter of Senator Ira Harris of New York, a close friend of the President's.

None could have dreamed that the future of this pair, young, handsome and elated over the honor done them, would involve both murder and madness. They were married soon after the assassination, but the horror of the night at Ford's cost the major his reason. Unbalanced for years, he went raving mad in 1894 and murdered Clara, who had been Mrs. Lincoln's companion on that unforgettable night. Soon afterward the major ended his own life in an asylum in Hanover, Germany. Tragedy flowed in all directions from the drama of classical proportions when Abraham Lincoln was assassinated and Mary went temporarily insane.

XVIII

Death in a Theater

M RS. LINCOLN WAS fighting a headache, but she looked assured
as she took her place in the upper right-hand box at Ford's
Theater and smiled amiably when the audience rose to applaud the
President before he settled into a large rocking chair and turned his
attention to the stage. They had been late in arriving, but a
thousand patrons of the theater acknowledged their presence in the
box heavily festooned with flags, with a picture of George
Washington as the centerpiece.

Curtains half-concealed them from view, and the actors alone
were aware of what was going on in the box. Their own line of vision
was limited, too, but they had a transverse view of the stage and the
play held their attention right into the third act. It was not a great
play; it was scarcely even a mediocre one, but Laura Keene was one
of their favorites, and both Lincolns were true lovers of the theater.
Many of their most enjoyable evenings had been spent in this box.
The theater had been a solace during some of the grimmest days of
the war.

Mary was becomingly dressed in a black-and-white striped silk
gown, with black lace veiling on her hair. She and the President
chatted between acts, and although it was years before Mary could
sort out her impressions of that evening, she eventually disclosed
that Mr. Lincoln was holding her hand at the moment that he was
shot and she felt it jerk as his head fell back.

The Lincolns were not given to demonstration in public, and

Mary, always conscious of appearances, wondered what Clara Harris might think of this display of affection. "She won't think anything of it," the President assured her, and Mary snuggled closer and settled down to enjoy the play. The third act was under way when John Wilkes Booth, who had been watching each move through a peephole, crashed into the box with a brass dagger and derringer pistol. He had picked what he thought to be the perfect moment, and he shot the President from a distance of five feet. Mary screamed, and the people in the theater were stunned to see a handsome unknown mount the railing of the box after a tussle with Rathbone before he jumped. He had gashed the young soldier's arm in the struggle, and he turned to slash at him once more as he shouted, "*Sic semper tyrannis,*" and leaped from the box. His spurred riding boot caught in one of the flags and he fell the last ten feet, injuring a leg.

"Stop that man!" Rathbone cried as Booth picked himself up and staggered out with a limp, which did not lessen his determination.

Mary clutched at her husband but remembered little more. Minutes passed before the audience was fully aware that the President had been shot, although his wife's scream had carried its own message. An actor at the prompting stand later said that he had seen the President lean back in the rocking chair without any struggle or movement, "save in the slight backward sway."

But when word spread that the President was dead or dying, there was intense excitement and the aisles were so choked with people that two hundred soldiers were called in to empty the theater. Dr. Charles A. Leslie, assistant surgeon of the United States Volunteers, was the first to give medical aid to the dying President, who was gently laid out on the floor. He quickly found that the wound was mortal, and when Dr. Charles Sabin Taft, Army surgeon and personal friend of the Lincolns, and Dr. Albert F. A. King arrived, all three worked to revive him. A clot of blood removed from his wound helped relieve the pressure on his brain and gave him a feeble pulse. Brandy and water were used for stimulation.

A lead ball less than half an inch in diameter had penetrated the back of his head on the left side, three inches from his left ear. Its course was oblique, and it lodged a few inches behind his right eye. Fragments of bone had been driven into his brain with the ball. About a hundred years later John F. Kennedy and his brother Robert would die from somewhat similar wounds.

Mary from the start was in a state of total collapse. She was numb and only partly conscious as her husband lay on the floor with doctors ministering to him. Laura Keene who, along with some of her fellow players, had recognized Booth, cradled Lincoln's head in her lap while the doctors worked over him. As Mary revived, her lamentations became part of the evening's horror, and she was heard to murmur: "His dream was prophetic."

Half an hour after the shot was fired, she followed as his body was carried across the street to William Peterson's house. His bearers had to force their way through the crowd that had gathered, and some followed them into the house as he was taken along a narrow hall into a back bedroom, to be laid diagonally across the bed because of his great height. The room was only fifteen by nine feet. It was simply furnished with a bureau, some chairs, a washstand, a small wood stove. The wallpaper was brown and white, the carpet a worn Brussels.

"Where is my husband? Where is my husband?" Mary cried when she was cut off by some of the invaders and could not see where he was being taken. She was led to the room where he lay, and she sank by the bed, covering his face with kisses. His eyes were half-open, and he was breathing with difficulty. Still wearing the frock coat and long boots in which he had gone to the theater, his stricken body looked huge on the white sheets that covered a corn whisk mattress resting on rope lacings. As the doctors prepared him for examination, all but the surgeons were ordered from the room. They still did not know if there were other wounds besides the fatal one in his head.

Every hour all night Mrs. Lincoln visited the room and studied her husband's face. It changed ominously as one eye began to bulge and his breathing grew worse. She waited in a room next door with Clara Harris and Mrs. Welles, and as the night wore on, she grew calmer from sheer exhaustion, or from sedatives.

Also gathered in the little room were all the members of the Cabinet except Chase, whose life had been threatened, and Seward who had been attacked and seriously wounded at his home by Booth's fellow conspirator, Lewis Powell. The news reached Sumner as he sipped wine with Senator John Conness at his house on Thirteenth Street. His fellow guest was William Stewart, of the newly admitted state of Nevada, who had tried to see the President that day and had an appointment for the next morning.

The three Senators jumped to their feet when Conness's black manservant ran in, shouting: "Mr. Lincoln is assassinated in the theater. Mr. Seward is murdered in his bed. There's murder in the streets." They took a hack to the White House, only to find that the guards there were still unaware of what had happened. They picked up Robert and drove to Ford's, then crossed the street to the house where the President lay. They could hear Mrs. Lincoln sobbing as they passed, and Robert was deeply moved when he found his father lying diagonally across the bed and obviously close to death. Sumner took Lincoln's hand and tried to speak to him, but one of the surgeons told him it was no use; he could not be heard. "He is dead," said the doctor.

"No, he isn't dead," said Sumner. "Look at his face, he is breathing." But he was assured that the President would never regain consciousness.

The night seemed endless to the men in the room, and who would dare guess what passed through the mind of Mary Lincoln as the dark hours merged into a miserable lowering dawn? Her gown was crumpled, her hair disheveled, her face was like tallow as nurses supported her when she repeatedly went to her husband's bedside. Gideon Welles noted in his diary that she would remain with him until overcome with "tears and lamentations." She pleaded for Tad to be sent for, thinking that Mr. Lincoln would speak to him if to no one else because he loved him so much.

But as the hours wore on and Mary saw the evidence in his changing face, she was at last persuaded that he would die. When this sank in, she appealed to him to speak, and between bursts of sobbing she used all the endearing terms that had ever passed between them in their life together, as if to draw him back to her side. When this brought no response, she begged him to take her with him.

A crowd stood outside the house, with the rain pelting down and the skies a dull pewter as dawn approached. A guard stood at the door to prevent any disturbance, for Washington was wakening up to the knowledge that President Lincoln was on the brink of death. The hall and other rooms in the house were packed with friends and well-wishers. Gideon Welles, who had been on guard since eleven the night before, left the stifling room to get some fresh air. On his return he saw at once that the final moment was approaching.

Robert stood leaning against Sumner at the head of the bed, and like his mother, he was sobbing but with more restraint. Finally Mary was called in for her last visit. She knew what it meant, and she threw herself on the bed in a passion of grief when she saw her husband's distorted face. She was slipping to the floor in a faint when a nurse lifted her up to the window to inhale the damp air. With more composure she returned to the bed and kissed her husband for the last time. As she passed along the hall, a reporter heard her cry: "Oh, my God, and have I given my husband to die?"

At seven twenty-two in the morning President Lincoln breathed his last, and Secretary of War Stanton made the statement that has come to be part of the history of the Civil War: "Now he belongs to the Ages." Two hours passed before Mrs. Lincoln was in any condition to be taken back to the White House, and she had a fresh outburst as she was led to her room. "Not there, not there," she cried.

Bells tolled in Washington and across the nation. Flags flew at half-mast. Government departments and all places of business closed. Social life was at a standstill, and all roads leading out of Washington were under guard in the quest for the killer.

"Oh, Mr. Welles, who killed my father?" Tad said, sobbing as he met the Secretary of the Navy on the White House stairs. Life had changed with shattering suddenness for this adored son of the President. For the next twenty-four hours he was inconsolable until a brilliant blue sky on Sunday caught his attention. According to newspaper reports of the time, Tad took this as a token that his father was happy.

"Do you think my father has gone to heaven?" he asked one of the White House callers.

When he was assured that no doubt he had, Tad answered excitedly: "Then I am glad he has gone there, for he never was happy after he came here. This was not a good place for him."

The ceremonial plans went ahead while Mrs. Lincoln surrendered completely to her grief, except for a few spasmodic attempts to impose her will. Mrs. Elizabeth Lee and Mrs. Welles, one of the few friends to whom she would listen, stayed with her much of the time. Mrs. Keckley was called in on the morning of Lincoln's death and from then on she devoted herself entirely to Mrs. Lincoln and Tad. On her arrival she found Robert bending over his mother, looking helpless, and Tad crouching at the foot of the bed, begging her to stop crying. According to Mrs. Keckley, Tad threw his arms around her neck and chokingly said: "Don't cry so, Mamma. Don't cry, or you will make me cry, too. You will break my heart."

This would quiet her momentarily, but Tad was soon taken away from her presence. Mrs. Keckley kept bathing her brow with cold water as one "terrible outburst" followed another. While the whole country shared step by step in the funeral ceremonies, Mary lay in a far-off world of her own, distraught and so disturbed that the doctors advised keeping her removed from it all.

But this was not altogether possible, and between convulsive bursts of sobbing Mary would voice some wish that Mrs. Welles would try to indulge. She had her son, Edgar T. Welles, delay the dismantling of the framework for the catafalque because the hammering when it was put up had cut clear through her consciousness.

When Judge Davis arrived to consult her about the burial place, he found that Mrs. Lincoln refused to see anyone, but she made it amply clear that she wanted the President to be buried in Chicago rather than in Springfield. Robert and the judge stood their ground for Springfield, so closely identified with Lincoln's rise to power. It was not until they agreed to take Willie's body west on the funeral train that she finally consented, knowing that then her husband, Willie, and Eddie, who had died in Springfield, all would rest together on home ground. But in the midst of her hysteria Mrs. Lincoln insisted that the removal of Willie's body should be done in secrecy, and as a result his coffin was quietly placed in the funeral car, in front of his father's.

Mrs. Lincoln heard only faint echoes of the solemn gathering in the East Room, of the departure of her husband from the White House in a mahogany coffin covered with Easter lilies, roses, magnolias and wreaths of lilac, for it was lilac time, as Walt Whitman noted, when the funeral train set off on its slow historic journey across the country. There were church services and all activities were suspended in the South as in the North, for the image of Abraham Lincoln loomed large in the public imagination and the horror of the assassination had rocked the country. Twenty-one guns were fired from Fort Clay in Mary's hometown of Lexington, and the church bells tolled at intervals until evening on the day of the President's funeral.

Tales of Mrs. Lincoln's ravaged condition spread quickly. Dr. Henry, who had passed some hours with her in the first days of her grief and shared her interest in the mystical, reported that she believed the President to be near at hand and to know what was happening. All who were around her heard her say repeatedly that she wished she, too, had been taken. None of this was unusual in the mourning tradition of the nineteenth century, but in Mary's case it assumed extravagant proportions.

She stayed out of sight for five weeks, but gradually her lamentation was broken up with intervals of packing. Although she was still unable to face the mountain of messages of condolence reaching the White House, her worldly sense revived sufficiently for her to show interest when she heard from Queen Victoria, the Empress Eugénie, and Louis Philippe d'Orléans, the comte de Paris. The queen's message from Osborne, dated April 29, 1865, read:

> Though a stranger to you I cannot remain silent when so terrible a calamity has fallen upon you and your country, and must personally express my *deep* and *heartfelt* sympathy with you under the shocking circumstances of your personal dreadful misfortune.
>
> No one can better *appreciate* than I can, who am myself *utterly brokenhearted* by the loss of my own beloved Husband, who was the light of my life—my stay—*my all*—what your sufferings must be; and I earnestly pray that you may be supported by Him to whom alone the sorely stricken can look for comfort, in this hour of heavy affliction.

There is little doubt that Mrs. Lincoln identified herself with Queen Victoria in their mutual sorrow, and in her reply she accepted the "tender sympathy" as coming from a heart which "from its own sorrow, can appreciate the intense grief I now endure."

The comte de Paris recalled the opportunities he had had of appreciating the "noble heart, the great qualities of M. Lincoln" and the gracious and friendly manner in which he had given him a commission in the Federal Army.

Mrs. Lincoln, still resentful of Andrew Johnson's conduct on inauguration day, was outraged when he failed to send her a message of sympathy immediately or to make any attempt to see her. At this time she was resisting the thought of returning to Springfield, and in a sudden outburst to Mrs. Keckley, as she sat rocking herself with folded arms, she exclaimed: "God, Elizabeth, what a change! Did ever woman have to suffer so much and experience so great a change? I had an ambition to be Mrs. President; that ambition has been gratified, and now I must step down from the pedestal. My poor husband! Had he never been President, he might be living today. Alas! all is over with me." However improbable, this was Mrs. Keckley's recollection of what Mrs. Lincoln said.

Major French decided that the death of her husband had made her even "crazier than she used to be," and he cited her purchase of a thousand dollars worth of mourning a month before the assassination as an inexplicable act. "What do you suppose possessed her to do it?" he wrote to his brother, H. R. French. "Please keep that fact in your own home. I will some time tell you what I have gone through since Mr. L's death. I cannot write it."

The disposition of the President's effects was subject to Mary's whims, and later there was a great deal of criticism of her strange behavior in this respect. Robert had his father's watch, gold pen, penknife and glasses. Mary was in haste to get rid of his most intimate things, saying that she could not bear to be reminded that he had worn them. When Seward heard that some of the President's initialed shirts were in a local store, he hurried to get them back. Four of his canes were given away—one to Sumner, one to Frederick Douglass, a third to the Reverend H. H. Garnet, and a fourth to William Slade, the last steward in the Lincoln administration and a messenger for the President. The shepherd plaid shawl that was such a distinctive part of his public image fell into Slade's hands, and his wife got hold of the black-and-white striped silk dress that Mrs. Lincoln had worn on the night of the assassination. Mrs. Keckley had the earrings, lace scarf and velvet cloak that could only remind Mary of a night of horror.

The last hat worn by the President was sent by Mrs. Lincoln to the Reverend Phineas D. Gurley, the minister who had officiated at the funeral services of Mr. Lincoln and his son Willie. Mary was greatly distressed when she found that the hat had not been delivered. When the personal possessions had been taken care of, she then had to cope with the piles of dresses, silks, laces, furs, gloves, bonnets, curtains and bolts of material that she had accumulated. Robert, in and out of the room where his mother and Mrs. Keckley packed, despairingly suggested that the used clothing being folded into boxes should be burned instead. But there was nothing that his mother would abandon. Every yard of silk or lace seemed to be vital to her well-being as she mulled over a fantastic collection of unused possessions.

When she left Washington, there was considerable speculation about the contents of the scores of trunks and between fifty and sixty boxes that she took from the White House. Mrs. Keckley and Robert knew that most of the contents were not worth packing, but Mrs. Lincoln reminded Lizzie that Robert gave no thought to the future. She considered these possessions insurance against leaner days, since she was still haunted by the knowledge of $70,000 that she owed at this time. Assuring Mrs. Keckley that the President had known nothing of these bills, she said that the "only happy feature of his assassination was that he died in ignorance of them."

The Lincolns, like other Presidential families, had received a rich endowment of gifts, and this was a baffling situation for Mrs. Lincoln in her disordered state. She paid special attention to the handicrafts of war veterans and the country quilts, but before Andrew Johnson took possession, things had been widely scattered. The vandalism of the five weeks after the President's death, when the Executive Mansion was comparatively unsupervised and Mrs. Lincoln did not stir from her quarters, was her excuse later for the disappearance of so many treasurers. The only souvenir she took for herself was her husband's shaving stand and she left a substitute. He had liked it because its height and shape had been right for his tall figure. But again she was under attack, and clear across the country she was accused of stripping the White House of valuables. The whole subject was freely aired in Congress when the Johnson administration sought funds to refurbish the White House.

Mary had resisted returning to Springfield when Judge Davis and Orville Browning had proposed that she go back to her old home, which was still owned by her family. She was estranged from Ninian and Elizabeth Edwards at this time, and the breach between her and her sisters had actually widened. The controversy about the funeral arrangements still raged, and many stories of Mrs. Lincoln's past had been revived in the city where she had passed most of her married life. She felt so uneasy about it all that Chicago was chosen as her home.

So many visitors had been turned away during her last few weeks in the White House that at the end she was left alone. Mary was a subdued figure as she left on May 22, 1865, ravaged, tearful, her memories of gala nights and historic moments all lost in the immediate strain of her departure. No President's wife ever left the White House more obscurely, more sadly than Mrs. Lincoln. She had no awareness now of the length of her bonnet strings or of the costume she wore.

Tad, Robert and Dr. Henry were with her as she walked down the public stairway, and Mrs. Keckley was by her side. Mrs. Lincoln had persuaded Lizzie to go with her, although she was reluctant to leave her spring business in Washington. But Mrs. Stephen Douglas, for whom she was then working, gave her consent. "Never mind me," said the beautiful Addie. "Do all you can for Mrs. Lincoln. My heart's sympathy is with her."

They traveled west in a chartered green car. Mary developed a headache as she left the capital, which was its most beautiful, in waves of bloom. On their arrival in Chicago they went to the Tremont House, the fashionable hostelry of the day, but its cost horrified Mrs. Lincoln. Within a week they moved to the Clifton House and then to less expensive quarters in the Hyde Park area, a new suburb. Robert was dismayed with the conditions he now faced as he arranged his books and looked around the sparsely furnished rooms. "I would almost as soon be dead as be compelled to remain three months in this dreary house," he said.

Tad alone was cheerful and interested in his new surroundings. "Ah, what a sad change has come to us all!" said his mother.

She was already the forgotten First Lady, except for the mud that was still being flung at her. It had to be the best or nothing for Mary Lincoln, and her wounded pride, as well as her endless grief, drove her at this point into the habits of a confirmed recluse. She shunned all social contacts and found escape in hallucinations and memories, a singularly rich resource where she was concerned.

Two days after she left Washington, a great review of the victorious federal forces was held, with Mrs. Grant and Mrs. Sherman sitting together in the reviewing stand opposite the White House. The Army of the Potomac marched on the first day, and the Army of the Tennessee on the second. Tattered, bloodstained flags were borne proudly, and Jesse Grant, Tad's friend, leaned over the railing and waved his Glengarry at the passing columns as shouts rang out: "Grant! Grant! Good-bye, old man."

Muskets gleamed like a wall of steel. Spring flowers had been fashioned into garlands. The black regiments had a special salute. Grant had arrived at the reviewing stand on foot to avoid a demonstration. He was now being compared to Napoleon, to Garibaldi, to Alexander. As Sherman flashed his sword in a salute to Grant, Mrs. Sherman and Mrs. Grant jumped to their feet and waved their handkerchiefs while torrents of applause greeted the most controversial of them all.

The White House, across the way, seemed still and empty with its great man gone, and Mrs. Lincoln was already only a shadow, a restless ghost, much loved by their leader but not by the men grouped around the new President. The echoes of the victory parade touched her with abrasive force as she coped alone with a new life, a diminished world.

XIX

A Diminished Empire

M UCH OF MRS. Lincoln's life had been associated with Springfield and nearby Chicago. There her roots had gone deep, and kinship for the prairies was now part of the Lincoln heritage, although she had come originally from Kentucky. Her husband had been nominated for the Presidency in Chicago. They had had days of triumph there, and she had always been well received by the people of Illinois. New York had been only a place to shop, attend the theater and be seen. She had no roots there and few friends, except for some of her husband's appointees. Mary was well aware that the women of New York did not like her, although the merchants had fawned over her.

The mere thought of Washington frightened her now that she had left the White House. Springfield at the moment had painful associations. Chicago, where her husband had finally thought of practicing law, seemed to be the place where she could best lose herself and where Robert might make headway in the legal profession. It was a vigorous, sparkling city at the close of the Civil War, growing fast from the deserted village it had been thirty years earlier.

Great new marble mansions were being built, and the spires of seventy churches broke the level line of the prairie. Lincoln and Sherman both were identified with its fast wartime growth. Its busy wharves, its storehouses, its factories and meat-packing houses presaged the metropolis of the future. Canals and waterways intersected the city and gave some charm to its straight rectangular streets. Potter Palmer had brought a touch of magnificence to an area that not so long before had had rough wooden shanties and loose planks for sidewalks. He and other merchants who had bought land on State Street were widening, paving and lighting streets, and ramshackle buildings were being torn down to make way for improvements. Marshall Field and Levi Leiter put up a six-story building at the corner of State and Washington streets with marble columns and wide aisles that delighted the women shoppers of the postwar era. Alexandre's gloves and Persian carpets alike could be bought under its bright lights, but Mrs. Lincoln no longer haunted the shops with her old zeal.

Fortunes were in the making in the booming Midwestern city, with factories sprawling toward the prairie, turning out axes, plows and reapers, shoes and cloaks and candles, whiskey, soap and cookstoves. The slaughter of pigs and cattle in the stockyards that had helped keep the Army fed continued, and thousands of workers processed the grain from the prairies.

All this was lost on Mrs. Lincoln, who tried various dwelling places, never feeling settled in any, never unpacking the boxes that held her treasures, never associating easily with her neighbors. Her tears flowed constantly. Her headaches grew worse, and she had many dim days when she seemed not to know where she was or what she was doing. But Tad had developed a new independence since his father's death. He dressed himself and no longer needed an attendant. The days of petting, pampering and receiving gifts from all and sundry because he was the President's son had come to an end. Tad now liked to go about with Robert, but his mother discouraged this, ever fearful of what might happen to him.

Robert had trouble coping with his mother's moods. He had a new sense of responsibility both for her and for Tad. At the same time he was starting a career of his own, and much was expected of him. He had had to give up all thought of the Harvard Law School, and he traveled in and out every day from Hyde Park to the offices of Scammon, McCagg & Fuller, where he read law. He did his best to help his mother make various moves that first summer, in the hope of finding a satisfactory way of living after her high-powered days in the White House. Although her own desire for seclusion cut her off from people, she seemed to feel the need for some homage and recognition. She wrote to a friend that there were many who could not "appreciate station and would like to see us live humbly. I am growing very weary of *boarding*. It is very unbecoming when it is remembered from whence we have just come."

Her consciousness of lost status made these days of transition difficult for her, and she wrote to Mrs. Welles on July 11, 1865, on making the best she could of her quarters in the Hyde Park region. The house in which she lived "had accommodated some of the very best Chicago people." Each family kept its own carriage and she walked every day in the park. She received few visitors, seeing no necessity "to pass through such an ordeal as yet." But it was evident that she felt the indignity of her position.

On October 14, 1865, Mary wrote again to Mrs. Welles, pointing out that Charles A. Dana had bought a house near hers costing $28,000. He was editing the Chicago *Republican*, a bitterly anti-Johnson paper, before beginning his long and brilliant career on the New York *Sun*. All their old friends seemed to be living handsomely, Mary wrote, while she was without a carriage for the first time in twelve years, but "with my darling husband, *any* lot, would have been cheerfully borne." Prices in Chicago were so high that all she could do was "to board genteely."

Mrs. Keckley had returned to Washington, since Mary could not afford to keep her and she had her own business to maintain. Tad attended a public school briefly, then in 1866 he was enrolled in the Brown School, near his home. Although at first he was slow to come to grips with his studies, she wrote optimistically to his old tutor, Alexander Williamson, on June 15, 1865, from the Hyde Park Hotel that Tad was at last seized with the desire to *read* and *write*—"which with his *natural* brightness, will be *half* the battle with him."

He was all love and gentleness, she assured Williamson, and she had no trouble managing him, but she was deeply upset by an article in the Chicago *Journal* saying that she had once threatened to *whip* Taddy for cutting up copper-toed shoes, something her boys had never worn. It was a new story to Mary "that in my life I have ever whipped a child." A gentle, loving word had always been enough, she wrote, and if anything, she had been too indulgent.

Mrs. Lincoln wrote to Williamson with complete frankness about her financial troubles. She had tried to get him a good government position through President Johnson, just as she had pleaded with Judge Harlan to do something for Dr. Henry, who had stayed close to her in Chicago for a time as physician and friend. But nothing was forthcoming for Dr. Henry. Sailing west to Olympia, Washington, in July, 1865, he was lost at sea. This was a great blow to Mrs.

Lincoln, for he had been close to her through many of her darkest moments.

In a letter addressed to Dr. Henry on July 26, 1865, that never reached him, she said that Mrs. Trumball had not called on her, nor would she receive her if she did. "She is indeed a 'whited sepulchre,' " Mary wrote of her old friend, Julia Jayne. This ended her communication with one of her most loyal friends—the man who had known both her and Julia in their younger days and who had helped bring Mary and Abraham Lincoln together when they seemed to be going their separate ways. Now she sought help from Williamson and on August 17, 1865, wrote to him: "My heart is indeed broken, and without my beloved husband, I do not wish to live. Life is indeed a heavy burden & I do not care how soon, I am called hence."

Mary had chosen Williamson to be her secret paid agent in the East to lobby for her in Congress and to persuade her creditors to reduce their bills or take back their goods. Between 1865 and 1868 she sent him more than sixty letters showing confusion, rancor and even desperation at times. She gave him peremptory orders, which he meekly tried to carry out. Although he was not to speak of her business to anyone or even to indicate that he was in touch with her, he was to promote the idea that she was in desperate straits. He was to approach members of the House about allowing her four years' salary for her husband's unfulfilled term of office, and he was to point out to them the shame of Mrs. Lincoln's being reduced to living in a boardinghouse.

On November 19, 1865, she warned him not to go near Seward about her business. He was to be quiet and cautious in all that he did, and he was to avoid Isaac Newton, Simeon Draper, Judge Harlan, Stanton, Joshua Speed, and Judge Davis, who was in charge of her affairs and the administration of Lincoln's estate. Evidently she was feuding with her husband's old friends and wished to do things in her own way without their interference.

Mary did not leave a stone unturned in suggesting to Williamson the men she thought he should approach. He moved between Washington, New York and Philadelphia, getting a dismaying view of her shopping expeditions and her mania for buying things on credit. The merchants must be placated, she said, and he had the task of persuading M. W. Galt & Company, the Washington jewelers, to take back some of her purchases. She insisted that she had never worn the pearl and diamond ring for which she was charged $440, or the diamond and pearl bracelet valued at $550, or other trinkets like a $100 gold card case that showed up in her bills.

Williamson tried to enlist the interest of wealthy Republicans such as William B. Astor, Cornelius Vanderbilt, Simeon Draper, Moses Grinnell, Moses Taylor, James Orne, Larz Anderson, "who had millions," and other rich men who had been helping to honor General Grant. But when his efforts failed, Mrs. Lincoln came out in the open with a humiliating series of letters to politicians, businessmen, journalists and old friends of her husband's. She threw herself on the mercy of Simon Cameron, telling him that although Judge Davis, her administrator, was a completely honorable man, he had no warmth. Mary asked Cameron to raise funds that would enable her to buy a suitable house. Cameron was sympathetic. They had always been on good terms when he was in her husband's Cabinet. But his appeals to Jay Cooke and other old friends of the President's brought no response. It was a long-drawn-out, painful process for one who had so recently been in a position to command attention. She felt betrayed on every side and suffered when her sale of the Presidential carriage brought fresh criticism.

Mrs. Lincoln was unrelenting about President Johnson and wrote to Mrs. Orne on March 15, 1866, that the "miserable *inebriate* Johnson, had cognizance of my husband's death—*Why*, was *that card* of Booth's, found in his box. . . . No one ever heard of Johnson, regretting my sainted husband's death, he never wrote me a line of condolence, and behaved in the most brutal way."

And why had Jefferson Davis not been brought to trial? Mary demanded, adding: "As sure, as you & I live, Johnson had some hand, in all this. . . . His fate will be to suffer. . . ."

On the day of the assassination Booth for some unknown reason had called at the Kirkwood House to see Johnson and had left his card when he found that both he and his secretary were out. A pamphlet theorizing about these events had reached Mary, and in her distraught state she had pounced on this distorted view of events but without sincere conviction.

It was true that Johnson had let her strictly alone after the President's death. When a letter finally was addressed to her on January 12, 1866, nine months after the assassination, it conveyed the profound sympathy of both houses of Congress but lacked a personal message. Sometime later it was found in a trash barrel outside Mrs. Lincoln's house in Chicago.

Mary continued to express her detestation of Johnson in letters to friends. She wrote to Sumner a year after her husband's death that he was a "faithless & unscrupulous President." To others she insisted that he was a "demagogue" and always was her enemy. She said he "desecrated her beloved's resting place" by visiting Lincoln's grave while making a grand tour of Illinois. Mary made a point of being out of reach when his party passed through, although her friend Mrs. Welles was with them.

But such was Mary's ambivalence when she wanted something that she was seeking favors from Johnson soon after her husband's death, and in particular a better post for Williamson than the one he held in the Treasury. There was no reply to this. At times she seemed to sense her own indiscretion and suggested to her friends that they burn her letters.

Aside from her excruciating and revealing correspondence with Williamson and her demanding letters to men in high office, Mary's letters during the first year of her widowhood combined lamentation and complaints with idolatrous praise of her husband. Perhaps more than most, she was conscious of his growing stature in world opinion. The nature of his death, his gargantuan presence, and the manner in which he had conducted the war and freed the slaves combined to make him a towering figure abroad as well as at home. Mary was particularly pleased when a committee in France, headed by Victor Hugo, gave a medal in his memory at a ceremony held in Paris on December 1, 1866. John Bigelow, American minister at the time, accepted it on behalf of Mrs. Lincoln. Forty thousand citizens were involved in this tribute to the Emancipator, but when the medal was not sent to her promptly, she became suspicious and wrote to Williamson that if "Seward, Hay or Nicolay could stop its reaching me—they would do so. They are a great set of scamps."

Both Hay and Nicolay were moving into the diplomatic field abroad, and Hay was becoming as popular in Paris as he had been in Washington. These young men had long been scamps in Mary's estimation, but her list of villains had grown since the President's assassination and now included French, Newton and others who had seemed to be her friends in the closing days of the administration. Ed McManus, who had been doorkeeper since Jackson's day, was dismissed in 1865 for spreading stories about her disagreements with the President and for gossiping about her trips to New York.

Mrs. Lincoln had never liked old Ed, and now she was furious with him. He was a "serpent," and she hastened to point out that scenes between her and Mr. Lincoln were novelties, in spite of what anyone said to the contrary. "Notwithstanding our opposite natures, our lives have been eminently peaceful," said Mary with assurance.

While she brooded over the wrongs done her, both real and imaginary, a scrapbook sent to her from England containing the speeches and tributes that noted Britons paid to her husband's memory kept her occupied for hours. Often she turned for consolation to a bundle of his letters, which she read over and over again. Mary wrote to Mrs. Welles of what they meant to her: "many of them written to me in the 'long ago,' and quite yellow with age, others more recent & one written from his office *only* the *Wednesday* before—a few lines playfully tenderly worded, notifying the hour of the day he would drive with me."

Mary finished this letter with a revealing paragraph: "Time, my dear Mrs. Welles, has at length convinced me that the loved idolized being, comes no more, ever. I must patiently await the hour when God's Love shall place me by his side again. I believe there are *no more* partings & no more bloodshed. For I have almost become blind with weeping and I can scarcely see sufficiently to trace these lines. . . ."

Like Queen Victoria she clung to every sign of deepest mourning. Her encompassing widow's weeds were traditional at the time, but the worn face behind the veil, the drooping bearing, were a new Mary. She had always held her head high and walked with pride, except on the days when she suffered from annihilating headaches. Her letters of this period reveal the passionate regret she felt at times for the occasions on which she had failed her husband, nagged him, and caused him concern. She wished that there had been time to ask his forgiveness for any "inadvertent moment of pain" she had caused him. Had his end come after an illness during which she had been able to nurse him, she "might have been able to convey to him her thankfulness for his lifelong devotion." She spent hours in frenzied worry, recalling the bad spots and wishing them undone. Had he remained at the White House on "that night of darkness, when the fiends prevailed, he would have been horribly *cut to pieces,*" she wrote to Carpenter.

Added to Mary's everlasting remorse was the burden of her debts. She had ground for concern about her financial future. Now that she was no longer the chatelaine of the White House, her creditors closed in on her with more insistence. The settlement of Lincoln's estate was a slow process, and the $22,000 allowed her by Congress for the President's unfinished year diminished fast as she tried to satisfy her most pressing creditors. She was deaf to family advice and was soon involved in a succession of ill-judged public appeals for support.

Horace Greeley opened a campaign in the New York *Tribune* to raise $100,000 for Mrs. Lincoln by one-dollar subscriptions, but by the end of May, 1865, the Springfield *Republican* announced that this plan had been abandoned because the President had left a much larger fortune than was at first supposed. Greeley denied this, but it caused Mary to ask that the subscription list be withdrawn after September 1 because of the uproar it was causing. She wrote to Norman S. Bentley, a prominent New York merchant, on July 5, 1865, that such men as Governor Edwin Dennison Morgan of New York and Samuel Hooper of Boston would rather give $50,000 apiece than to have her poverty so widely discussed in the newspapers. She now favored private circulation of an appeal, involving larger sums and no publicity.

But the diverse efforts to help Mrs. Lincoln financially merely added to the confusion and misunderstanding that always seemed to surround her. They were poorly managed and soon had political implications. Her own unpopularity and her past extravagance did not help her at this point. She gave more and more thought to money and would not listen to Judge Davis, who was the administrator of her husband's estate. Lincoln had not left a will, and although Judge Davis' final report filed in 1868 showed that the estate had increased to more than $110,000, there were lean days for Mrs. Lincoln in the interim while things were being settled. At the time of his death the President, according to Judge Davis' findings, had cash and government bonds totaling roughly $70,000, which, with the Springfield property, made an estate of $110,000. Divided into three parts for her and her sons, each eventually got $36,765.60, which allowed them $1,700 a year in income. All three received the same amount, and during his administration of the estate Judge Davis sent Tad's share to Robert, to be used for his brother's benefit, but the final settlement took time. Meanwhile, Mary was haunted by debts totaling nearly $70,000 and was making frantic efforts to conciliate her creditors.

She believed that Chicago should honor Abraham Lincoln's memory by doing what Galena and Philadelphia had done for General Grant. "Roving Generals have elegant mansions *showered* upon them," she wrote bitterly to Williamson, "and the American people—leave the family of the Martyred President, to struggle as best they may!" Mary felt that her situation reflected on Mr. Lincoln for not having provided for his family.

By the end of 1865 she was in a state of confusion and depression just as the Grants were settling in a spacious house on I Street in Washington and were being entertained by President Johnson and his daughters, Mrs. Martha Patterson and Mrs. Mary Johnson Stover. Mrs. Keckley was now sewing for the new hostesses in the White House, and Mary suffered when she read that the "ruins and tatters of the last days of the Lincoln administration" had been concealed by fresh linen covers. She felt that the new occupants would have little appreciation of the china and glass she had bought.

Her trunks and boxes were in storage two miles from where she lived, and Robert had warned her not to go near them until she had a house of her own. In the end she used part of the $22,000 allowed her by Congress for the purchase of a marble-fronted house at 375 West Washington Street. But she soon found that she could not afford to live in it or to keep it up. During the eight years that she held on to it, the rent she received for this white elephant did no more than cover taxes and upkeep. She and her sons occupied it for only a year.

She was thrown into fresh paroxysms at the end of 1866 over the removal of the bodies of her husband and Willie from a receiving vault to a hillside in Oak Park, which would be their permanent resting place. The squabbling over the location had been painful. The Springfield Monument Association had chosen a site in the center of the city for the Lincoln shrine. Mary was unalterably opposed to this idea and threatened to have her husband's body sent back to Washington to rest in a vault under the Capitol rather than let the proposed plan be carried out.

She could not forget what Mr. Lincoln had said to her shortly before his death, as if he already felt that his end was near. While at City Point in the last days of the war they came to a wooded cemetery as they drove by the James River. Mr. Lincoln suggested that they get out for a stroll. He seemed to find peace as they walked under the sheltering trees, with the fragrance of the spring foliage around them. As he studied the tombstones, he said in his thoughtful way, "Mary, you are younger than I. You will survive me. When I am gone, lay my remains in some quiet place like this."

Oak Ridge Cemetery had the beauty and peace of which Mary thought he would have approved. A paramount consideration also was her determination to be buried by his side. Like Mrs. Grant, when Ulysses died, nothing could shake her in this resolve. When John Todd Stuart showed her the niche where she would rest, she burst into tears and prayed that her appointed time would not be distant.

Mary was now at odds with old friends whom she called the "Springfield clique." There had been so much trouble about the burial place that she felt the entire community was against her. Even John Stuart and Judge Davis no longer had her total trust. She had no communication with her sisters, and her widowed cousin, Mrs. Elizabeth Todd Grimsley, had married the Reverend John M. Brown in 1867 and was devoting herself to church affairs.

That same summer Mrs. Lincoln and Tad were summoned to Washington to testify before Judge Edwards Pierrepont at the trial of John Suratt, son of Mrs. Mary Suratt at whose house the conspirators involved in the assassination plot had met. Tad recalled having seen a man on the *River Queen* who seemed to him to resemble Suratt. Robert took him to Washington to testify, but Mary pleaded illness as she rested in Racine, Wisconsin.

By this time she was involved in her ill-judged efforts to raise money by selling her White House clothes. In March she had written to Mrs. Keckley asking for help.

She said she could not live on her income of $1,700 a year and would have to give up the house she had bought and settle again in a cheap boardinghouse. Since she had many costly things that she would never use again, why not sell them? With her old air of authority Mrs. Lincoln said that, humiliating though it was, she would come to New York at the end of August, and Lizzie must help her with the transaction. It was all to be done with the utmost secrecy, and Mrs. Lincoln would call herself Mrs. Clarke. The original intention was to have the articles disposed of privately, but they fell into the hands of sharpers who tried to use the Lincoln name to advantage.

After some confusion in their plans Mrs. Keckley arrived from Washington and met Mrs. Lincoln at the St. Denis Hotel. The plan was no surprise to Lizzie, who had heard her say more than once in the White House that she might one day sell clothing and jewelry to raise money for her debts. This may even have been an unconscious factor in the multiplicity of her purchases. Clothes and money had become true obsessions with her since she had left Springfield for Washington. Her critics viewed her plan as cupidity rather than dementia. But the arrangements were naïve and haphazard. Mary sent Mrs. Keckley with a valuable diamond brooch and some other jewelry to W. H. Brady and Company, a firm at 609 Broadway that had caught her attention in the advertising columns of the *Herald.*

After some haggling over price Brady's partner, Seth C. Keyes, spotted Mrs. Lincoln's name inside one of the rings. Lizzie snatched it away from him and returned to the hotel with the jewelry, but Brady and Keyes followed up and finally persuaded Mrs. Lincoln to let them see her shawls, dresses and fine laces, which she frankly said she must sell in order to live. They assured her that they would raise $100,000 for her in a few weeks' time, and it was nothing new for Mary to be taken in by persuasive sycophants. They moved to a better hotel, and Brady and Keyes kept in close touch with them.

Mary found it strange to be in New York, where she had once paraded through the smartest shops with all the authority of her position, and now to be engaged in this furtive mission. She tried to preserve her anonymity by being extra-heavily veiled when she went out walking or drove in Central Park. When she and Mrs. Keckley visited some secondhand shops, they found that the dealers offered them next to nothing for their wares. Up to this point only Brady and Keyes knew the identity of Mrs. Clarke, and Mrs. Keckley did everything she could to cover up for Mrs. Lincoln.

But a reporter spotted the half-erased letters of her name on one of her trunks at Grand Union Hotel, to which they had moved, and that brought the press into the picture. The first reporter to reach Mrs. Lincoln wrote that she had changed from the "sprightly body she was when her very presence illumined the White House with gayety" to a sad and sedate figure, seeking seclusion and maintaining communication only with her most intimate friends. She was described as sitting in her hotel reading and writing letters that she regretted as soon as she had sent them—and with good cause, since Mary now found herself in a serious political tangle because of the indiscretion of some of these communications.

Keyes and Brady had urged her to write for help to some of the influential men whom her husband had backed, and one of these was Abram Wakeman, who had been appointed Postmaster and Surveryor of the Port of New York through Seward and Thurlow Weed. In a letter to Brady Mrs. Lincoln pointed out that Wakeman was indebted to her for getting this "lucrative" office, and surely he would not hesitate to return in a small manner the favors she and her husband had showered on him.

Wakeman, who had flattered her and been one of her courtiers when she was First Lady, was unresponsive. Hamilton Fish, former governor of New York and about to become Grant's Secretary of State, ignored a letter from Keyes. Then the brokers made public letters Mrs. Lincoln had written, attacking Seward; Thurlow Weed, journalist and politician who had supported Lincoln's war policies; and Henry J. Raymond, editor of the New York *Times.* She suggested that her husband had tested these men and found them wanting.

The Democratic *World* picked up the issue, and howls rose across the country when the paper flaunted this embarrassing correspondence on October 3, 1867. On the following day Weed slashed back in the New York *Commercial Advertiser,* saying that if the American Congress had failed to meet the pecuniary expectations of President Lincoln's widow, it was because she had "failed, during his life and since his death, to inspire either respect or confidence." Had she behaved otherwise, she would have been rewarded with the liberal endowments accorded the families of Grant and Farragut.

Not to be outdone by its rival, the *World,* Horace Greeley's *Tribune* suggested that Mrs. Lincoln must be deranged and would end her life in an insane asylum. Mary was profoundly shaken by this. "They would doubtless like me to begin it *now,*" she wrote angrily to Mrs. Keckley after reading this verdict on her behavior.

All the old charges against her were revived. Meddlesome Mary Lincoln. Mad Mary Lincoln. The trunks taken from the White House were again pictured as having been packed with loot belonging to the government. Her mail was no longer screened by the kindly Stoddard, and she caught the whirlwind full blast. The clothes transaction which had started it all and now floundered miserably was more or less lost in the political storm over the letters. Mary decided to go back to Chicago and leave the bargaining to Mrs. Keckley.

Fleeing from the scene, she ran into fresh embarrassment on the train bound for Chicago. She was brooding over the raw exposure in the *World* when she heard two passengers discussing what they had been reading about her in that morning's paper. One said to the other, according to the letter she wrote at once to Mrs. Keckley:"Are you aware that Mrs. Lincoln is in indigent circumstances, and has to sell her clothing and jewelry to gain means to make life more endurable?"

The other man replied: "I do not blame her for selling her

clothing, if she wishes it. I suppose *when sold* she will convert the proceeds into five-twenties to enable her to have means to be buried."

"That woman is not dead yet," was the reply.

But within a few hours' time she wished that she were, for at Fort Wayne she had an embarrassing encounter with Charles Sumner, who happened to be on her train. Here was the man who had loomed so large in her life, who had been her favorite courtier, who had shared some of the great moments of her history as the war ended. She had left her railroad car to get a cup of tea in the station dining room. Suddenly she was being ushered to a table where a "very elegant-looking gentleman" sat beside a middle-aged lady. Sumner recognized her at once.

"My black veil was doubled over my face," Mrs. Lincoln wrote. "I had taken the seat next to him. . . . I immediately *felt* a pair of eyes gazing at me. I looked him full in the face, and the glance was earnestly returned. I sipped my water, and said, 'Mr. S(umner), is this indeed you?' His face was as pale as the tablecloth. We entered into conversation. . . . He said, 'How strange you should be on the train and I not know it.'"

Mary slipped away, saying that she had to get tea for a sick friend on the train. But when she returned to her car, Sumner was there, carrying a cup of tea in his own "aristocratic hands." He was so agitated that he spilled half of it over her own *"elegantly gloved"* hands. His sad look convinced Mary in her sensitive state that he was thinking of the sordid operations at 609 Broadway. How things had changed for both of them!

"His heart was in his eyes, notwithstanding my veiled face," she wrote. "Pity for me, I fear, has something to do with all this. I never saw his manner *so* gentle and sad. . . . I did not see him again, as he returned to the lady, who was his sister-in-law from the East. . . . When he left me, *woman-like* I tossed the cup of tea out of the window, and tucked my head down and shed *bitter tears.*"

Sumner, who had married Mrs. Alice Mason Hooper, the widowed daughter-in-law of Samuel Hooper of Massachusetts, in 1866, had separated from her after a year, and a divorce would go through in 1873. It seemed to Mary the irony of fate that she should have had this painful encounter with the man whom she had most admired in Washington outside of her husband. Her state of mind was chaotic when she reached Chicago, but "darling little Taddie was waiting for me, and his voice never sounded so sweet."

Mary ended this letter by apologizing for the way in which she had treated Lizzie the night before she left New York. She had blamed her for the mess they were in. "Of course you were as innocent as a child in all you did," she wrote. "I consider you my best living friend, and I am struggling to be enabled some day to repay you."

But Robert was waiting for her return. He and Judge Davis had been distracted by her actions in New York and the embarrassing letters. Mary always denied the story that she had told the brokers they could have the letters published, but in the short time she had been in the East she had provoked a major storm.

Writing to Mrs. Keckley on October 6, she said: "I pray for death this morning. Only my darling Taddie prevents my taking my life."

Robert had acted like a maniac, "looking like death and almost threatening my life" because of the letters involving his father. She was writing from the depths of a broken heart after a sleepless night of mental suffering, and she could not refrain from weeping when she saw Robert looking so miserable. "Tell Mr. Brady and Keyes not to have a line of mine once more in print," she warned Lizzie. Two days later she wrote again to say that the Republicans were "falsifying her" and added: "What a *vile, vile* set they are. . . . I assume I would be mobbed if I ventured out. What a world of anguish this is—and how I have been made to suffer. . . . You know yourself how innocently I have acted and from the best and purest motives."

Newspaper stories saying that she was totally deranged now began to multiply across the country. She was accused of padding White House bills and of riling Seward with her questionable handling of the expenses for the famous Napoleon dinner. It was pointed out that her loyalty to the North had always been in question. A political battle was fought all over again by the New York press, a revival of the smear campaign that had preceded Lincoln's second term. It was not the first time that her sanity had been questioned, but she wasted away now as this grim suggestion leaped at her from the headlines. Her clothes began to sag on her customarily plump figure. On October 13, 1867, she wrote again to Mrs. Keckley, quoting the Springfield *Journal* that she had been known "to be deranged for years, and should be *pitied* for all her *strange acts.*" In bitterness of spirit she commented, "I should have been all right if I had allowed them to take possession of the White House."

Such was her distress that she was having daily chills in her comfortable new house, and she felt forsaken by God and man. With her incurable self-pity Mary wrote to the sympathetic Mrs. Keckley: "I am feeling so *friendless* in the world." She conveyed the same thought to Williamson in a letter written on October 29, 1867: "I am left to do the best I can for myself." By this time her link with Williamson was almost severed, and she wrote apologetically about the clothes transaction in New York. "What I did—was undertaken with the idea that no one save the agent, Lizzie & myself would know of it—I am sure from what you knew of the circumstances you were not unprepared for my action." Their correspondence dwindled, then died in that year; neither one was happy about the frantic efforts they had made to raise funds.

Mrs. Lincoln's White House garments were put up for auction in New York early in October, 1867, and the curious trooped into the showrooms to stare at her possessions. They had come to gaze rather than to buy, and the New York papers gave a dismal picture of Mary's gowns and shawls being carelessly fingered and criticized. Twenty-five dresses were tossed about, and most of them suffered from too much handling. There were comments on torn seams and on the low décolletage that Mrs. Lincoln preferred. Some of the dresses had never been worn, and their basting threads were still visible. Furs, laces and jewelry were displayed in a glass case, and Mary's exquisite point-lace shawl was exhibited by itself.

Her sable boa, her paisley shawls, her opera cloaks, her feather cape, her five lace shawls and three camel's hair shawls, her gold bracelets and other possessions seemed to be of little value to anyone. She had told Brady that, although her things were valued at more than $24,000, she would be willing to let them go for $16,000; but like everything else in her life the end was bathos. No one really cared for her things; no one genuinely admired them, perhaps because they did not admire her. They came to look because they belonged to a sensational First Lady who was again in the headlines.

Appalled by the news of the auction, Robert wrote to his fiancée, Mary Harlan, on October 16, 1867: "The simple truth, which I cannot tell to anyone not personally interested, is that my mother is on one subject not mentally responsible. I have suspected this for some time from various indications and now have no doubt of it." He had sought advice from his most trusted friends but had been told there was nothing he could do but hold his peace. When asked why he did not take charge of his mother's muddled affairs, he said that it was hard "to deal with one who is sane on all subjects but one."

Robert was wholly baffled by her monomania. "You could hardly believe it possible, but my mother protests to me that she is in actual want and nothing I can do or say will convince her to the contrary," he wrote. His strongest ally was Judge Davis, who noted on her return from New York that Mrs. Lincoln had the "insane delusion that poverty stared her in the face." When he asked her why she had done what she had in the East, she told him that it was because she was in danger of "becoming a pauper."

The old clothes scandal was so shattering that Mary reported to Mrs. Keckley that Robert had called on her with Judge Davis and that they were going to push through the settlement of the estate. "R. is very spiteful at present," she wrote, "and I think hurries up the division to cross my purposes. . . . He is very *deep*."

She asked Mrs. Keckley not to leave New York for Washington until the finest of the things that had not been sold were returned to her. She particularly wanted the *single* white camel's hair shawl and the two paisleys. And a few days later, on November 15, 1867, she wrote that she felt assured her husband's "watchful, loving eyes were watching over us, and he is fully aware of the wrong and injustice permitted his family by a country he lost his life in protecting."

Had Congress allowed her the four years' salary of her husband's unfulfilled term, she would have been able to live as the widow of the great President Lincoln should and to have left at least half of her estate to the freedmen, she assured Mrs. Keckley. "It appears to me a very remarkable coincidence, that most of the good feeling regarding my straitened circumstances proceeds from the colored people, in whose cause my noble husband was so largely interested."

A movement by the blacks to raise funds for her through the African churches had been abandoned, although Frederick Douglass and the Reverend Henry H. Garnet, both of whom had been warmly received at the White House by the President after the Emancipation Proclamation had been issued, had backed her cause in New York and Rochester. The influence of Mrs. Keckley was apparent in much of this, but the new year brought Mrs. Lincoln an unexpected blow from the woman who had been her friend and confidante throughout the war years.

When she learned that the clothes she had worn to the theater on the night of the assassination were to be exhibited in the capitals of Europe, she was stricken and wrote to Mrs. Keckley from Clifton

House on January 12, 1868: "Your letter announcing that my clothers were to be paraded in Europe—those I gave you—has almost turned me wild. R[obert] would go *raving distracted* if such a thing was done. . . . For the sake of *humanity,* if not *me* and my children, *do not* have those black clothes displayed in Europe. The thought has almost whitened every hair on my head."

Mary herself had considered showing her White House gowns in Europe when they first went on sale. She wistfully countered the criticism she incurred then by saying that no one in Europe thought anything of the Empress Eugénie selling her spectacular gowns. Women longed to touch the much discussed creations that had figured in the history of the French court.

But when it came to a vulgar display of bloodstained garments she had worn at Ford's Theater, Mary was filled with horror. She had given them to Lizzie, who had turned them over to Wilberforce College, an educational institution for black people that she was trying to help. The European plan was blocked immediately, but soon afterward Robert had ample opportunity to express his sense of outrage when Mrs. Keckley's book, *Behind the Scenes,* came out in the spring of 1868. Her name was not used at first on the title page, and obviously it had been ghosted or compiled from Lizzie's recollections and the letters she had received from Mrs. Lincoln.

Various names were discussed, including that of James Redpath, who had helped other Civil War writers with their work. Hamilton Busbey was also regarded as a strong possibility, as was Jane Swisshelm. To the end of her life Mrs. Keckley said, as she did in her preface, that the sole purpose of the book was to give the public a better understanding of Mrs. Lincoln. But her intimate picture of the Lincolns at home together, of Mary's comments on politicians, generals and Washington beauties, and of the debts that weighed on her roused another fierce storm. Many of those mentioned in the book were alive when it came out, and they were indignant.

The fact that the revelations came from a mulatto helped kill the book at the time as a compilation of backstairs gossip, but historians later found that it stood up well and gave a picture of the Lincolns in their intimate hours that no one else had presented. Much of its horror for Mrs. Lincoln and Robert lay in Lizzie's use of the letters that had passed back and forth about the sale of clothes in New York and the inferences of blackmail by the brokers to force some of President Lincoln's appointees into helping his widow. In the end Lizzie swore that her collaborator had promised not to use the letters. But her frantic attempts to apologize to Mrs. Lincoln and Robert failed, and Robert had G. W. Carleton and Company recall the book from the market. He bought up every copy he could find, with his friends' help.

It was a peculiarly blighting experience, coming at a time when his mother was already highly sensitized and in a dangerous state of mind. There would be other books, other revelations, but Mrs. Keckley had known Mrs. Lincoln as well as her own sisters had, and the wound cut deep. The intimacies so freely discussed by Mrs. Keckley were not in the mood of the Victorian era. Mrs. Lincoln's sense of dignity and privacy was stripped bare, and its coming from one who had had every chance to observe her at close range made her inconsolable. Lizzie was a century ahead of her time in turning her knowledge into profit, but it was not that she did not love Mrs. Lincoln. She, too, was malleable in the hands of others, and she was bitterly aware of the mistake she had made when she had to face the storm it caused. Her later years were not happy ones, and she died obscurely in a shabby boarding house.

Meanwhile Mary, with the help of Robert and Judge Davis, set her house in order and decided to seek escape in a "land of strangers." She would go abroad, to get away from "persecution, from the vampyre press." In May, 1868, she wrote to Mrs. White, who also was now a widow, that her plan to flee "does not argue *a debt of $70,000!!* as the colored historian asserts"—her one bitter reference to the woman she then chose to ignore.

Mary could now assure her friends that she did not owe a dollar in the world, and this miracle had indeed come to pass. Her complicated affairs had assumed such proportions in the press that Republican friends had come to the rescue. Some of the merchants had been persuaded to take back goods or settle for smaller amounts. Mary disposed of furniture, books and other possessions until all her most pressing responsibilities had been met, but much had been done behind the scenes to help her. Brady received more than $800 in commission on the sale of her clothes, and all but the few things that had been bought were returned to her.

It was a big clearing up of what had seemed like a hopeless situation, and Mary dramatized it a little to her friends by writing about her "dinnerless days." The chain of debts that had weighed on her had been removed, but it had not made her any less money-conscious. She now had the promise of Senator Sumner that he would do everything in his power to push through an adequate pension for her in Congress, and he devoted much of 1868 to this end. She was well aware that the furor from which she had just emerged might be disastrous to her in the cold world of politics. She no longer had Abraham Lincoln to temper the steel of public attack. As Katherine Helm put it: "While her husband lived she could smile and jest at the unpleasant things said of them both; but now her smiles were tears, her jests sobs. She was truly a victim of the cruel times in which she lived, a suffering, innocent creature, whose only crime was her prominence."

XX

Herndon and Ann Rutledge

MARY LINCOLN MADE many enemies during her lifetime, but
the man who tarnished her image beyond repair and contributed heavily to her ultimate collapse was William H. Herndon,
a fellow Kentuckian who had shared her husband's law office for
twenty years and knew him well. He pictured her as having made
Lincoln's home a hell on earth, as having harrassed and nagged him
night and day, as having married him only in revenge for his failure
to show up on the first date set for their wedding, an incident
vouched for by Herndon alone. Most wounding of all, and vaguely
commented on by her sister Elizabeth, he insisted that Lincoln had
never loved her.

Within a year and a half after the assassination Herndon was
telling America and the sorrowing widow that Ann Rutledge was
the girl Lincoln had loved and that he had gone mad with grief
when she died. Mary had never heard of her, and the news reached
her at a time when she was still in a fog over her husband's death. It
was more than she could bear, and although the revelations
stretched over a period of years, as Herndon assembled the material
that dimmed the picture of a great romance, the blistering years for
Mrs. Lincoln were between 1867 and 1874. She was dead when his
books became the early classics on Abraham Lincoln; they were rich
in memorabilia, reminiscences and intimacy but devastating and
questionable where she was concerned. Much of the material

reached her in one way or another before her death, and it left her an angry and shattered woman.

To her everlasting regret he used her own words, trustingly given in a friendly interview before she was aware of what Herndon was doing, to bolster his belief in her husband's lack of Christian faith. Her anger over this was laced with despair and a feeling of guilt that she should have in any way helped stoke the fires being lit around Lincoln's memory. The public conception of the assassinated President was completely changed by the flood of Herndon material that reached into the most personal areas of his life.

Mary's devotion to her husband and children was the guiding light of her existence. It was so strong as to seem obsessive. Nothing had ever mattered to her as much as the political advancement of her husband and the well-being of her sons. To read that her house was "cold—exclusive and aristocratic, with no soul—fire—cheer or fun in it," to be described as the "female wild cat of the age," to be branded materialistic, avaricious and insolent was more than she could bear; still more did she shrink from the slightest reflection on her husband's memory.

Herndon and Jesse W. Weik's compilations were devastating in their revelations, although they made a rich historical record for others to study and improve on. Various changes and modifications in later editions did not remove the original slurs. Mrs. Lincoln and Herndon had never liked each other, from the moment when he compared her sinuous grace to that of a serpent after their first dance together. He opposed Lincoln's marrying her, feeling that the tie-up to Springfield's aristocracy would not help him politically on the popular front. Mary, in turn, thought him an unsuitable partner for her husband. He was rough, unkempt, bibulous and erratic in his ways. She was used to smooth young lawyers like John Todd Stuart and John J. Hardin, and it was noted that she never invited Herndon to dine at her house, as she did the others. Yet during the Springfield years she preserved the amenities where he was concerned, recognizing the fact that he was useful to her husband in many ways and that he was unusually well informed on all manner of subjects. She visited the office occasionally and greeted Herndon in a pleasant manner, but later said that her husband regarded him merely as the "office drudge." Mary had no clue to the smouldering hate in Herndon's heart as he coped with his huge family and a wife whom he dearly loved. When she died, he married a young girl and was devoted to her, too, but in Mary's estimation he had gone downhill and was seedy when he showed up at the White House in 1861, seeking favors from the new President.

However, Mary seemed to have no apprehension when he sought to interview her for a book he was preparing on her husband's life. He had been in correspondence with Robert about a biography of his father. It seemed natural enough that he should be the collector and chronicler of the Lincoln history. None had worked more closely with him. Herndon was well known in Springfield and throughout Illinois. When Robert reported to Judge Davis in August, 1866, that he had found a box of his father's papers in Springfield, Herndon was permitted to see them. This was the starting point of years of research in Springfield, through the Sangamo Valley and the early haunts of Lincoln, to assemble the material that had a stunning impact when it finally reached the public and presented the President and Mrs. Lincoln in an entirely new light.

When Herndon wrote to Mary in the summer of 1866 asking for a brief account of the family life in the White House, she answered from 375 West Washington Street, Chicago, on August 28: "The recollections of my beloved husband's, *truly* affectionate regard for *you,* & the knowledge of your great love & reverence, of the best man, that ever lived, would of itself, cause you, to be cherished, with the sincerest regard, by my sons & myself."

Mary suggested a meeting in the St. Nicholas Hotel in Springfield on September 4, 1866, at ten o'clock in the morning. She was going to be in town that day "to visit the tomb—which contains my all in life—my husband," but she did not want anyone but Herndon to know of her presence.

The interview seemed to go smoothly, although after the damage had been done, Mary recalled that Herndon had been his usual "disagreeable self." Evidently he had been imbibing and his "appearance & the air he brought with him, were so revolting that I could scarcely ask him to be seated. . . . The flowing bowl, must have been entirely *exhausted*—when he wrote that intellectual production."

Herndon took penciled notes of the "substance" of Mrs. Lincoln's conversation, and the Chicago *Tribune* commented that Herndon's memoranda of their talk gave the "best photograph of Lincoln's real life and character that has yet been produced." It caught him from many angles, and inevitably the question of Mrs. Lincoln's influence on her husband came up in the course of their talk. She assured Herndon that Mr. Lincoln was a "terribly firm man when he put his foot down" and no one could influence him after he had fully made up his mind.

"I could always tell when in deciding anything he had reached the ultimatum," she said. "At first he was very cheerful, then he lapsed into thoughtfulness, bringing his lips together in a firm compression. When these symptoms developed I fashioned myself accordingly, and so did all others have to do sooner or later."

But Mary said, and with truth, that her husband placed great reliance on her knowledge of human nature, often telling her when he was on the verge of making an important appointment that he had no knowledge of men and their motives. She said that he greatly disliked Andrew Johnson and that he intended to remove Seward when peace was declared. When she told him on one occasion that Seward's friends said he was the power behind the throne and could rule the President, Mr. Lincoln replied: "I may not rule myself, but certainly Seward shall not. The only ruler I have is my conscience —following God in it—and these men will have to learn that yet."

Mary acknowledged that the newspaper attacks on her husband gave him pain. Sometimes he would stop her as she read them to him, saying he had heard enough, even though he might add: "But yet I care nothing for them. If I'm right I'll live and if wrong I'll die anyhow; so let them fight at me unrestrained." This was his attitude in general, and Mary recalled that when trying to prove to her husband that Chase was his enemy, he replied in his quiet way: "Be good to them who hate you . . . and turn their ill-will into friendship."

Herndon made a point of pinning Mrs. Lincoln down on her husband's religious faith. He himself was an agnostic and had passed endless hours with Lincoln discussing every aspect of Biblical faith. Mary told him honestly that Mr. Lincoln had not been a church member but that he was a religious man with a "kind of poetry in his nature." From this came Herndon's interpretation that he was not technically a Christian. When Mary was later quoted as having been the author of this statement, she was inconsolable, since it raised the cry of infidel among his enemies.

She had much to say about his devotion to her and to their sons. "He was the kindest man, most tender husband, and loving father in the world," said Mary. "He gave us all unbounded liberty. He often said, 'It is my pleasure that my children are free and happy, and unrestrained by parental tyranny. Love is the chain whereby to bind a child to its parents.' "

Mary spoke of her husband's growth during his years in office, and she impressed on Herndon the manner in which he had risen "grandly" to meet each crisis. "I never saw a man's mind develop itself so finely," she said. His manners, too, had become polished, in Mary's estimation. And none could deny that she had had a hand in this. With a traditional touch of vanity she lopped five years off her age for Herndon's sketch, saying that she was born in 1823 instead of in 1818.

Realistic biography had not yet become a national habit, and Herndon worked in devious ways to round up information. He had the help of Lincoln's family and close friends at first, but a chill developed with some when he began lecturing and writing about Lincoln and Ann Rutledge within eighteen months of the President's assassination. Robert caught the full implication of the romantic story that Herndon had brought to light, and he knew what it would mean to his mother. He wrote to Judge Davis, citing one lecture entitled "Abraham Lincoln & Ann Rutledge" and urging immediate action to stop Herndon from "making an ass of himself." Robert did not believe this story and was concerned about the "impropriety" of using it, even if it were true.

He confronted Herndon in his office in December, 1866, but Herndon had never taken Robert seriously, calling him a "little cold soul—his mother's child," and he gave no ground on this occasion. Robert told him that he did not doubt his good intentions, but since everyone interpreted his lecture as a slur on Mrs. Lincoln, he must ask him to drop it. This interview was followed by a letter from Robert begging Herndon not to publish anything that would cause pain to his father's family.

Herndon stood his ground, but by this time the press and the public were on the trail of a romantic story about Lincoln and nothing could stem the tide. Suddenly people were asking: Who is Ann Rutledge? Had Lincoln really gone mad when she died? And where did this leave Mrs. Lincoln? Curiously enough, Mary was one of the last to know about it. Living like a recluse in Chicago, she did not hear the news that had been circulating for more than three months until March, 1867. This was a staggering blow and bewildering in its unexpectedness. To hear through a public lecture by Herndon that Mr. Lincoln had never loved her, that he had known no joy in the twenty-three years of his married life, that he had loved Ann Rutledge with "all his soul, mind and strength" was more than Mary could bear. Her pride, her honor, her love all were at stake.

Above all, she worried about what it would do to her husband's reputation.

She was ill prepared to cope with this thunderbolt. Herndon, whom she had always despised, had torn to ribbons the sanctity of her home and made a mockery of her much publicized devotion to her family. She wrote at once to Judge Davis asking him to see Herndon and "direct his *wandering* mind to the truth. . . ." She admitted that it would not have been strange had Mr. Lincoln been interested in Ann: "As you justly remark, each & every one had had a little romance in their early days—but as my husband was *truth itself*, and as he always assured me, he had cared for no one but myself . . . I shall assuredly remain firm in my conviction that Ann Rutledge is a myth, for in all his confidential communications such a romantic name was never breathed. . . . Nor did his life or his joyous laugh, lead one to suppose his heart, was in any unfortunate woman's grave, but in the proper place with his loved wife & children."

Judge Davis visited Mrs. Lincoln in Chicago and tried to mollify her. He assured her that he had advised Herndon not to publish the story, and now he urged her to ignore it. For days after his visit Mary pelted him with letters urging action, and on March 8, 1867, she wrote that Herndon was a "dirty dog" who would rue the day he had failed to take the judge's advice, for in future his life would not be worth living. "He may well say his *prayers*," she added vengefully.

Herndon, in turn, had written: "Mrs. Lincoln . . . hates me on the same grounds that a thief hates a policeman." His story traveled far and could not be eradicated from the historical record, but he lacked the essential evidence that later came to light of the affectionate letters the Lincolns had exchanged over the years. All tended to show his pride in her, his faith in her opinions, his sympathy when she was beset by insane moods and impulses. In the final analysis, through these letters Mary emerged convincingly as the true love of Lincoln's life.

But the Ann Rutledge story was only the starting point of the Herndon barrage. The eventual revelations added many fresh touches to the image of Abraham Lincoln and his wife. All were of intense interest to the public, but the first and most lasting impression was the story of Ann and the unhappy homelife the President was thought to have had.

Since Mrs. Lincoln's unpopularity during the war years was a matter of record, people were willing to believe that she had tormented and nagged the President, made his home a hell on earth, and had been subject to maniacal moods. The most damaging references to her were published in the Herndon-Weik compilations after her death, but most of these reached her through Ward Hill Lamon's *Life of Abraham Lincoln*, published in 1872. While Herndon continued to collect material for his own book, Lamon bought copies of the letters, interviews and memorabilia that Lincoln's partner had assembled up to the autumn of 1869. When Lamon's book came out, with the literary aid of Chauncey Black, who was hostile to Lincoln, it proved to be a preview of Herndon's revelations.

It was not until Ruth Randall embarked on a thorough study of Mrs. Lincoln's history in the 1940's that justice was finally done her. With the opening of the Herndon-Weik papers Mrs. Randall was able for the first time to put truth and myth into perspective. She was already deeply committed to Lincoln history through her work with her husband, James G. Randall, and she was able to run to earth many of the fantastic stories concerning Mrs. Lincoln. Other writers of an earlier date who were not swayed by the Herndon material were William O. Stoddard, Isaac N. Arnold, and Henry B. Rankin.

Although years elapsed before the Herndon revelations appeared in book form, Mary kept close watch on the early books and articles about her husband. They came thick and fast, and although she was concerned when she heard that Henry Raymond had asked to see Lincoln's papers, she was well pleased with his book. She had great expectations of Josiah G. Holland's biography of her husband. He was the managing editor of the Springfield *Republican* in Massachusetts and had some reputation as a historian. With considerable tact Mary made clear to him where he had gone astray in his appraisal of her husband, and she was particularly disturbed by his version of Lincoln's abortive duel with Shields, but her comments were mild.

The early books and articles that she studied with care were written close to the time of the assassination and hence were friendly and uncritical in tone, but as the years passed six thousand volumes, dealing with every aspect of Lincoln's history and nature, had been published. None stirred up such waves as the Herndon-Weik revelations.

Mary's most articulate defender when the first of Herndon's charges became public was Lincoln's old friend, the Reverend

James Smith, whose letters from Dundee, Scotland, on the President's religious faith and his love for his wife were well publicized. Actually Mary masterminded this correspondence, sending the minister notes on what she wanted said about her husband's religious views and pinpointing the time of publication. There was little that Mary did not know about the inner workings of the journalistic world, bitter though her own experiences had been with it.

Smith was already incensed over a peremptory letter he had received from Herndon asking him for specific "written evidence" that he had converted Lincoln to Christianity during their days together in Springfield. He wanted the President's exact words and not Smith's interpretation of what had occurred between them. This was legal practice, but it seemed out of place to the Reverend Mr. Smith.

On top of this letter came Herndon's lecture attacking Mrs. Lincoln and reflecting on the President's unhappy homelife, which caused Smith to point out that he had watched them at their own fireside and thought that Mr. Lincoln's heart was "overflowing with love and affection" for his wife. He found it absurd of Herndon to suggest that no words of love or affection ever appeared in Lincoln's letters to his wife, which were frequently signed "Yours truly." The Lincoln correspondence in time proved this to be false, since he often signed his letters to Mary "Yours affectionately." And if the Ann Rutledge story were true, as Herndon told it, then he was making the President out to have been "worse than a dishonest man."

Always the champion of both Lincolns, Smith wrote furiously, "Oh, Sir, was it not enough that Mrs. Lincoln should be overwhelmed and stricken to the earth by the dreadful ... blow which had fallen upon her, in the cruel death of her husband, but you must come upon the scene and mingle your poisoned chalice into the cup of woe which she must drink even to the dregs."

Herndon's letter to Smith and the minister's reply appeared together in the Chicago *Tribune*, and Mary suffered over these revelations. But this was only the beginning of what later came to pass. As Herndon and Weik rounded up their material through the years, it was extraordinary how many close friends of the Lincolns spoke ill of them. In addition to exhausting the files of the *Sangamon Journal*, later the Illinois *State Journal*, and all the other newspaper sources he could trace, Herndon for years followed trails and sought out people who had had even a remote association with the

President or his wife. The good and the bad, the true and the untrue made a mixture that later historians sought to unravel and appraise.

Mary had never been popular in Springfield, and her years in the White House had clouded her image still further. Political rivalry and jealousy dating back to Lincoln's early days in Illinois tended to dim the picture where even he was concerned. He had yet to reach full stature in the eyes of the world, and glimmers of gossip and reproach invaded the reverential afterglow that followed his assassination. Ninian Edwards had turned against him when Lincoln failed to give him an appointment in the federal government, and so he called him an ungrateful, not a warmhearted man. Mrs. Edwards was more scathing than loyal in discussing her sister and gave some support to Herndon's story of the marriage date that was supposedly broken. She said she believed Lincoln loved Mary but that he went crazy "because he wanted to marry and doubted his ability & capacity to please and support a wife."

James H. Matheny, best man when the ceremony finally took place, jested about the earlier debacle, to which he seemed to give credence, and noted that "Mrs. Lincoln often gave Lincoln hell in general. . . . *Ferocity*—describes Mrs. L's conduct to L." Even John Todd Stuart, who had taken Lincoln into his law firm and had been a close friend of Mary's before the two men became politically estranged, described her husband as a "kind of vegetable" and said other unflattering things about him. Although the assassination had changed the picture where Lincoln was concerned, the bitterness of the Civil War remained and both of the Lincolns were easy prey to attack. Because the story of Ann Rutledge was a mortal blow to Mrs. Lincoln, it was played to the limit by her enemies.

Few historians today accept the details that Herndon recorded about Lincoln and Ann Rutledge. Most are willing to concede that he knew her and had a friendly interest in her well-being. According to Mrs. Randall, when a full investigation and critical analysis were made of the Rutledge material in the 1940's, so many inconsistencies and contradictions came to light that little remained except the certainty that Lincoln had boarded at Ann's home, the Rutledge Tavern, during his early months in New Salem; that her fiancé was a friend of his; that he encouraged Ann to pursue her education; and that, like other neighbors, he grieved when she died.

Mary insisted when she first heard the story that Ann Rutledge was a myth, that she had never existed, and that Mr. Lincoln had always told her that she, Mary, was the only woman he had ever loved. But Ann May(e)s Rutledge did exist. She was born in Kentucky in 1816 and died in New Salem in 1835 of typhoid, known at the time as brain fever. Her story had a sentimental quality in keeping with the mood of the 1830's, and it was a piquant thought that beautiful blue-eyed Ann, with the reddish-blonde hair, should have died of a broken heart because of her divided love between Lincoln and John McNamar, the man to whom she was engaged. It remains a strong legend today as thousands of sightseers from different parts of the world each year walk through the bosky vales of New Salem, view the old cabins, and picture Lincoln strolling with the girl who was said to have charmed him by singing old ballads. This was a fresh and provocative view of a man who was being canonized when the tale was made public.

Herndon's pertinacious quest for Ann Rutledge reminiscences was carried out around New Salem thirty years after her death, and relatives and neighbors to whom he talked contradicted one another freely. In the intervening years Lincoln had emerged as a great man, and some of Herndon's informants retracted or changed their stories as a storm blew up about these revelations. But the natives of New Salem still cherish this romance and see no extravagance in Edgar Lee Masters' poem inscribed on Ann's tombstone, with its significant line: "Beloved of Abraham Lincoln."

Although he told his story in detail, Herndon at no time quoted Lincoln on the subject; it was never the great man's habit to discuss personal affairs in the office, friendly though the partners were on political issues and their legal work. It was more significant that Lincoln never mentioned Ann to Joshua Speed, his confidant where affairs of the heart before his marriage were concerned. David Donald, who studied every aspect of Herndon's life in writing his biography, gave a guarded view of the Rutledge story: "Whether Lincoln and Ann were in love, whether they were engaged . . . are conjectures on which Herndon's own witnesses differed sharply. His further inference that Lincoln's entire life was shaped by this romance, that Ann's death caused him to throw himself in politics, and that Lincoln never loved another woman, rest upon no particular proof." James G. Randall made further havoc with the legend in "Sifting the Ann Rutledge Evidence" in *Lincoln the President: Springfield to Gettysburg*. And Paul M. Angle remained unconvinced.

But this was one of the major scars of Mrs. Lincoln's life, and the perpetuation of the legend in books, plays and films has tended to cloud the authentic love story of Mary Todd and Abraham Lincoln. Ann's father was the founder of New Salem, a man concerned with scholarship and a pillar in the little community. As the village grew, he turned his home into a tavern, where Lincoln lodged in 1832. He could scarcely have failed to notice the pretty daughter of the house, but she was already engaged to John McNamar, who had come from the East, hoping to make a fortune. John bought property and within three years owned a farm and had a half interest in a local store. When he decided to go back East and bring his family to New Salem, the Rutledges moved to his farm seven miles from New Salem, believing that Ann would soon be marrying "Mack," as he was known.

Lincoln saw less of Ann after this. Time passed, and McNamar failed to return as he coped with illness in his family and settling his father's estate. According to Herndon, Lincoln had fallen deeply in love with Ann, and she had written to McNamar, asking to be released from her engagement. Beyond that, Lincoln was pictured as telling Ann that he had no money but would marry her when he had finished his law studies. Such was Herndon's tale, substantiated only by some family proof that Lincoln had shown interest in Ann's education and had urged her to go to college.

McNamar was still away when Ann died on August 25, 1835. No visitors were allowed to go near her except Lincoln, for whom she asked. "What was said, what vows and revelations were made during this interview, were known only to him and the dying girl," Herndon commented. When she died a few days later, she was buried seven miles from Petersburg. Because of her fame, a handsome monument was raised to her memory in the course of time.

John McNamar returned after Ann's death, and in the general effort to establish Lincoln's role in her life, he carved her initials on a board, along with the inscription: "I never heard . . . any person say that Mr. Lincoln addressed Miss Ann Rutledge in terms of courtship neither her own family nor my acquaintance otherwise." The errant suitor and Lincoln remained friends.

Herndon's account of Lincoln's actions at the time of Ann's death matches the other shadowy details of this woodland romance, if romance it ever was. He was described as wandering up and down the river and into the woods in a state of great distress, and one friend quoted him as saying that the "snows and rains falling upon her grave filled him with indescribable grief." Mrs. Randall deduced that Herndon confused this with Lincoln's despair before he married Mary Todd and his collapse in the winter of 1841. He was staying at Mrs. Bennett Abell's cabin in New Salem when Ann Rutledge died, and she told Herndon that Lincoln was not crazy but "he was very disponding." But those who knew Lincoln best in these surroundings, as later in his life, were not unused to his melancholy moods.

Mrs. Abell knew him well, for however wraithlike the Ann Rutledge romance appears to have been, there was no doubt about the reality of Lincoln's halfhearted attempts to marry her sister, Mary Owens, whom he had first seen in 1833, when she came from Kentucky for a visit. The young lawyer, with marriage on his mind, found her intelligent and attractive. Three years later Miss Owens returned for a longer stay, with her sister openly playing the role of matchmaker and finding her quarry cooperative. Remembering Mary's pleasant manners and interesting conversation, Lincoln wrote that he was "most confoundedly well pleased with the project . . . and saw no good objection to plodding through life hand in hand with her."

Like Mary Lincoln, Miss Owens was of Southern birth. She was highly educated, a good conversationalist and coquettish in manner, a combination that seemed irresistible to Lincoln. But on her return visit he was startled to find that her teeth were gone and that her girth had become formidable in the intervening three years. A friend of Miss Owens described her to Herndon as being "tall, portly, had large blue eyes and the finest trimming I ever saw. She was jovial, social, loved wit and humor, had a liberal English education, and was considered wealthy."

But Lincoln did not seem to generate any real warmth in Mary Owens. She was scornful of his boorish manners and, unlike Mary Todd, had no understanding of his inner nature. By her own admission she did not think his rudeness was due to lack of goodness of heart; it was simply a question of training too different from hers. They thought alike politically at the time, although after Lincoln became President, the breach between North and South marked a dividing line in their outlook.

For a time things moved along at a leisurely pace. Lincoln missed Mary Owens when he had to spend ten weeks doing legislative work in Vandalia, and he urged her to write to him. When the legislature adjourned, he was back in Springfield and could drive over to New Salem to visit her. But Springfield, like Vandalia, was a lonely place for a young lawyer in those days, and he wrote to Mary on May 7,

1837, that he had never been more "lonesome" anywhere. Only one woman had spoken to him since his arrival. They had tentatively discussed her coming to Springfield as his wife, but he now wrote to her discouragingly, knowing what she wanted from life. It was not what he could give her. "I am afraid you would not be satisfied. There is a great deal of flourishing about in carriages here, which it would be your doom to see without sharing in it. You would have to be poor without the means of hiding your poverty. Do you believe you could bear that patiently? Whatever woman may cast her lot with mine, should anyone ever do so, it is my intention to do all in my power to make her happy and contented, and there is nothing I can imagine that would make me more unhappy than to fail in the effort. I know I should be much happier with you than the way I am, provided I saw no signs of discontent in you."

Again he pleaded for a letter to cheer him in the "busy wilderness of Springfield" and said that it gave him the "hypo" to hear that Mrs. Abell was thinking of selling her place at New Salem and moving away. The "hypo" was Lincoln's favorite term for the blues, to which he was no stranger. His loneliness and desire for feminine companionship underlay his letters to Mary Owens. At the same time the stability of marriage for an ambitious young lawyer may have entered into his calculations. But it was not an impassioned affair on either side. He did not touch Mary Owens' heart as he did Mary Todd's a few months later. After considerable correspondence and a number of meetings Mary Owens decided not to marry young Mr. Lincoln.

Like Ann Rutledge, her story was fair game for Herndon. On May 1, 1866, a year after the President's death, he wrote to her, asking for recollections for his book. By that time she was Mrs. Jesse Vineyard, of Weston, Missouri, the mother of five, and unquestionably she had followed Lincoln's course in the White House with interest. She had not seen him since they parted company in 1838, when, to all intents and purposes, she had jilted him.

Mrs. Vineyard was dubious about letting Herndon have Lincoln's letters to her, but in the end she did, trusting to his discretion not to misuse them. At the same time she wrote to him: "From his own showing you perceive that his heart and hand were at my disposal; and I suppose that my feelings were not sufficiently enlisted to have the matter consummated."

A string of searching questions by Herndon evoked one much quoted comment that "Mr. Lincoln was deficient in those little links which make up the chain of woman's happiness—at least it was so in my case." Among other lapses she was critical of his failure to help her across a treacherous stream when they were out riding with friends. As his companions helped all the girls across, Lincoln rode straight on, leaving Mary to her fate. "I suppose you did not care whether my neck was broken or not," she said as she caught up with him. He told her that he knew she was "plenty smart enough" to take care of herself—a compliment that she did not particularly appreciate. This was one of a number of incidents that persuaded Mary Owens that Abraham Lincoln was not good husband material, although he kept assuring her, "I want in all cases to do right; and most particularly so in all cases with women."

When the break came after much irresolution on his part and two rejections on Mary's, Lincoln wrote a jesting but curiously bitter letter to Mrs. Orville Browning on April 1, 1838. He referred to Miss Owens as being "over-size . . . a fair match for Falstaff." She made him think of his "old mother and this was not for withered features—for her skin was too full of fat to permit of its contracting into wrinkles—but from her want of teeth, and weatherbeaten appearance in general."

The satire that ran through this letter suggested considerable pain. Mary's two rejections, he wrote, had mortified him in a hundred different ways. "My vanity was deeply wounded by the reflections, that I had so long been too stupid to discover her intentions, and at the same time never doubting that I understood them perfectly; and also, that she whom I had taught myself to believe nobody else would have, had actually rejected me with all my fancied greatness; and to cap the whole, I then, for the first time, began to suspect that I was really a little in love with her. But let it all go. I'll try and outlive it. Others have been made fools of by the girls; but this can never with truth be said of me. I most emphatically, in this instance, made a fool of myself. I have now come to the conclusion never again to think of marrying, and for this reason: I can never be satisfied with anyone who would be blockhead enough to have me."

This was the mood Lincoln was in when he looked across the ballroom floor and had his first glimpse of Mary Todd. His fate was set in that hour, and so was hers.

XXI

Escape to Europe

H URT BEYOND ENDURANCE by the ceaseless animosity and criticism that pursued her, Mrs. Lincoln seemed to know instinctively that she was losing her balance and must seek peace abroad. She wrote to a friend that she had brooded so much that travel was the only way to prolong her life. Beyond that was her old ambition to have her backward Tad receive some formal education and to give him the benefit of foreign travel. This was something that the President had planned for all of them when his term of office ended.

Just before sailing, she attended Robert's marriage to Mary Harlan, the girl she had long ago decided was the ideal mate for her oldest son. She was staying at Barnum's Hotel in Baltimore preparatory to sailing for Europe when she was suddenly called to Washington for the wedding, which was held at Judge Harlan's house. The ceremony had been speeded up so that Mary could attend before starting her secret trip to Europe. Tad had begged her to stay for the wedding, although her relations with Robert had been more than chilly since the President's death, and she had recently been at Cresson in the mountains of Pennsylvania trying to muster strength for the voyage. But in spite of her ill health and depression the marriage of her oldest son could not fail to stir her from her apathy.

Mrs. Lincoln had not been back to the capital since leaving the White House, and she dreaded the sight of the familiar domes and streets. Judge Harlan, with Mary and Robert, met her at the depot, and old friends like Gideon Welles called to see her. Washington seemed to make Tad uneasy and difficult to handle. His mother concluded that this was because of his associations there. But he showed great interest in Bob's marriage. The wedding ceremony was held on September 25, 1868, with Bishop Matthew Simpson, of the Methodist Church, officiating and thirty guests in attendance.

There was much interest in Mrs. Lincoln, looking handsome in a fashionable dress, heavily braided and richly trimmed, and Mary Harlan was an attractive bride. Mrs. Lincoln watched every move with an attentive eye, but the visit to Washington proved to be too much for her. On her return to Baltimore she had one of her "seizures" as she was being seated in the dining room of Barnum's Hotel. In her own words: "I found my head becoming dizzy and everything appeared black before me. A very distinguished looking gentleman gave me his arm and led me to my room door. . . ."

After that she took her meals upstairs until she and Tad sailed for Bremen on the *City of Baltimore* on October 1, 1868. Her name was not on the passenger list and she was veiled beyond recognition, but she did not wholly escape the vigilant press. On October 6 the New York *Tribune* noted that Mrs. Lincoln had departed in peace for Europe, intending to enter her son in school abroad. In time she would be sharply criticized for enrolling Abraham Lincoln's son in English and German schools. The feeling was strong that an American President's son should be educated in his native land.

Few recognized the dignified figure in deep mourning, moving restlessly from place to place in Europe between 1868 and 1871, as the widow of Abraham Lincoln. His memory was still fresh, but she was already forgotten, and the presence of Tad at her side meant nothing except to Americans established in the foreign field or travelers from home. This was the way she wanted it, and she shrank from recognition, for she had reached the stage where she felt she could stand no more.

On reaching Frankfurt, Tad was enrolled with German and English boys at Dr. D. Hohagen's Institute, where he remained from October, 1868, to April, 1870. It was a new experience for Tad to be in an atmosphere of order and discipline, and at first he clung to his mother. She stayed at the fashionable Hotel d'Angleterre and immediately established the pattern of seclusion that was becoming second nature to her. Although her presence was noted by American residents, both permanent and transient, she showed no inclination to accept their invitations. William Walton Murphy, the American consul in Frankfurt, made her welcome at once, and she occasionally saw General Robert Allen, an old Springfield friend, and Mrs. Henry Mason, whose husband was a founder of the Mason and Hamlin Organ Company. All lived at her hotel and were anxious to do what they could for Abraham Lincoln's widow.

She showed keen interest in the European nobles who abounded in Frankfurt, and they all left cards and sought to entertain her. Because of her health and deep mourning she declined their formal invitations but showed childish excitement when she came face-to-face with a crown princess. Both were in a shop buying fans. Mrs. Lincoln had not changed in one respect, and she was soon ordering dresses from Popp, one of the top couturiers of the period. He dressed Queen Victoria's daughters, as well as many British peeresses and rich American women traveling abroad. With her strong kinship for royalty Mary soon had him make up some heavy mourning silks, lavishly trimmed with crepe. She was gratified to find that the heaviest English crepe, for which she had paid ten dollars a yard in America, cost only fifty cents in Frankfurt.

But the prices in general dismayed her as she paid her hotel bills and picked up bibelots for Christmas. Tad increasingly liked his school and had recovered from his early homesickness. Although his mother was within easy range, she was no longer at hand to humor him in every whim, and this seemed to do him good. The school was sufficiently spartan to toughen him and to give him a better sense of proportion about his own importance. But Tad had memories that none of the other pupils could boast, and his English-speaking schoolmates regarded him with a touch of awe and affection.

Mary managed to cover a great deal of ground in Europe and to send her friends piquant and entertaining letters about her travels, the people she met, and the political situation at home and abroad.

Much as she liked Frankfurt, with its cosmopolitan air and worldly visitors from neighboring countries, the weather proved too rigorous for her fragile constitution, and after being severely ill during her first winter there, she moved south to Nice. She was soon rejoicing in her surroundings, a new Mary conscious of the "flowers growing in the gardens, oranges on the trees, my windows open all day, looking out upon the calm, blue Mediterranean."

She found this a glorious change, for she had lived so long in darkness, and on February 17, 1869, she wrote to Mrs. Felician Slataper in one of her fast swings from depression to elation: "Was there ever such a climate, such a sunshine, such air? You cannot turn for flowers, beautiful bouquets thrust into your very face. I never return from my walks without my hands being filled and yet to me, they bring sad, deeply painful memories."

Mary had dreamed of Willie the night before—a common occurrence with her now. "Time brings to me no healing on its wing and I shall be only too glad when my mission, which I know to be my precious child Taddie, is complete, to be rejoined to my dearly loved ones who have 'gone before.' "

Tad and Daniel Slataper had played together at Cresson, Pennsylvania, before the Lincolns sailed for Europe, and they continued to correspond from time to time. Mrs. Slataper had four children, and they had found a mutual link in their sons. She was the wife of an Austrian-born consulting engineer who lived in Pittsburgh and had a summer cottage at Cresson. Mrs. Slataper was anxious to know how Mary and Tad were faring in Europe, for she had helped her make her decision to go abroad for her health.

Mary's interest in spiritualism had been quite marked before she sailed, and she seemed at times to understand the irrationality of her thoughts and to shy away from the occult. She longed to have her "strength of mind return to her even partially," she wrote, indicating that she was fighting the ghosts that waylaid her and knew their danger.

She was observant of people around her as she traveled and was critical of Americans abroad. She wrote to Mrs. White from Nice on March 16, 1869, that they were everywhere, and on her morning walks in the sunshine she could always recognize them, often by their loud voices and their *"velvet costumes"* worn as early as ten or eleven in the morning. She did not approve of this sort of dress for travelers who were either sight-seeing or trying to improve their health, she wrote, adding that everything looked desolate to her without her husband.

In the gay atmosphere of the Riviera, with the postwar matrons and their daughters from America arriving with smart new Parisian clothes and fortunes to spend, Mary pondered sadly on the aftermath of the war, which had been so close to her life. Paris was alive with Americans building diplomatic fences, with profiteers who had made wartime fortunes, with people from the North and South who were holidaying after the great struggle they had survived. She saw much of it through a haze of memory—familiar names, generals now out of uniform, diplomats whom she had entertained in the White

House, correspondents who had written about her. She shrank instinctively from it all and preferred to dwell with her sorrows.

The note of self-pity was a constant refrain, but her visitors were sometimes amazed that she stood up so well to her new way of life, often in cramped quarters and without any of the comforts to which she had always been accustomed. But she was still Mrs. Lincoln to the men and women who had known her husband and revered him.

Her health improved greatly on the Riviera, and she was back in Frankfurt by the end of March, 1869. This time she avoided the expensive Hotel d'Angleterre and settled on the fourth floor of the modest Hotel de Holland, climbing the stairs and living in spartan quarters. She felt she could not afford a maid, and Tad stayed out of school to nurse her when she was ill. He had his father's tenderness in this respect, and she told Mrs. Orne of his "dark, loving eyes watching over her and reminding her of his dearly beloved father's." He brought her soft flannel ordered by her doctors to wear against her skin during a serious illness in Frankfurt. It was Tad's fate to see his mother through many crises, and he was used to her sobs and moans. At times he bolstered her shattered ego with his quaint and comforting ways. He persuaded her to abandon her mourning for a day while she helped him celebrate his birthday.

Tad could be more persuasive with his mother than anyone else in her life, and she was encouraged about him during the Frankfurt days. His speech had noticeably improved, and she was impressed with the progress he was making with his German tutor. His classes left her free to roam by herself and to seek relief from her rheumatism at Marienbad, but occasionally Tad had permission to make brief trips with his mother. He went with her to Heidelberg and Baden, and they drove together in the Black Forest. Mary had always believed in the benefits to be gained from spas, and this was her chance to join the hordes of Americans and Britons who sought relief and recreation at the German resorts. On her way to Bohemia she stopped at Nuremberg to visit the castles and churches, and she wrote enthusiastically about Oberursel and a church there dating back to 1610. She was so impressed with this place that when Tad finished at Dr. Hohagen's Institute, she entered him for two months at a school in Oberursel. From Baden they visited La Favorita, where one of Germany's traditional White Ladies held legendary sway.

A fresh interest was added to Mary's life when she became a grandmother in the autumn of 1869. Robert and Mary named their daughter Mary Todd Lincoln, and this mellowed her attitude toward them. She shopped with enthusiasm for "Little Mamie" and sent gifts to Robert's wife, including a fashionable Marie Louise wrap. Her worldly sense was still alive, and she urged the younger Mary to go out every day and enjoy herself in the sunshine. "You are so very young, and should be as gay as a lark," she wrote. "Trouble comes soon enough, my dear child, and you must enjoy life, whenever you can. We all love you so very much—and you are blessed with a devoted husband and darling child. . . ."

Mary urged her daughter-in-law to make use of anything that she had left at their house, including a double India shawl that she had never worn. Her head ached from the tears she had shed that morning while thinking of their little household in Chicago, she wrote. The doctor had just been to visit her, and he was surprised to find her sitting up after the severe illness she had had.

The constant change in scene and atmosphere served at times to divert Mrs. Lincoln from her ceaseless lamentation, but her letters continued to reflect the discomforts as well as the beauties of her restless touring. There seemed to be no end to her sufferings from headaches, neuralgia and depression. But things were better when, during his school vacation in the summer of 1869, Mary took Tad on the traditional tour then being enjoyed by Americans abroad. For seven weeks they covered the ground that Longfellow, Hawthorne, Washington Irving and other compatriots had written about with assorted impressions. Mary was an intelligent and strenuous sightseer, who missed few of the cultural highlights or natural beauties of the countries they visited. She was her old sparkling self, alive and discerning, and she took special delight in historical landmarks and in the association of nobles and grandees.

Her five days in Paris were the fulfillment of an old dream, but Tad's frail legs grew weary as they paraded through endless corridors, studying the world's great art. Mary's lifelong interest in history and her wide reading had prepared her well for the sights of Paris. She found time, too, to visit the shops and buy some clothes.

When she and Tad landed in Britain, strictly incognito, the Reverend James Smith sailed down from Scotland to meet them in London and take them north. "Beautiful, glorious Scotland, has spoilt me for every other country," Mary wrote after the conventional round of Abbotsford, Dryburgh Abbey, six days in Edinburgh, then Glasgow and a trip on the Clyde. Mary, who knew Sir Walter Scott's work almost by heart, toured the Rob Roy country, saw Loch Katrine, and drove through the majestic Pass of Glencoe. Since it was not the Scottish season, Queen Victoria was not in residence when she passed by Balmoral, but had she been, Mary felt sure her majesty would have welcomed a "sister in grief," she wrote to Mrs. White from Kronberg on August 30, 1869.

She particularly enjoyed her visit to the wild west coast, exploring Fingal's Cave and growing sentimental over Burns' birthplace and Highland Mary's grave. These surroundings brought a flood of recollections as she thought of the number of times she had listened to Mr. Lincoln reading Burns' poetry. She and the Reverend Mr. Smith passed some nostalgic hours over this.

On their way back to Frankfurt they stopped in Belgium and visited Waterloo. Tad was a veteran of other battlefields, so this stop was of prime interest to him. He had known several members of Napoleon's family in Washington, and war was a real and terrible thing to him, young though he was. He had grown up to the roll of drums and the crack of muskets.

The years 1869 and 1870 sped by in a whirl of travel, illness and transatlantic communications. Mrs. Lincoln followed an erratic and restless course. She crossed the English Channel several times and made many return visits to spots that she particularly liked, but Frankfurt remained her headquarters as long as Tad was in school there. She considered entering him in a school in Italy at this juncture, feeling that both might benefit from the climate. Her doctors were always advising her that what she needed was the sunshine of Italy or the south of France. But her fast-growing son had become desperately homesick. Constant colds debilitated him, and he was tired of all the irregularities of their wandering existence. His mother was worried about his education and the need for better instruction in English, since his accent by this time had become slightly Germanic. So they returned to England, and Mary at once found her way to the most comfortable spa within easy reach of London.

Leamington for a time proved to be the best stopping place of all that she had tried. It seemed a garden spot with the glory of the copper beaches in October. Close to Kenilworth, Warwick and Stratford-on-Avon, the historical and literary associations of the region were satisfying to Mrs. Lincoln. Best of all, she had found a "quiet, patient and gentlemanly scholar" to tutor Tad, who soon was studying seven and a half hours a day six days a week. This was a stiff regime for delicate Tad, but Mary was pleased with the results when she gave him a three-hour examination at the end of each week and, with full belief in her own scholarship, noted a great improvement in his work. He already spoke German well. Now he was coming to grips with English history and literature, both visually and from his books. All this was satisfying to his mother, who never ceased to foster the academic spirit in the young. His father had always thought that his frail Tad should be allowed to run free and wild, that no pressures should be applied. But she had now learned that Tad *could* be educated, at whatever cost to his frail constitution.

Both began to suffer acutely from the English climate, and Mary made a big decision when she wrote to her daughter-in-law, suggesting that Tad be sent back to America just before Christmas so that Bob might enter him in an American school. But she soon changed her mind, for she could not bear to part with him, and she wrote again to Mary, pointing out that she feared to trust her "beautiful, darling *good boy*" to the elements in that season of the year.

No doubt Mary had been getting some practical advice from the American visitors she had when she returned to London and settled in comfortable quarters at 9 Woburn Place, just off Russell Square. It had been reassuring for Tad to see General Sheridan calling on his mother and showing an interest in his growth and development. This was a link with his father and the life that he understood. The comte de Paris came calling to take her driving, just as if they all were in Washington again. Mary was glad to report to Charles Sumner that his friend John Lothrop Motley, Minister to Great Britain had called on her. Benjamin Moran, Secretary of the Legation, had also given her courteous attention, and John Evans, governor of Colorado Territory during the Civil War, who had brought his son to England to place him in a school, discussed Tad's future with her and gave her advice. Adam Badeau, who had been General Grant's military secretary, also came back into her life at this time, but not happily.

There are differing versions of Mrs. Lincoln's life in London at this time. The publicity surrounding her fight for a pension had revived some of the scandalous charges to which she had been exposed in her White House days. There were many powerful people in London who had favored the Confederate cause and who were by no means friendly to the widow of Abraham Lincoln. To some she seemed to be her old proud self, no longer able to maintain the status she had always desired and thus preferring to live as a recluse and shun her fellow countrymen, except those of whose friendship she was sure. To others she seemed elusive, morbid and strange. But some old friends, visiting her in London, found her as she had always been—witty, intelligent, alive to current affairs and considerate of their comfort.

Adam Badeau wrote patronizingly in the New York *World* of January 8, 1875, that he was a consul in London while she was there, and that when he learned of her living in an obscure quarter and being neglected, he invited her to his house. "She declined in fine style, her note of thanks betraying how rare such courtesies had become to her," he noted.

But it seems unlikely that Mrs. Lincoln, knowing him to have been President Grant's friend and amanuensis and remembering the scene at the battlefield, would enjoy seeing much of Badeau. Paul L. Shipman, a former editor of the Louisville *Courier*, who, with his wife, had been seeing a good deal of Mrs. Lincoln in London, wrote an indignant letter to his old paper, refuting everything that Badeau had said about Mrs. Lincoln's isolation and strange behavior in London.

Shipman pointed out that, far from living in an obscure quarter, she was within five minutes' walk of the British Museum in a region noted for its fine mansions and established families. Nor had she been neglected. Bishop Matthew Simpson, who had delivered the eulogy at President Lincoln's burial in Springfield, was one of her visitors, as well as Motley, the comte de Paris and many others who had known her in Washington. He had personally taken her to hear Charles H. Spurgeon, the Baptist preacher who was stirring up England with his books and sermons.

Had her health been better and had she been able to go out more, the Shipmans would have done a great deal more for her, but they usually had to see her at her hotel, since she and Tad always seemed to have severe colds. Mrs. Shipman was an old friend of Mary's mother and of the Joshua Speeds. She had remarried and was on her wedding trip with Paul Shipman. Since she was expecting a baby, she was not able to get out too much. She had tried to look up Mary in Germany, but they had missed connections. Now they were making up for it in London, and Mrs. Shipman noted that Mrs. Lincoln was as mercurial and vivacious as of old. She was full of "repartee and dash . . . a more affectionate heart I never knew." Moreover, she was frank, and when she thought the occasion demanded it, she was still capable of making a cutting remark. She bore herself, in Mrs. Shipman's opinion, as a "warmhearted, whole-souled high-spirited Kentucky woman, which she was."

Shipman, who had not known Mrs. Lincoln in her earlier days as his wife had, found her "sympathetic, cordial, sensible, intelligent, and brimming with bonhomie." Not a trace of eccentricity showed in her conduct or manners. She was simply a "bright, wholesome attractive woman," and he could not reconcile the Mrs. Lincoln of the newspapers with the Mrs. Lincoln he saw in London.

This was a period of comparative peace for her as she viewed the historic landmarks of London. While wandering about the streets, she looked in shop windows for trifles to send to her grandchild, and she wrote to Robert's wife begging them to come over with the baby. Mrs. Lincoln flatteringly wrote that she only hoped Tad in time would marry someone who suited her in the role of daughter-in-law as well as Mary had. Tad, she said, was still being tutored by the man he had had in Leamington, and for the first time in his life he seemed to realize the necessity of a good education.

But Robert was not responsive to Mary's plea that they join her in London. His own affairs were prospering. He had bought a handsome house on Wabash Avenue and was building up his own career. He was still quite shaken by the shattering publicity of the pension fight, and Judge Davis continued to wrestle with the complicated details of the Lincoln estate.

Mary's health slipped badly in the London climate. By February, 1871, she had made arrangements to leave Tad in an English school at Brixton attended by Governor Evans' son, while she journeyed to Italy with a companion. She was flooded with high spirits as she traveled through the Tyrol, saw Milan Cathedral and "The Last Supper," and sailed around Lake Como, enjoying every moment of its beauties and of the romantic villages on the hillsides. All her life she had longed to visit Florence, and in the White House she had entertained many of the writers and artists whose lifeblood it seemed to be. Now she could see the Pitti Palace and Fiesole for herself. She wrote to her friends of viewing the king's residence and the room "where the beautiful Princess Marguerite sleeps." Before leaving Florence, she visited the studio of Larkin Goldsmith Mead, the sculptor who was working on the Lincoln Monument for Springfield.

She could think of home again with some equanimity, since she had won the long and bitter battle for a pension that had disheartened her during the days she spent abroad. In December, 1868, while she was still in Frankfurt, she had formally applied to the Senate for a pension. She stated her case in a brief letter asking for this boon to relieve her "pecuniary cares." Her request, Mary wrote, was in consideration of the "great services which my deeply lamented husband has rendered to the United States, and of the fearful loss I have sustained by his untimely death . . . his martyrdom, I may say."

Senator Sumner drew up the pension bill, and in January, 1869, it was introduced to the Fortieth Congress by Benjamin Wade, who had once spurned Mrs. Lincoln's most famous party at the White House. The bill failed to pass the first time, but when General Grant became President, it came up again at an extra session of the Forty-first Congress. Here, according to Senator Sumner, it was deliberately smothered, and it took more than a year to have it forced onto the floor for general debate. Various efforts were made to kill it on the grounds that President Lincoln was not a military officer; that there was no precedent for the action; that it was not in line with government policy; and that Mrs. Lincoln was not destitute.

Mary was back in the headlines as she moved restlessly from place to place in Europe, worrying night and day about the ingratitude of her country and her own financial insecurity. Her pride and her cupidity were equally involved, but in retrospect the treatment she received was infused with the venom that seemed to be her lot. The press again assailed the half-forgotten First Lady. Although the New York *Times*, the *Tribune* and the *Herald* all were behind her in what she and many others considered a "matter of common justice," other papers revived the most damaging old stories about her until she doubted that the measure could ever pass. The smears included the fantastic tale that she had been a party to the assassination plot against her husband and had been exiled as a punishment. It seemed that anything could be said about Mary Lincoln at home or abroad.

The Senate was more obstinate than the House about the pension, for many of the Senators remembered her well and harbored prejudices dating back to the Lincoln administration. But Mary was a determined and formidable fighter for what she wanted and, in this instance, for something that she felt the country owed her. Letters streamed from her pen to politicians, businessmen and soldiers who she felt might back the bill. In one of her strange reversals of mood she wrote flatteringly to men she had once denounced. She even begged the help of some who she thought had not been altogether loyal to her husband, but they had power in the new administration and so might be able to help her.

Mrs. Lincoln was frankly bewildered by the largesse accorded other widows whose husbands had been notable figures in the Civil War while she was being slapped down by Congress. She was particularly critical of the Presidential influence used to raise a large sum for the widow of Grant's Chief of Staff, General John A. Rawlins, who died of tuberculosis just after being appointed Secretary of War. While this was going on, she, the widow of Abraham Lincoln, was enduring privations that she "would not venture to whisper to any one," Mary wrote to a friend.

Her letters at this time reflected her bitterness about the honors and gifts bestowed on General Grant, whom she had never liked. She insisted that his services to his country were "not superior" to her husband's, but within eighteen months three mansions had been given him, a library in Boston, a salary of $13,000 a year, and a special gift of $100,000. From there he had gone on to the Presidency at $25,000 a year.

Mrs. Lincoln could not refrain from comparing the honors heaped on Grant with the "darkness and gloom in the unhappy family of the fallen chief." Nor could she help gloating a little when Mrs. Grant's name figured in the gold scandal of 1869. Jim Fisk and Jay Gould had tried to corner the gold market until they were headed off by the President. Abel Rathbone Corbin, an elderly lobbyist and speculator married to Grant's sister, Virginia, had used his White House connections in his partnership with Gould and Fisk, and Mrs. Rathbone had been seen in a theater box with Mrs. Grant at the time of the scandal.

The Grants were exonerated when an inquiry followed, but Mary wrote to Mrs. James H. Orne from Frankfurt, on February 11, 1870: "As, in the midst of all my wickedness & transgressions I never indulged in gold speculations, perhaps a more dreadful woman than *Mrs. L.* may yet occupy the W.H."

Mary had been getting strong support from Mrs. Orne and her husband, a wealthy carpet manufacturer from Philadelphia who had been a generous contributor to the welfare of the federal soldiers during the war. The Ornes had been Lincoln's friends and were even closer to the Grants. Mrs. Orne's brother, Charles O'Neill, was active in Congress, and he did what he could in the fight for Mrs. Lincoln's pension.

When her husband's victorious general became President, Mary simply could not believe that he would be indifferent to her fate, regardless of her well-known antipathy to him. After all, he had revered Mr. Lincoln. But her sense of neglect knew no bounds when Congress gave President Grant a generous appropriation to refurnish the White House while she, "the wife of the great chieftain whose life was sacrificed for his country [was] living in an uncarpeted apartment—ill in bed without a menial to hand her a cup of cold water." Her health, Mary added, had been completely broken down by the deprivations she had been called upon to endure.

This was apparent to Mrs. Orne when she stayed briefly at the Hotel d'Angleterre in Frankfurt in 1869 with her two daughters, a maid and valet. When she saw how Mrs. Lincoln was living and how wretched her health seemed to be, she took up her cause in earnest and gave firsthand reports to Sumner as he backed the pension bill in the Senate. She found Mary on the fourth floor of the modest Hotel de Holland instead of at the Hotel d'Angleterre, where she had previously stayed. She studied the "small cheerless desolate looking room with but one window—two chairs and a wooden table with a solitary candle" and thought how absurd this was for the "petted indulged wife" of President Lincoln. Mrs. Orne, who lived in a world of the utmost luxury and who had known Mrs. Lincoln in her White House days, wrote to Sumner that if her "*tormentors* and *slanderers* could see her—they surely might be satisfied." Subsequent letters to Sumner from Baden-Baden and from Paris after she saw Mrs. Lincoln were urgent and persuasive.

Mary was overjoyed to be again with Mrs. Orne, whom she considered a "sweet and affectionate woman." They talked, laughed and wept together until guests in adjoining rooms complained about the noise the two American ladies were making at three o'clock in the morning. There was much ground to cover, and Mary's emotions had been bottled up for so long that she became almost hysterical in enlarging upon her woes. Although she was a skilled interpreter of the news she picked up from American papers, Sally Orne gave her an inside view of what was happening around Grant. Mary was critical of some of his appointments in the foreign field. She wondered how the young wife of Elihu B. Washburne, who had been appointed Ambassador to France after a brief interlude as Secretary of State, would cope with the social duties of that exacting embassy. It did not surprise her that General Sickles, who had moved vigorously into the Grant camp, was having a turbulent time as Minister to Spain. Mary had always enjoyed his company but was well aware of his unpredictability.

Mrs. Orne brought warmth and excitement into her lonely life in the days that followed, giving her a taste of the affluence that had once been hers. They went about together until it was time for Sally to move on with her daughters to the next stop. Mary teased her a little about her frivolity, for Mrs. Orne was a worldly woman, enjoying all the pleasures of her travels. They met again at Kronberg, the summer resort of the Prussian royal family in the Taunus Mountains. The ruined castles, the majestic scenery, the precipitous parapets were thrilling to Mary, who had always been intensely responsive to the glories of nature.

After she and Mrs. Orne parted, a barrage of letters followed, and much as Sally sympathized with Mary, she was embarrassed at times by the urgency of her demands where the Grants were concerned. But she tried to fulfill them to the letter, and she let Mary read and approve the appeal she sent to Julia Grant on her behalf. Mrs. Orne was well aware of the chill between the two women, but in Mary's opinion the letter could not have been surpassed for "gentle, womanly persuasion & nobleness of feeling." She hoped that in some way it would "change her lot, pecuniarily."

When a reply was not immediately forthcoming, Mary wrote again, saying she hoped Mrs. Grant had had the grace to answer her letter. Wild with impatience, she quickly followed this with an urgent letter about Grant—"that small specimen of humanity." Where was the general's memory of her husband who had made him "just what he is," Mary asked impatiently. "Will not your husband, your brother, your *true good men* in Congress—make him G.—manifest himself." This was followed by the suggestion that Mrs. Orne write directly to Grant and have her brother deliver the letter to the President when Congress convened.

Things seemed to be at a standstill, and Mary became desperately ill at this point. She had periods of delirium, and when she was finally able to sit up in bed, her hands shook so that she could scarcely write. But she summoned up strength to scribble a note to Sally on April 3, 1870, about the generosity that had been shown Mrs. Stanton on the death of her husband. There had been quick action there, involving substantial financial support. After a full-scale review of her own condition she urged Sally to "forgive & burn this blotted,—*tear*-stained letter." But this and similar warnings on many of Mrs. Lincoln's letters went unheeded.

Like many of her traveling compatriots, it was her custom to visit the English Reading Room in Frankfurt to study the American and British newspapers. Few of the visitors performed this task with more intensity and intelligence than Mary Lincoln. Her round pale face and heavy mourning gave no clue to her quick-witted absorption of the news, and the name Lincoln in print always struck terror in her heart. Late in May she came on an item that caused her to collapse on the spot. A bill granting her $3,000 a year had passed in the House without debate, but when it was read in the Senate and Lyman Trumbull spoke for it, action was taken at once to table it indefinitely. It was argued that Congress had already allowed her $22,000 of her husband's $25,000 salary for one unfinished year in office and that she had inherited a substantial fortune from his estate. The Senate committee report even implied that Mrs. Lincoln had appropriated public property for her own use, that she had been the recipient of public subscriptions, and that $60,000 or thereabouts should be enough for any American widow. The fact that final settlement had not yet been made of Lincoln's estate and that she was living on a comparatively small sum was overlooked. The Senate report was loaded with innuendo of a damaging nature, and it suggested that she was living on a royal scale in Europe.

Mary's spirits reached a new low with this rebuff, and her doctors insisted that she go to Marienbad for the waters. As she became stronger, she sent James Orne an emotional letter, pointing out that she was "often wanting a meal" instead of being rich, as those "cruel, wicked, reckless assertions" implied. Her broken heart "cried aloud . . . to be at rest by my darling husband's side." Surely he could never have anticipated such a return for saving his country from a rebellious foe, she added in agony of spirit.

Orne evidently took action, in addtion to sending her spending money for the time being, and late in April, 1870, she wrote to Congressman O'Neill that General Grant had sent a letter to the pension committee, supporting the bill. This news had reached her indirectly through Henry Seligman, who had returned to Frankfurt from America, where he and his brother, Joseph, had helped finance the Civil War through the powerful banking house of Seligman & Stettheimer. The two brothers, having revered Abraham Lincoln, were concerned about his widow's fate, and Joseph is believed to have helped her clear up her debts and to have paid her fare in Europe. Now he came to her aid again, linking his efforts with Orne's in support of the pension bill at stake.

Judge Davis and Robert Lincoln suffered great embarrassment as Mary pulled strings in all directions. The rhetoric in the Senate was considerable before the matter was settled. In July a storm broke loose when Sumner, trying to force the issue after the negative vote, found himself defending Mrs. Lincoln against the ugly charges coming at her from all sides, in some instances from men who had been among her husband's closest friends. He dramatized the contrast between her past and her present way of life. Her open carriage drawn by six milk-white horses, her promenades, dinners and balls were recalled; the attentions paid her by the diplomatic corps and her hospitality to members of Congress were pointed up. There was even mention of her bloodstained cloak on the night of the assassination.

"Surely the honorable members of the Senate must be weary of casting mud on the garments of the wife of Lincoln. . . . She loved him. I speak of that which I know. He had all her love," said the majestic Senator from Massachusetts.

He spoke with cause, for Richard Yates of Illinois, once close to the President, had suggested infidelity on Mary's part, an appalling thought to this devoted wife. Leading the opposition to the bill, he made the point insinuatingly that a woman should be true to her husband. He would not go into details, he said, and he blessed the name of Abraham Lincoln, but Mrs. Lincoln and her family "all through the war had sympathized with the Rebellion" and so she should not be given a reward.

The old clothes scandal had an airing, and Senator Reuben Fenton, who had had a chance to observe Mrs. Lincoln abroad as well as at home, conceded that she had sometimes been indiscreet and had thereby lost standing with the public, but it should never be forgotten that she was the widow of the Great Emancipator.

Senator Simon Cameron, who had failed her when she had appealed to him earlier for financial aid, now spoke movingly for Mary. He recalled the arrival of the Lincolns in Washington and said that the gossips of the capital, both men and women, had done all they could to hurt the President and his wife. "They could not destroy him," said the Senator, "but they did . . . destroy the social position of his wife."

Some of the Senators were touched, feeling the shade of Lincoln among them; others clung stubbornly to their convictions about his widow. After Cameron had spoken, the vote was taken. The struggle came to an end on July 14, 1870, and Mrs. Lincoln was granted a lifetime pension of $3,000. The vote was twenty-eight to twenty, with twenty-four Senators absenting themselves. In 1882 Congress would increase her pension to $5,000 a year and give her an additional $15,000 to meet her obligations, but by that time she had none. She was well off, and the financial stress, both real and fancied, had lifted in so far as it ever did with Mrs. Lincoln. Today Presidents' widows have a fixed pension of $20,000, but in Mary's time their allowance was left to the whim of Congress.

The news of her victory reached her at Innsbruck, where she had taken Tad for a change of scene and air. It came in a telegram from James Orne, and she wrote at once to Senator Sumner, expressing her gratitude for the fight he had dominated from first to last. There were many others to thank, and Mary wrote with warmth to them all, including her old enemies, Norman B. Judd and Lyman Trumbull.

Although she considered $3,000 a niggardly pension, she showed uncharacteristic restraint and vowed that she would never utter a "murmuring word" about it, a resolution that she soon found hard to keep. The fact that it was a moral victory as well as a material one gave her a sense of relief, and she had moments of her old vivacity and lightheartedness. She felt that she could now stay in better quarters and spend more money for comforts and entertainment. Old friends who saw her at this time noticed that she took an interest in the world around her and was less obsessed with her own woes. Her letters reflected a different and more nearly normal attitude. The hatred and rancor that she had vented so freely seemed to evaporate in a new benignity. She was considering a trip to Italy when it became evident that the Franco-Prussian War was closing in on them. Mary hurried to Frankfurt to settle her business affairs there and crossed to England with Tad.

Peace of mind was not a natural attribute of Mary Lincoln's, but she came close to it in England during the winter of 1870–71 when she finally acknowledged that she was weary of sight-seeing after wandering "over the greater portion of Europe." The undercurrent of anxiety over her pension had been constant for so long, dimming her days and haunting her nights, that when this worry ended, she began to think longingly of America, where she had been so happy, so miserable, so loved and so hated.

She resumed her old habit of reading by the hour, and she wrote to Mrs. Eliza Slataper from Leamington about the books that she was enjoying and particularly *The Gates Ajar* by Mrs. Humphrey D.

Ward, which was having great success at the moment in England. But the climate wore her down as the winter advanced, and it proved to be disastrous for Tad. Although he made excellent progress in his studies, he yearned to return home and to join his brother, Bob. In his eighteen years Tad had done a great deal of living, and as he approached manhood there was pathos in his constant battle to feel well. Although he was liked by his fellows, he was always an alien spirit among them.

His debility startled his mother when she returned to London after a brief visit to Frankfurt in the spring of 1871. It was clear to her that they must go home without further delay. Tad's pleural condition did not clear up, and no doubt Sheridan, who had been observing him at close range, had a hand in forcing the issue. The general, too, was heading home, and they all sailed together on the *Russia* on April 29, 1871.

In this company Mrs. Lincoln could scarcely be overlooked, but she did her best on landing not to draw attention to herself. She still shrank from the thought of the old wounds reopened during the pension fight, and she had a well-founded dread of seeing her name in a newspaper. In the end she was persuaded to see a New York *World* reporter, whose story appeared on May 12, 1871. She had had some of her worst moments from this crusading paper, but Mary could never help being spontaneous in her comments.

Dressed in deep mourning when she was interviewed at the Everett House, she was as stout as ever, it was noted. She looked pale and weary and said that she was suffering from a severe headache, but she answered questions courteously for as long as she could.

When asked if she meant to return to Europe, she said she did not know. She had enjoyed the time abroad and liked the European style of living, but she was glad to be back in America. The voyage had been tiresome and monotonous, although her fellow passengers were a "social and agreeable" set of people. There were three generals aboard, including Sheridan, three captains, an earl and a countess on their way to visit the Governor-General of Canada, and they all had been pleasant and polite to her.

The passage had been extremely rough, and they thought they were "doomed to destruction" during a tremendous gale. All the women and most of the men had to stay in their berths for three days, and when they came out on deck, the waves were mountainously high, and the swell was so strong that they were tossed about like leaves. But the sun shone brightly all the time and the sky was clear.

Mary told of Tad's happiness in Frankfurt, and she said that they had liked the Germans and had been kindly treated by them, although their habits and outlook appeared strange at first. Their six months in England had been the best of all, she added. When asked if the memory of President Lincoln was respected abroad, Mary spoke up proudly: "Everywhere. His shocking death seems to have overcome all prejudice. . . . People spoke of him as if they honored him greatly, and I know that the manner of his death made all persons his friends."

The thought of her husband was too much for Mary at this point, and she said that she could not continue with the interview. Tad would carry on for her. But once his mother was out of the room, he showed reluctance to do anything of the sort. He made it clear that he disliked "getting into the newspapers," as he put it. Tad answered a few questions with an air of hesitancy, and he called it an "abominable shame" that there had been so much trouble about his mother's pension.

When questioned about the report that she might marry again, he was indignant and exclaimed: "That's all nonsense. I wish folks wouldn't talk so much about my mother. There's no truth whatever in that report. People say pretty near what they like nowadays."

While the Lincolns were abroad, the *World* of November 13, 1869, had given publicity to a satirical sketch that had appeared first in a Maine paper, but had soon reached London and other European cities. Mary, according to this piece of buffoonery, was to marry a Count Schneiderbutzen, grand chamberlain to the Duke of Baden, and the court tailor was cutting "Abe Lincoln's clothes" to fit the diminutive bridegroom.

Mrs. Lincoln was frantic when this piece of Gilbert and Sullivan nonsense came to her attention. She wrote at once to Mrs. Orne from Frankfurt, calling it a most "malignant invention" since she "knew no such person." Her predilection for titles was well known, and there had been earlier rumors of a German baron seen in her company, so that the story about the grand chamberlain took hold at a time when the pension fight was hot and she felt that every cross-current might affect it. "You can conceive how much my feelings have been wounded, when American papers, are placing my name, with some imaginary 'Baron or Count' whom I have never seen," she wrote to Mrs. White just before Christmas, 1869.

Tad's indignation was well-founded, since he knew the falsity of all this. Although in a sense he had been the victim of his mother's doting and sometimes selfish course where he was concerned, he had never wavered in his devotion and protective love for her. His own development abroad had been quite dramatic. The New York *Semi-Weekly Tribune* of May 26, 1871, described him as "having grown up a tall, fine-looking lad of 18, who bears but faint resemblance to the tricksey little sprite whom visitors to the White House remember as the most comic feature of that dull place during the exciting years of the war." His speech was clearer, he had acquired a working knowledge of French and German, and in looks he now closely resembled the Bob Lincoln of the early days of the war.

Tad was clear-eyed, of medium height, and his flushed cheeks suggested a ruddy state of health to his interviewer, but as things turned out, this may well have been the bloom of fever. Mary traveled west with high hopes for her beloved Tad, who she thought might now take his place in the world with the help of Robert. Both were charmed by "little Mamie," but they stayed only briefly at Robert's home before moving to Clifton House. Tad's pleural condition had grown worse with a fresh cold he had picked up on the crossing. Once more Mary had a desperately sick son on her hands.

XXII

Mrs. Lincoln Held Insane

T
AD'S DEATH A few weeks after their return from Europe was the final blow that led to Mrs. Lincoln's being adjudged insane after the cumulative terrors of the years finally overwhelmed her at the age of fifty-six. It was one shock too many, and it robbed her of her main interest in life. Without Mr. Lincoln, without Tad, she moved gradually into the shadows.

Since her youngest son had been ill so often, yet had picked himself up and gone on with considerable gallantry, she assumed he would recover once more. But she had never seen him in a more serious condition, and on June 8, 1871, she wrote to Mrs. White that Tad had been "*very, very* dangerously ill" and she had been up with him for ten consecutive nights. He could not rest or lie down because of edema. Robert, only dimly aware of the respiratory distress of his mother and brother while they were in Europe, was appalled by Tad's suffering, which continued for six weeks.

Dr. Charles Gilman Smith, attending Tad, told Robert that his brother could not live more than a few days, since his heart and lungs were failing. Then for three mornings, while fresh breezes swept the city, he seemed to improve. He was stronger, and the edema was reduced. He brightened and showed his last gleam of interest when a picture of Robert's little girl was shown to him. A close, oppressive day followed and he sank rapidly. Dr. H. A. Johnson and Dr. N. S. Davis were called in as consultants. They would face Mrs. Lincoln later at her sanity trial.

On the fourteenth Tad seemed to rally again, and at eleven in the evening he was sleeping peacefully, so Robert felt that it was safe to leave him with his mother and two nurses while he went to his neglected home. But he was called back at half past four in the morning, to find Tad in great distress, struggling to breathe. Between half past seven and eight in the morning he suddenly pitched forward in his chair and was gone.

This was the ultimate wound for Mrs. Lincoln. There was no peace for her now or ever again. She collapsed and was helpless, but worn out after weeks of anxiety and ceaseless vigilance, she was quieter than when Willie and her husband died. Soon she was almost beyond consciousness and was being cared for by a nurse.

Tad's body was taken from the Clifton House to Bob's home on Wabash Avenue, where a brief funeral service was conducted by a Baptist minister. The cortege then went on to the Edwards' home in Springfield, and funeral services were held in the First Presbyterian Church, so closely identified with Lincoln history. Although the precise cause of Tad's death was never established, it was thought that pleurisy developing in the eighteen-year-old boy and lasting six months might well have been tubercular in origin. Tad's high flush and excitable ways were recalled. He had been plagued by colds during the two years that he and his mother had been abroad, and she had felt that he had been undernourished for a time in Germany. Other posthumous speculations include emphysema, so familiar today, and a virus unrecognized at the time.

There was great sorrow across the nation over Tad's death. He had been a familiar figure at his father's side during the crucial and well-publicized days of the Civil War. His ways had often been troublesome, but he had been much loved, too. His mother, now fifty-three, gray-haired and heavy-footed, was beyond consolation: "I feel that there is no life for me, without my idolized Taddie," she wrote. "One by one I have consigned to their resting place, my idolized ones, & now, in this world, there is nothing left me, but the deepest anguish & desolation."

After a brief stay in Chicago she began to move about again, and little was heard of her. She wrote few letters, and in October, 1871, she discouraged Mrs. Slataper from visiting her. "Bleeding wounds would only be opened afresh," she wrote. "In God's good time I *may* grow calm, yet I very much doubt it. As grievous as other bereavements have been, not one great sorrow ever approached the agony of *this*. My idolized and devoted son, torn from me, when he had bloomed with such a noble, promising youth."

Mary wrote that she had been suffering from heart palpitation and had been ordered to take a complete rest, but a stay in Waukesha, Wisconsin, had not improved matters much, She lived in seclusion in a private home there, and Senator Reuben E. Fenton and his daughter, who had been kind to her in Europe, called repeatedly and were "determined to penetrate my sorrows." But she felt so miserable that she found it impossible even to look at a strange face, said the overwrought Mary. There were no other boarders and she drank the waters, a habit that had often helped her during her stay in Europe.

Without Tad, Mary had lost her anchor. She had no idea what to do or which way to turn. On her arrival in New York with Tad, she and Mrs. White had discussed the possibility of taking adjoining houses close to Central Park, but Tad had longed for the companionship of his brother Bob, and Mary realized that her own life strings were tied to the Middle West.

Robert and his wife were worried by her strange actions and whims after Tad's death. She had reverted to brooding over money, although she now had ample means. Early in 1872 Robert first employed Mrs. Richard Fitzgerald, Eddie Foy's mother, to act as nurse and companion for his mother while she moved about in the old restless way. She needed a good deal of physical care, since she suffered from edema, which she called "bloating," in the idiom of the day. She was profoundly uncomfortable. Had she lived a century later she might have been helped physically in this respect. But between her physical ills and her mental quirks she was sunk in the depths of sorrow and desperation. It annoyed her to have Mrs. Fitzgerald act as companion and guard. As always, she longed to be totally free and to roam at will. But there seemed to be no escape for her anywhere, and the sum of her sorrows had reached a new crescendo.

Unable to cope with her eccentricities, Mrs. Fitzgerald left her several times, but Mrs. Lincoln's family repeatedly implored her to return. Elizabeth and Ninian Edwards shared Robert's conviction that she needed protective care as she followed an erratic course between the time of her return from Europe and her confinement in 1875.

Mrs. Fitzgerald went south with Mrs. Lincoln several times, and she startled the distraught woman's family with her tales of Mary's conviction that gas was an invention of the devil, that she was being poisoned, that she heard rappings on the walls and voices coming through to her, that she was still living in the White House, that she was in touch with her husband and sons. She shrank from light, kept her shades drawn, and would have no illumination but the flicker of candles.

Although she never referred in any of her letters to the Great Fire of October, 1871, when a large part of Chicago was burned, her fear of fire and smoke became acute. Robert and his wife took their first trip abroad in the following year, getting away from the chaos of the half-demolished city, but during this period Mary was lost in a fog of sorrow over Tad. It was evident that she lived in a state of mortal fear. She could not sleep but paced the floor and thought the walls were falling in on her, a schizophrenic pattern. She lived the completely introverted life, moving restlessly from place to place, suspicious of everyone, critical of the costs of the hotels where she stayed, and constantly preoccupied with her money and possessions. Her earlier flow of letters thinned to communication with a few of her most trusted friends, and wherever she went, a drooping figure in black, she tried to avoid being recognized as Mrs. Lincoln.

The key to Mary's troubled existence was inevitably the question of her sanity and what her life as a President's wife might have been had she not been the victim of such major sorrows. As a central figure in the tragedy of the assassination she could neither be ignored nor forgotten, but her image today has crystallized into that of an insane woman. Actually her condition evolved through the years by slow stages, and it might never have reached such a pitch but for the tragedies that followed one another in quick succession. There was something prophetic about her wild tantrums as a child. These became more marked during her years as a wife and mother in Springfield. Then came her troubled and sometimes fantastic behavior in the White House, and finally the major trauma of the assassination, followed by Tad's death.

Allowing for the fact that few women in history have been so slandered, snubbed and scorned, it is also true that she reaped a rich harvest in worldly benefits and prestige for one so ambitious and proud. She had risen to high estate at a time when the attention of the world was focused on a nation caught in the blazing passions of civil war. The riches and prestige of her husband's office were behind her, and she shared in life's prizes as well as its griefs, but she was as unable to cope with success as with disaster. She was incomprehensible to the women of her generation, but because she was the wife of an overpowering figure in American history, she was something more than a shadowy First Lady caught in the bitter suffering of war.

Her immoderate swings of mood, her extravagance, her need to hoard and possess, her unreasonable jealousy of her husband were not unheard-of characteristics in women of any age. Nor were the devastating headaches that troubled her so often. But when a sense of disorientation set in and she was haunted by delusions, hallucinations and visitations, the picture changed to something more serious, until it reached the ultimate pitch of confinement for insanity.

Mrs. Lincoln was in Florida when her obsessive fear for her family centered on Robert, her one remaining child. She had had many sleepless nights, with her thoughts constantly on her lost sons. Now in one of her visions she seemed to see him as ill. She telegraphed to Dr. Ralph N. Isham, a Bellevue graduate and well-known figure in medical circles in the Middle West, asking him to go to Robert at once and attend to him until she arrived, since she believed he was ill.

Dr. Isham, a family friend and the nephew of Robert's law partner in the firm of Isham & Lincoln, took her at her word, but he found the young man in perfect health. Both realized that she must be hallucinating, and they sent her a reassuring message telling her to remain in Florida. This did not stop her. She may not have received this message, for she took off hurriedly after sending Robert a second telegram suggestive of her disturbed state of mind: "My dearly beloved son, Robert T. Lincoln—Rouse yourself and live for your mother, you are all I have, from this hour all I have is yours. I pray every night that you may be spared to your mother."

Robert saw at once when he met her at the depot that she was beset by fear, but she looked tanned and healthy from her stay in the South. She studied him with amazement. Nothing seemed to be wrong. Robert was his usual sturdy self, carefully tailored, and attentive to her needs. With the utmost gravity she told him that someone had tried to poison her when she breakfasted in Jacksonville on the way up. She also insisted that her pocket book had been taken from her by a wandering Jew whom she had met in Florida, but she was convinced that he would return it. At intervals she talked to him quite intelligently about conditions in the South and some of the things that she had seen.

Although Robert had intended to take her to his house, he knew that she and his wife were not on good terms at the moment, and his mother said she would rather go to the Grand Pacific Hotel. He was sufficiently concerned about her to take a room next to hers and to watch her closely for the next few days. It was clear to him that she was in an unnatural state of fear and restlessness, but she slept soundly the first night because she was worn out from her journey.

Robert testified later at the sanity hearing to the extraordinary events that followed. After the first night she returned to her restless prowling and the ungrounded fears that had haunted her since Tad's death. She roamed about in her nightdress, and after rousing Robert twice in one night in a shivering state of fear, she begged to be taken into his room for protection. Sure now that his mother was in a dangerous condition, he gave her his bed and slept on the lounge. Her actions were so eccentric that the hotel employees and guests were watching her with some alarm. When she sat by a wall and talked mumbo jumbo, ostensibly to the man who had taken her pocket book, the "voices" of schizophrenia were at work. She worried about fire, and a plume of smoke seen from a window upset her. She told Robert after the fact that Chicago was going to be burned down and that her trunks and boxes must be moved to some safe place, perhaps in a small town. She urged him to take charge of them at once. Obviously echoes of the Great Fire haunted her.

Mary next went on one of her mad spending sprees—$600 worth of lace curtains (a particular phobia of hers since her White House days), $700 worth of jewelry, three watches costing $450, a heavy bolt of silk and $200 worth of soaps and perfumes. Once they were bought, she never touched them. They were piled up around her, fulfilling her pathological passion for buying and hoarding. Robert would have indulged her in this, since there seemed to be no way of stopping it, but he worried about the securities worth $57,000 that she carried in pockets in one of her petticoats. Unknown to his mother, he had a Pinkerton detective assigned to guard her and to follow her when she went on buying expeditions—not knowing what the outcome might be.

The climax came on April 1 when Mary left her room half-clad and headed for the elevator that would have taken her down to the hotel lobby. Robert ordered it stopped and tried to persuade her to return to her room. She would not get out and she accused him of interfering. When he put his arms around her to force her back into the hall, she became wildly excited and screamed: "You are going to murder me."

At this point Robert consulted his mother's cousin, John Todd Stuart, and Judge Davis, both of whom already had ample knowledge of her eccentricities. It was difficult for Mary afterwards to forgive these men, whom she had always regarded as her friends, for counseling Robert to initiate lunacy proceedings. It was clear to all three men that she was no longer accountable for her actions and that her estate would soon be dissipated if she continued to spend so wildly—the compulsion that seemed to slake her anxiety. Robert feared that she might do herself bodily harm.

When news of the proposed sanity proceedings for Mrs. Abraham Lincoln became public, there was sympathy but no element of surprise, for it had been common talk for a long time that Mary was behaving in curious ways. Here and there tales cropped up of strange actions, and her White House history was recalled through this foggy spectrum. Her simplest action in the past assumed significance. Many felt sympathetic, adding up the sum of her woes and the monstrous fact of the assassination. Some were inclined to see Robert as an ungrateful and unfeeling son. But he and the Edwards had already done what they could to protect her, chiefly through Mrs. Fitzgerald. And in the two months since her return she had been overwhelmed by the classic symptoms of her illness—ghostly rappings, conversations with the unseen, voices telling her what to do, desperate fears and general disorientation. She had grown thin and haggard, and her once clear blue eyes were clouded with fear.

Before taking decisive action, Robert rounded up the opinions of a number of doctors who had attended his mother at one time or another. Each had something significant to add to the picture, and they all were brought to court, presumably to give medical evidence, although none was a specialist in mental diseases.

Benjamin F. Ayers and Leonard T. Swett had Mrs. Lincoln in tow when she entered the Cook County Court, unconscious of the ordeal that lay ahead of her. Swett, tall and bearded, dangling a gold-headed cane, was a familiar figure from the past, for he had been one of the men involved in the nomination of Abraham Lincoln for the Presidency. Wherever she looked in the courtroom, she saw men who had been friends of her husband's. Quiet and dignified in a simple black costume, Mary was suddenly aware of the jury of men lined up to be her judges. It was a courtroom scene that would go down in history for its poignant quality—the wife of Abraham Lincoln losing her freedom at the hands of their oldest son. Many would resent this action as time went on, and her own family chilled in the end to Robert. But history seemed to vindicate him, and Mary forgave him before she died.

Judge Marion R. M. Wallace, a Democrat and former friend of the President's, presided and Mary learned to her amazement that Swett was the prosecuting attorney who would examine the witnesses, and Isaac N. Arnold, another old friend, would defend her. The jury was composed of merchants, bank officials, foundrymen and real-estate operators. They were Lyman J. Gage, who would later serve as Secretary of the Treasury under William McKinley and Theodore Roosevelt, Charles B. Farwell, J. McGregor Adams, S. B. Parkhurst, C. J. Henderson, James A. Mason, D. H. Cameron, William Stewart, S. M. Moore, H. C. Durand, Thomas Cogswell, and Dr. S. C. Blake, formerly city physician but at this time in private practice.

The atmosphere was highly charged as Mrs. Lincoln sat with quiet dignity, listening attentively to the evidence and seeming to weigh it. Her composure was so striking and so much at variance with her excitable nature that some wondered if she had been given a sedative before the ordeal began. When the evidence stung her in a sensitive spot, she would sit up as if to protest but would then sink back resignedly and wave her white ivory fan.

Mrs. Lincoln showed no surprise as a strange parade of witnesses gave testimony—faces vaguely familiar to her and suddenly menacing as they turned her simplest actions into demented deeds. The hotel employees recalled one damaging incident after another, from her strange behavior over her food in the dining room to her delusions and posturings in the privacy of her room. The sight of Maggie Gavin, her chambermaid, was reassuring to Mrs. Lincoln. Here was a friend who had been kind to her and would surely not mock her. But Maggie drew the most damaging picture of all, calling the President's widow "balmy," recalling her fear of smoke and fire, the trunks in her room packed with goods, her persistent hatred of General Grant and her insistence that men were following her everywhere. When things became unmanageable, Maggie said that she gave Mrs. Lincoln laudanum drops. Counsel for the defense promptly asked if this might not have been one of the causes of some of the "hallucinations." Maggie conceded that when Robert visited his mother, he tried to make things easier for her, and when he spoke of her, he showed great concern. This scrap of testimony seemed to give Mrs. Lincoln a moment of warmth in the chilly atmosphere.

Robert soon cleared up the mystery of the men his mother thought were following her, according to Maggie and other witnesses. He acknowledged that for the last three weeks he had had Pinkerton detectives trailing her for her own protection. This established the fact that she was followed into shops and watched as she made her purchases and that the men who sat outside her hotel door and followed her into the dining room were not imaginary, as they all had concluded, but flesh and blood.

Mary seemed transfixed as she listened to her son Robert, once a naughty, unresponsive but much loved boy, now a stolid and impressive lawyer. She showed neither surprise nor resentment when he described her acts on her return from Florida, her delusions about his health, her wild spending, her eccentric behavior. But there was a flicker of response when he somberly acknowledged that she had always been kind to him. The watching reporters commented on Robert's pale face and tear-filled eyes as he testified that, since his father's death, his mother had not been wholly responsible. Her recent purchases had dismayed him, since she already had trunks filled with garments that she never wore and jewelry that she never touched, except perhaps for the "mourning brooch" visible to spectators in the courtroom.

Mrs. Lincoln's attention was closely riveted on Robert when he said that she had securities worth $57,000 tucked away in pockets in her petticoats. She refused to let him bank this money, although he considered it a threat to her safety because of her irresponsible actions. Moreover, she was spending it so fast that soon none would be left. He had been advised to bring these proceedings by Judge David Davis of the Supreme Court and his mother's cousin, John Todd Stuart, when he was fully convinced that it was no longer safe to let her go about without restraint. She had been a constant source of anxiety to him for a long time, and she would not visit his house because of her confused relations with his wife.

A variety of tradesmen heaped high the fires on Mrs. Lincoln. They testified to irrational purchases that her son later returned. She baffled them with her insistence on buying out their stock of any item that caught her fancy. One salesman pictured her playing hide-and-seek among the clothes' racks to elude the men who she believed were following her. Still more shattering was the medical testimony from men who had been sympathetic in their treatment of her but now were her most formidable accusers. Dr. Willis Danforth, professor of surgery and gynecology at the Chicago Homeopathic College, described the most curious symptoms attributed to Mary.

They seemed always to accompany her blinding headaches. When he attended her on her return from Europe in 1873, she told him of an Indian pulling wires out of her eyes and removing the bones from her face. In the following years he found her suffering from what he called debility of the nervous system. This time she talked of someone taking steel springs from her head. She could not rest or sleep, and she felt sure that she was about to die, insisting that Mr. Lincoln had forewarned her of her coming end—a welcome thought to Mary Lincoln. Evidently this was one of the occasions when she thought she was in communication with her lost husband.

She also told of table rappings that warned her when she would die. These seemed to come in response to her anxious questions, for she longed to join her husband and sons. But other women across the country were doing much the same thing in the postwar years, with their Ouija boards, table rappings and desperate efforts to communicate with the dead. It was a current craze, but it was much exaggerated in Mrs. Lincoln's case, and Dr. Danforth was specific in testifying that she was of unsound mind and was incapable of managing her property.

The other physicians merely gave their opinions on evidence presented at the hearing and not from personal treatment of her symptoms. Dr. N. S. Davis was a New Yorker who was commonly known as the father of the American Medical Association, and at the time of Mrs. Lincoln's trial he was the best-known medical man in Chicago. Dr. H. A. Johnson, like Dr. Davis, was identified with Rush Medical College. Dr. Charles Gilman Smith, a Harvard and University of Pennsylvania graduate who had settled in Chicago, had attended Tad in his final illness, with Dr. Davis and Dr. Johnson as consultants. These men had seen Mrs. Lincoln in moments of deep agony, if they had not actually ministered to her.

From first to last there was no question of the outcome of the hearing, and Mary accepted the verdict of insanity with proud unconcern. This was not one of the great moments of her extraordinary life, but it was perhaps the bravest. Spectators could not fail to be touched by the plight of Abraham Lincoln's widow, once the great lady of the White House in some of its most historic days. She stoically accepted the recital that she was fifty-six years old, that the disease in her case was not hereditary, that she was not subject to epilepsy, that she was not a pauper, but that she was a "fit person to be sent to the State Hospital for the Insane."

Robert seemed deeply moved when he tried to take his mother's hand as the jury left the courtroom. Observers thought they saw tears running down his cheeks. But Mary turned away from him with a baffled murmur: "O Robert, to think that my son would ever have done this!" The newspapers the next day described her as being "stolid and unmoved." Whether she was stunned into silence or she wished to show her judges that she had self-control remains a question. It is also possible that she did not even know where she was. The next day all America learned that Mrs. Abraham Lincoln had been pronounced insane. The *Inter-Ocean* of May 20, 1875, giving a full account of the court proceedings, summed things up in memorable banked headlines:

MRS. LINCOLN

THE WIDOW OF THE MARTYRED PRESIDENT ADJUDGED INSANE IN THE COUNTY COURT

ONE OF THE SADDEST SPECTACLES EVER WITNESSED IN A COURTROOM IN THIS CITY

EMINENT MEDICAL MEN PRONOUNCE HER TO BE OF UNSOUND MIND AND INCAPABLE OF SELF-CARE

THE DREAD AFFLICTION OWES ITS ORIGIN TO THE ASSASSINATION OF THE LAMENTED PRESIDENT

SHE WILL BE REMOVED TO-DAY TO A PRIVATE ASYLUM AT BATAVIA, ILL.

Mrs. Lincoln was taken to the Grand Pacific Hotel by Swett and Arnold in a closed carriage to stay overnight under guard. Ironically enough, she was declared in the verdict not to harbor homicidal or suicidal tendencies, but before the night was over, she had attempted suicide. This was one of the things that Robert had feared.

The thought of suicide was not completely alien to her history, although until her total collapse she had usually worked off her tempestuous emotions in torrents of grief or rage. Her letters at times suggested her wish to die, but such sentiments were not uncommon in the harsh days of the Civil War, and they did not seem to have special significance in Mrs. Lincoln's case. Her sisters thought she was given to extravagant language and self-dramatization. Yet no sooner was the lunacy verdict flashed across the country than the public learned that she had followed it with a suicide attempt.

Mary eluded her attendants on the first night and tried to buy laudanum at a drugstore in the Grand Pacific Hotel. She said that she needed it for neuralgia in her arm. The chemist, alert to the situation and knowing her well, told her to return in half an hour, when he would have it ready for her. He followed her when she left his shop, heading straight for another pharmacy nearby. His colleague caught the warning and refused Mrs. Lincoln's request, but she tried a third place before returning to the hotel. The chemist who had guessed her purpose from the start was ready for her with a phial falsely labeled "Laudanum and Camphor." She drank this and in ten minutes was back for more. Stalling for time, since Robert had been summoned, he placated her with another innocuous dose.

The original plan to send her at once to the Bellevue Nursing and Rest Home in Batavia, Illinois, went through, and for the first time Mrs. Lincoln came under the care of a doctor with specialized training in mental diseases. Dr. R. J. Patterson was head of the institution, and since Mrs. Lincoln's name was of national importance, it was obvious that she had to be handled with care and consideration.

The newspapers were alert to every move involving her incarceration, and there was a growing tide of feeling that Abraham Lincoln's widow should not be in confinement. Robert had been appointed conservator of his mother's estate, and once again the struggle over money began. This obsession and others did not subside during Mary's stay at Batavia. As such institutions went, Bellevue was a good one for its era. It was pleasantly situated deep in the countryside, with shady trees around it. When Mrs. Lincoln arrived in the private car of a railroad president who still remembered who she was, May blossoms flowered all around her. But she did not see them, nor did she hear the birds sing, such was her trancelike state.

She was a patient from May 20 until September 10, 1875, but under protest. Wholly resistant to her surroundings, she brooded endlessly over Robert's role, and the son she had loved so deeply became her major enemy. The loss of her securities had made a deep impression, and her resentment over her helpless state became stronger with every week that passed. When news of her attitude reached her old friend Mrs. Sally Orne, then summering at Saratoga Springs, she appealed to Robert for news of his mother.

He wrote to her on June 1, 1875, that six physicians had warned him against delaying proceedings lest he make himself morally responsible for "some very probable tragedy, which might occur at any moment." He acknowledged the fact that friends in the East had criticized the public proceedings in court. They thought that his mother's case might have been handled in a less conspicuous way.

But he assured Mrs. Orne, who had considerable understanding of his problem because her own son-in-law had recovered from what was called hopeless insanity, that his mother was improving under Dr. Patterson's care. She lived in the private quarters of the house and took her meals with his family or by herself, as she chose. She walked and drove with them, but he was informed that there did not seem to be much hope of a speedy recovery. Robert wrote, none too realistically, that he was on the best of terms with his mother and he added: "So far as I can see she does not realize her situation at all. Indeed my consolation in this sad affair is in thinking that she herself is happier in every way, in her freedom from care and excitement, than she has been in ten years."

This was how Robert saw things, but Mary's view was different. She had a bright and cheerful room, but she kept it in total darkness except for occasional candlelight. She disliked the metal frame that guarded her window, and it irked her to have an attendant always at her heels. She worried constantly about her trunks, then in storage in Milwaukee, and it did not take her long to find her way with an attendant to the local shops and to litter her room with unopened packages.

Batavia was not a great shopping center, but she still longed to buy materials, although she had become indifferent to what she wore. A sixteen-year-old girl, who later became Mrs. G. W. Gardner of Aurora, drove regularly to the rest home to sew for the well-off inmates. She found Mrs. Lincoln looking "gray-haired and very pale." The black dress the President's widow was wearing seemed to this bright-eyed teen-ager a shabby costume for one who had been so famous for her sartorial style. The young seamstress could scarcely believe that this great lady, now a shrinking recluse, owned many trunks filled with clothes and dress fabrics. In the end she made Mrs. Lincoln a simple summer dress of black-and-white striped material. Mary had always liked stripes, and she had worn this black-and-white combination on the night of the President's assassination.

Mrs. Lincoln sent letters in all directions, pleading for help, just as she had from Europe about her pension. She charged Robert with having her confined in order to get hold of her estate. This and other delusions persisted, and Dr. E. Swain, a Civil War dentist who lived close to the sanitarium found when he was with her that she thought she was still in the White House. A visiting reporter left Bellevue somewhat awed by Mrs. Lincoln's conviction that her husband was beside her and that she was looking after him in the old motherly way. Rappings and voices continued to haunt her, and she clung to the darkness of her room.

The Aurora *News-Beacon* recorded her efforts to get free. Her correspondence with two old friends, Judge and Mrs. James B. Bradwell, caught the attention of the Chicago press, and tired Mrs. Lincoln was again in the papers, to Robert's great embarrassment. Myra Bradwell was Chicago's first woman lawyer, a fighter who took up her cause with conviction and zeal. She and her husband believed Mary to be sane, and they felt that she was capable of living in the outside world. They visited her regularly, took messages and packages in and out, and sometimes stayed overnight at Bellevue. Her conversation amazed them with its scope and clarity, except when her personal phobias came to the surface.

But Dr. Patterson put a stop to this after receiving what he called a "threatening and insulting letter" from Judge Bradwell, who kept insisting that Mrs. Lincoln should be freed. On July 2, 1875, the Illinois *State Journal* reproduced a New York *Tribune* dispatch in which Dr. Patterson answered some of the charges by saying: "No restraint other than a prudent supervision is necessary. At present her derangement exhibits itself mainly in a general mental feebleness and incapacity. No encouragement is held out that Mrs. Lincoln will ever become permanently well."

But the storm mounted, and Mr. and Mrs. Edwards threw their support to the Bradwells, irrespective of Robert's wishes. By degrees they all came around to thinking that it might be better to let Mary return to her sister's home in Springfield. On August 28, 1875, Dr. Patterson weakened and addressed a letter to the Chicago *Tribune* in which he admitted that Mrs. Lincoln was much improved, both mentally and physically, but that he had not at any time regarded her as a person of sound mind.

"I am still unwilling to throw any obstacles in the way of giving her an opportunity to have a home with her sister," he wrote. "But I am willing to record the opinion that, such is the character of her malady, she will not be content to do this, and that the experiment, if made, will result only in giving the coveted opportunity to make extended rambles, to renew the indulgence of her purchasing mania, and other morbid manifestations. . . ."

It was obvious that Dr. Patterson was hauling down the flag as a growing tide of support washed around Mrs. Lincoln and the public questioned the need to have her confined when she seemed to be rational in all but a few areas. It was an accepted fact that she had always been slightly eccentric, but she had coped impressively with the demands of the White House years and had been well regarded by men of world renown. Was her case one that required locks and bars? Was she a victim of Robert's acute embarrassment and his strong feeling for worldly possessions, which in some ways resembled his mother's?

One of Mrs. Lincoln's favorite ministers took up her cause and made a speech at a church convention that stirred the clergy on her behalf. The feeling was that she must be helped, and this time she had Ninian and Elizabeth Edwards strongly on her side. Dr. Patterson gave in as the storm grew, and he and Robert quietly agreed that Mrs. Lincoln should be released without any publicity and returned to the care of the Edwards family in Springfield. When Ninian gave her this news, Mary wanted to know if Robert had had a hand in it. She brightened when the day of departure came and scattered presents among the patients in her usual generous way. This had been one more strange and searing episode in her extraordinary life. She was released on September 10, 1875, after four months' confinement, and little more was heard of her while she lived quietly for the next nine months in the Edwards' house, where Lincoln had wooed and married her.

During this period she proved her capacity to live at home, so that on June 15, 1876, her case was reopened and Mrs. Lincoln was pronounced sane. This was a news item of great interest, discussed across the land, for by this time the public that had once abused her savagely had come to believe that she might have been the victim of a great injustice. Mr. and Mrs. Edwards, Mrs. Wallace, Judge

Davis, John Todd Stuart, Isaac Arnold and even Robert had come to the conslusion that the uproar must be stopped. Mary's will was like iron, and she would continue to agitate and keep the issue alive until her fortune was restored to her. Too many outside forces were working for her now. Her continued confinement had become a national scandal.

The second hearing before Judge Wallace in Cook County Court was brief, and everything went in her favor. Neither Robert nor Dr. Patterson was present. Leonard Swett, who had been her prosecutor at the first hearing, now spoke on her behalf. The main issue was the restoration of her right to manage her own finances. Ninian Edwards, who had often been at loggerheads with Mary when Lincoln was alive, stood by her staunchly now. He testified that in the nine months she had been in his home, all had agreed that she was able to take charge of her own affairs. She had not spent as much as had been allotted her during this period, and he felt that she should be allowed to resume the status of a sane person.

The jury returned almost instantaneously with its finding that Mrs. Lincoln had been "restored to reason" and was capable of managing her estate. Robert was discharged as her conservator, and she was wholly free, with access to her own funds. This meant everything to Mary. Her son was out of her life for the time being, but the bitterness she had felt during her weeks of confinement came to the surface when she was freed, in a scorching letter she sent to Robert from Springfield on June 17, 1876.

It began with the stern salutation: "Robert T. Lincoln" and she ordered him to send her without delay all her paintings, including her Moses in the bulrushes, and the fruit picture that hung in his dining room. She wanted her silver set and the large silver waiter given her by New York friends. She also must have the silver tête-a-tête and other articles "your wife appropriated and which are *well known* to you."

Mary listed with specific care the garments she wanted returned. Her laces, her diamonds, her other jewelry, her unmade silks, her white lace dress, her double lace shawl and flounce, her lace scarf, two black lace shawls, one black lace deep flounce, white lace sets —all should be sent to her at once. She assured Robert that she had checked her list against corresponding lists held by two lawyers and that she intended to have it published. As a final reproach she wrote that she was constantly receiving letters from friends who condemned his conduct in the bitterest terms.

"You have injured yourself, not me, by your wicked conduct," she wrote. "Two prominent clergymen have written me, since I saw you . . . that they think it advisable to offer up prayers for you in church on account of your wickedness against me, and High Heaven. . . . Send me all that I have written for, you have tried your game of robbery long enough."

Mary assured her son that the "respectable" people of Chicago were behind her and she did not feel that he was worthy to wipe the dust off Judge Harlan's feet. Apparently Robert's father-in-law had been lending comfort to Mary, too. And as for her sister: "Trust not the belief that Mrs. Edwards' tongue has not been rancorous against you all winter and she has maintained to the very last, that you dared not venture into her house & our presence."

It was a crucifying letter and was the measure of Mary's feeling toward her son for what he had done to her. Again possessions were the issue, the cause to which she had clung through everything. As a rising young lawyer Robert was embarrassed by his mother's genius for getting into the newspapers. Proud Ninian Edwards and his wife were equally upset by the publicity, but they felt that Robert had brought it all on their heads by having his mother confined. When it was all over, Robert destroyed many of his mother's letters, and the Bradwell correspondence disappeared altogether, leaving various gaps in the complete history of this period. Mrs. Bradwell's fight was backed by her legal skill and knowledge, and she considered Mrs. Lincoln well able to handle her own affairs and live as a free woman—a judgment that was confirmed in the years that followed.

Long after her death the impression prevailed that she should never have been exposed to a public trial or to testimony which in some instances was uninformed, debatable and intensely cruel. Her bitterness toward Robert knew no bounds, but the events leading up to his action show clearly that his hand was forced. He broke with the Edwards family when he took this drastic step, for difficult though they knew Mary to be, they shrank from the stigma of an insanity verdict for the widow of Abraham Lincoln and for a member of their own proud clan.

When she was declared sane and her fortune was restored to her, there was no further squandering of her resources, no mad buying of everything that caught her fancy. Mary was chastened. She was quiet, but she was sadder than ever. Her old wit was gone; she rarely smiled. Her face had a heavy drooping look and she moved without any of her old spring. Mr. and Mrs. Edwards did everything they could for her, and their grandson, Edward Lewis Baker, Jr., the son of Julia Edwards Baker, seemed to remind her of Tad and Willie. He was a handsome youth of eighteen, gentle and kind, and he endeared himself to his shrinking great-aunt, closeted on the second floor of Ninian's house. Efforts were made for a reconciliation with Robert, who came to see her, but she could not view him with anything but resentment.

Mary soon saw that she was an embarrassing member of the family and could not feel at ease. The people of Springfield were kind to her. Some remembered her as a young bride, as the wife of ambitious Abraham Lincoln, as the President's wife. But with her quick intelligence she sensed the slightest hint of pity or patronage and shrank from it. "I cannot endure to meet my former friends, Lizzie," she said to Mrs. Edwards when she could bear no more of this attitude. "If I should say the moon is made of green cheese they would heartily and smilingly agree with me. I love you, but I cannot stay. I would be much less unhappy in the midst of strangers."

She felt that she had lost status in the world, and pride drove her to go where she might not be known. Ninian and Elizabeth accepted her decision as inevitable and young Lewis saw her off to Europe. The old Mary Lincoln revived for a time, and her intelligence burned its way through the confusion of the preceding years. She found some inner peace for herself away from people, away from interference, away from familiar scenes. For a time she seemed to regain her old intelligent interest in the world around her and to dwell less on her woes.

The doctors involved in her case followed her course with close attention. They could not forget Mrs. Lincoln, nor could the American public cease to think of Robert as an ungrateful son to the woman his father had loved and protected. Reviewing the medical evidence, Dr. W. A. Evans came to the conclusion that Mrs. Lincoln's mind was as disorganized after 1876 as it had been in 1875, and that by 1882 it was even more so. He rounded up all the elements in her history bearing on her sanity and defined her case posthumously in the light of the psychiatry of the 1930's.

Her multiple purchases, her extravagance, her hallucinations, her shifting moods, all were characteristic of the schizophrenic pattern. But Dr. Evans did not agree with Dr. Patterson that her passion for travel had special significance—the restless impulse that drives the disturbed from place to place, always seeking escape or peace and failing to find either. It was the fashion for women of that era who could afford it to visit Europe, to improve their health at the spas, and to seek culture at the art centers. Actually, until 1868 Mrs. Lincoln, who longed to go abroad, had traveled only in the United States, but when she finally reached Europe, she moved from place to place like a haunted spirit. Through the greater part of the 1870's she might truly be described as a wanderer without motive or destination, except that her physical ills were great and she was always in quest of warmth and sunshine.

Dr. Evans placed more reliance on the testimony of Dr. T. W. Dresser, Mrs. Lincoln's family physician for years, who stated her case simply when he wrote: "While the whole world was finding fault with her temper and disposition, it was clear to me that her trouble was a cerebral disease." In other words, Dr. Dresser was convinced all along that Mrs. Lincoln was insane.

Yet Dr. Evans personally believed that it was not until close to the end of her life that she developed any considerable degree of dementia. He classified her case as "involutional" and cited her habit of shutting herself away from the world when she failed to accomplish what she wanted. Her determination and aggressiveness, her poor judgment arising from her strong prejudices and dislikes, her paradoxical combination of miserliness and extravagance and her restless nature—all tied in with his diagnosis. He analyzed her as being explosive but reasonable, angry but tender, kind but miserly, cultivated yet crude, a composite of conflicting elements.

Various people who had known Mrs. Lincoln in her great days reached into the past to recall the occasions on which they had first noticed her idiosyncracies, but some of this might well have been hindsight, after she had been committed as insane. Mrs. Grimsley and Mrs. Edwards could recall many irrational acts by Mary. Some of these went back to her girlhood years. Katherine Helm, in particular, had the firsthand testimony of her clever and clearheaded mother, Emilie Todd Helm. Springfield friends were disposed to have seen strange manifestations during her second decade in their city.

Since the White House was constantly in the public eye during the Civil War, the slightest deviation in conduct was noted by the correspondents who swarmed around Washington. Stoddard was convinced that something was seriously wrong in 1861, almost as soon as Lincoln took office. In that same year her balance was so shaky that Lincoln gave his wife's mental state as one reason for sending Robert to college instead of to war.

Several of the more observant women writers of the day took note of Mrs. Lincoln's strange actions. Mrs. Laura C. Holloway, a social commentator of the period, wrote that from the time of Mr. Lincoln's death his wife was a mental wreck and would never recover. Mrs. Swisshelm, by no means a well-balanced character herself, wrote with understanding: "I think she was never entirely sane after the shock of her husband's murder; but on most subjects she was entirely clear."

This coincided with the opinion of many who conceded her eccentricities but forgave her her sins because of the magnitude of her sorrows, and chose to remember her intelligence, kindness, wit and charm when she was at her best. She was a woman of great complexity and remains so today. Her divided personality drove her to extremes, but she had a husband who treated her at all times with extraordinary understanding. He was the first to realize the depths of her instability, and when she stumbled through the dark avenues of madness and death, he above all others knew how to deal with her. Mary Todd Lincoln was both cursed and blessed in her marriage. This made Robert's action all the more incomprehensible to her after the years of understanding she had known with his father.

XXIII

The Struggle Ended

MRS. LINCOLN'S SECOND trip to Europe in 1879 was an escape from the annihilating effects of her incarceration and in a sense the revival of her own identity. Her pride had been mortally wounded, her status impaired, and the breach with Robert was complete. But during her stay abroad she found a certain measure of peace in the anonymity and variety of her travels. Her fears diminished; her tantrums were rare. The migraine headaches no longer plagued her as she aged, but her health in general had not improved. Yet she enjoyed sight-seeing, and letters from Paris, Pau, Avignon, Le Havre, Biarritz, St. Jean-de-Luz, Marseilles, Bordeaux and Naples were brightened with her impressions of what she saw.

People had ceased to assail her. Instead, they pitied her but Mary could not easily tolerate this, remembering the great days of the past. Even in her White House years she had been conscious of tales that she was demented, but Robert's act seemed to have fixed this image convincingly in the public mind. It left her no choice but to avoid observation, an effect she could more easily achieve abroad and away from people she knew.

Her memories sustained her through lonely hours in hotels and boardinghouses, where she continued to write letters with some of her old spontaneity but with a notable decline in her handwriting as rheumatism plagued her. She still dwelt lovingly and constantly on her memories of Mr. Lincoln, Tad and Willie. It was strange to cover some of the ground she had shared so recently with her adored son and to realize that he was gone. The seeds of her madness were deeply rooted there. But she had found an outlet for her motherly instincts in Mrs. Edwards' grandson, Edward Lewis Baker, Jr., the youth who had been kind to her during the trying days in Springfield. He saw her off when she sailed for Europe, and she kept up an illuminating correspondence with him, sharing her thoughts and experiences as she moved from place to place and giving him advice on his future.

Mary's letters during this period were sprightly and no longer so self-absorbed. She urged young Edward to stay out of politics and to go to college. He should enjoy his youth, so quickly over, and should travel, first in America and then abroad. She offered to finance him on a trip to the Pyrénées, which she had recently visited and liked. This was the old energetic and imaginative Mrs. Lincoln, eager to see the young make the most of their lives.

Again she found Americans all over Europe, as on her earlier visit. The postwar riches were still in evidence although money had become tighter since the crash of 1873. But parents still took their young on the grand tour and bought clothes in Paris. The spas were popular, and Mrs. Lincoln was an authority in this field because she had tried so many on both sides of the Atlantic. After landing at Marseilles, she went first to Vichy and then proceeded to her favorite, Pau. After a trip through the Pyrénées she went south to Naples, staying at the fashionable Hotel de Russie. In April she lingered in Sorrento, where the flowers, the music, the blue waters of the Mediterranean seemed heaven after the long cold winter. In May she was at the Hotel d'Italia in Rome, which she had planned to visit with Abraham Lincoln. But she suffered there from the damp and was glad to move on to Marseilles and more of the Mediterranean sunshine. After another stay at Vichy she returned to Pau, the resort that seemed to suit her best of all. She was able to live quietly there, without running into too many Americans, and this was what she most desired, although her letters to young Baker suggest that at this point she was beginning to think she should mingle more with people and "behave in a more *civilized* manner in the future."

In adopting this tone Mary might have been trying to convince her family in Springfield that she was living in a more normal way. They had done their best to keep her from shutting herself off from human contacts, and she knew that her sister would feel she was not better if she pursued the same course abroad. She had lost all her earlier resentment of Elizabeth and Ninian and kept assuring young Baker of her gratitude for their help after Robert's precipitous move. The other relative she could not forgive was her cousin and the playmate of her youth, John Todd Stuart.

Robert did not even know where she was. He wrote to the Reverend Henry Darling of New York that she was somewhere in Europe but had ceased to communicate with him. "I do not know her present address although, of course, I can by writing to some of her friends obtain it in case of need," he wrote. But she showed excitement when she found an item in the *American Register*, a weekly published in Paris, that her son was being mentioned as a Presidential possibility. The pulse of ambition stirred in her again, and forgetting her hurt for the moment, she even began to speculate about his Cabinet and to picture "*Little Mamie* with her charming manners & presence," in the White House. History was repeating itself, for the article she read so avidly mentioned the fact that Robert T. Lincoln and Stephen A. Douglas, Jr., both were prominent in their respective political parties, with the certainty of being candidates before long for the Presidency.

She mentioned this in a letter to Edward Lewis Baker in June, 1879, and speculated on Cabinet possibilities; but when Hayes was nominated, she was so isolated that she did not get the news for some time. This annoyed her because she took pride in following political developments in America. Her old critical spirit held sway when she learned that David M. Key had been appointed to the Cabinet. He had served in the Confederate Army and was therefore a secessionist who should not be rewarded, in Mrs. Lincoln's estimation.

Her mind was at all times extraordinarily active, and she kept churning up old issues and remembering past hurts. Her husband's gift for forgetting and forgiving had not rubbed off on Mary, who was implacable in her prejudices. In January, 1880, she was commenting on the fact that Mrs. John Tyler was applying vigorously for a government pension. She considered this an "impudent request" from a woman who had been so "forceful a Secessionist," with money and property in both the North and South. The pension question was still omnipresent in Mrs. Lincoln's mind, whether it related to Mrs. Garfield or to the dashing Julia Tyler, familiarly known as the Rose of Long Island.

Mary continued to jab at her son Robert in her letters to young Baker and to encourage Lewis to attend college. She felt that his leaning toward journalism would get him into politics, and she considered this undesirable for him. His father had long been proprietor and editor of the Illinois *State Journal*. Like Tad, Baker was drowned in the details of his great-aunt's sufferings, even while she commented on the political picture. She seemed to have made him a substitute for Taddie, who had tended to her ills, nursed her, listened to her, and been a sounding board for her political views and her reactions to world events.

On the whole her letters at this time suggest how far she had traveled from the confusion and hysteria that preceded her incarceration. Although nearly every communication had some allusion to her husband and sons, it was clear that she was now able to think beyond her woes and was following world news with the interest so characteristic of her past history. Her conversation at times was sharp, informed and allusive, in the old manner, and were it not for her ill health, her travels would have brought her great satisfaction. She never ceased to be an intelligent sightseer, approaching each new area well read and well versed in its history.

When she was well enough, she liked to take walks by herself, to gather flowers, as her husband had done on the banks of the James, to read books and newspapers, but to avoid talking to others whenever possible. She could now pass a tempting shopwindow without feeling compelled to go inside and buy up all the stock. Apparently she had gone through the manic swing from uncontrolled extravagance to pathological miserliness. Although she was relatively well off, her extreme frugality was a matter of comment at the hotels where she stayed. Her anxiety about money was never wholly allayed, and she still thought she might die in want.

The particular target of her business urgency was Jacob Bunn, a well-known Springfield banker and merchant who had been a friend of her husband's. When she sailed for Europe the second time, she committed all her financial affairs to his care. Her fortune had grown substantially, thanks to the disposition of her affairs by Judge Davis, and she had sound bonds and securities. Nearly a hundred letters addressed to Bunn from Europe show her shifting moods and also her business acumen, now that she was free and independent. At first she linked him in her mind with the Springfield group that had cost her her freedom, but as time went on, she and Bunn became good friends. She amazed him with her perspicacity in money matters as she followed the market fluctuations and every shift in exchange.

Mrs. Lincoln kept a banking base as she moved from place to

place, and she had many stormy encounters with American and British consuls who functioned too slowly for one as quick-witted as she was in this period. In 1878, when Bunn lost his own fortune, he suggested that she turn her affairs over to someone else, but she wrote from Pau, begging him to continue his stewardship. "My husband esteemed you so highly, and I should have *no confidence* in any one else," she wrote.

Bunn's martyrdom continued, but in spite of the petty aggravations and an endless spate of complaints and advice, in the end he was impressed with the meticulous way in which the notoriously spendthrift Mrs. Lincoln handled her fortune once she had got it out of Robert's hands. There were no more debts, and every obligation was promptly met. Between 1865 and 1882 her government bonds and top-grade securities had greatly increased in value and she had made a point of not breaking into her capital. It had taken years to get the estate straightened out, and she had played an active part in some of the negotiations, getting rid of dubious stock and concentrating on sound investments. But she had help from many sources. In the final analysis no one wanted to see the widow of Abraham Lincoln in financial difficulties, although many of the problems had been created by her own headstrong and irrational acts.

She was living in simple lodgings in Pau when her health seemed to deteriorate. Dr. Evans and other medical experts have since decided that she was probably suffering from diabetes. During the summer of 1878 she was plagued by boils, and she lost weight rapidly. She had been obese for a number of years, but she now weighed only 110 pounds. She drank a great deal of Vichy water and wrote that she was beset by "continual running waters, so disagreeable and inconvenient." She was constantly thirsty, and her symptoms pointed clearly to diabetes with agonizing boils, fluctuating vision, and a constant backache. Although she was at a low ebb physically, her letters flowed out in all directions, some of them almost illegible where her script had once been clear and graceful.

She had quieted down in all respects. There were no battles to be fought with real or imaginary foes. She was too exhausted for the ranting hysteria of her earlier years. In a sense Mrs. Lincoln was a burned-out shell, living in the past and seeking always for some physical comfort that seemed to be denied her, as her pains became obsessive. Her steady decline showed in her letters, but the last straw was an accident she had at Pau in December, 1879. She was trying to hang a picture over a mantelpiece when the stepladder on which she was standing collapsed. Her spine was injured and the lower part of her body was paralyzed. She was in pain constantly, and her back was strapped with plasters. She weighed less than 100 pounds by the middle of January, 1880. Her Washington friends would not have known her.

She was miserable all that winter, and spring brought no relief. In June she was moving some of her things from a fourth story hotel room in Pau, and in being helped by a maid her left side, in her own words, "gave way." The concierge lifted her, and a physician was summoned. Mrs. Lincoln was back in plasters, and she found no relief after that. Her thoughts turned to home. She was tired of the French, whom she now described as "unprincipled, heartless, avaricious people." Except for a few, she "detested them all!" And at times she longed for waffles, butter cakes, corn bread and buckwheat cakes. . . . "a long period of absence from America, is not agreeable—but to an oppressed, heart broken woman it is simply an *exile*," she wrote to young Baker. Soon the Edwards family learned that Mary would be back with them. She conceded that she was "too ill and feeble in health" to go on and would sail home on *l'Amérique* on October 16, 1880. Lewis was to meet her in New York, and she would be glad if Mrs. Edwards would come, too.

Her fashion sense had not deserted her, and gaunt but dignified, she had abandoned the crinoline for the fashionable but much-less becoming bustle. Sarah Bernhardt, a fellow passenger, noticed how sad and resigned she looked, although she had no idea at first that the shrinking figure in black was Mary Todd Lincoln. But she soon learned her identity when the ship lurched and she and Mary were thrown together at the top of a stairway. Noticing that the aging woman was about to fall down the stairs, she caught her firmly by the skirt and saved her from a dangerous tumble.

In *Memories of My Life* Sarah Bernhardt told later of Mrs. Lincoln's confused state. "She thanked me in such a gentle, dreamy voice that my heart began to beat with emotion," the actress recalled.

"You might have been killed, madame," I said, "down that horrible staircase."

"Yes," said Mrs. Lincoln, "but it was not God's will."

Each identified the other at this point, when Mary whispered that she was President Lincoln's widow. Sarah Bernhardt's comment was revealing. She wrote: 'I had just done this unhappy woman the only service that I ought not to have done her—I had saved her from death."

Mary may well have felt the same way about it, for life was flickering low for her at this point. The falls she had had at Pau had been culminating disasters in her ill-starred life and had added greatly to her physical suffering. She shrank from any reminder of the theatrical people she had once loved, and she never entered a theater after her husband's death.

Her sister Elizabeth did not meet her, but young Lewis was at quarantine to board her liner. A crowd had gathered at the dock, and hundreds more waited in the street outside the gates. When the gangplank was swung aboard, Sarah Bernhardt and Madame Colombier of her troupe were the first to descend. Their fellow passengers cheered them as they left, but none on the ship or ashore paid any attention to the gray-haired woman in black who had been First Lady during the years of the Civil War. As she walked on Lewis's arm toward the gates, a policeman tapped her on the shoulder and asked her to stand back as a carriage for Madame Bernhardt moved slowly through the waiting crowd.

Although the New York *Sun* suggested that this must have humiliated Mrs. Lincoln, in fact she was relieved to escape unnoticed. Lewis took her to the Fifth Avenue Hotel, where they registered simply as Edward Lewis Baker and Aunt. This was by Mary's wish. When they reached Springfield, the Edwards family was appalled to see how she had failed. Although they had been cheered by her earlier letters from Europe, they saw at once that she had slipped back into the old chaotic and unreasonable state. There were many scenes, and although they all tried to humor her at first, the situation became difficult. Once more she rebelled over not being a free agent. Mrs. Edwards installed her comfortably on the second floor of the mansion where so much history had been made, but she stayed indoors for the better part of a year. At times she refused even to see her sisters, Elizabeth Edwards and Frances Wallace, and on rare occasions when they persuaded her to drive with them, she hid behind the curtains or sank low in the back of the carriage where she could not be seen. She stubbornly resisted doing what anyone else suggested, and they all saw that it was best to let her alone. But sixty-four crates and trunks threatening to collapse the floor of one of their rooms made no sense to the disciplined Elizabeth Edwards. She wrote to Emilie Todd Helm that Mary's enjoyment of a darkened room was not her idea of the good life. She felt that her sister exaggerated her condition to get attention. The situation as a whole wearied her, and she could see that Mary was getting restless again and might wish to wander.

This same idea apparently had been conveyed to Robert, who wrote rather skeptically to Mrs. Orne after visiting his mother that "my own judgment is that some part of her trouble is imaginary." A reconciliation had been planned for this visit in May, 1881, and Robert asked his mother to forgive him. Whatever mental reservations she may have had, she was won all over again by his small daughter. She recalled that Mr. Lincoln had longed for a girl when one son after another was born to them, and she felt that this child would have been infinitely dear to him.

Amicable relations were restored with Robert after this visit. He was prospering as a lawyer and had become an important man in his own right. His mother's obsessions were no longer the nightmare they had been to him, except when her name sprang to life in the newspapers. His wife was torn between concern for her own mother and her mother-in-law. Mrs. Harlan had been an invalid for years, and Judge Harlan was apologetic for how often he called Robert's wife to attend her.

But once again Mrs. Lincoln made dismaying headlines for her family. She made two trips to New York, seeking medical treatment for her back. On the first she consulted Dr. Lewis A. Sayre, a leading orthopedic surgeon, who had originally come from Lexington and knew her family. He diagnosed her condition as inflammation of the spinal cord with partial paralysis of the lower part of the body. He found that she could not walk safely without the aid of a chair, and even with this support she was likely to fall. Dr. Sayre suggested that she employ a nurse or maid to help her get around, but she pleaded poverty and said that she could not afford anything of the sort.

On her second trip to New York she was in such a state of collapse that when she arrived at the Clarendon Hotel, the coachman picked her up in his arms and carried her to her room. She was equally helpless when she took treatments at Dr. E. P. Miller's therapeutic establishment on West Twenty-sixth Street in New York. Physiotherapy was being practiced widely at this time, and Dr. Miller's Turkish, electric and Roman baths were both fashionable and expensive. Mrs. Lincoln, well able to pay for it all, was in a state of mortal fear over the costs. Her medical bills, the baths, her accommodation and five dollars a month that she paid for a room in which to store her trunks preyed on her mind.

With Congress allowing Mrs. Garfield a pension of $5,000 a year, Mary plunged into another fight to have her $3,000 pension increased. Two old friends went into action on her behalf. Rhoda White Mack, the daughter of her old friend Mrs. James W. White, and the Reverend Noyes W. Miner, both visited her and were touched by her helpless state. Dr. Sayre had inadvertently said that her living costs had not been high, but Mrs. Mack was skeptical about this.

The Reverend Mr. Miner was the brother of another old friend, Mrs. Hannah Shearer, and after visiting Mrs. Lincoln, he made a plea for her at a pastors' conference. When he asked her what he could do to help, she suggested lobbying for her in Congress. She gave him the names of men he might approach on her behalf. "Overpower them all, by your good words," Mary implored him. But she warned him against approaching her son, Robert. However, since her plight had again come to the attention of the press and the ministry was stirred up about it, Robert was soon aware of what was going on.

This time his mother's case got instant attention in Congress. The injustice of the treatment she had had on the pension issue had become a public scandal, and there was fast action. Her pension was raised from $3,000 to $5,000 a year, and she received an immediate gift of $15,000, presumably to help meet her medical bills. Aside from the moral satisfaction, this made little difference to Mary. It did not change her conviction that she was in want. Her notes became wild incoherent scrawls, and there was clear evidence of her disorientation.

Susan B. Anthony and other suffrage workers were staying at Dr. Miller's fashionable establishment while she was there, but Mrs. Lincoln was resolutely cold to feminist leanings. For one who had campaigned zealously in her early days in Lexington and Springfield, who had wielded more than her share of political power, she deplored the efforts of the women who were battling for the vote. On her return from her first trip to Europe she had written to Mrs. Madeleine Vinton Dahlgren, wife of Admiral John A. Dahlgren and an old friend, that she agreed with the sentiments in her "spirituelle brochure" opposing the movement.

Mary wrote that the women of America were in the fullest possession of every right—"even of that one which I think the French call, 'le droit insolence.'" She would recommend that "our strong minded sisters" go to Savoy or Saxony and see women hitched to the plow or harnessed with dogs drawing little carts through the streets.

Although agreeing wholly with Mrs. Dahlgren's campaign against the suffrage pioneers, Mary declined to head a proposed counter petition. She had never signed a protest against anything in her life, and "I know not whether it is indolence or because I am so thoroughly anti-protestant," wrote the woman who had been a fighter all her life. But with Victoria Woodhull staging her own particular kind of battle for the Presidency, Mrs. Lincoln was skeptical and disapproving. She assured Mrs. Dahlgren that the movement should be treated with "wholesome neglect," for if Congress did give women the vote, those who would avail themselves of it would "behave in so inconsequent a manner as to reduce the whole matter to an absurdity."

Thus Mrs. Lincoln, who had played the liberationist game for a lifetime, dismissed with Victorian disdain the surging movement and its eloquent pioneers. No doubt she had long since forgotten having written to Mercy Levering just before Christmas, 1840, about her role in the William Henry Harrison campaign: "This fall I became quite a *politician,* rather an unladylike profession, yet at such a *crisis,* whose heart could remain untouched while the energies of all were called in question?"

This was wholly characteristic of Mary's complex nature, and she was not unobservant, through the mist of her own immediate agony, of Susan Anthony's long, lean figure striding about at Dr. Miller's. Her pain-racked days in the city where she had once been feted and had bought so riotously at A. T. Stewart's, Lord & Taylor's, and Arnold Constable's soon came to an end. Beaten at last, she wrote to Lewis that she would be returning to Springfield, but she dreaded the journey in her paralyzed state. When she arrived, her family's apprehensions were confirmed; it was clear to them that she had greatly deteriorated.

After this she lived in a strange world of pain and incoherence. She had been seeing mediums in New York, and again there was evidence of visions and hallucinations. She thought that she talked to Tad and Willie, and she slept always on one side of the bed, believing that Mr. Lincoln was by her side. Night and day she wore a money belt, as well as secreting cash and bonds in odd places. The young people who came and went at the Edwards' home thought of her as a pathetic, crazy old lady, but Lewis remained kind and understanding.

Her boils became almost unbearable in July, 1882, and her family thought of moving her to the seashore because of the trouble she had breathing in humid weather. But she had passed the stage where she could be helped in any way known to medicine at that time. Soon she was unable to walk across a room and she was tended like a baby. Her ramblings went on, but they meant nothing except to the spiritualists who sometimes came to her. They were wholly centered on the griefs and disasters of the past.

The July heat was stifling when she made one last desperate effort to walk across her room, but that evening she had a stroke. All through the next day, a quiet Sunday in Springfield, she lay in a coma, and at 8:15 in the evening of July 16, 1882, Mary Todd Lincoln was dead, her struggles and her sorrows behind her. She was in her sixty-fourth year, and what she had called the "waiting" was over for one of the most unhappy and abused women in the world's history.

Dr. T. W. Dresser signed her death certificate "paralysis," which was more generally defined at the time as apoplexy. Mrs. Edwards locked her sister's sixty-four trunks filled with the treasures she had so senselessly hoarded, until Robert arrived. She had $3,000 in gold in her top drawer and $75,000 in bonds.

Friends streamed through the Edwards' parlor where the coffin rested, close to the spot where Mary Todd and Abraham Lincoln had been married forty years earlier. At last Mary looked at peace, her sorrows erased in the calm of death. She seemed wraithlike in plain white silk. Her folded hands, so vivaciously used for gestures in her White House days when they were plump and dimpled, were swollen now, so her ring with the inscription "Love is eternal" was buried with her but it was no longer on her hand.

Springfield, where so much of Mary Lincoln's early history lay, paid her honor on the day of her funeral. Business houses and public offices were closed in memory of the wife of Springfield's great man. Much was forgiven her; much had already been forgotten. The funeral was delayed for the arrival of Robert, who was now Secretary of War. Services were held in the First Presbyterian Church. Reverend James A. Reed delivered the eulogy and, taking note of the Mrs. Lincoln they had known before her acknowledged illness, said: "It is not only charitable but just to her native mental qualities and her noble womanly nature, that we think of her & speak of her as the woman she was before her noble husband fell a martyr by her side."

He likened the Lincolns to two tall and stately pines which had grown so close together that their roots and branches had intertwined as they faced mountain storms. When the taller of the two was struck by a flash of lightning, the shock was too much for the other. "They had virtually both been killed at the same time," said Dr. Reed. "With the one that lingered it was only slow death from the same cause ... when Abraham Lincoln died, she died. The lightning that struck down the strong man, unnerved the woman.... So it seems to me today, that we are only looking at death placing its seal upon the lingering victim of a past calamity."

There was drama in the church as Robert stood with bowed head listening to the eulogy of the mother who had given him so much love and support and had caused him so much sorrow. The church was stifling, with waves of fragrance coming from the masses of flowers sent in memory of Mrs. Lincoln. Springfield's tribute to a learned First Lady was a book—the book of life—made of carnations, rosebuds, tuberoses with the name Mary Lincoln interwoven with forget-me-nots.

Governor Shelby M. Cullom of Illinois and other state and civic dignitaries drove in the long cortege to Oak Ridge Cemetery, where Mary Lincoln lies today with Abraham Lincoln and her sons, in a woodland setting of peace and beauty. Thousands make pilgrimages to this tomb each year, with varying feelings about Mary. Her history lives after her in the most controversial way.

The news that Mrs. Lincoln was dead brought mixed memories to many across the country, and in the final analysis the comments were kindly. All took account of her mental state, and even Judge Davis, who had known her so long and so well as he coped with her business affairs and acted as friend and protector, wrote after her death: "Poor Mrs. Lincoln. She is at last at rest. She has been a deranged woman ever since her husband's death. In fact she was so, during his life."

Friend and foe in Springfield closed ranks in her behalf at the end. On his return to Washington from his mother's funeral Robert wrote to Mrs. James Garfield on July 30, 1882, a letter which showed convincingly that before her death they had become fully reconciled. Mrs. Garfield, too, was the widow of an assassinated President, and she must have read with satisfaction his declaration: "Her death was very sudden & unexpected to me but it was a painless release from much mental & bodily distress. I have a great satisfaction that a year ago I broke down the personal barrier which her disturbed mind had caused her to raise between us, so that in the end her estrangement had ceased."

Thus death softened the picture, even where Robert was concerned, and this had been one of her deepest wounds. But it did not clarify things for historians, who would continue to explore and debate the motivations of Mary Todd Lincoln's complex nature.

XXIV

Lincoln Alone Understood

T HE DISASTERS OF Mary Lincoln's life have been made the apologia for the extraordinary course she followed and the persistence of her image in the public consciousness. To accept an encompassing verdict of insanity in her case is to excuse all and in a sense to discount her remarkable gifts as an individual. But her attacks were intermittent, and her eccentricities were only a small part of her story, which was rich in all the elements of human drama, stark and terrible though its manifestations were.

She was unique among Presidents' wives—a Southern-born woman committed heart and soul to the Northern cause at the most crucial period in the nation's history. The bitter animosities of the period flowed around her like a river of poison, and she was married to the most abused of men until time and achievement gave him an aura of grandeur.

By the time she reached the White House few remembered, and she herself never alluded to, the great gulf that stretched between them in training, education, social background, and general cultivation. They were as different in temperament as they were in their physical makeup. Even Herndon, Mrs. Lincoln's most ruthless critic, took note of how much these differences entered into the daily irritations of their life together. In paradoxical terms, considering many of his statements about her, he wrote: "In her domestic troubles I have always sympathized with Mrs. Lincoln. The world does not know what she bore, or how ill-adapted she was to bear it. Her fearless, witty, and austere nature shrank instinctively from association with the calm, imperturbable, and simple ways of her thoughtful and absent-minded husband."

But Herndon also acknowledged that with all his simple ways Lincoln at one moment might be as "pliable and expansive as gentle air; at the next as tenacious and unyielding as granite itself," and he understood the disparate pull between Lincoln's instinctive earthiness and Mary's highly developed sense of decorum. Only the fact that their physical love seemed to have an enduring and special quality enabled them to rise above the situations that often created tension between them.

Mary was worldly because she had always dealt with worldly men. She knew how they talked both in and out of their cups, and crass language did not necessarily dismay her, but she also had a fundamental dash of Victorian primness that took firm root while she was in the White House and under observation. In her marriage she had to accustom herself to the rough edges of a new vocabulary and to buffoonery that set her teeth on edge.

Mary threw all her energy and influence behind her husband when he emerged on the national scene through clouds of doubt and abuse. She considered him all too trustful of his fellow men, and she believed that she could help him in appraising those he chose for office. He had listened to her on the lesser issues of the past and had found her judgment sound. Even Herndon conceded that she was an astute judge of human nature, understanding men's motives better than her husband did. Mary was quick to detect those who sought to use him. In the best sense she was a stimulant, for she prodded him into action when he seemed to lag. Herndon believed that her drive rested to some extent on the realization that her husband's rise to power would elevate and strengthen her at the same time, and so she kept him moving in an effort "to win the world's applause."

It is evident that Mrs. Lincoln found some appeasement for her own ambition in the crucial days of the Civil War, when she presided with grace at a dinner table peopled with princes, diplomats and world-famous statesmen; when the most recalcitrant Cabinet members bowed to her; and when the most difficult generals remembered that she was Mrs. Lincoln.

But in the end she drove too hard, interfered too much, and was condemned for her nagging and pretentious ways. Her letters from abroad after her husband's death show how much she regretted some of her more impulsive acts and how she wished them undone.

Lincoln had brushed off slander and bitter attack with the detachment characteristic of his nature, but with Mary they had sunk in and stung. Where he could ward off a savage blow with a jest, she dissolved in rage and tears. The slightest wound to her husband was more terrible than any to herself, for her early devotion turned to idolatry during their years in the White House—or perhaps the picture was magnified after his death as he reached full stature in the eyes of the world. Mary had not always thought of him as a saint or even as a man easy to live with, but that was how she saw him at the end.

The degree of influence that she exercised over her husband remains a debatable question, with most historians agreeing that it was minor after they reached the White House, but potent in the years before. Carl Sandburg noted that there was always a "moving undertow of their mutual ambitions" between Mr. and Mrs. Lincoln. "Though his hope of achievement and performance was sometimes smothered and obliterated in melancholy, it was there burning and questing, most of the time," he added. Meanwhile the deep desire for "high place, eminence, distinction" never seemed to leave Mrs. Lincoln. But even those who believed her to be a vixen and shrew conceded that she was an "exceptional mother, brooding over her offspring with a touch of the tigress."

Lincoln's deep-rooted ambition did not show, but his fortitude and persistence were evident long before Mary Todd came into his life, and she never pretended that she had helped him on his way. Rather, in her later years she tortured herself with memories of the trouble she had given him with her tantrums and illnesses. Her remorse was as devastating as the temper that ruled her and led to unforgettable scenes. Her devotion to his needs was obsessive. She liked to wait on him in the White House as she had done in their home in Springfield. He accepted her wifely attentions with good-natured amusement, and he missed them when she was away and he was left to the ministrations of a housekeeper.

But most of the time Lincoln lived in another world, a tired, harassed man who could give her little time in the war years and talked less and less to her of military affairs and his troubles. Had it not been for the boys, it is likely that she would have had still less of his attention in these harrowing years. Meanwhile, her own days were filled with a busy round of social activities that he knew little about, and he was scarcely aware of the flatterers and sycophants who took up so much of her time. Gallantry was a sure way to hold Mary Lincoln's attention.

But more often than the public realized, she was prostrated with her headaches, neuralgia or the well-developed malarial symptoms common to many of the Civil War matrons who underwent this particular misery in the capital and fled from it when they could. Mary was not alone in suffering acutely from a variety of aches and pains and the general malaise that developed when things went wrong, as they usually did in these years of desperation. Some of the wives were in better health and had more self-control than others, but when one of Mrs. Lincoln's unpredictable moods took hold, she went to extremes. Since she was in middle life while in the White House and was subject to gynecological woes, her family and certainly her husband made ample allowance for her unreasonable outbursts and hysteria. Clearly Mrs. Lincoln's chemistry was out of balance and she had to express herself in her own way.

The sparkling moods and witty repartee that had been attractive in her youth wore thin under the cares and sorrows of the war years, except when things were going her way. Then she would blossom out with a touch of the old brilliance. Although she had a few close women friends, she was not popular with the wives of the official set, except for Mrs. Gideon Welles, who had lost six children and had some understanding of Mary's sorrows. But she kept up a lively correspondence with a number of women who valued her friendship. Some were old Springfield neighbors. Others were the wives of rich men prominent in the Republican Party. She seemed to long for chatty, gossipy letters rich in feminine interests. Mary was always adored by children, and her interest in them extended far beyond the boundaries of her own home. Her concern for the oppressed blacks was constant, in spite of the criticism it brought her at the time. Her kindnesses to obscure people were legion but unnoticed.

Some of the men around the President thought that his wife's nagging was just what he needed to stir him into action. Henry B. Rankin, one of her warmest advocates, wrote that, but for Mary Todd, Lincoln might never have become President. This close friend and long time admirer believed that she possessed in a high degree the qualities that her husband lacked. "She was not in any sense a virago and Abraham Lincoln loved her," said Rankin, praising the unfaltering faith and indomitable spirit with which she had stood by him when "storms were breaking, and when fair-weather friends deserted him."

In *Legends That Libel Lincoln* Montgomery S. Lewis wrote that Mrs. Lincoln did not nag her husband into greatness but stood by his side "shoulder to shoulder," helping him in every way within her power, sharing his disappointments, showing her faith by encouraging him to strive for new and higher goals. Then, for seventeen years she lived in a mist, "doing strange, regrettable things."

William E. Barton, who knew her well and gave her history deep study, believed that she nagged Lincoln unmercifully but that this was beneficial, since he was a "man too fond of ease to have been successful in political life if wedded to a woman who made an ideal home." This cool-eyed observer of the Lincolns thought that once in a while when the President's "sluggish but vehement temper got the better of him," he said and did things which afterward caused him bitter self-reproach.

Barton was convinced that Mary Todd married Abraham Lincoln as deliberately as such a woman ever could do anything. She was a creature of whims, but she made her choice and selected him from among her many suitors for two reasons: He was likely to gratify her ambition, and she sincerely cared for him. Their love was mutual, in Barton's opinion, and he wrote of this unlikely combination of personalities: "In his big, undemonstrative, imperturbable way, Lincoln loved his wife, and was enormously proud of her. . . . He was proud of her beauty, her wit. Like other big men who have little wives, he enjoyed 'the long and short of it' in their matrimonial combination." Mrs. Keckley noticed that he sometimes called her his "child wife" and that Mrs. Lincoln found this comforting.

The young lawyers who traveled the circuit with Lincoln in his Springfield days made many comments on his manners and strange ways. Henry C. Whitney, who often shared the same room and even the same bed with Lincoln, wrote of Mary that the world did not know how much he was indebted to her for "words of cheer—of hope—of comfort and solace, when all seemed dark. . . . Lincoln thoroughly loved his wife. I had many reasons to know this in my intimacy with him, and she therefore wrought a great influence over him."

Lloyd Lewis wrote many years later of the Lincoln combination that the "woman Lincoln loved, and who loved him, had a fiery scolding way that could be managed only with tolerant persuasion.

His treatment of her was typical of his genius for management, for he guided the electorate as he handled his wife."

In his *Abraham Lincoln* Lord Charnwood, a British visitor, seemed to think that the President did not take a firm enough hand with his wife. He wrote of them: "The worst that we are told with any certainty amounts to this, that like the very happily married writer of *Virginibus Puerisque* Lincoln discovered that marriage is a 'field of battle and not a bed of roses'—a battle in which we are forced to suspect that he did not play his full part. . . ."

Badeau acknowledged in his final analysis of Mrs. Lincoln that no one could rightly judge her as the unwitting cause of many of the President's miseries who chose to forget that she had "eaten on the insane root that takes the reason prisoner." Yet this did not mitigate his own harsh appraisal of her qualities.

In assembling various opinions about Mrs. Lincoln, including medical afterthoughts, Dr. Evans came to the conclusion that she had not influenced her husband in the White House days. "Lincoln politics, plans, and methods of the presidential period were Lincolnesque and gave no evidence of his wife's influence," he wrote with finality. Dr. Evans considered that as a woman Mary was too serious, with no capacity to laugh at herself. She knew how to ridicule others but never herself. He felt that her likes and dislikes were so strong that they begot likes and dislikes in others. Among her weaknesses he listed her inability to withstand restraint, her hysterical tendencies, and a disposition to disregard the point of view and feelings of others. Added to this, she was prone to give offense, to resent criticism, to give way to anger, to remember hurts and to be revengeful.

Strangely enough, for one so devoted to flowers, house decoration, music and attractive costuming, Dr. Evans came to the conclusion that Mrs. Lincoln was lacking in an artistic sense and in a true love of beauty in color, form or sound. He did not think that inheritance was a dominating factor in her mental collapse, but he did believe that the circumstances of her life were overwhelming for a woman of her temperament.

In a sense her life pattern was molded by death, from the loss of her mother before she was seven until Tad died in 1871. After that the shadows closed in on her altogether, for she no longer had the steadying influence of Lincoln to give her the support and protection that had carried her through one crisis after another.

Mary's devotion to her husband and her sons was classic in its proportions—or obsessive, according to one's thinking. It was the motivating force of her life. No President was ever more blindly loved than Abraham Lincoln. No President's wife was ever the victim of more misunderstanding and abuse. There was an element of great frustration in her history, too. She was highly educated for the period and intensely ambitious, not just on the social side but where intellect counted. She saw herself not only as the nation's leading hostess but as her husband's critic and adviser—an effective woman in her own right.

Her besetting sin perhaps was vanity, in the Biblical sense of the word, and this in her case had many manifestations. Until her mind clouded over altogether, she could pinpoint her own mistakes with perception and clarity, but she would repeat them because her superabundant energies constantly needed an outlet. Dr. Barton told much about Mary Lincoln when he described her as being "affectionate, ardent, passionate, and to a hot temper she joined a stubborn will." But she herself gave the true key to her life history when she described the fallen President as "lover—husband—father—*all*."

Had it not been wartime, it is conceivable that Mrs. Lincoln might have emerged as one of the most effective First Ladies, for she had intelligence, dash, good looks, ambition, a power complex, and a strong social sense. But to her own undoing she could not cope with stress and her sorrows were manifold. She shared with Mrs. Garfield, Mrs. McKinley and Mrs. Kennedy the loss of a husband in office. Each took the blow in her own way, according to her particular strength or temperament. But Mary was already badly shaken by the death of Willie, by the storms that roared around her husband's administration, and by her strong sense of guilt over her debts and the troubles she had caused the President.

Her virtues were forgotten and her sins were magnified in the final holocaust, but beyond doubt she was greatly and compassionately loved by Abraham Lincoln, and her story is firmly and lastingly embedded in the historical picture of America at war with itself.

Notes

CHAPTER I

A Bluegrass Girl

Katherine Helm, *The True Story of Mary, Wife of Lincoln*; Emilie Todd Helm, "Mary Todd Lincoln," *McClure's Magazine*, September, 1898; G. H. Edwards, *Historic Sketches of the Edwards and the Todd Families and Their Descendants 1821–1895*; William H. Townsend, *Lincoln and His Wife's Home Town*; Dr. W. A. Evans, *Mrs. Abraham Lincoln: A Study of Her Personality and Her Influence on Lincoln*; Charles W. Hackensmith, "Family Background and Education of Mary Todd," *The Register*, Kentucky Historical Society, July, 1971; George W. Ranck, *History of Lexington*; J. Winston Coleman, Jr., *Historic Kentucky* and *Lexington During the Civil War*; Teresa L. Reed thesis, *Mary Todd Lincoln*; Charles H. Atherton and J. H. Atherton correspondence, 1832, University of Kentucky Library; Katherine E. Wilkie, "Tradition May Malign Mary Todd," *Blue Grass Heritage Survey* made by Theta Sigma Phi, and *Mary Todd Lincoln, Girl of the Blue Grass*; William E. Barton, *The Women Lincoln Loved*; obituary of Madame Mentelle, Kentucky *Statesman*, September 14, 1860; Todd and related press items: Kentucky *Gazette*, July 27, 1798, March 6, 1800, and March 26, 1834; Lexington *Intelligencer*, March 6, 1838, and October 24, 1834; Kentucky *Reporter*, July 4 and 11, 1825, and July 8 and October 14, 1829; Lexington *Daily Press*, November 14, 1871, and July 18, 1882; Lexington *Herald*, April 17, 1949, March 19, 1957, and June 18, 1971; information supplied by Mrs. William H. Townsend, Charles W. Hackensmith, J. Winston Coleman, Jr., Teresa L. Reed, Mrs. Mary Genevieve Murphy and Miss Katherine Lambert.

CHAPTER II

Across a Dance Floor

Katherine Helm, *The True Story of Mary, Wife of Lincoln*, using diary and family letters of her mother, Emilie Todd Helm, on the meeting and courtship of the Lincolns; correspondence of Mary Todd and Mercy Levering, Illinois State Historical Library; correspondence of Lincoln and Joshua Fry Speed, Illinois State Historical Library; Mary Leighton Miles, "Fatal First of January, 1841," *Illinois State Historical Journal*, April, 1927; Octavia Roberts, "We All Knew Ab'ham," *Abraham Lincoln Quarterly*, March, 1946; Mrs. Ninian Edwards' statement to Jesse Weik in 1883 and to William H. Herndon in 1887 regarding wedding arrangements, in *Abraham Lincoln*, by William H. Herndon and Jesse W. Weik; Joshua F. Speed's statement to Herndon regarding engagement, September 17, 1866, *ibid.*; Carl Sandburg and Paul M. Angle, *Mary Lincoln, Wife and Widow* (including original documents); Ruth Painter Randall, *The Courtship of Mr. Lincoln* and *Mary Lincoln; Biography of a Marriage*; William H. Townsend, *Lincoln and His Wife's Home Town;* Dr. W. A. Evans, *A Study of Her Personality and Her Influence on Lincoln*; C. W. Hackensmith, "The Much Maligned Mary Todd Lincoln," *The Filson Club History Quarterly*, July, 1970, Vol. 44; Montgomery S. Lewis, *Legends That Libel Lincoln*; Roy P. Basler, "The Authorship of the 'Rebecca Letters,' " *Abraham Lincoln Quarterly*, June, 1942; Albert J. Beveridge, *Abraham Lincoln 1809–1858*, Vol. 1; William E. Barton, *Life of Abraham Lincoln* and *The Women Lincoln Loved*; Henry B. Rankin, *Intimate Character Sketches of Abraham Lincoln*; Mrs. John T. Stuart, "Recollections of Lincoln," mss., Illinois State Historical Library; Mary Edwards Raymond, "Some Incidents in the Life of Mrs. Benj. S. Edwards," privately printed pamphlet, Illinois State Historical Library; Carlos W. Goltz, *Incidents in the Life of Mary Todd Lincoln*; Mrs. Elizabeth Keckley, *Behind the Scenes*, on Stephen A. Douglas courtship; Mrs. Lincoln to Mrs. Gideon Welles, December 6, 1865, Welles mss., Library of Congress; Dr. Anson G. Henry mss., Illinois State Historical Library; Carl Sandburg, "Mary Todd Lincoln," *Woman's Home Companion*, September, 1932; *Sangamon Journal*, September 2, 9 and 16, 1842; Mary Lincoln to Francis B. Carpenter, Chicago, December 8, 1865; "The Documents" in Sandburg and Angle's *Mary Lincoln, Wife and Widow*; Lincoln's uncertainty about marrying, *ibid.*, Appendix; Ida M. Tarbell, *The Life of Abraham Lincoln*, Vol. I; J. Duane Squires, "Lincoln's Todd In-Laws," *Lincoln Herald*, Fall, 1967; Mrs. Lincoln to Josiah G. Holland, December 4, 1865, University of Chicago Library.

CHAPTER III

Mary Todd Becomes Mrs. Lincoln

Emilie Todd Helm, "Mary Todd Lincoln," *McClure's Magazine*, September, 1898; statements by Ninian Edwards, Mrs. Elizabeth Edwards, James H. Matheny and James Gourley in Herndon-Weik mss., Library of Congress; Frances Todd Wallace, "Lincoln's Marriage," Springfield interview, September 2, 1895, and *Lincoln's Marriage*, privately printed, 1917; Eugenia Jones Hunt, "My Personal

Recollections of Abraham and Mary Todd Lincoln," *Abraham Lincoln Quarterly*, March, 1945; Mary Edwards Brown, "Abraham Lincoln Married 78 Years Ago Today," Illinois *State Register*, November 4, 1920; Lincoln-Joshua F. Speed correspondence, including Lincoln's letter to Speed re "hypo," February 3, 1842, Illinois State Historical Library; Mrs. John T. Stuart correspondence with her daughter Elizabeth, Stuart-Hay papers, Illinois State Historical Library; Katherine Helm, *The True Story of Mary, Wife of Lincoln*; Carlos W. Goltz, *Incidents in the Life of Mary Todd Lincoln*; William H. Townsend, *Lincoln and His Wife's Home Town*; Orville Hickman Browning, *The Diary of Orville Hickman Browning*; Albert J. Beveridge, *Abraham Lincoln 1809–1858*, Vol. I; Montgomery S. Lewis, *Legends That Libel Lincoln*; Dale Carnegie, *Lincoln the Unknown*; Paul M. Angle, *Here I Have Lived*; Ward Hill Lamon, *Life of Abraham Lincoln, from His Birth to His Inauguration as President*; Emanuel Hertz, *The Hidden Lincoln*; David Donald, *Herndon's Lincoln*; Reverend N. W. Miner, *Personal Recollections of Abraham Lincoln*, mss. Illinois State Historical Library; Henry C. Whitney, *Life on the Circuit with Lincoln*; Harry E. Pratt, *The Personal Finances of Abraham Lincoln*; Isaac N. Arnold, *The Life of Abraham Lincoln*; Gamaliel Bradford, *Wives* and "The Wife of Abraham Lincoln," *Harper's Monthly*, September, 1925; W. A. Evans, *Mrs. Abraham Lincoln: A Study of Her Personality and Her Influence on Lincoln*; Ruth Painter Randall, *Mary Lincoln: Biography of a Marriage*; Chicago *Times Herald*, September 8, 1895, quoting Mrs. George McConnell of Jacksonville, Illinois, on Mrs. Lincoln's solicitude for children; Mrs. Leigh Kimball Brainerd, "New Facts About the Home Life of Mrs. Lincoln," Louisville *Courier-Journal*, March 5, 1899; William Dodd Chenery, "Mary Todd Lincoln Should Be Remembered for Many Kind Acts," Illinois *State Register*, February 27, 1938; C. C. Ritzie, "In Defense of Mrs. Lincoln," *Illinois State Historical Society Journal*, April, 1937, John Alexander McClernand, mss. Illinois State Historical Library.

CHAPTER IV

A Congressman's Wife

Benjamin Platt Thomas, *Lincoln 1847–1858, Being the Day-by-Day Activities of Abraham Lincoln from January 1, 1847 to December 31, 1858*; Emilie Todd Helm, "Mary Todd Lincoln," *McClure's Magazine*, September, 1898; Katherine Helm, *The True Story of Mary, Wife of Lincoln*; Lincoln to Mary, from Washington, April 16, 1848, Illinois State Historical Library; Lincoln to Mary from Washington, June 12, 1848, and July 2, 1848, photostat, *ibid.*; Mrs. Lincoln to "My dear husband," from Lexington, May, 1848, Illinois State Historical Library; Fayette Circuit Court records of Todd-Parker litigation in William H. Townsend's *Lincoln and His Wife's Home Town*; Honoré Willsie Morrow, *Mary Todd Lincoln*; Ward Hill Lamon, *Recollections of Abraham Lincoln 1847–1865*; Henry C. Whitney, *Life on the Circuit with Lincoln*; Henry B. Rankin, *Intimate Character Sketches of Abraham Lincoln*; Albert J. Beveridge, *Abraham Lincoln 1809–1858*; Vol. 2; Paul M. Angle, *Here I Have Lived*; Isaac N. Arnold, *The Life of Abraham Lincoln*; Carl Sandburg, *The Prairie Years*; James Gourley statement to Herndon, Herndon-Weik mss., Library of Congress; Dr. Anson Henry mss., Illinois State Historical Library; Lexington *Observer & Reporter*,

August 29, 1846, and January 26, 1850; Illinois *Daily Journal*, July 23, 1849; "Mrs. Lincoln's Influence on President Felt," Civil War Round Table conferences, Lexington *Herald*, March 19, 1957, February 16, 1964, February 13, 1968, and November 16, 1969; *Biography of Ninian W. Edwards, First Governor of Illinois Territory*, edited by E. B. Washburne; Josephine Craven, "Lincolns in Springfield," *National Republican*, February, 1931; Richard Allen Heckman, *Lincoln Versus Douglas*; Gustav Koerner, *Memoirs*; Horace White, *The Lincoln and Douglas Debates*, speech before Chicago Historical Society, February 17, 1914; "Political Debates Between Hon. Abraham Lincoln and Hon. Stephen A. Douglas," Illinois *State Journal*, July 21, 1858; Horace White, *The Life of Lyman Trumbull*; Edwin E. Sparks, ed., *The Lincoln Douglas Debates of 1858*; Carl Schurz to Mrs. Schurz, Alton, Illinois, July 25, 1860, *Abraham Lincoln Quarterly*, June, 1942; Cooper Union speech, February 27, 1860, New York newspaper files, March, 1860.

CHAPTER V

Farewell to Springfield

Emilie Todd Helm, "Mary Todd Lincoln," *McClure's Magazine*, September, 1898; Elizabeth Todd Grimsley, "Six Months in the White House," *Journal of the Illinois State Historical Society*, October, 1926, to January, 1927; Mrs. W. M. Bailache to her mother, November 12, 1860, *Abraham Lincoln Quarterly*, June, 1942; Henry B. Rankin, *Personal Recollections of Abraham Lincoln*; Henry Villard, *Memoirs* and *Lincoln on the Eve of '61*; Orville Hickman Browning, *The Diary of Orville Hickman Browning*; Gustav Koerner, *Memoirs*; Donn Piatt, *Memories of the Men Who Saved the Union*; Benjamin Platt Thomas, *Lincoln 1847–1858, Being the Day-by-Day Activities of Abraham Lincoln from January 1, 1847–December 31, 1858*; John G. Nicolay, *A Short Life of Abraham Lincoln*; Ward Hill Lamon, *Life of Abraham Lincoln, from His Birth to His Inauguration as President*; Helen Nicolay, *Lincoln's Secretary: A Biography of John G. Nicolay*; Paul M. Angle, *Here I Have Lived*; Lincoln's farewell to Springfield, February 11, 1861, Official Documents; Carl Sandburg, *The Prairie Years*; William O. Stoddard, *Abraham Lincoln: The True Story of a Great Life*; Horace White to Herndon, January 16, 1891, in Herndon-Weik mss., Library of Congress; Emanuel Hertz, *The Hidden Lincoln*; Willard L. King, *Lincoln's Manager, David Davis*; Alexander K. McClure, *Abraham Lincoln and Men of War-Times*; Ruth Painter Randall, *Mary Lincoln: Biography of a Marriage*; Stefan Lorant, *Lincoln: A Picture Story of His Life*; Louisville *Daily Journal*, January 11, 1861; Dorothy Meserve Kunhardt, "Lincoln's Neighbors: A Dramatic Find," *Life*, February 9, 1959; Washington *Evening Star*, February 13, 1861; Cleveland *Plain Dealer*, February 16, 1861; New York *Times*, February 19, 1861, and March 5, 1861; New York *Herald*, February 17, 18, 1861; *Frank Leslie's Illustrated Newspaper*, March 2, 1861; Carl Sandburg, *Lincoln Collector*; Alban Jasper Conant, "A Portrait Painter's Reminiscences of Lincoln," *McClure's Magazine*, March, 1909; Robert E. Sherwood, *Abe Lincoln in Illinois*.

CHAPTER VI

Mrs. Lincoln in the White House

Elizabeth Todd Grimsley, "Six Months in the White House," *Journal of the Illinois State Historical Society*, October, 1926, to January, 1927; Elizabeth Keckley, *Behind the Scenes*; Nicolay and Hay, *Abraham Lincoln*, Vols. 4 and 5; Margaret Leech, *Reveille in Washington 1860–1865*; Ben: Perley Poore, *Perley's Reminiscences of Sixty Years in the National Metropolis*, Mrs. E. F. Ellet, *The Queens of American Society* and *Court Circles of the Republic*; Laura C. Holloway, *The Ladies of the White House*; Edna M. Colman, *Seventy-five Years of White House Gossip: From Washington to Lincoln*; John Lothrop Motley, *The Correspondence of John Lothrop Motley*, George William Curtis, ed.; Charles Francis Adams, *Diary of Charles Francis Adams*; Laura Catherine Redden Searing (Howard Glyndon), "The Truth About Mrs. Lincoln," *The Independent*, August 10, 1882; Roy P. Basler, ed., *Abraham Lincoln: His Speeches and Writings*; Julia Taft Bayne, *Tad Lincoln's Father*; William H. Russell, *My Diary North and South*; Ishbel Ross, *Proud Kate* and *Rebel Rose*; Helen Nicolay, *Lincoln's Secretary*; Katherine Helm, *Mary, Wife of Lincoln*; Emilie Todd Helm, "Mary Todd Lincoln," *McClure's Magazine*, September, 1898; Mrs. Lincoln to Mrs. John Henry Shearer 1859–64, *Journal of the Illinois State Historical Society*, Spring, 1951, Vol. 44; *Kentucky Statesman*, April 16, 1861, and May 24, 1861; Noah Brooks, *Washington, D.C., in Lincoln's Time*; Elizabeth Todd Grimsley to John Stuart, May 24, 1861, in *Concerning Mr. Lincoln*, Harry E. Pratt, ed.; Teresa L. Reed thesis, *Mary Todd Lincoln*.

CHAPTER VII

A Nation Divided

Mrs. Lincoln to Captain John Fry regarding weapons for Kentucky, June, 1861, mss., Library of Congress; Mrs. Lincoln to Mrs. John Shearer, October 6, 1861 (courtesy of Mrs. Katrina van Asmus Kindel of Grand Rapids, Michigan); Elizabeth Todd Grimsley, "Six Months in the White House," *Journal of the Illinois State Historical Society*, October, 1926, to January, 1927; Helen Nicolay, *Lincoln's Secretary*; John G. Nicolay and John Hay, *Abraham Lincoln: A History*, Vol. 6; Margaret Leech, *Reveille in Washington, 1860–1865*; William H. Russell, *My Diary North and South*; William O. Stoddard, *Inside the White House in War Time*; Ruth Painter Randall, *Colonel Elmer Ellsworth: A Biography of Lincoln's Friend and the First Hero of the Civil War*; *Kentucky Statesman*, April 30, 1861; Carl Sandburg, *The War Years*; Hudson Strode, *Jefferson Davis*, Vol. 2; *New York World*, August 8, 1861; *New York Herald*, August 18, 19, 22, 23 and 25, 1861; *Frank Leslie's Illustrated Newspaper*, August 24, 1861; *New York Daily Tribune*, February 25, 1861, August 15, 22 and 31, 1861, and December 9, 1861; *Chicago Daily Tribune*, August 31, 1861; *Philadelphia Bulletin*, August 31, 1861; Tyler Dennett, ed., *Lincoln and the Civil War in the Diaries and Letters of John Hay*; Jane Grey Swisshelm, *Half a Century*; Mrs. Lincoln to James

Gordon Bennett, October 25, 1861, University of Chicago Library; Mary Lincoln to Elizabeth Grimsley, September 29, 1861, Philip D. Sang, "Mary Todd Lincoln: A Tragic Portrait," *Journal of Rutgers University Press*, April, 1961; Montgomery S. Lewis, *Legends That Libel Lincoln*; Elizabeth Keckley, *Behind the Scenes*; William E. Barton, *The Life of Abraham Lincoln*, Vol. 2.

CHAPTER VIII

Spendthrift First Lady

John A. Briggs to John Sherman, February 20, 1861; Sherman mss., Library of Congress; Benjamin B. French to his brother, H. F. French, July 5, 1861, French mss., Library of Congress; Elizabeth Todd Grimsley, "Six Months in the White House"; Harry E. Pratt and Ernest E. East, "Mrs. Lincoln Refurbishes the White House," *Lincoln Herald*, February, 1945; Robert Gerald McMurtry, "Lincoln White House Glass and China," *Lincoln Herald*, June, 1947; Ruth Painter Randall, *Mary Lincoln: Biography of a Marriage*; Mary Clemmer Ames, *Ten Years in Washington*; Bess Furman, *White House Profile*; Elizabeth Keckley, *Behind the Scenes*; Ward Hill Lamon, *Recollections of Abraham Lincoln*; Margaret Leech, *Reveille in Washington, 1860–1865*; Orville Hickman Browning, *The Diary of Orville Hickman Browning*; New York *Commercial Advertiser*, November 16, 1861; Benjamin B. French to his brother, H. F. French, October 13, 1861, and March 23, 1862, French mss., Library of Congress; Benjamin B. French to his sister-in-law, Pamela French, on President Lincoln's reaction to Mrs. Lincoln's bills with Thomas H. Carryl & Bros., December 24, 1861, *ibid.*; Benjamin B. French to Pamela French, May 15, 1864, September 4, 1864, and February 8, 1865, *ibid.*; Mary Lincoln to Mrs. Grimsley, September 29, 1861, Philip D. Sang, "Mary Todd Lincoln: A Tragic Portrait," *Journal of Rutgers University Press*, April, 1961; Mary Lincoln to Benjamin B. French, July 26, 1862, Illinois State Historical Library; Virginia Kinnaird, "Mrs. Lincoln as a White House Hostess," Illinois State Historical Society, privately printed, 1939; Mrs. Lincoln to Alexander Williamson, January 26, 1866, Sandburg and Angle, *Mary Lincoln, Wife and Widow* ("The Documents"); Teresa L. Reed thesis, *Mary Todd Lincoln*.

CHAPTER IX

Adviser to the President

New York *Herald*, August 8, 1861, February 14, 17 and 19, 1862; New York *World*, February 12, 1862; New York *Times*, February 15, 1862; Albany *Atlas and Argus*, October 15, 1861; Henry Villard, *Memoirs*; Ben: Perley Poore, *Perley's Reminiscences of Sixty Years in the National Metropolis;* William Howard Russell, *My Diary North and South;* Mrs. Lincoln to Elizabeth Todd Grimsley, September 29, 1861, *ibid.;* Matthew Hale Smith, *Sunshine and Shadow in New York;* George Bancroft, *The Life and Letters of George Bancroft,* M. A. De Wolfe Howe, ed.; *The Diary of Edward Bates, 1859–1865,* Howard K. Beale, ed.; T. Harry Williams, *Lincoln and the Radicals;* Rose O'Neal Greenhow, *My Imprisonment and the First Year of Abolition Rule at Washington;* Ishbel Ross, *Rebel Rose;* John Hay to John G. Nicolay, November, 1861, March, 1862, and April 9, 1862; Tyler Dennett, ed., *Lincoln and the Civil War in the Diaries and Letters of John Hay;* Noah Brooks (Castine), Sacramento *Union,* December 4, 1863; Anson G. Henry to Isaac Newton, April 21, 1864; Lincoln Papers; W. O. Stoddard, *Inside the White House in War Time;* Ward Hill Lamon, *Recollections of Abraham Lincoln, 1847–1865;* Orville Hickman Browning, *The Diary of Orville Hickman Browning;* Mrs. Lincoln to Simon Cameron, September 12, 1861, and January 2, 1863, Simon Cameron mss., Library of Congress; President Lincoln to Simon Cameron, November 13, 1861, *ibid.;* New York *Herald,* February 19, 1862; Mrs. Lincoln to James Gordon Bennett, October 4, 1862, Brown University Library; Helen Nicolay, *Lincoln's Secretary;* John Hay, "Life in the White House in the Time of Lincoln," *Century Magazine,* November, 1890; Gideon Welles, *Diary of Gideon Welles;* Elizabeth Keckley, *Behind the Scenes;* Mrs. Lincoln to Mrs. James W. White, August 30, 1869, photostat, Library of Congress; Benjamin B. French to Pamela French, May 15, 1864, September 4, 1864, and February 8, 1865, French mss., Library of Congress.

CHAPTER X

Accused of Treason

Katherine Helm, *The True Story of Mary, Wife of Lincoln;* William H. Townsend, *Lincoln and His Wife's Home Town;* Elizabeth Todd Grimsley, "Six Months in the White House"; Robert Gerald McMurtry, *Ben Hardin Helm, "Rebel" Brother-in-law of Abraham Lincoln, with a Biographical Sketch of His Wife and An Account of the Todd Family of Kentucky;* Address by Gerald McMurtry at annual meeting of Lincoln Fellowship of Madison, Wisconsin, February 12, 1958; President Lincoln's telegram to Mrs. Lincoln, September 24, 1863, Illinois Historical Society Library; Mrs. Lincoln's telegram to President Lincoln, September 22, 1863, *Harper's Magazine,* February, 1897; David Davis interview with Emilie Todd Helm, quoting President Lincoln on death of Helm; Margaret Leech, *Reveille in Washington, 1860–1865;* Elizabeth Keckley, *Behind the Scenes;* Emilie Todd Helm, "Mary Todd Lincoln," *McClure's Magazine,* September, 1898; Emilie's diary in Katherine Helm's *The True Story of Mary, Wife of Lincoln;* W. O. Stoddard, *Inside the White House in War Time;* Ruth Painter Randall, *Mary Lincoln: Biography of a Marriage;* Cincinnati *Daily Commercial,* August 27, 1862; Boston *Transcript,* October 2, 1861; Chicago *Daily Tribune,* October 21, 1861, and February 16, 1862; J. G. Nicolay and John Hay, *Abraham Lincoln: A History,* Vol. 9; Emilie Todd Helm to President Lincoln, October 31, 1864, Lincoln

Papers; Martha Todd White to President Lincoln, December 19, 1863, and March 14, 1865, Lincoln Papers; *Diary of Gideon Welles*, April 29, 1864, Library of Congress; President Lincoln to Mrs. Lincoln, September 20, 22 and 24, 1864, and December 7, 1864, Illinois State Historical Library; Mrs. Ninian Edwards, Mrs. C. M. Smith and Mrs. Frances Wallace's criticism of Mrs. Lincoln, Herndon-Weik mss., Library of Congress; Elizabeth Todd Grimsley to John Todd Stuart, March 20, 1861, Illinois State Historical Library; Levi O. Todd to President Lincoln, September 12, 1864, Lincoln Papers; Kenneth A. Bernard, "Glimpses of Lincoln in the White House," *Abraham Lincoln Quarterly*, December, 1952; Julia Taft Bayne, *Tad Lincoln's Father*; Ward Hill Lamon, *Recollections of Abraham Lincoln, 1847-1865*; Montgomery S. Lewis, *Legends That Libel Lincoln*; Elizabeth Todd Grimsley, "Six Months in the White House," *Journal of the Illinois State Historical Society*, October 1926 to January, 1927; Ishbel Ross, *Rebel Rose*; James D. Horan, *Desperate Women*; John G. Nicolay to Major General Benjamin Butler re Mrs. J. Todd White, April 19, 1864, Benjamin Butler mss., Library of Congress; President Lincoln to Mrs. Margaret Preston (formerly Margaret Wickliffe), August 21, 1862, Brown University Library.

CHAPTER XI

Four Young Lincolns

John Hay, "Tad Lincoln," Illinois *State Journal*, July 21, 1871; Julia Taft Bayne, *Tad Lincoln's Father*; Francis B. Carpenter, *Six Months at the White House* and *The Inner Life of Abraham Lincoln*; Charles A. Dana, *Recollections of the Civil War*; W. O. Stoddard, *Inside the White House in War Time*; President Lincoln to Mrs. Lincoln, June 9, 1863, Illinois State Historical Library; Howard Glyndon, "The Truth About Mrs. Lincoln," *The Independent*, August 10, 1882; Helen Nicolay, *Lincoln's Secretary*; Noah Brooks, *Washington in Lincoln's Time*; Edna M. Colman, *Seventy-Five Years of White House Gossip: From Washington to Lincoln*; Ruth Painter Randall, *Lincoln's Sons* and *Mary Lincoln: Biography of a Marriage*; David C. Mearns, *The Lincoln Papers: The Story of the Collection with Selections to July 4, 1861*, Vol. 1; Elizabeth Todd Grimsley, "Six Months in the White House"; Katherine Helm, *The True Story of Mary, Wife of Lincoln*, quoting from Emilie Todd Helm's diary; Mrs. James C. Conkling to Clinton Conkling, February 1, 1861, from Harry E. Pratt, ed., *Concerning Mr. Lincoln: In Which Abraham Lincoln Is Pictured as He Appeared to Letter Writers of His Time*; Elizabeth Keckley, *Behind the Scenes*; Mrs. Lincoln to Mrs. John C. Sprigg, May 29, 1862, Charles Goltz, *Incidents in the Life of Mary Todd Lincoln*; Carl Sandburg, *Abraham Lincoln; The War Years*; President Lincoln to Joshua Speed, October 22, 1846, regarding young Robert, Illinois State Historical Library; Orville Hickman Browning, *The Diary of Orville Hickman Browning*; Howard K. Beale, ed., *The Diary of Edward Bates, 1859-1866*; Dr. W. A. Evans, *Mrs. Abraham Lincoln: A Study of Her Personality and Her Influence on Lincoln*.

CHAPTER XII

Mater Dolorosa

W. O. Stoddard, *Inside the White House in War Time*; Ben: Perley Poore, *Perley's Reminiscences of Sixty Years in the National Metropolis*; Margaret Leech, *Reveille in Washington, 1860–1865*; *Leslie's Weekly*, February 5, 1862; Elizabeth Keckley, *Behind the Scenes*; Julia Taft Bayne, *Tad Lincoln's Father*; Benjamin B. French to H. F. French, February 27, 1862, French mss., Library of Congress; New York *Tribune*, February 6, 1862; Anna L. Boyden, *War Reminiscences or Echoes from Hospital and White House*; Mrs. James C. Conkling to Clinton Conkling, February 24, 1862, Illinois State Historical Library; Mrs. Ninian Edwards' first statement to Herndon, Herndon-Weik mss.; Mrs. Lincoln to Mrs. John C. Sprigg, May 29, 1862, Sandburg and Angle, *Mary Lincoln, Wife and Widow* ("The Documents"); Mrs. Lincoln to Mrs. Gideon Welles, February 21, 1863, *ibid.*; Carlos W. Goltz, *Incidents in the Life of Mary Todd Lincoln*; *Diary of Edward Bates*, February 24, 1862; *Diary of Gideon Welles*, Vol. 1; Katherine Helm, *Mary, Wife of Lincoln*, quoting Emilie Todd Helm; Emilie Todd Helm, "Mary Todd Lincoln," *McClure's Magazine*, September, 1898; Mary Clemmer Ames, *Ten Years in Washington: Or, Inside Life and Scenes in Our National Capital as a Woman Sees Them*; Frank Klement, "Jane Grey Swisshelm and Lincoln, A Feminist Fusses and Frets," *Abraham Lincoln Quarterly*, December, 1950; Edna M. Colman, *Seventy-five Years of White House Gossip: From Washington to Lincoln*; Mrs. H. C. Ingersoll, "Abraham Lincoln's Widow," Springfield (Mass.) *Republican*, June 7, 1875; New York *Herald*, March 18, 1862, quoting *Liberator* and *Jeffersonian Democrat*; Reverend Noyes W. Miner, "Mrs. Abraham Lincoln, a Vindication," mss., Illinois State Historical Library; Ruth Painter Randall, *Mary Lincoln: Biography of a Marriage*; Howard Glyndon (Laura Redden Searing), "The Truth About Mrs. Lincoln," *The Independent*, August 10, 1882; Mrs. Lincoln to President Lincoln, November 2 and 3, 1862, Nicolay mss., Library of Congress; Mrs. Lincoln to Mrs. John H. Shearer, November 20, 1864, *Journal of the Illinois State Historical Society*, Spring, 1951; *National Republican*, January 26, 1863; Lincoln to Mrs. Lincoln, December 21, 1862, Lincoln Papers; Lincoln to Mrs. Irvin McDowell, March 21, 1862, Carl Sandburg, *Abraham Lincoln: The War Years*, Vol. 2; Francis B. Carpenter, *Six Months at the White House*; Dr. W. A. Evans, *Mrs. Abraham Lincoln: A Study of Her Personality and Her Influence on Lincoln.*

CHAPTER XIII

The Bible and the Occult

Jay Monaghan, "Was Abraham Lincoln Really a Spiritualist?" *Journal of the Illinois State Historical Society*, June, 1941; Nettie Colburn Maynard, *Was Abraham Lincoln a Spiritualist?*; Orville Hickman Browning, *Diary of Orville Hickman Browning*;

Elizabeth Keckley, *Behind the Scenes*; Sandburg and Angle, *Mary Lincoln, Wife and Widow*; Mrs. Lincoln to Mrs. Gideon Welles, July 11, 1865, Gideon Welles mss., Library of Congress; Noah Brooks letter, May 10, 1865, *The Character and Religion of President Lincoln*, privately printed, 1919; Dr. W. A. Evans, *Mrs. Abraham Lincoln: A Study of Her Personality and Her Influence on Lincoln*; Ward Hill Lamon, *Recollections of Abraham Lincoln*; William H. Herndon, "Lincoln's Religion," broadside, Illinois *State Register*, December 13, 1873; "Mrs. Lincoln's Denial and What She Says," broadside, January 12, 1874, Copy, Massachusetts Historical Society; Reverend James Smith to William H. Herndon, January 24, 1867, and William H. Herndon to the Reverend James Smith, December 20, 1866, both letters printed in Chicago *Tribune*, March 6, 1867; Emanuel Hertz, *The Hidden Lincoln*; Katherine Helm, *The True Story of Mary, Wife of Lincoln*; Emilie Todd Helm, "Mary Todd Lincoln," *McClure's Magazine*, September, 1898; Margaret Leech, *Reveille in Washington, 1860–1865;* William E. Barton, *The Life of Abraham Lincoln*; William H. Townsend, *Lincoln and His Wife's Home Town*; Ruth Painter Randall, *Mary Lincoln: Biography of a Marriage*; Reverend Noyes W. Miner, *Mrs. Abraham Lincoln. A Vindication*, mss., Illinois State Historical Library; Joshua Speed, *Reminiscences of Abraham Lincoln and Notes of a Visit to California, ibid.*

CHAPTER XIV

From Darkness into Light

Benjamin B. French, "At the President's Reception," January 1, 1863, mss., Brown University Library; Benjamin B. French to Pamela French, February 19, 1863, mss., Library of Congress; Mrs. Lincoln to Mrs. Gideon Welles, February 21, 1863, Gideon Welles mss., Library of Congress; Mrs. Lincoln to Mrs. Charles Heard, March 4, 1863 (courtesy of Mrs. Katrina van Asmus Kindel); Virginia Kinnaird, "Mrs. Lincoln as a White House Hostess," mss., Illinois State Historical Library; Mrs. James Conkling to Clinton Conkling, March 9, 1864, *ibid.*; Anson G. Henry to Mrs. Henry, April 12, 1863, *ibid.*; W. O. Stoddard, *Inside the White House in War Time*; Elizabeth Keckley, *Behind the Scenes*; Mrs. E. F. Ellet, *Court Circles of the Republic*; Margaret Leech, *Reveille in Washington, 1860–1865*; Noah Brooks (Castine) Sacramento *Union*, May 8, August 5 and December 4, 1863; *The Diary of Edward Bates 1859–1866*; Noah Brooks, *Washington in Lincoln's Time*; William Howard Russell, *My Diary North and South*; Princess Salm-Salm, *Ten Years of My Life*; Leslie J. Perry, "Lincoln's Home Life in Washington," *Harper's New Monthly Magazine*, February, 1897; Anna L. Boyden, *War Reminiscences or Echoes from Hospital and White House*; Chicago *Daily Tribune*, July 2, 1863; President Lincoln to Robert Lincoln, July 11 and 14, 1863, Illinois State Historical Library; William E. Baringer, *The Abraham Lincoln Quarterly*, September, 1946; Katherine Helm, *The True Story of Mary, Wife of Lincoln*; "Mrs. Lincoln at Mount Washington," Cincinnati *Daily Gazette*, August 14, 1863; President Lincoln's telegrams to Mrs. Lincoln, June 11 and 15, 1863, Illinois State Historical Library; President Lincoln to Mrs. Lincoln, June 9, 1863, Roy P. Basler, *The Collected Works of Abraham Lincoln*, Vol. VI; Benjamin B. French to H. F. French, June 28, 1863, and October 4, 1863, French mss., Library of

Congress; President Lincoln's telegrams to Mrs. Lincoln, September 20, 21, 22 and 24, 1863, Illinois State Historical Library; Thomas Graham and Marva Belden, *So Fell the Angels*; Gettysburg Address, Mrs. Lincoln's telegram to Lincoln, November 18, 1863, copy, Lincoln National Life Foundation; President Lincoln to Edward Everett, November 20, 1863, mss., Massachusetts Historical Society; Ward Hill Lamon, *Recollections of Abraham Lincoln*; Tyler Dennett, ed., *Lincoln and the Civil War in the Diaries and Letters of John Hay*; Montgomery S. Lewis, *Legends That Libel Lincoln*; Mrs. Lincoln's telegrams to President Lincoln, December 4, 6 and 7, 1863, *Harper's New Monthly Magazine*, February, 1897; President Lincoln's telegrams to Mrs. Lincoln, December 5, 6 and 7, 1863, Katherine Helm, *Mary, Wife of Lincoln*; Carl Sandburg, *Abraham Lincoln: The War Years*; Ruth Painter Randall, *Mary Lincoln: Biography of a Marriage*.

CHAPTER XV

A Second Term

Benjamin B. French to H. F. French, January 31, 1864, mss., Library of Congress; Benjamin B. French to Pamela French, April 10 and September 4, 1864, *ibid.*; Tyler Dennett, ed., *Lincoln and the Civil War in the Diaries and Letters of John Hay*; Helen Nicolay, *The President's Secretary*; Thomas Graham and Marva Belden, *So Fell the Angels*; Elizabeth Keckley, *Behind the Scenes*; Francis B. Carpenter, *Six Months at the White House*; Stephen Massett to President Lincoln, June 6, 1864, Lincoln Papers; Allen Thorndike Rice, ed., *Reminiscences of Abraham Lincoln by Distinguished Men of His Time*; Henry B. Rankin, *Intimate Sketches of Abraham Lincoln*; Mrs. Lincoln to Mrs. Gideon Welles, May 27, 1864, mss., Library of Congress; Mrs. Lincoln to Mrs. Keckley, "My Tired & Weary Husband," *Abraham Lincoln Quarterly*, September, 1946; Adam Badeau, *Military History of Ulysses S. Grant*; Bruce Catton, *Mr. Lincoln's Army* and *This Hallowed Ground*; Charles A. Dana, *Recollections of the Civil War*; Ishbel Ross, *The General's Wife*; Mrs. Lincoln to President Lincoln, April 28, 1864, Katherine Helm, *Mary, Wife of Lincoln*; President Lincoln's telegrams to Mrs. Lincoln, April 28 and June 24, 1864, August 31, 1864, *ibid.*; John H. Cramer, "Lincoln Under Enemy fire," *Gideon Welles Diary*, Vol. 2; David Donald, *Charles Sumner & the Rights of Man*; Roy P. Basler, "Patent Office Fair, February 22, 1864," *The Collected Works of Abraham Lincoln*, Vol. 7; "All About the Domestic Economy in the White House," Illinois *State Register*, October 30, 1864; William Dodd Chenery, "Mary Lincoln Should Be Remembered for Many Kind Acts," Illinois *State Register*, February 17, 1938; C. C. Ritzie, "In Defense of Mrs. Lincoln," *Journal of the Illinois State Historical Society*, April, 1937; Ruth Painter Randall, "Mary Lincoln: Judgment Appealed," *Abraham Lincoln Quarterly*, September, 1949; Teresa L. Reed thesis, *Mary Todd Lincoln*; Dr. W. A. Evans, *Mrs. Abraham Lincoln: A Study of Her Personality and Her Influence on Lincoln*; Henry B. Rankin, *Personal Recollections of Abraham Lincoln*; Eunice (Hunt) Tripler, *Some Notes of Her Personal Recollections*, Louis A. Arthur, ed.; Orville Hickman Browning, *The Diary of Orville Hickman Browning*; William H. Crook, *Memories of the White House*; Noah Brooks, *Washington in Lincoln's Time;* Nicolay and Hay, *Abraham Lincoln: A History*, Vol. 9; Mrs. Lincoln to Mrs. Mercy Levering Conkling, November 19, 1864, Illinois State Historical Library.

CHAPTER XVI

Peace at Last

Zachariah Chandler to Mrs. Chandler, January 10, 15 and 21, 1865, Chandler mss., Library of Congress; Marquis de Chambrun's letters to his mother, Marthe de Corcelle, December 20, 1864, and June 13, 1865, Marquis de Chambrun, *Impressions of Lincoln and the Civil War* and "Personal Recollections of Mr. Lincoln," *Scribner's Magazine*, January, 1893; Wayne C. Temple, "Mrs. Lincoln's Jewelry," *Lincoln Herald*, Spring, 1962; Edward Dicey, *Six Months in the Federal States*; President Lincoln to General Grant, January 19, 1865, Roy P. Basler, *The Collected Works of Abraham Lincoln*, Vol. 7; Mrs. Lincoln to Charles Sumner, March 23, April 10 and 11, 1865, Sumner mss., Houghton Library, Harvard University; Mrs. Lincoln to Abram Wakeman, April 13, 1865, in David Donald, *Lincoln's Herndon*; Mrs. Lincoln to Abram Wakeman, March 20, 1865, Washington *Evening Star*, January 19, 1930; Anson Henry to Mrs. Henry, February 8 and March 13, 1865, mss., Illinois State Historical Library; Mrs. Lincoln to Mrs. Anson Henry, August 31, 1865, *ibid.*; Dr. Anson G. Henry, *Lincoln Herald*, Vol. XLV, Nos. 3 and 4, 1943; Second inaugural, March 4, 1865, Roy P. Basler, *Abraham Lincoln: His Speeches and Writings*, Vol. 8; Salmon P. Chase to Mrs. Lincoln, March 4, 1865, *ibid.*; Noah Brooks (Castine) on Andrew Johnson, Sacramento *Daily Union*, April 10, 1865; New York *Herald*, March 8, 1865; Margaret Leech, *Reveille in Washington, 1860–1865*; William H. Crook, *Memories of the White House*; Otto Eisenschiml and Ralph Newman, *The American Iliad*, Horace Porter, *Campaigning with Grant*; Adam Badeau, *Grant in Peace*; *Memoirs of General William T. Sherman*; *Personal Memoirs of Ulysses S. Grant*; Jefferson Davis, *The Rise and Fall of the Confederacy*; Hudson Strode, *Jefferson Davis*, Vol. 2; R. Ernest Dupuy and Trevor H. Dupuy, *The Compact History of the Civil War*; William H. Townsend, *Lincoln and His Wife's Home Town*; Ishbel Ross, *The General's Wife*; Captain John S. Barnes, "Sidelights on Life of Lincoln," Lincoln National Life Foundation; Ida Tarbell, *Life of Lincoln*, Vol. 2; President Lincoln to Stanton, April 1 and 2, 1865, Lincoln Papers; Mrs. Lincoln to President Lincoln, April 2, 1865, Illinois State Historical Library; Carl Schurz to Mrs. Schurz, April 2, 1865, Joseph Schafer, ed., *Intimate Letters of Carl Schurz, 1841–1869*; Mrs. Lincoln to Stanton, April 6, 1865, Illinois State Historical Library; Ward Hill Lamon to Herndon, Herndon-Weik mss.; Ishbel Ross, *First Lady of the South*; Elizabeth Keckley, *Behind the Scenes*, Sandburg and Angle, *Mary Lincoln, Wife and Widow.*

CHAPTER XVII

One Final Day Together

Mrs. Lincoln to Charles Sumner, April 10, 11 and 13, 1865, Sumner mss., Houghton Library, Harvard University; Mrs. Lincoln to Mrs. Gideon Welles, July 11, 1865, Gideon Welles mss., Library of Congress; Honoré Willsie Morrow, "Lincoln's Last Day with His Wife," *Cosmopolitan*, February, 1930; Charles Adolphe de Pineton (Marquis de Chambrun), "Personal Recollections of Mr. Lincoln,"

Scribner's Magazine, January, 1893, and *Impressions of Lincoln and the Civil War*; Adam Badeau, *Grant in Peace*; Margaret Leech, *Reveille in Washington, 1860–1865*; Ruth Painter Randall, *Mary Lincoln: Biography of a Marriage*; Mrs. Lincoln to Francis F. Carpenter, November 15, 1865; Sandburg and Angle, *Mary Lincoln, Wife and Widow* ("The Documents"); Dr. Anson G. Henry to Mrs. Henry, April 19, 1865, Illinois State Historical Library; Elizabeth Keckley, *Behind the Scenes*; Katherine Helm, *Mary, Wife of Lincoln*; Ward Hill Lamon, *Recollections of Abraham Lincoln*; William T. Stewart, *Reminiscences of William T. Stewart of Nevada*; Isaac N. Arnold, *The Life of Abraham Lincoln*.

CHAPTER XVIII

Death in a Theater

New York *Tribune*, April 14, 1865, "The President Shot—Secretary Seward Attacked"; *Gideon Welles Diary*, Vol. 2, Library of Congress; J. F. Usher to Mrs. Usher, April 16, 1865, copy, Library of Congress; Benjamin B. French to Pamela French, May 21, 1865, mss., Library of Congress; Charles Sumner to the Duchess of Argyle, April 24, 1865, *Memoirs and Letters of Charles Sumner*, Edward Lillie Pierce, ed., Vol. 4; David Donald, *Charles Sumner and the Coming of the Civil War*; Carl Sandburg, *Abraham Lincoln: The War Years*, Vol. 4; Sandburg and Angle, *Mary Lincoln, Wife and Widow*; Katherine Helm, *The True Story of Mary, Wife of Lincoln*; Honoré Willsie Morrow, "The Woman Lincoln Loved," *Cosmopolitan*, May, 1927; Ruth Painter Randall, *Mary Lincoln: Biography of a Marriage*; Elizabeth Keckley, *Behind the Scenes*; Marion Wefer, "Another Assassination, Another Widow, Another Untitled Book," *American Heritage*, August, 1967; Dorothy Meserve Kunhardt and Philip B. Kunhardt, Jr., "Assassination," *American Heritage*, April, 1965; Stefan Lorant, *Lincoln: His Life in Photographs*; Frank A. Flower, *Edward McMasters Stanton*; William E. Barton, *Life of Abraham Lincoln*, Vol. 2; Henry B. Rankin, *Personal Recollections of Abraham Lincoln*; W. J. Ferguson, "Lincoln's Death," *Saturday Evening Post*, February 12, 1927; Orville H. Browning, *The Diary of Orville Hickman Browning*; William H. Townsend, *Lincoln and His Wife's Home Town*; *National Unionist*, April 21, 1865; Willard L. King, *Lincoln's Manager, David Davis*; Charles A. Dana, *Recollections of the Civil War*; Ward Hill Lamon, *Recollections of Abraham Lincoln*; Howard H. Peckham, "James Tanner's Account of Lincoln's Death," *Abraham Lincoln Quarterly*, December, 1942; Mrs. Elizabeth Dixon to Mrs. Louisa Wood, May 1, 1865, *The Collector*, March, 1950; Dorothy Hemenway Van Ark, "New Light on Lincoln's Death," *Saturday Evening Post*, February 12, 1944; Reverend Noyes W. Miner, "Mrs. Abraham Lincoln, A Vindication," mss., Illinois State Historical Library; Dr. Anson G. Henry to Mrs. Henry, April 19 and May 8, 1865, Illinois State Historical Library; Queen Victoria to Mrs. Lincoln, April 29, 1865, Empress Eugénie to Mrs. Lincoln, April 28, 1865, Louis Philippe d'Orléans to Mrs. Lincoln, May 5, 1865, condolence letters in Katherine Helm, *The True Story of Mary, Wife of Lincoln*, and photostat copies in Manuscript Division, Library of Congress; Mrs. Lincoln to Queen Victoria, May 21, 1865, *ibid.*, original in the White House; President Andrew Johnson to Mrs. Lincoln, January 12, 1866, in Sandburg and Angle *Mary Lincoln, Wife and Widow*

("The Documents"); Dr. W. A. Evans, *Mrs. Abraham Lincoln: A Study of Her Personality and Her Influence on Lincoln*; Teresa L. Reed thesis, *Mary Todd Lincoln*; scrapbooks on funeral ceremonies across the country and news dispatches from abroad.

CHAPTER XIX

A Diminished Empire

New York to Chicago trip, New York *Herald*, May 23, 1865; Mrs. Lincoln to Mrs. Welles, July 11 and October 14, Gideon Welles mss., Library of Congress; Mrs. Lincoln to Alexander Williamson, June 15 and August 17, 1865, and January 26, 1866, Sandburg and Angle, *Mary Lincoln, Wife and Widow* ("The Documents"); Mrs. Lincoln to Francis P. Carpenter, November 15 and December 8, 1865, *ibid.*; Mrs. Lincoln to Mrs. James H. Orne, August 31, 1865, Illinois State Historical Library; Willard L. King, *Lincoln's Manager: David Davis*; David Davis mss., Illinois State Historical Library; Harry E. Pratt, *The Personal Finances of Abraham Lincoln*; Horace Greeley subscription campaign in New York *Tribune*, Illinois *State Journal*, April 22 and May 8, 1865; Mrs. Lincoln to Noah Brooks on finances, December 26, 1865, Lincoln Papers, Library of Congress; Mrs. Lincoln to Noah Brooks, May 11, 1866, in *Washington in Lincoln's Time*; selection of tomb site in Springfield, Illinois *State Journal*, December 22, 1865; Mrs. Lincoln to Mrs. Welles, July 11, October 14, and December 29, 1865, Gideon Welles mss., Library of Congress; William E. Barton, *Life of Abraham Lincoln*, Vol. 2; Mrs. Lincoln to Mrs. Keckley on sale of her clothes, September 17, 1867, and other letters involving their transactions, in *Behind the Scenes*; Mrs. Lincoln's letters to W. H. Brady regarding sale of clothes, printed in New York *World*, October 3 and 7, 1867; Mrs. Lincoln to Mrs. Keckley, October 6, 1867, and January 12, 1868, giving her reactions to clothes scandal, *Behind the Scenes*; John Hill Wheeler, October 12 entry in "Diary for 1867," Wheeler mss., Library of Congress; Seth C. Keyes to Hamilton Fish, October 31, 1867, Hamilton Fish mss., Library of Cngress; press comment on clothes sale: New York *World*, October 12, 1867, New York *Herald*, October 10, 1867, New York *Commercial Advertiser*, October 4, 1867, Boston *Transcript*, October 23, 1867, Detroit *Free Press*, October 16, 1867, and Pittsburgh *Commercial*, November 4, 1867; Mrs. Lincoln to Mrs. James W. White, October 18, 1867, Illinois State Historical Library; Ruth Painter Randall, *Mary Lincoln: Biography of a Marriage*; C. W. Hackensmith, "The Much Maligned Mary Todd Lincoln," *Filson Club History Quarterly*, July, 1970; Dr. W. A. Evans, *Mrs. Abraham Lincoln: A Study of Her Personality and Her Influence on Lincoln*; Robert Lincoln to Mary Harlan, October 16, 1867, in Katherine Helm, *The True Story of Mary, Wife of Lincoln*; Mrs. Lincoln to Mrs. Keckley on meeting Charles Sumner on train, October 6, 1867, in *Behind the Scenes*; Jeanne H. James and Wayne C. Temple, "Mrs. Lincoln's Clothing," *Lincoln Herald*, Summer, 1960; Wayne C. Temple, "Mrs. Lincoln's Visit to Springfield in 1866," *Lincoln Herald*, Winter, 1960; Mrs. Lincoln to Mrs. James H. Orne, March 15, 1866, courtesy of David Kirschenbaum, Carnegie Bookshop, New York.

CHAPTER XX

Herndon and Ann Rutledge

Mrs. Lincoln to William H. Herndon, August 28, 1866, Herndon-Weik mss., Mrs. Lincoln to David Davis, March 4, 6 and 8, 1867, Davis mss., Illinois State Historical Library; Robert T. Lincoln to David Davis, January 25, 1866, *ibid.*; Robert T. Lincoln to Herndon, December 13 and 24, 1865, Herndon-Weik mss.; "Abraham Lincoln, Miss Ann Rutledge, New Salem Pioneering, and the Poem," broadside of Herndon's lecture in Springfield, November 16, 1866, copy in Illinois State Historical Library; 'Lincoln's Religion," broadside in Illinois *State Register*, December 13, 1873; "Mrs. Lincoln's Denial and What She Says," broadside, January 12, 1874, copy in Massachusetts Historical Society; Mrs. Lincoln denies interview "as stated by Herndon" to John Todd Stuart, Illinois *State Journal*, December 9, 1873; David Donald, *Herndon's Lincoln*; Ruth Painter Randall, *Mary Lincoln: Biography of a Marriage*; James G. Randall, *Lincoln the President*, Vol. 2; *Lincoln's Domestic Life*, Herndon monograph in Herndon-Weik mss.; Herndon to Francis P. Carpenter, December 11, 1866, *ibid.*; Emanuel Hertz, *The Hidden Lincoln*; Paul M. Angle, "Lincoln's First Love," *Lincoln Centennial Association Bulletin*, December, 1927; Jay Monaghan, "New Light on Lincoln-Rutledge Romance," *Abraham Lincoln Quarterly*, September, 1944; Earl Schenck Miers, "Lincoln as a Best Seller," *Abraham Lincoln Quarterly*, December, 1948; Ida Tarbell, "Lincoln's First Love," *Collier's*, February 8, 1930; Francis Newton Thorpe, 'Ann Rutledge," *Harper's Weekly*, February 13, 1909; Edwin Cyrus Miller, "The Myth of the Ann Rutledge Love Affair," *Kiwanis Magazine*, February, 1944; Isaac N. Arnold to Herndon, November 22 and 26, 1866, Herndon-Weik mss.; Herndon to James Smith, December 20, 1866, and Smith to Herndon, January 24, 1867, in Chicago *Tribune*, March 6, 1867; Ward Hill Lamon, *The Life of Abraham Lincoln*; Dr. W. A. Evans, *Mrs. Abraham Lincoln: A Study of Her Personality and Her Influence on Lincoln*; Montgomery S. Lewis, *Legends That Libel Lincoln*; Lloyd Lewis, *Myths After Lincoln*; Stefan Lorant, *The Life of Abraham Lincoln*; Mary S. Vineyard (Mary Owens) to Herndon, May 23, 1866, Herndon-Weik mss.; Mrs. John T. Stuart, *Recollections of Lincoln*, mss., Illinois State Historical Library; Lincoln to Mary Owens, May 7, 1837, August 16, 1837, photostats, *ibid.*; Lincoln to Mrs. Orville H. Browning, April 1, 1838, photostat, *ibid.*; Sandburg and Angle, *Mary Lincoln, Wife and Widow*; David Donald, 'Herndon and Mrs. Lincoln," *Books at Brown*, April, 1950; William H. Herndon, "Analysis of the Character of Abraham Lincoln," *Abraham Lincoln Quarterly*, September and December, 1941.

CHAPTER XXI

Escape to Europe

Mrs. Lincoln to Miss Martha Stafford, Cresson, Pa., July 18, 1868 (courtesy of Mrs. Katrina van Asmus Kindel); Mrs. Lincoln to Mrs. James W. White, Altoona, Pa., August 19, 1868, University of Chicago Library; Robert T. Lincoln's marriage to Mary Harlan, *Gideon Welles Diary*, Vol. 3; Mrs. Lincoln sails to Europe, New York

Tribune, October 6, 1868; Mrs. Lincoln's letters from Europe (1869–71) to Mrs. James W. White and Mrs. James H. Orne, in Katherine Helm, *The True Story of Mary, Wife of Lincoln*; and Sandburg and Angle, *Mary Lincoln, Wife and Widow*; Mrs. Lincoln to Mrs. Robert T. Lincoln, *ibid.*; Mrs. Lincoln to Mrs. Paul Shipman, June 29 and October 27, 1870, and January 13, 1871, *ibid.*; Justin G. Turner, "The Mary Lincoln Letters to Mrs. Felician Slataper," *Journal of the Illinois State Historical Society*, Spring, 1956; Mrs. James H. Orne to Charles Sumner, Baden-Baden, September 12, 1869, Sumner mss., Houghton Library, Harvard University; Mrs. Lincoln to Charles Sumner, York, September 7, 1870, *ibid.*; F. Lauriston Bullard, "Mrs. Lincoln's Pension," *Lincoln Herald*, June, 1947; Ruth Painter Randall, *Mary Lincoln: Biography of a Marriage*; Mrs. Lincoln to Mrs. Orne, December 16, 1869, denying engagement to German baron, Illinois State Historical Library; Mrs. Lincoln to Mrs. Orne, August 30, 1869, and January 13, 1870, *ibid.*; Mrs. Lincoln to Mrs. White, May 2, 1868, University of Chicago Library; Mrs. Lincoln's pension, *Congressional Globe* (records of Fortieth and Forty-first Congresses), May, June and July, 1870; Mrs. James H. Orne to Charles Sumner, Paris, November 27, 1870, Sumner mss.; *Journal of Benjamin Moran*, September 4, 1870, mss., Library of Congress; Mrs. Lincoln and Tad return to the United States: New York *World*, May 12, 1871, Chicago *Tribune*, May 16, 1871, New York *Tribune*, May 26, 1871; Mrs. Lincoln to Eliza Stuart, May, 1871, in Katherine Helm, *The True Story of Mary, Wife of Lincoln*; Robert T. Lincoln to his wife, July 11 and 14, 1871, *ibid.*; death of Tad, Chicago *Tribune*, July 16 and 18, 1871; "Mary Todd Lincoln Summers in Wisconsin," *Journal of the Illinois State Historical Society*, June, 1941; Mrs. Lincoln to Mrs. James W. White, June 8, 1871, University of Chicago Library.

CHAPTER XXII

Mrs. Lincoln Held Insane

Robert T. Lincoln to Mary Harlan, October 16, 1867, in Katherine Helm, *The True Story of Mary, Wife of Lincoln*; Eddie Foy and Alvin F. Harlow, "Clowning Through Life," *Collier's*, December 25, 1926; David Davis mss., Illinois State Historical Library; Mrs. Lincoln's telegram to Dr. Ralph N. Isham about Robert's health, March 12, 1875; Robert T. Lincoln's petition to Judge M. R. M. Wallace to have his mother adjudged insane and Dr. Ralph N. Isham's accompanying certification, May 18, 1875; Mrs. Lincoln pronounced insane, May 19, 1875, Cook County proceedings, photostats in Illinois State Historical Library; *The Inter-Ocean*, Chicago, May 20, 1875; Chicago *Tribune*, May 21, 1875, suicide attempt; William E. Barton, *The Life of Abraham Lincoln*, Vol. 2; Homer Croy, *The Trial of Mrs. Abraham Lincoln*; James S. Rhodes and Dean Jauchius, *The Trial of Mary Todd Lincoln*; Ruth Painter Randall, "When Mary Lincoln Was Adjudged Insane. New Light on the Tragic Case of a President's Widow Who Saw Her Own Son as a Hated Enemy," *American Heritage*, August, 1955; John M. Suarez, "Mary Todd Lincoln. A Case History," reprinted from the *American Journal of Psychiatry*, January, 1966; Robert T. Lincoln to Mrs. James H. Orne, June 1, 1875, and Mrs. Orne's reply, August 8, 1875, in Katherine Helm, *The True Story of Mary, Wife of Lincoln*; Judge and Mrs.

James B. Bradwell's fight for Mrs. Lincoln's release, in Dr. W. A. Evans, *Mrs. Abraham Lincoln: A Study of Her Personality and Her Influence on Lincoln*; Dr. R. J. Patterson's defense, Illinois *State Journal*, July 2 and September 1, 1875; Mrs. Lincoln pronounced sane at second hearing, Chicago, June 15, 1876, Cook County court records; Mrs. Lincoln to Robert T. Lincoln, June 19, 1876, in Philip D. Sang, "Mary Todd Lincoln: A Tragic Portrait," *Journal of Rutgers University Library*, April, 1961; Rodney A. Ross, "Mary Todd Lincoln, Patient at Bellevue Place, Batavia," *Journal of the Illinois State Historical Society*, Spring, 1970.

CHAPTER XXIII

The Struggle Ended

Mrs. Lincoln to Mrs. Paul Shipman, Frankfurt am Main, June 29, 1870, and Leamington, October 27, 1870, in Sandburg and Angle, *Mary Lincoln, Wife and Widow* ("The Documents"); Paul Shipman refuting Adam Badeau in Louisville *Courier-Journal* in Katherine Helm, *The True Story of Mary, Wife of Lincoln*; Adam Badeau, New York *World*, January 8, 1875; and *Grant in Peace*; *Journal of Benjamin Moran*, Manuscript Division, Library of Congress; Mrs. Lincoln's letters to Jacob Bunn, 1876–80, Illinois State Historical Library; David Davis mss. *ibid.*; Mrs. Lincoln's letters from Europe to Edward Lewis Baker, Jr., Illinois State Historical Library; "Mrs. Lincoln's Pecuniary Condition," edited by friends and relatives, Illinois *State Journal*, November 26, 1881; Mrs. Lincoln's return to America on *l'Amérique*, New York *Sun*, October 28, 1880; Sarah Bernhardt, *Memories of My Life*; Reverend Noyes W. Miner, *Mrs. Abraham Lincoln, a Vindication*, mss., Illinois State Historical Library; Mrs. Lincoln to Reverend Noyes W. Miner, in Sandburg and Angle, *Mary Lincoln, Wife and Widow* ("The Documents"); Mrs. Lincoln to Madeleine Vinton Dahlgren (Mrs. John A. Dahlgren), Spring, 1871, *ibid.*; Dr. W. A. Evans, *Mrs. Lincoln: A Study of Her Personality and Her Influence on Lincoln*; Robert T. Lincoln to Mrs. James H. Orne, June 2, 1881; obituary and funeral notices: Illinois *State Journal*, July 17, 1882, Illinois *State Register*, July 20, 1882, Chicago *Tribune*, July 20, 1882, New York *Times*, July 18, 1882, New York *World*, July 17, 1882, Lexington *Daily Press*, July 18, 1882; funeral oration by Reverend James A. Reed, in Sandburg and Angle ("The Documents"); Reverend N. W. Miner to Jesse Weik, January 3, 1889, Herndon-Weik mss.; Mrs. Charles E. Putnam to her sons, St. Clair and Clement Putnam, December 8, 1882, on Mrs. Lincoln's last hours, copy in Illinois State Historical Library; William E. Barton, *Life of Abraham Lincoln*, Vol. 2; Honoré Willsie Morrow, *Mary Todd Lincoln*; Robert T. Lincoln to Mrs. James Garfield, July 30, 1882, Garfield mss., Library of Congress.

CHAPTER XXIV

Lincoln Alone Understood

Gideon Welles mss., Library of Congress; *The Diary of Edward Bates*; Roy P.

Basler, *The Lincoln Legend: A Study in Changing Conceptions*; *Herndon's Life of Lincoln . . .* by William H. Herndon and Jesse W. Weik, with introduction and notes by Paul M. Angle; William H. Townsend, *Lincoln and His Wife's Home Town*; Katherine Helm, *The True Story of Mary, Wife of Lincoln*; Honoré Willsie Morrow, *Mary Todd Lincoln*; Emilie Todd Helm, "Mary Todd Lincoln," *McClure's Magazine*, September, 1898; Carl Sandburg and Paul M. Angle, *Mary Lincoln, Wife and Widow*; Mrs. Lincoln's letters from Europe to Mrs. James H. Orne and Mrs. James W. White; James G. Randall and David Donald, *The Divided Union*; Elizabeth Keckley, *Behind the Scenes*; C. C. Ritzie, "In Defense of Mrs. Lincoln," *Journal of the Illinois State Historical Society*, April, 1937; Stefan Lorant, "The Tragic Love Story of Mrs. Lincoln," *McCall's* magazine, May, 1953; "One of the Most Lied About Women in the World," *Literary Digest*, April 28, 1928; Teresa L. Reed thesis, *Mary Todd Lincoln*; Dale Carnegie, 'The Woman in Lincoln's Life," *Reader's Digest*, January, 1937; Leslie J. Perry, "Lincoln's Home Life in Washington," *Harper's New Monthly Magazine*, February, 1897; Ruth Painter Randall, "Mary Lincoln: Judgment Appealed," *Abraham Lincoln Quarterly*, September, 1949; Ruth Painter Randall, "Mr. Lincoln: A Portrait by His Wife," *New York Times Magazine*, February 11, 1951; Ruth Painter Randall, "Mrs. Lincoln Revealed in a New Light," *New York Times Magazine*, February 12, 1950; Montgomery S. Lewis, *Legends That Libel Lincoln*; William E. Barton, *The Woman Lincoln Loved*; Henry C. Whitney, *Life on the Circuit with Lincoln*; Lloyd Lewis, *Myths After Lincoln*; Ida M. Tarbell, *The Life of Abraham Lincoln*; Mary Day Winn, *Adam's Rib*; Adam Badeau, *Grant in Peace*; Dr. W. A. Evans, *Mrs. Abraham Lincoln: A Study of Her Personality and Her Influence on Lincoln*.

Bibliography

ANGLE, PAUL M., *Here I Have Lived.* A history of Lincoln's Springfield, 1821–65. Springfield, Illinois, Abraham Lincoln Association, 1935.

———, and MIERS, EARL SCHENCK, eds., *The Living Lincoln: the man, his mind, his times and the war he fought, reconstructed from his own writings.* New Brunswick, New Jersey, Rutgers University Press, 1965.

———, and SANDBURG, CARL, *Mary Lincoln, Wife and Widow.* Part I by Carl Sandburg. Part II by Paul Angle. New York, Harcourt, Brace, 1932.

ARNOLD, ISAAC N., *Life of Abraham Lincoln.* Chicago, Jansen, McClurg, 1885.

ATKINSON, ELEANOR, *Lincoln's Love Story.* New York, Doubleday, Page, 1909.

BADEAU, ADAM, *Grant in Peace.* Hartford, Connecticut, Scranton & Company, 1887.

———, *Military History of Ulysses S. Grant from April, 1861 to April, 1865,* 2 vols. New York, D. Appleton, 1881.

BANCROFT, GEORGE, *The Life and Letters of George Bancroft.* M. A. De Wolfe Howe, ed. 2 vols. New York, Scribner, 1908.

BARINGER, WILLIAM E., *Lincoln's Rise to Power.* Boston, Little, Brown, 1937.

BARTON, WILLIAM E., *Life of Abraham Lincoln,* 2 vols. Indianapolis, Bobbs-Merrill, 1925.

———, *The Soul of Abraham Lincoln,* New York, George M. Doran, 1920.

———, *The Woman Lincoln Loved.* Indianapolis, Bobbs-Merrill, 1927.

BASLER, ROY P., ed., *Abraham Lincoln: His Speeches and Writings,* edited with critical and analytical notes by Basler; preface by Carl Sandburg. Cleveland and New York, World Publishing, 1946.

———, ed., *The Collected Works of Abraham Lincoln,* assistant editors, Marion Dolores Pratt and Lloyd A. Dunlap. Vols. 4, 5, 6 and 7. New Brunswick, New Jersey, Rutgers University Press, 1953.

———, *The Lincoln Legend: A Study in Changing Conceptions.* Boston and New York, Houghton Mifflin, 1935.

BATES, EDWARD, *The Diary of Edward Bates 1859–1866,* Howard Beale, ed. Washington, D.C., Government Printing Office, 1933.

BAYNE, JULIA TAFT, *Tad Lincoln's Father.* Boston, Little, Brown, 1931.

BELDEN, THOMAS GRAHAM and MARVA, *So Fell the Angels.* Boston, Little, Brown, 1956.

BERNHARDT, SARAH, *Memories of My Life.* New York, D. Appleton, 1907.

BEVERIDGE, ALBERT J., *Abraham Lincoln 1809–1858*, 2 vols. Boston, Houghton Mifflin, 1928.

BIRMINGHAM, STEPHEN, *Our Crowd*. New York, Harper & Row, 1967.

BOWERS, CLAUDE G., *The Tragic Era*. Boston, Houghton Mifflin, 1929.

BOYDEN, ANNA L., *War Reminiscences or Echoes from Hospital and White House*. A record of Mrs. Rebecca H. Pomroy's experiences in wartime. Boston, E. Lothrop, 1884.

BRADFORD, GAMALIEL, *Wives*. New York, Harper & Brothers, 1925.

BROOKS, NOAH, *Abraham Lincoln*. New York, G. P. Putnam's Sons, 1909.

———, *Statesmen*. New York, Scribner, 1893.

———, *Washington in Lincoln's Time*. New York, Century Company, 1895.

———, *Washington, D.C. in Lincoln's Time*, edited with new commentary by Herbert Mitgang. 2 vols., Chicago, Quadrangle Books, 1971.

BROWNING, ORVILLE HICKMAN, *The Diary of Orville Hickman Browning*, edited with introduction and notes by Theodore Calvin Pease and James G. Randall. Springfield, Illinois State Historical Society, 1925.

CARNEGIE, DALE, *Lincoln the Unknown*. New York, Century Company, 1932.

CARPENTER, FRANK B., *Six Months at the White House*. New York, Hurd & Houghton, 1866.

CARRUTHERS, OLIVE, *Lincoln's Other Mary*. Appendix by R. Gerald McMurtry. Chicago, New York, Ziff-Davis, 1946.

CATTON, BRUCE, *Mr. Lincoln's Army*. Garden City, New York, Doubleday, 1951.

———, *This Hallowed Ground*. Garden City, Doubleday, 1951.

CHAMBRUN, MARQUIS DE (CHARLES ADOLPHE DE PINETON), *Impressions of Lincoln and the Civil War*, trans. by General Aldebert de Chambrun. New York, Random House, 1952.

CHANDLER, MARY G. (WARE), *The Elements of Character*. Boston, Crosby, Nichols, 1854.

CHARNWOOD, LORD, *Abraham Lincoln*. New York, H. Holt, 1916.

CHASE, SALMON PORTLAND, *Inside Lincoln's Cabinet: The Civil War Diaries of Salmon Portland Chase*, David Donald, ed., New York, Longmans, Green, 1954.

CLEMMER, MARY (MRS. AMES), *Ten Years in Washington: Or, Inside Life and Scenes in Our National Capital as a Woman Sees Them*. Hartford, Connecticut, A. D. Worthington, 1873.

COLEMAN, J.WINSTON, JR., *Historic Kentucky*. Lexington, Henry Clay Press, 1968.

———, *Lexington During the Civil War*. Lexington, Commercial Printing Company, 1938.

COLEMAN, MRS. CHAPMAN, *The Life of John J. Crittenden*, edited by his daughter. Philadelphia, Lippincott, 1871.

COLMAN, EDNA M., *Seventy-five Years of White House Gossip: From Washington to Lincoln*. Garden City, Doubleday, Page, 1925.

CRAMER, J. H., *Lincoln Under Enemy Fire: The Complete Account of His Experiences During Early's Attack on Washington*. Baton Rouge, Louisiana State University Press, 1948.

CROOK, WILLIAM H., *Memories of the White House: The Home Life of Our Presidents from Lincoln to Roosevelt*, compiled and edited by Henry Rood. Boston, Little, Brown, 1911.

CROY, HOMER, *The Trial of Mrs. Abraham Lincoln*. New York, Duell, Sloan and Pearce, 1962.

DAHLGREN, MADELEINE V., *A Washington Winter*. Boston, J. B. Osgood, 1883.

———, *Etiquette of Social Life in Washington*. Washington, D.C., Mohun Bros., 1876.

DANA, CHARLES A., *Recollections of the Civil War*. New York, D. Appleton, 1898.

DAVIS, JEFFERSON, *The Rise and Fall of the Confederate Government*, 2 vols. New York, D. Appleton, 1881.

DE LEON, T. C., *Belles, Beaux and Brains of the 1860's*. New York, G. W. Dillingham, 1907.

DENNETT, TYLER, ed., *Lincoln and the Civil War in the Diaries and Letters of John Hay*. New York, Dodd, Mead, 1939.

DICEY, EDWARD, *Six Months in the Federal States*. London and Cambridge, Macmillan, 1963.

———, *Spectator of America*, edited and with an introduction by Herbert Mitgang. Chicago, Quadrangle Books, 1971.

DODGE, MARY ABIGAIL (GAIL HAMILTON), *A New Atmosphere*. Boston, Ticknor and Fields, 1865.

DONALD, DAVID H., *Herndon's Lincoln*. New York, Alfred A. Knopf, 1948.

——, *Charles Sumner and the Coming of the Civil War.* New York, Alfred A. Knopf, 1960.
DUPUY, R. ERNEST, and DUPUY, TREVOR N., *The Compact History of the Civil War.* New York, Hawthorn Books, 1960.
EISENSCHIML, OTTO, and NEWMAN, RALPH, *The American Iliad: The Epic Story of the Civil War as Narrated by Eyewitnesses and Contemporaries.* Indianapolis, Bobbs-Merrill, 1947.
ELLET, MRS. E. F., *The Court Circles of the Republic.* Hartford, Connecticut, Hartford Publishing, 1869.
——, *The Queens of American Society.* New York, Charles Scribner, 1867.
EVANS, W. A., Mrs. *Abraham Lincoln: A Study of Her Personality and Her Influence on Lincoln.* New York, Alfred A. Knopf, 1932.
FURMAN, BESS, *White House Profile.* Indianapolis, Bobbs-Merrill, 1951.
GOLTZ, CARLOS W., *Incidents in the Life of Mary Todd Lincoln.* Sioux City, Iowa, Deitch Lamar, 1928.
GRANT, ULYSSES S., *Personal Memoirs of Ulysses S. Grant,* 2 vols. New York, Century, 1895.
GREELEY, HORACE, *The American Conflict.* Hartford, Connecticut, O. D. Chase, 2 vols., 1864 and 1866.
GREEN, T. M., *Historic Families of Kentucky.* Chicago, Robert Clarke, 1889.
GREENHOW, ROSE O'NEAL, *My Imprisonment and the First Year of Abolition Rule at Washington.* London, Richard Bentley, 1863.
GRIMSLEY, ELIZABETH TODD, "Six Months in the White House," *Journal of the Illinois State Historical Society,* Vol. 19 (October, 1926 to January, 1927).
HACKENSMITH, C. W., "The Much Maligned Mary Todd Lincoln," *The Filson Club History Quarterly,* Vol. 44 (Louisville, July, 1970).
——, "Family Background and Education of Mary Todd," *The Register of the Kentucky Historical Society* (Frankfort, Kentucky, July, 1971).
HECKMAN, RICHARD ALLEN, *Lincoln Versus Douglas.* Washington, D.C., Public Affairs Press, 1967.
HELM, KATHERINE, *The True Story of Mary, Wife of Lincoln,* containing the recollections of Mary's sister Emilie (Mrs. Ben Hardin Helm), extracts from her wartime diary, numerous letters and other documents. New York, Harper & Brothers, 1928.
HERNDON, WILLIAM H., and WEIK, JESSE W., *Herndon's Life of Lincoln* . . ., with introduction and notes by Paul M. Angle. Cleveland and New York, World Publishing, 1942.
——, *Abraham Lincoln: The True Story of a Great Life,* with introduction by Horace White, 2 vols. New York, D. Appleton, 1909.
——, *Abraham Lincoln,* 3 vols. Chicago, Belford, Clarke & Company, 1889.
HERTZ, EMANUEL, *The Hidden Lincoln.* From the letters and papers of William H. Herndon. New York, Viking, 1938.
HOLLOWAY, LAURA C. (LANGFORD), *The Ladies of the White House.* Philadelphia, Bradley, 1883.
HUBBARD, FREEMAN H., *Vinnie Ream and Mr. Lincoln.* New York, Whittlesey Houss, McGraw-Hill Book Company, 1949.
JAUCHIUS, DEAN, and RHODES, JAMES A., *The Trial of Mary Todd Lincoln.* Indianapolis, Bobbs-Merrill, 1959.
KECKLEY, ELIZABETH, *Behind the Scenes . . . or Thirty Years a Slave, and Four Years in the White House.* New York, G. W. Carleton, 1868.
KING, WILLARD L., *Lincoln's Manager: David Davis.* Cambridge, Mass., Harvard University Press, 1960.
KINNAIRD, VIRGINIA, "Mrs. Lincoln as a White House Hostess." From papers in the Illinois State Historical Society, transactions for the year 1938. Springfield, printed by the State of Illinois, 1939.
KOERNER, GUSTAV, *Memoirs.* Cedar Rapids, Iowa, Torch Press, 1909.
LAMON, WARD HILL, *Life of Abraham Lincoln, from His Birth to His Inauguration as President.* Boston, J. R. Osgood, 1872.
——, *Recollections of Abraham Lincoln, 1847–1865,* Dorothy Lamon Teillard, ed. Chicago, A. C. McClurg, 1895.

LEECH, MARGARET, *Reveille in Washington, 1860–1865*. New York, Harper & Brothers, 1941.

LEWIS, LLOYD, *Myths After Lincoln*. New York, Harcourt, Brace, 1929.

LEWIS, MONTGOMERY S., *Legends That Libel Lincoln*. New York, Rinehart, 1946.

LOGAN, MARY S., *Thirty Years in Washington*, Mrs. John A. Logan, ed. Hartford, Connecticut, A. D. Worthington, 1901.

LORANT, STEFAN, *Lincoln. A Picture Story of His Life*. New York, Harper & Brothers, 1952.

——, *Lincoln: His Life in Photos*. New York, Duell, Sloan and Pearce, 1941.

——, *The Life of Abraham Lincoln*. New York, McGraw-Hill, 1954.

McMURTRY, ROBERT GERALD, *Ben Hardin Helm, "Rebel" Brother-in-law of Abraham Lincoln, with a Biographical Sketch of His Wife and an Account of the Todd Family of Kentucky*. Chicago, privately printed for the Civil War Round Table, 1943.

McNAMAR, MYRTLE, *Gentle Ann: A Tale of the Sangamon*. New York, Beacon Publications, 1943.

MAYNARD, NETTIE COLBURN, *Was Abraham Lincoln a Spiritualist?* Philadelphia, R. C. Hartcranft, 1891.

MEANS, MARIANNE, *The Woman in the White House*. New York, Random House, 1963.

MEARNS, DAVID C., *The Lincoln Papers: The Story of the Collection with Selections to July 4, 1861*. Introduction by Carl Sandburg. Garden City, Doubleday, 1948.

MESERVE, FREDERICK HILL, and SANDBURG, CARL, *The Photographs of Abraham Lincoln*. New York, Harcourt, Brace, 1944.

MILES, MARY LEIGHTON, "The Fatal First of January, 1841," *Journal of the Illinois State Historical Society*, Vol. 20 (April, 1927).

MORAN, BENJAMIN, *The Journal of Benjamin Moran 1857–1865*, 2 vols., Sarah Agnes Wallace and Frances Elma Gillespie, eds. Chicago, University of Chicago Press, 1948–49.

MORROW, HONORÉ WILLSIE, *Mary Todd Lincoln*. New York, William Morrow, 1928.

MOTLEY, JOHN LOTHROP, *The Correspondence of John Lothrop Motley and George William Curtis*. New York, Harper & Brothers, 1889.

NEWMAN, RALPH, and EISENSCHIML, OTTO, *The American Iliad: The Epic Story of the Civil War as Narrated by Eyewitnesses and Contemporaries*. Indianapolis, Bobbs-Merrill, 1947.

NICOLAY, HELEN, *Lincoln's Secretary*. A biography of John G. Nicolay. New York, Longmans Green, 1949.

NICOLAY, JOHN G., *A Short Life of Abraham Lincoln*. New York, Century Company, 1902.

——, and HAY, JOHN, *Abraham Lincoln: A History*, 10 vols. New York, Century, 1890.

OSTENDORF, LLOYD, *The Photographs of Mary Todd Lincoln*. Springfield, Illinois State Historical Society, 1969.

PHELPS, MARY MERWIN, *Kate Chase. Dominant Daughter*. New York, Thomas Y. Crowell, 1937.

PIATT, DONN, *Memories of the Men Who Saved the Union*. New York, Belford, Clarke, 1887.

POORE, BEN: PERLEY, *Perley's Reminiscences of Sixty Years in the National Metropolis*, 2 vols. Philadelphia, Hubbard Brothers, 1886.

PORTER, HORACE, *Campaigning with Grant*. New York, Century Company, 1897.

PRATT, HARRY E., ed., *Concerning Mr. Lincoln: In Which Abraham Lincoln Is Pictured as He Appeared to Letter Writers of His Time*. Springfield, Illinois, 1944.

——, *The Personal Finances of Abraham Lincoln*. Springfield, Illinois, 1943.

PRINDIVILLE, KATHLEEN, *The First Ladies: Stories of the Presidents' Wives*. New York, Macmillan, 1964.

RANCK, GEORGE W., *History of Lexington, Kentucky*. Cincinnati, Robert Clarke, 1872.

RANDALL, JAMES GARFIELD, *Lincoln, the President*, 4 vols. New York, Dodd, Mead, 1945–55.

——, *Mr. Lincoln*, Richard N. Current, ed. New York, Dodd, Mead, 1957.

——, and DONALD, DAVID, *The Divided Union*. Boston, Little, Brown, 1961.

RANDALL, RUTH PAINTER, *Mary Lincoln: Biography of a Marriage*. Boston, Little, Brown, 1953.

——, *The Courtship of Mr. Lincoln*. Boston, Little, Brown, 1957.

——, *Lincoln's Sons*. Boston, Little, Brown, 1955.

——, *Colonel Elmer Ellsworth: A Biography of Lincoln's Friend and First Hero of the Civil War*. Boston, Little, Brown, 1960.

RANKIN, HENRY B., *Intimate Character Sketches of Abraham Lincoln.* Philadelphia, J. B. Lippincott, 1924.

———, *Personal Recollections of Abraham Lincoln.* New York, G. P. Putnam's Sons, 1916.

REED, TERESA L., *Mary Todd Lincoln.* Senior honors thesis, Transylvania University, 1971.

RHODES, JAMES A., and JAUCHIUS, DEAN, *The Trial of Mary Todd Lincoln.* Indianapolis, Bobbs-Merrill, 1959.

RICE, ALLEN THORNDIKE, *Reminiscences of Abraham Lincoln by Distinguished Men of His Time.* Edited and collected for *The North American Review*, New York, 1888.

ROSS, ISHBEL, *First Lady of the South: The Life of Mrs. Jefferson Davis.* New York, Harper & Brothers, 1958.

———, *Ladies of the Press.* New York, Harper & Brothers, 1936.

———, *Proud Kate: Life of Kate Chase.* New York, Harper & Brothers, 1953.

———, *Rebel Rose: Life of Rose O'Neal Greenhow, Confederate Spy.* New York, Harper & Brothers, 1954.

———, *The General's Wife: The Life of Mrs. Ulysses S. Grant.* New York, Dodd, Mead, 1959.

RUSSELL, WILLIAM H., *My Diary North and South*, Fletcher Pratt, ed. New York, Harper & Brothers, 1954.

SALM-SALM, PRINCESS, *Ten Years of My Life.* New York, R. Worthington, 1877.

SANDBURG, CARL, *Abraham Lincoln: The Prairie Years*, 2 vols. New York, Harcourt, Brace, 1926.

———, *Abraham Lincoln: The War Years*, 4 vols. New York, Harcourt, Brace, 1939.

———, and ANGLE, PAUL M., *Mary Lincoln, Wife and Widow*, including letters and documents. New York, Harcourt, Brace, 1932.

SCHURZ, CARL, *Intimate Letters of Carl Schurz, 1841-1869*, Joseph Schafer, ed. Madison, State Historical Society of Wisconsin, 1928.

SCRIPPS, EDWARD W., *Damned Old Crank: A Self-Portrait of E. W. Scripps Drawn from His Unpublished Writings*, Charles R. McCabe, ed. New York, Harper & Brothers, 1951.

SHERIDAN, PHILIP H., *Personal Memoirs of P. H. Sheridan*, 2 vols. New York, Charles W. Webster, 1888.

SHERMAN, WILLIAM T., *Home Letters of General Sherman*, M. A. De Wolfe Howe, ed. New York, Charles Scribner's Sons, 1909.

SHERWOOD, ROBERT E., *Abe Lincoln in Illinois.* New York, Charles Scribner's Sons, 1939.

SIMMONS, DAWN LANGLEY, *A Rose for Mrs. Lincoln.* Boston, Beacon Press, 1970.

SINGLETON, ESTHER, *The Story of the White House*, 2 vols. New York, McClure Company, 1907.

SMITH, MATTHEW HALE, *Sunshine and Shadow in New York.* Hartford, Connecticut, J. B. Burr, 1869.

SPARKS, EDWIN E., *The Lincoln-Douglas Debates of 1858.* Springfield, Illinois, Torch Press, 1908.

SPEED, JOSHUA FRY, *Reminiscences of Abraham Lincoln and Notes of a Visit to California.* Louisville, John P. Morton, 1884.

STEPHENSON, NATHANIEL, *Lincoln: An Account of His Personal Life.* Indianapolis, Bobbs-Merrill, 1922.

STEWART, WILLIAM M., *Reminiscences of Senator William M. Stewart of Nevada.* New York and Washington, Neale Publishing, 1908.

STODDARD, WILLIAM O., *Abraham Lincoln: The True Story of a Great Life.* New York, Fords, Howard & Hulbert, 1884.

———, *Inside the White House in War Time.* New York, C. L. Webster, 1890.

———, ed., *The Table Talk of Abraham Lincoln.* New York, Frederick A. Stokes, 1894.

STONE, IRVING, *Love Is Eternal.* Garden City, N.Y., Doubleday, 1954.

STRODE, HUDSON, *Jefferson Davis*, 3 vols. New York, Harcourt, Brace, 1955-64.

STRONG, GEORGE TEMPLETON, *George Templeton Strong's Diary*, Allan Nevins and Milton Halsey Thomas, eds. New York, Macmillan, 1952.

SUMNER, CHARLES, *Memoirs and Letters of Charles Sumner*, Edward Lillie Pierce, ed. Vol. 4. Boston, Roberts, 1877-93.

SWANBERG, W. A., *Sickles the Incredible.* New York, Charles Scribner's Sons, 1956.

SWISSHELM, JANE GREY, *Half a Century*. Chicago, Jansen, McClurg, 1880.

TARBELL, IDA M., *The Life of Abraham Lincoln*, 2 vols. New York, Macmillan, 1923.

———, *In the Footsteps of the Lincolns*. New York, Harper & Brothers, 1924.

TEMPLE, WAYNE C., "Mary Todd Lincoln's Travels," *Journal of the Illinois State Historical Society* (Spring, 1959).

———, ed., *Lincoln, as Seen by C. C. Brown*. Prairie Village, Kansas, Crabgrass Press, 1963.

THOMAS, BENJAMIN PLATT, *Lincoln 1847–1858, Being the Day-by-Day Activities of Abraham Lincoln from January 1, 1847 to December 31, 1858*. Springfield, The Abraham Lincoln Association, 1936.

———, *Lincoln's New Salem*. Springfield, The Abraham Lincoln Association, 1934.

TOWNSEND, WILLIAM H., *Lincoln and His Wife's Home Town*. Indianapolis, Bobbs-Merrill, 1929.

———, *Lincoln the Litigant*. Boston, Houghton, Mifflin, 1925.

TRIPLER, EUNICE (HUNT), *Eunice Tripler: Some Notes of Her Personal Recollections*, Louis A. Arthur, ed. New York, Grafton Press, 1910.

TURNER, JUSTIN G., and TURNER, LINDA LEVITT, *Mary Todd Lincoln. Her Life and Letters*. New York, Alfred A. Knopf, 1972.

VILLARD, HENRY, *Memoirs of Henry Villard*. Boston, Houghton, Mifflin, 1904.

———, *Lincoln on the Eve of '61. A Journalist's Story*, Harold G. and Oswald Garrison Villard, eds. New York, Alfred A. Knopf, 1941.

WALTON, CLYDE C., *Illinois' Lincoln Letters*. Springfield, printed by the Illinois State Historical Library, 1967.

WELLES, GIDEON, *Diary of Gideon Welles*, 3 vols., John T. Morse, Jr., ed. Boston, Houghton, Mifflin, 1911.

WHITNEY, HENRY C., *Life on the Circuit with Lincoln*, with introduction and notes by Paul M. Angle. Caldwell, Idaho, Caxton Printers, 1940.

WHITTON, MARY ORMSBEE, *First First Ladies*. New York, Hastings House, 1948.

WILKIE, KATHERINE ELLIOTT, *Mary Todd Lincoln, Girl of the Blue Grass*. Indianapolis, Bobbs-Merrill, 1954.

WILLIAMS, T. HARRY, *Lincoln and His Generals*. New York, Knopf, 1952.

———, *Lincoln and the Radicals*. Madison, University of Wisconsin Press, 1941.

WINN, MARY DAY, *Adam's Rib*. New York, Harcourt, Brace, 1931.

WRIGHT, CARRIE DOUGLAS, *Lincoln's First Love: A True Story*. Chicago, A. C. McClurg, 1901.

Index